TWENTIETH-CENTURY AMERICA

A Brief History

Thomas C. Reeves

New York • Oxford
OXFORD UNIVERSITY PRESS
2000

Oxford University Press

Oxford   New York
Athens   Auckland   Bangkok   Bogotá   Buenos Aires   Calcutta
Cape Town   Chennai   Dar es Salaam   Delhi   Florence   Hong Kong   Istanbul
Karachi   Kuala Lumpur   Madrid   Melbourne   Mexico City   Mumbai
Nairobi   Paris   São Paulo   Singapore   Taipei   Tokyo   Toronto   Warsaw

and associated companies in
Berlin   Ibadan

Copyright © 2000 by Oxford University Press, Inc.

Published by Oxford University Press, Inc.,
198 Madison Avenue, New York, New York 10016
http://www.oup-usa.org

Oxford is a registered trademark of Oxford University Press

Library of Congress Cataloging-in-Publication Data
Reeves, Thomas C., 1936–
    Twentieth-century America : a brief history / Thomas C. Reeves.
        p.   cm.
    Includes bibliographical references and index.
    ISBN 0-19-504484-3 (pbk.). — ISBN 0-19-504483-5 (cloth).
    1. United States—History—20th century. I. Title.
    E741.R33   2000   98-50366
    973.92—dc21   CIP

1 3 5 7 9 8 6 4 2
Printed in the United States of America
on acid-free paper

CONTENTS

PREFACE

This book is designed for those who want a succinct, comprehensive, and reasonably objective examination of recent American history. It is aimed at general readers and college undergraduates who want a core textbook that can be supplemented by primary sources and additional readings.

In my more than thirty years of teaching American history, I have rarely been satisfied with the reading material available for the classroom. Most survey textbooks are bulky and attempt to cover nearly everything that happened. Students are often bewildered and weary from the start, being faced with tens of thousands of facts, dates, and charts they presumably must memorize. The attempt here has been to select materials more carefully, trying to present solid coverage of an era without burying readers in detail and trivia.

Some elements of our past readers find important are no doubt neglected in these pages—show business celebrities of the 1990s, for example. But such omissions, if they prove serious, can be rectified in the classroom by the instructor and covered in additional reading assignments. All any introduction or survey can do in any case is to raise names, events, and issues that will warrant further study. The cliché is true: Education is a lifelong adventure.

Some textbooks offer alternative viewpoints from historians on major issues. That leads almost inevitably to student confusion and even cynicism. Which historian is right? they ask. It is important for students of the past to learn that historians differ on many things. History is not a science; and even scientists disagree, often vehemently, on certain topics. But much of the confusion about historical viewpoints can be avoided by the careful synthesis of a single author.

It has become fashionable since the 1960s to infuse textbooks with an abundance of polemics, especially after the story reaches the post World War II period. This is not only a disservice to the historical calling, it seems to me, but it again hampers classroom effectiveness. Students who object to the slant often complain they are being indoctrinated and refuse to take the reading seriously. Those who agree also often lose interest, knowing in advance what the interpretation of events and people will be. There is, of course, nothing wrong with historical interpretation. It is present in this volume and in all history books. But every effort is made here to be responsible and accurate, avoiding any sort of "line" that guides the narrative. Objectivity is an illusive but worthy goal for the historian.

For brevity, some students and professors turn to volumes that are outlines or near-outlines of historical events. This approach often omits too much, encourages hasty rote memorization, and makes the subject of history something to be endured as a mere academic hurdle. Such books, almost by definition, fail to engage readers in the often exciting stories that historians cull from the past to make sense of things.

This then is an effort to fill what I have long thought was a gap in the training of Americans about their own history. The format is based on the fifteen-week semester, one chapter a week, but instructors and general readers may choose, of course, to engage the book in a variety of ways.

I have chosen to bring the story as up to date as publishing deadlines permit. Students are particularly interested in the near past and often are assigned books that end the story before they were born or fully conscious of the world around them. Moreover, I wanted to present a complete look at this dynamic century.

This book talks much about American politics, a topic that fell out of fashion in the 1960s. It is encouraging to see many historians again realizing the importance of public policy and policymakers on all of our lives. But life is, of course, much more than politics, and readers will encounter here a wide variety of topics that have made our country and our century what they are. Over the past three decades, historians have expanded the perimeters of history to include the lives of people of all sorts and conditions. This strikes me as a wise and productive step, one that I have followed with enthusiasm.

The recommended readings at the end of each chapter were selected primarily to appeal to students. The emphasis was on books that were readable, provocative, and responsible. Most textbooks list hundreds of books, thereby pleasing as many professors as possible and leaving students baffled. In my experience, students almost always ignore bibliographies, and one can hardly blame them. A great many important books, to be sure, are omitted from the brief lists cited here, but these selections are a beginning. Those with eager minds will be encouraged to reach further into the vast riches of historical scholarship.

I am deeply grateful to Nancy Lane and Gioia Stevens, my editors at Oxford University Press. This book is dedicated to Katherine Garrison.

                                                            TCR

Chapter One

BY 1900

THE FAITH OF AMERICANS

A mericans toasted the arrival of the new century in 1900 with speeches, articles, and books declaring a firm faith in the nation's future. The pride and determined optimism that had long characterized Americans seemed more strident than ever. In only a few decades, after all, much of the nation's rural landscape had given way to a welter of factories and cities, providing jobs and promising a degree of prosperity only dreamed of in the past. New inventions were improving everyday living. Immigrants were pouring into the country, and population was booming. The West, free of Indian resistance, seemed more inviting than ever. Farm income was better than it had been in years. Educational opportunities were expanding. New professional organizations were emerging, raising the standards in such vital fields as medicine and law. The nation was now a world power.

There were loud voices stressing the unhappy features of the departing era: monopolies, the gap between rich and poor, recurrent recessions and depressions, wretched factory conditions, urban blight, and political corruption. Several farseeing observers complained about racial and sexual discrimination and the ravaging of our natural resources. But few thought these problems permanent. Most Americans seemed eager to express their belief in progress. As in Thomas Jefferson's administration, when the nineteenth century began, they were confident that the future was bright and that they lived in a nation uniquely blessed by the Creator.

The great majority of Americans assumed they lived in a Christian, Protestant country; the faith was an integral part of everyday life. For example, not only was Bible reading in the public schools routine, but in 1890 twenty-two of twenty-four *state* universities surveyed conducted chapel services, twelve required attendance, and four mandated church attendance as well. In 1892 United States Supreme Court Justice David Brewer declared, "This is a reli-

1

gious people. This is historically true. From the discovery of this continent to the present hour there is a single voice making this affirmation . . . this is a Christian nation." Economic abundance, religion, patriotism, and optimism were intertwined and everywhere in evidence in the United States at the dawn of the twentieth century.

Industrialization

The most significant development by 1900 was the Industrial Revolution. It began in this country in the second decade of the nineteenth century and had started to blossom after the Civil War. By the 1880s the value of manufactured goods surpassed that of farm products, and more people worked in nonagricultural occupations than on farms. The capital invested in American manufacturing increased from $1 billion in 1860 to $10 billion in 1900. The value of American manufacturing products grew from $2 billion to $13 billion in the same period, making the United States the leading industrial nation of the world. In 1889 the Dow Jones industrial average made its debut. It was comprised of twelve business behemoths and began trading at 40.94.

The largest steel producer in the nation, the Carnegie Company, saw its profits swell from $1.6 million in 1880 to $40 million in 1900. That same year, the company was worth $320 million—a 500-percent increase over the original investment made just twenty-seven years earlier. In 1901, company properties were valued at $492 million.

John D. Rockefeller and his associates founded their first oil refineries in 1863 with a capitalization of $1 million. In 1889 the net value of Standard Oil properties was $196.7 million. By 1911 the company's net value had ballooned to $660.4 million.

Inventions and technological advances were at the core of industrialization. Between 1860 and 1890, Americans took out an unprecedented 440,000 patents. The Bessemer process of converting iron into steel, for example, not only made Carnegie a multimillionaire but contributed to the transformation of American life with steel railroad tracks, plows, bridges, skyscrapers, scalpels, sewing machines, and automobiles. Thomas Edison's development of the electric light bulb in 1879 introduced a wave of startling advances and helped create an electrical equipment industry that produced goods worth $21.8 million in 1890. Alexander Graham Bell's genius enabled the New York metropolitan area to have more telephones in 1888 than the entire United Kingdom. There were already 100,000 of George Eastman's Kodak cameras in circulation by 1900, and the Brownie box camera introduced that year was priced at a mere $1.00. Some eight thousand automobiles were moving about the country, at a time when the nation had only a single mile of smooth paved road.

The telegraph, transatlantic cable, typewriter, rotary press, gasoline motor, refrigerator car, and linotype machine were among many pathbreaking innovations that contributed significantly to the industrialization of America. Wireless telegraphy, the airplane, the motion picture *The Great Train Robbery*, the diesel engine, and Henry Ford's Model T would appear within the first decade of the new century.

Railroad development was a vital stimulant to industrialization. Railroad mileage in the United States increased from 79,082 in 1877 to 166,703 in 1890, the latter figure amounting to about a third of the world's total. Moreover, track gauges were uniform by 1890 and the integration of a railroad network was virtually complete. This network, which encompassed 200,000 miles by 1900, enabled people and goods to travel from one corner of the nation to another, permitted factors of production such as iron ore and coal to be combined readily, opened a national market for corporations, and stimulated mass production. Historian John A. Garraty would later write of the railroad system, "its rails, tying section to section, were the bone and sinew, its locomotives and cars the pumping heart and life-bearing blood of the nation."

By the turn of the century the rise of the modern corporation was also an integral part of America's industrial revolution. Business leaders were increasingly abandoning individual ownership of companies, with its personal risks and limited capital, in favor of creating state-chartered corporations. Vast sums of money could be raised through the sale of corporate stock to investors. Stockholders and officials enjoyed limited liability: they were legally responsible for corporate debts only to the extent of their personal investments. And stockholders elected a board of directors, which in turn appointed managerial personnel to run the corporation, an arrangement that enabled a small group of people to manage the complex policies of a large enterprise with efficiency and dispatch. (In the new century corporations would be run by professionals who held little or no stock in the economic empires they managed.) With the growth of national and international markets, and the rapid expansion and diversification of industry, the corporation soon became the dominant economic institution of the Western world.

Corporate Mergers

Business leaders had long sought effective methods for minimizing competition (while at the same time publicly extolling its virtues). In the 1870s they employed the pool, a quiet agreement to set prices and rates and to divide markets. This proved ineffective, for in hard times executives would not stick by their agreements, and pools were unenforceable at law. Standard Oil officials then pioneered the trust, which became common in the 1880s. With this device, stockholders of competing companies gave their voting stock to a central board of trustees in return for trust certificates. The board then had the power to determine prices and market policies. An entire industry could be dominated in this way. By 1881 Standard Oil controlled nearly 90 percent of the nation's oil-refining capacity.

The trust angered many Americans, who had long believed in individualism, opportunity, and competition. It also clashed with the common law and a number of state statutes. In 1890 Congress passed the Sherman Antitrust Act, a half-hearted attempt to outlaw combinations in restraint of trade. The Act was not enforced vigorously at first. And in 1895 the Supreme Court, long dominated by pro-business judges, sharply restricted its effectiveness.

When the State of New Jersey passed a general incorporation act in 1889, business leaders began to abandon the trust in favor of the holding company, a single corporation that could legally hold the controlling share of the securities of other corporations. This tactic triggered an unprecedented wave of mergers between 1895 and 1905 that transformed American business.

Mammoth corporations appeared. In 1901 the United States Steel Corporation brought together 158 companies with a capitalization of $1.4 billion—three times the amount spent annually by the federal government. Now familiar names such as General Electric, Westinghouse, American Sugar, Swift and Company, Goodyear, American Tobacco, Eastman Kodak, International Harvester, and Singer enabled industrialists to escape price competition and maximize their profits. The American Sugar Company controlled 98 percent of the nation's refining capacity. The National Biscuit Company controlled 90 percent of the biscuit and cracker market. Two firms dominated the manufacture of locomotives. Three hundred supercorporations together owned $20 billion—over 40 percent of all the industrial wealth of the United States.

A small group of eastern investment bankers, sometimes called the "Money Trust," underwrote almost all of these mergers. By the early 1900s these bankers had become an extremely powerful force in the economy, controlling hundreds of directorships in major corporations. Financial giant John Pierpont Morgan, who engineered the creation of U.S. Steel, said, "I like a little competition, but I like combination better."

Urbanization

The industrialization of America led to the growth of large cities. By 1900 about nine-tenths of all manufacturing took place there, and cities dominated the nation's economic, political, and cultural life.

The population of the United States had soared from 31.4 million in 1860 to 75.9 million in 1900. During these same years the number of Americans living in communities of 2,500 or more jumped from 6 million to 30 million—almost 40 percent of the population. A rapid trend toward urban living was apparent: Minneapolis grew from 2,500 to 200,000; the population of Los Angeles increased from 5,000 to 100,000; New York-Brooklyn, Chicago, and Philadelphia each had more than a million residents. In 1900 thirty-eight cities had populations of more than 100,000 people.

European immigration accounted for much of the increase. Some 14 million immigrants had entered the country between 1860 and 1900, and in the early years of the new century they would average a million a year. In 1900 the foreign-born comprised 14 percent of the total population. They now came largely from southern, central, and eastern Europe. Often unskilled and poor, they frequently had no choice but to seek their fortunes in the industrial and commercial activities of the cities. They were also attracted to cities by the presence of fellow country people who could help them adjust to the challenges of their new homeland. Every major city had its ethnic neighborhoods where English was spoken as a second language—if at all. In 1900 nearly 13 percent of the foreign-born were illiterate.

Even more of the new city dwellers were migrants from rural areas. They were prodded by shrinking opportunities in agriculture and the lure of factory wages. They also eagerly sought the many social, cultural, and intellectual stimulations of urban areas.

The technology of cities was a particular source of pride by 1900. Business executives often rode elevators to and from their offices in steel-framed skyscrapers. Electric lights lit some streets, offices, and homes. (Gas would be the principal source of energy, however, until after 1910.) Electric streetcars expanded city limits and opened suburbs. Water, gas, and sewage systems were constantly improving. Telephones linked people together as never before. (The Chicago World's Fair of 1893 featured a long-distance telephone connected with New York City.)

A new urban middle class was developing at the turn of the century, consisting of salaried professionals, technicians, government employees, sales-

Newly arrived immigrants struggle through the maze at Ellis Island. **Source:** *Courtesy of the National Park Service, Statue of Liberty National Monument*

people, and clerical workers. Their number increased from 756,000 in 1870 to 5.6 million in 1910. Emerging from rural or lower income urban backgrounds, these people had great faith in the future and envisioned unlimited prosperity and economic independence for those committed to virtuous living and hard work.

Prosperity

It seems clear that by the early years of the century Americans owned more material goods than ever before. Prices declined steadily from the end of the Civil War to the mid-1890s, due largely to lower production costs brought about by mass-production techniques and technological developments. Real wages of workers rose more than 50 percent between 1860 and 1890, and would go up another 33 percent by 1910. Per capita income in 1900, estimated at $569, was the highest in the world. Unemployment levels dropped after the Spanish-American War, and job opportunities seemed unprecedented to many contemporaries.

Farmers had much to be optimistic about, as well. Scores of technological improvements, from the twine-binders to the latest spraying equipment, had almost cut in half the time and labor costs of crop production between 1830 and 1896. The price of farm machinery had dropped sharply after 1880. Production was climbing dramatically: between 1860 and 1915 corn soared from 800 million bushels to 3 billion; wheat increased from 173 million bushels to 1 billion. Prices of farm products would rise by nearly 50 percent between 1900 and 1910. Foreclosure rates had dropped. New land was under cultivation. Commercial, specialized farming was clearly the future for rural America.

Education

Prosperity also meant that many Americans, in the cities and on the farms, could partake of the expanding educational opportunities of the period. In 1900 15.5 million people attended public schools, up from 6.8 million thirty years earlier. The national illiteracy rate had declined from 20 percent to 10.7 percent in the same period. At the turn of the century one out of twenty-five young men between the ages of 18 and 21 received some form of higher education. Fifty years earlier the figure had been one out of sixty.

In 1900 there were almost a thousand colleges and universities, with 240,000 students and 24,000 professors. The state-chartered universities, such as Wisconsin, Michigan, and California, led the way in opening the doors of higher education to the intellectually able, regardless of their socioeconomic status. Course offerings increasingly emphasized practical and applied subjects over the traditional classical curriculum associated for centuries with privileged elites. By 1900 several prominent technical institutions, including the Massachusetts Institute of Technology, Case, Carnegie, and Stevens, fashioned their educational offerings to meet the nation's industrial needs.

The emergence of several prominent medical schools, such as Johns Hopkins (1893), and the reorganization of the American Medical Association in 1901 brought modern, scientific medicine to the nation for the first time. In the first two decades of the new century, the national death rate dropped by more than 20 percent. The appearance of state bar associations, the formation of the American Economic Association in 1885, and the creation of the National Education Association in 1905 revealed the fact that many professions were busily raising their educational requirements and restricting access to their ranks.

A World Power

By 1900 the United States had shed its long antimilitary and anti-imperialist tradition and become a world power. The origins of this development are complex. Some advocates of a combative, expansionist foreign policy had argued that American industry needed overseas markets. Senator Albert Beveridge declared, "American factories are making more than the American people can use; American soil is producing more than they can consume. Fate has written our policy for us; the trade of the world must and shall be ours." Some were convinced that Americans were obligated to share the blessings of Christianity and Western civilization with the less fortunate and "inferior." Josiah Strong, in his best-selling book *Our Country* (1886), proclaimed that the Anglo-Saxon was "divinely commissioned to be, in a peculiar sense, his brother's keeper." Others were certain that the nation was threatened by European powers and had to rearm and expand for purposes of self-defense. Common to all proponents was an intense nationalism.

Senator Henry Cabot Lodge of Massachusetts, New York's Theodore Roosevelt, and Alfred Thayer Mahan, author of the influential book *The Influence of Sea Power Upon History* (1890), were among those calling for the creation of a strong navy and merchant marine, the construction of an American-controlled canal through Central America, and control of several Pacific islands, including Hawaii, as stepping stones to Asia. The construction of a modern navy, with steel rather than wooden ships, got under way in the early 1880s during the presidency of Chester Alan Arthur. Arthur's successor, Grover Cleveland, accelerated the naval buildup.

American military victories during the 113-day Spanish-American War in 1898 were decisive. This struggle was waged to help Cubans free themselves from Spanish rule and seek revenge for the sinking of the battleship *U.S.S. Maine* in Havana harbor. When the fighting stopped, Spain ceded Puerto Rico and Guam and left the United States in control of the Philippine Islands. Following a lengthy debate, the Philippines were annexed and America became an imperial power. Senator Beveridge declared that God "has made us the master organizers of the world to establish system where chaos reigns. He has made us adept in government that we may administer government among savages and senile peoples." Many Americans agreed, including business leaders, Protestant clergymen, and long-time expansionists. Among those who disagreed were a number of Filipinos, led by Emilio Aguinaldo, who fought a bloody war for their independence from 1899 to 1902, a conflict that took the lives of 4,300 Americans and untold thousands of Filipinos.

In August 1898 the United States annexed Hawaii as a further link in its path to the Far East. A year later John Hay, McKinley's expansionist secretary of state, issued the first Open Door note, declaring America's commitment to commercial equality in China and asking European powers to respect the same principle. American troops were involved in putting down the Boxer Rebellion of 1900, a peasant uprising that attempted to drive all foreigners from China, and Hay again declared his country's determination to maintain a strong presence in that country. It was obvious that the United States was determined to make its voice heard throughout the world during the new century.

Laissez Faire

By 1900 politicians, business leaders, educators, and reformers, among others, continued to praise the virtues of laissez faire. In practice, however, this dogma of the classical economists opposing government interference in economic affairs was frequently ignored. Rhetoric about the blessings of unchecked competition, a self-regulating economy, and the evils of state intervention, while often sincere, disguised the actual role played by corporations and government at all levels in the development of the industrial nation.

Congress, for example, protected American industries from overseas competition by passing high tariffs. Rates were raised so often during the Gilded Age that revenue from customs duties produced annual Treasury surpluses from 1866 to 1893. Moreover, federal and state spending for internal improvements, such as the modernization of rivers and harbors, was generous. With the passage of the Homestead Act of 1862, millions of acres of public land were given or sold at low prices to speculators and settlers. Federal, state, and local assistance was critical to the construction of nationwide railroad lines: between 1862 and 1872, for example, Congress loaned railroad entrepreneurs $64.6 million and gave them 200 million acres of public domain. The Supreme Court forbade state regulation of interstate railroads, sharply limited the powers of railroad regulatory agencies, protected corporations through the Fourteenth Amendment (designed originally to assist freed slaves), and declared the income tax unconstitutional. Federal and state courts, along with federal and state troops, were often used to break strikes; between 1885 and 1895 states mobilized their military forces 118 times to resolve labor conflicts.

By the turn of the century government intervention into the economy was a reality that few knowledgeable Americans could ignore. Nevertheless, laissez faire was extolled throughout the land. Many sincerely believed that it was the key to past and future prosperity. Those who had benefited handsomely from the government policies of the late nineteenth century, however, often had less exalted motives for preaching the dogma. The facts of government assistance detracted from the self-image of the rich and powerful, who boasted tirelessly of the direct relationship between their alleged personal virtues and wealth. They also feared that if the less fortunate saw how government might be used to help the few, they might begin demanding assistance for the majority of Americans.

Social Darwinism

Many influential Americans of the Gilded Age firmly believed that Charles Darwin's theory of evolution, published in 1859, explained the functions of human society as well as nature. Progress, they argued, depended upon the "survival of the fittest." Englishman Herbert Spencer (whose books sold more than 300,000 copies in the United States during the late nineteenth century) and Americans William Graham Sumner and John Fiske told wealthy, middle-class, conservative, and ambitious citizens what they wanted to hear: certain moral attributes such as industriousness, temperance, and frugality produced prosperity and power; it was against the "laws of nature" and the health of the nation for the state to come to the rescue of those who were losers in the struggles of life. Spencer, for example, argued against public health measures: it was right that disease should "weed out" the unfit. Reformers, he contended, were dangerous sentimentalists who opposed science.

The less intellectually inclined majority may not have known about Spencer or Sumner but they clung to a gospel of success shared by Social Darwinists. Countless lectures and sermons and a vast literature of schoolbooks, self-help handbooks and magazines, Protestant tracts, and inexpensive rags-to-riches novels had taught millions to believe that success came more or less automatically to those who exhibited honesty, frugality, sobriety, industry, perseverance, punctuality, initiative, loyalty, obedience, and similar virtues. (The novels of Horatio Alger, which taught these values, adding the element of good fortune, sold some 200 million copies between the Civil War and World War I.) Godliness was in league with riches. Those who failed to improve their lot in life, it was thought, had earned their fate and deserved their punishment. Henry Ward Beecher, a highly influential urban clergyman, declared: "no man in this land suffers from poverty unless it be more than his fault—unless it be his *sin*." Wickedness was in league with poverty.

Examples of social and economic mobility could be seen everywhere, and most people no doubt believed themselves on their way up. Many were aware of the much-publicized fact that Andrew Carnegie had started out as a bobbin boy in a steel mill earning $1.20 a week. He had followed the rules, it was said, and so must others who would equal or better his wealth. Thomas Edison was another prominent example of the self-made man.

John D. Rockefeller, the nation's first billionaire, told people simply that God had given him his money. In 1900 many Americans believed him.

THE OTHER SIDE OF THE COIN

For all of the optimism, prosperity, power, and scientific, technological, and educational advances, however, much of American life at the turn of the century was unworthy of celebration. Everywhere one could see glaring examples of exploitation, corruption, and injustice, and much of the fear, ugliness, and pain was directly related to industrialization, urbanization, and the other new developments that were generally associated with progress. Increasingly, men and women were becoming sensitive to the nation's social and economic problems and were challenging the assumptions that dominated American life and thought. Indeed, a powerful age of reform was on the horizon.

Living Standards

Despite a general rise in the standard of living for all Americans at the time, the disparity of wealth between rich and poor was enormous, and the gap was increasing.

As early as 1877 Rockefeller was earning approximately $720 an hour—more than the annual salary of most of his employees. Surveys revealed that by the 1890s there were more than 4,000 millionaires in the country, up from a few hundred several decades earlier. In 1900 Andrew Carnegie's personal income was $23 million (on which there was no income tax). One percent of the population owned more of the nation's wealth than did the remaining 99 percent. Railroad tycoon Cornelius Vanderbilt and his family owned seven homes in the heart of New York City worth a total of $12 million. During the summer months, some of the wealthy enjoyed incredibly lavish dinners and balls at palatial estates dotting the shores of Newport, Rhode Island. Wealthy Americans spent more money on art between 1880 and 1910 than had ever been spent by a similar group in world history.

On the other hand, one contemporary study estimated that of the nation's 12.5 million families in 1890, 11 million received an annual income of $380, considerably below the $500-a-year poverty line. Steelworkers earned about $450 a year, textile workers less than $350. The average industrial worker could not support a family adequately. Robert Hunter's book *Poverty*, published in 1904, estimated that approximately half of America's families owned no property, and that between 10 and 20 million Americans were living in poverty.

The instability of the nation's rapidly expanding economy often brought panic and pain to the majority of Americans. Industrialization produced sharp, unpredictable swings between prosperity, recession, and depression. In 1900 things were booming, but people had not forgotten the seven-year depression that had haunted the 1870s or the massive collapse of the economy in 1893 that within a year had caused 20 percent of the work force to be unemployed. Recessions in 1904, 1907, and 1913–14 lay in the immediate future.

Wealthy businessmen often used economic downturns to accelerate the merger movement, to modernize plants at low cost, to purchase raw materials inexpensively, and to attract customers by low rates and prices. Most Americans simply suffered through the recessions and depressions, hoping desperately that good times would somehow return and that their hard work and virtuous living would pay off.

Modern studies of socioeconomic mobility reveal that in good times or bad the rags-to-riches theme of the period was largely a myth. The wealthy came mostly from middle-class or upper-middle-class families. A small minority of people had always held most of the nation's wealth and would continue to do so. The dream of countless Americans of rising by their abilities from the lower and blue-collar classes to become rich and famous were almost entirely illusory. Still, mobility was more possible in the United States than anywhere else, and the hope of rising even a notch or two beyond one's current socioeconomic level was usually enough to temper extreme discontent about the maldistribution of wealth. Socialism, anarchism, and other radical ideologies did not appeal to the vast majority of Americans—and never would.

Working Conditions

The life of a typical industrial worker was harsh and often brutal. A ten-hour day and a six-day week were standard by 1890. Some steelworkers put in twelve-hour days, seven days a week; canners worked nearly seventy-seven hours a week. By 1900 the work week averaged 57.3 hours. Almost a million workers a year suffered industrial accidents without compensation. Between 1890 and 1917, 72,000 railroad employees were killed on the tracks, and close to 2 million were injured; an additional 158,000 were killed in the yards. In accord with the teachings of laissez faire, government failed to regulate or inspect working conditions to any meaningful degree.

By 1900 more than five million women worked in industry, some in southern textile mills for wages as low as 4 cents an hour. About 1.7 million children under the age of 16 worked full-time. Children labored sixteen hours a day in some canneries. Young farm laborers often toiled twelve hours a day. Children in North Carolina mills were paid as low as 10 and 12 cents a day.

Work was frequently monotonous as well as exhausting and dangerous. Business leaders and efficiency-minded reformers were increasingly attracted to the teachings of Frederick Winslow Taylor, chief engineer of the Midvale Steel Company and the pioneer in time and motion studies. As early as 1881 Taylor was arguing that by analyzing jobs and supervising labor more efficiently, factory owners could increase output, lower prices, and increase wages. His "scientific management" proposals contributed to the development of the assembly line. Workers found themselves repeating a single task all day at a rapid and often agonizing pace set by "scientific" employers. The standardization of work procedures was to be a common feature of industrial America in the new century. Peter Drucker has ranked Taylor with Darwin and Freud as one of the most important thinkers of modern times.

Labor unions were of little or no assistance to most workers. Numerous unions, containing no more than 1 or 2 percent of the labor force, had come and gone in the nineteenth century. Massive labor disturbances during the Gilded Age (there were close to 37,000 strikes between 1881 and 1905, involving 7 million workers) yielded few benefits.

In 1900 the American Federation of Labor, a loose alliance of craft unions founded in 1886, was the dominant labor force in the nation. It had a half million members and within four years would see its ranks swell to 1,676,000. The latter figure still represented only 12 percent of the nonagricultural work force, however, and that percentage would drop during the next few years.

Traditional individualism and the gospel of success undoubtedly prevented many workers from joining unions; prosperity was linked in the popular mind with personal qualities rather than collective actions. Workers also feared retaliation by their employers, who had used dismissals, lockouts, injunctions, and armed violence to break strikes, and who were soon joining organizations like the National Association of Manufacturers to crush unionization once and for all. Moreover, the craft unionism advocated by the AFL's founder and perennial president, Samuel Gompers, could appeal to only a small percentage of the work force. Gompers did not believe in organizing by industry and was prejudiced against women. (By 1910 there were some 8 million women working outside the home, and only 125,000 were organized.) Radicals opposed Gompers for his hostility to ideology, his frank conservatism, and his abiding concern with higher wages, shorter hours, and job security.

The Cities

However wealthy, important, and popular urban areas had become by 1900, the large cities of America, and a great many of the smaller ones, were crowded, chaotic, noisy, filthy, ugly, and corrupt. The pioneering architect Louis Sullivan described Chicago, his hometown, as "this flat smear, this endless drawl of streets and shanties, large and small, this ocean of smoke . . . Seventy years ago it was a mudhole—today it is a human swamp."

Urban density stunned many observers. A burgeoning population increased the value of land, technology permitted the construction of tall buildings, and cities lacked zoning laws. The result was the tenement, into which landlords crammed as many rent payers as possible. Two-thirds of New York City's 3.5 million people lived in tenements. In 1900 one city block housed thirty-nine tenements with a population of nearly 2,800. In 32 acres of the eleventh ward there were 986.4 persons per acre—that is, about 30,000 people in five or six city blocks, the worst crowding in the world.

The tiny tenement rooms were poorly lighted and ventilated, and less than 10 percent of the buildings had either indoor plumbing or running water. Foul odors filled the air. Juvenile delinquency and crime were rampant. Disease and death were constant companions; in one Chicago district in 1900 three of every five babies died before their first birthday. "In the tenements," wrote Jacob Riis, the chronicler and photographer of slum life, "all the elements make for evil."

Despite recent improvements, garbage piled up in the streets of some cities for days and even weeks. Drinking water was sometimes taken from the same river or lake into which sewage was poured. Factories polluted the air. Roads went unpaved. Educational and recreational facilities were extremely inadequate. City planning was still in its infancy. The cries of those who suffered in urban areas would be loud in the age of reform that was to come.

Much of the suffering, of course, was endured by the immigrants; in 1900 60 percent of the population of the nation's twelve largest cities were the foreign-born or their children. Most of the immigrants had been recruited by business as a source of cheap labor. Once in the United States they found themselves locked into a strange and baffling world of back-breaking jobs or chronic unemployment, grinding poverty, repulsive tenements, and discrimination. Many Americans were not only hostile to the newcomers, they sought to shut off the flow of immigrants altogether. Organized labor wanted to avoid job competition; racists wished to protect "Anglo-Saxon purity"; conservatives worried about labor radicalism and the future of democracy; many Americans disliked Jews and feared the growth of Roman Catholicism. Even

Industrial Pittsburgh at the turn of the century. **Source:** *Library and Archives Division, Historical Society of Western Pennsylvania, Pittsburgh, PA*

those who were in general sympathy with the immigrants were likely to be critical of their alliance with big city bosses.

Most of the larger cities, and many smaller ones, were dominated in 1900 by infamous political machines headed by bosses. One learned critic wrote in 1890, "With very few exceptions the city governments of the United States are the worst in Christendom—the most inefficient, and the most corrupt." Among other things, bosses and their minions stole public funds, loaded the public payroll with cronies (Philadelphia's boss controlled 5,630 public jobs), exacted payments from vice peddlers, sold favors and public utility franchises, took kickbacks from government contractors, and won elections by fraud. In 1905 George Washington Plunkett of New York City's Tammany Hall, a powerful Democratic party machine, spoke of "honest graft," boasting: "I seen my opportunities and I took 'em."

In exchange for their loyalty and votes, the city bosses provided immigrants with much-needed social services that were unavailable from other sources in the laissez faire years. Among other things, the bosses found jobs and places to live for newcomers, cut red tape, provided timely handouts and presents, bailed youngsters out of jail, and threw parties for slum children on hot summer days. Urban reformers discovered that immigrants often staunchly resisted efforts to curtail the power of political machines. Cleveland progressive Frederick D. Howe later lamented, "Faithfulness to the boss was the only civic idea. To the poor, politics meant bread and circuses." Many business owners and managers, accustomed to dealing with the bosses profitably, also resisted reform.

Agrarian Turmoil

While farmers enjoyed reasonably good times in 1900, few of them could forget how recent and shaky their prosperity was. The 1870s had been filled with uncertainties and depression; the 1880s were plagued by blizzards and drought; the 1890s contained a massive financial panic. Farm prices had declined from 1870 to 1895.

A number of complex business problems confused and frustrated farmers. The list included high interest rates; widely fluctuating national and international price levels; high transportation, storage, and marketing costs; and high prices for agricultural machinery. Many agrarians blamed their difficulties on evil conspiracies in big cities among bankers, railroad presidents, corporation executives, industrial workers, and immigrants. In the late nineteenth century, bewilderment, fear, and anger were shared by farmers throughout the nation.

In the 1870s over a million and a half agrarians had joined the Granger movement to improve their lot. In the 1880s the Farmers Alliance had offered hope. In 1892 Alliance representatives and others united to form the Populist party, a "third party" effort with a national platform and a presidential ticket.

The Populists advocated measures sought by angry farmers for two decades. They proposed such striking reforms as the nationalization of banks, federal ownership of railroads and telephone and telegraph systems, immigration restriction, a graduated income tax, the free coinage of silver (to create inflation and ease the monetary problems of farmers), and an end to all government aid to private corporations. Populism was a direct assault upon the traditions of laissez faire, and many Americans thought it dangerously radical. Farmers and labor leaders, among others, failed to rally behind Populist candidates at the polls in 1892, and with the return of prosperity a few years later Populism disappeared. By 1900 farmers had repeatedly failed to organize effectively in their own defense, and their future was decidedly uncertain.

Women

Despite the fact that 20 percent of all women over the age of 15 were employed outside the home in 1900, women were expected to conform to a value system centering exclusively upon domestic matters. They were to be pious, modest, submissive, unintellectual, and thoroughly domestic in their tastes and activities. It was a way of life in which, as one later study put it, women "would always be subordinate, venerated, admired, and ignored."

Medical science taught that women were physically, emotionally, and intellectually inferior to men. The fashionable presence of "nervous disorders" among a great many urban middle-class women seemed to confirm this view. In fact, the health of these women was undoubtedly impaired to some degree by urban pollution, lack of exercise, and current clothing styles. Tight corsets, worn even by small girls, were frequently painful and often damaging. A cultured urban woman in the Gilded Age wore an average of 37 pounds of street clothing in winter months, 19 pounds of which suspended from her waist. One gown could weigh as much as 50 pounds.

The code of proper female conduct, which the great majority of women apparently accepted and defended, was especially severe on the subject of sex. Young girls were advised to avoid romantic novels, dancing, and chatter about young men on pain of disease, hysteria, or worse. Physicians and purity manuals told the married woman to remain cold and passive to her husband's sexual impulses. Continence was sanctioned as the ideal marriage relationship. Most doctors and authorities on family life condemned the distribution of contraceptive information. In any case, such information was almost uniformly illegal and considered immoral.

By 1900 growing numbers of urban middle-class women were expanding their range of activities, largely within the sphere of what was considered "proper" and "feminine." Prosperity, a declining birthrate (3.56 per woman in 1900 as opposed to 7.04 a century earlier), the increasing availability of higher education (by 1902 over half the University of Chicago undergraduates were women), labor-saving devices, and the practice of hiring immigrants as inexpensive domestic servants gave leisure time to thousands of women. For the most part, business and the professions remained closed to them, but in any case most women were unenthusiastic about assuming traditionally male roles. They chose instead to devote their talents and energies to teaching, nursing, charity work, and reform movements that defended the family. The temperance crusade and efforts to abolish prostitution received strong support. By 1900 Frances Willard's Women's Christian Temperance Union had 160,000 members.

Feminists, who for decades had been working to further women's rights, now saw the ballot as the key to the struggle for equality. In 1890 they had formed the National American Woman Suffrage Association, headed at first by such veteran leaders as Susan B. Anthony and Elizabeth Cady Stanton. Only four lightly populated western states had given women full suffrage by 1900. The strongest opponents of the movement were women themselves, fearful that sex roles might be altered and that the family might in some way be damaged. When Massachusetts voted on the suffrage issue in 1895, four times as many men were in favor of it as women.

Minorities

Some 90 percent of African Americans lived in the South at the turn of the century and were the victims of poverty, discrimination, violence, and ignorance. (As late as 1910 almost a third of all blacks were illiterate.) The high hopes of abolitionists for the future of freed slaves had been abandoned even before the official termination of Reconstruction in 1877. Throughout the country, blacks were a despised minority, believed by almost all whites to be inferior in every way and deserving of their fate.

In the South, three-fourths of the black farmers were sharecroppers or tenant farmers, and the lagging price of cotton after the Civil War made land ownership increasingly difficult. While almost half of the population of Georgia was black in 1880, African Americans owned less than 2 percent of the state's landed wealth.

Southern blacks were subject to arrest virtually at the whim of white law enforcement officers; convicts were often "farmed out" to work on white-owned farms and railroads. African Americans were disfranchised; the number of registered black voters in Louisiana fell from 130,000 in 1896 to 1,300 in 1904. Violence against blacks was commonplace. According to the Tuskegee Institute, there were 4,733 lynchings between 1882 and 1950, nearly 90 percent of them in the South. The worst year was 1892, when there were 292. Railroads advertised special trains to the lynching scenes; ten thousand spectators gathered at one of them. Victims were also tortured in public, some of them flayed alive and slowly burned to death. In 1900 mobs took over all of New Orleans, killing and terrorizing blacks.

African Americans were also rigorously segregated. The "Jim Crow" laws that had appeared in the North before the Civil War had spread and intensified throughout the South by 1900, segregating such things as railway waiting rooms, streetcars, elevators, toilets, drinking fountains, parks, doorways, and, in New Orleans, houses of prostitution. The Richmond *Times* demanded in 1900 that segregation be "applied in every relation of southern life" because "God almighty drew the color line and it cannot be obliterated."

Much of the antiblack mood in the South was a reaction to the effort by Populists to unite poor whites and blacks against their economic and political oppressors. Conservative leaders preached racial hatred to preserve their power, and the lessons proved effective. The severe depression of the 1890s also summoned the need for a scapegoat, a role blacks had long filled in the South and elsewhere.

In the North, America's involvement with imperialism enhanced widely held assumptions about white supremacy. Scholars such as Louis Aggasiz of Harvard assured Americans that science confirmed the innate inferiority of blacks. The United States Supreme Court sanctioned segregation in public facilities by declaring the Civil Rights Act of 1875 unconstitutional and by establishing in *Plessy* v. *Ferguson* (1895) the "separate but equal" doctrine. Journalists and novelists cranked out such best-sellers as *"The Negro a Beast"; or "In the Image of God", The Leopard's Spots: A Romance of the White Man's Burden—1865–1900*, and *The Negro, A Menace to American Civilization.*

Throughout the North, African Americans retained their civil and political rights, but they were frequently discriminated against in public places, barred by trade unions, and forced to live in inferior, segregated housing.

The widely acknowledged spokesman for blacks in 1900 was Booker T. Washington, founder and president of the Tuskegee Institute in Alabama. In a much-heralded speech of 1895 that came to be known as the Atlanta Compromise, Washington promised white leaders of the North and South that blacks would accept their social and political inferiority. All they wanted, he said, was the opportunity to advance economically to the fullest extent of their skills. Throughout his career, in speeches, articles, and in his popular book *Up From Slavery*, Washington preached the gospel of success, stressed practical education, and emphasized the importance of material prosperity. He would tell a group of white educators in 1912, "We are trying to instil into the Negro mind that if education does not make the Negro humble, simple, and of service to the community, then it will not be encouraged."

Most African Americans, it seems, looked up to Washington as a personal model of the self-made man and accepted his teachings as the only option open to them in an age of rampant racism. One perceptive scholar has referred to the period 1877 to 1901 as "the nadir" in the modern life of American blacks.

Not all blacks supported Washington's subservient approach, however. (We now know that even Washington was privately more militant than his admirers ever imagined.) Boston newspaperman William Monroe Trotter and the brilliant intellectual William E. B. Du Bois urged blacks to seek first-class education (both were Harvard trained) and strive for complete equality. In 1909 Du Bois and others formed the National Association for the Advancement of Colored People. While lacking mass support, the NAACP would later become a leading force in the drive for black equality.

By 1900 Native Americans were a defeated, impoverished, and largely dependent people. The ever-increasing expansion of white settlers and railroads into Indian territory, and the slaughter of the Great Plains buffalo, nearly complete by 1870, had gravely weakened their traditional culture. ("Kill every buffalo you can," advised an army officer. "Every buffalo dead is an Indian gone.") After more than two hundred pitched battles and countless skirmishes against whites, Indian resistance ended in 1890. At Wounded Knee, South Dakota, in one of the great tragedies of the Gilded Age, United States Army troops massacred two hundred Dakota men, women, and children.

The Dawes Act of 1887 had broken up reservations into individually owned allotments in the hope of transforming Native Americans into self-sustaining farmers. The attempt soon proved futile, and most of the land wound up in the hands of white speculators. Efforts to educate American Indians in the ways of whites were largely unsuccessful. Government policy in the nineteenth century, much of which was well intentioned, had clearly failed to solve what was generally called the "Indian problem."

Other minorities bore the brunt of the nation's intolerance, as well. The Chinese on the Pacific Coast, who resisted acculturation and were willing to work for low wages, were the objects of intense discrimination and periodic outbursts of violence. The Chinese Exclusion Law of 1882 had suspended the importation of laborers for ten years and denied American citizenship to all Chinese.

About 100,000 people of Mexican birth lived in California and the Southwest by 1900. They were scorned for their culture, religion, and language, exploited by employers eager for cheap labor, and shunted into slums.

Politics

Most students of late-nineteenth-century politics, at the time and later, have been extremely critical of those who governed on the local, state, and national levels. James Bryce, a learned Scotsman who traveled throughout the country, concluded in 1888 that "politician" was "a term of reproach." Modern scholars have tempered this judgment, but there is no escaping the fact that the politics of the period contained a considerable quantity of corruption, greed, incompetence, and confusion.

The two major parties were evenly balanced in public support until 1896, when the GOP (Grand Old Party, or Republicans) began to dominate. Party platforms stuck largely to generalities, and the differences between Republicans and Democrats seemed difficult to decipher. In fact, the GOP was more interested in an active federal government than its opponents; it backed high tariffs, centralized banking, huge grants to railroads, and stern Reconstruction policies. Still, most voters determined their party loyalty according to sectional ties, family traditions, religious considerations, and local issues. The post-Reconstruction South, for example, was solidly Democratic; Americans of Scandinavian descent tended to be Republicans.

Both parties seemed primarily intent on winning office, serving an assortment of business interests, and grabbing government jobs. The spoils system was the glue that held the political parties together during these decades. A victorious big city mayoral candidate, for example, could replace hundreds of his incumbent opponent's officeholders with campaign workers, not worrying about the qualifications of his supporters. Once in office, these political allies were required to kick back a fixed percentage of their salaries to party coffers. This system, obviously, was not designed for the good of the taxpayers, and it frequently led to government inefficiency and corruption. In 1883 civil service reformers had won a hard-fought victory against the spoilsmen on the federal level, and more than 94,500 positions were covered by the Pendleton Act in 1900.

Election fraud was common throughout the nation. In often-pivotal Indiana, for example, campaign workers sometimes stood on street corners buying votes. Illegal voters were imported into critical states. Ballot boxes were stuffed. Blacks were kept from the polls by intimidation and violence.

Congress was the dominant force on the national level, and it was plagued with numerous deficiencies. Party discipline was nonexistent, procedures were antiquated, bitter factional feuds were recurrent, and disorder often threatened to become chaos. Ethical standards were low, and congressmen were frequently the servants of special interests.

The presidents from Johnson to McKinley were content to abide by the prevailing belief that they were merely to administer the nation's laws. They avoided legislative affairs for the most part and chose not to exert vigorous leadership. Had they decided otherwise, their opportunities would have been limited, for one party controlled both Congress and the White House only twice, 1889–91 and 1893–95. Several chief executives, such as Hayes and Harrison, were regularly ridiculed for their indecision and weakness. Johnson was impeached, avoiding conviction by a single vote. Grant's administrations were alarmingly corrupt. Two presidents after Lincoln, Garfield and McKinley, were assassinated, while another, Arthur, was mortally ill while in office. The Gilded Age was a low point in the history of the presidency.

In 1900 President McKinley ran against William Jennings Bryan, the Democratic candidate four years earlier. McKinley stood for "honest money" and a high tariff; the "boy orator" from Nebraska again advocated the free silver issue, a scheme to cut the value of U.S. currency in order to create inflation and help those short of funds and burdened with debt. Times were good, most people seemed contented, and the Republicans spent lavishly to ensure their victory. McKinley, and his running mate, 41-year-old Governor Theodore Roosevelt of New York, won easily, carrying the electoral vote 292 to 155. Republicans, with a single interruption, were to enjoy the support of the majority of Americans for the next almost thirty years.

SEEDS OF REFORM

For all of the public contentment evident at the turn of the century, a wide variety of men and women were actively seeking reform. In fact, all of the basic ideas associated with what is known as the Progressive Era were in evidence by 1890. These reformers denounced trusts, plutocrats, and corporate crooks, attacked laissez faire and Social Darwinism, cried out against the miseries of urban living, condemned factory conditions and child labor, sought better treatment of women and minorities, and took steps to rid government of inefficiency and corruption. The intellectual and political atmospheres crackled with new ideas and proposals. In books and articles, in college and university classrooms, in pulpits, in courts of law, on city streets, and in election campaigns people were at work exposing the painful realities of the late nineteenth century and urging Americans to build a more equitable, honest, organized, and democratic society. "Progress" was a popular word, and progressivism was beginning to capture the nation's imagination.

SUGGESTED READING

Edward Bellamy, *Looking Backward, 2000–1887* (1888); Charles W. Calhoun (ed.), *The Gilded Age: Essays on the Origins of Modern America* (1996); Roger Daniels, *Coming to America: A History of Immigration and Ethnicity in American Life* (1990); John S. and Robin M. Haller, *The Physician and Sexuality in Victorian America* (1974); Robert Kanigel, *The One Best Way: Frederick Winslow Taylor and the Enigma of Efficiency* (1997); Harold C. Livesay, *Andrew Carnegie and the Rise of Big Business* (1975); Thomas C. Reeves, *Gentleman Boss: The Life of Chester Alan Arthur* (1975); Ole Rolvaag, *Giants in the Earth* (1927); Alan Trachtenberg, *The Incorporation of America: Culture and Society in the Gilded Age* (1982); C. Vann Woodward, *The Strange Career of Jim Crow* (1974).

Chapter Two

PROGRESSIVISM AND THE SQUARE DEAL

The Progressive movement is an umbrella term to cover a number of reform efforts, from all across the nation, that began to come together about 1900, in a period of prosperity and rising expectations. The progressives lacked a single economic policy; they disagreed among themselves about political reforms, cultural issues such as prohibition, and racial equality; and they proposed a variety of plans and panaceas. Some reformers had self-interest in mind, while others were concerned primarily with the general good. Several were committed to efficiency and order, and sought to place experts in positions of authority. The progressives were united, however, in their desire to document and right the wrongs caused by industrialization, urbanization, and immigration. Like virtually all Americans, they also agreed about the inherent goodness of capitalism, private property, democracy, and individual freedom.

The progressives were greatly influenced by Protestant Christianity, and they saw most problems as moral problems. They believed that "practical idealism" and "applied Christianity" could remake America. They believed in the power of environment to shape lives and in the ability of men and women to create a just, democratic, happy, and sensible society. Most reformers were willing to use the power of government—at all levels—to accomplish their ends.

From the Gilded Age until America's entrance into the First World War, people from various classes, ethnic origins, occupations, and sections of the country attempted to restrain the power of big business, bolster national morality, democratize politics, and help the underdog by laying the foundations of the welfare state. Their extremely fruitful activities would alter the pattern of American life and reverberate throughout the rest of the century, directly influencing the New Deal, the Fair Deal, the New Frontier, the Great Society, and beyond.

21

THE REFORM SPIRIT

The first calls for reform in the 1870s and 1880s, such as Henry George's *Progress and Poverty*, which called for a tax on the unearned increase in the value of land, and Edward Bellamy's utopian novel *Looking Backward*, received considerable attention. At the same time, writers began to abandon the romantic style that had dominated pre-Civil War literature in favor of examining life as it really was. The creation of believable and complex characters from all social classes and the vivid description of the nation's most serious social problems jolted millions of readers and stirred reform activity well into the 1900s.

Mark Twain, for example, in such books as *The Gilded Age* (1873) and the classic *Huckleberry Finn* (1884), contributed biting commentary on the pomp, greed, and inhumanity of his time. Novelist and editor William Dean Howells castigated grasping businessmen and contrasted the lives of rich and poor in such books as *The Rise of Silas Lapham* (1885). Hamlin Garland's *Main-Travelled Roads* (1891) described the loneliness and poverty of rural life. Stephen Crane, in *Maggie, A Girl of the Streets* (1893), depicted the tragic life of a young girl trapped in an urban slum.

The immense depression of 1893–97 shocked the American people as never before into the realization that something was gravely wrong with at least a portion of the political and economic system. Henry Demarest Lloyd's *Wealth Against Commonwealth* (1894) won readers by carefully documenting the elimination of Standard Oil's competition and denouncing Social Darwinism and laissez faire. Frank Norris skillfully blasted the Southern Pacific Railroad in *The Octopus* (1901) and condemned the wealthy in *The Pit* (1903). Jack London, a Marxian socialist who once wrote fifty books in seventeen years, including *The Call of the Wild* (1903), described the Darwinian struggle for life and told of the plight of urban workers. Upton Sinclair's *The Jungle* (1906) was a socialist plea containing shocking accounts of daily life in the meat-packing industry.

By 1900 the nation had 2,226 newspapers, half of the world's total, and 14,000 weeklies with a circulation of 42.5 million. The owners and editors of newspapers and magazines had discovered the popularity of vivid stories exposing corruption and focusing upon those who suffered in the slums. Starting in late 1902, and for about a decade thereafter, a number of new and inexpensive magazines specialized in this genre. While the quality of the articles often varied and sometimes bordered on yellow journalism, this literature on the whole was factual, well written, and often courageous.

In such magazines as *McClure's, Munsey's, Everybody's*, and *Collier's*, Ida Tarbell ("the terror of the trusts") revealed the inner workings of Standard Oil, Lincoln Steffens dissected urban political machines, Ray Stannard Baker detailed railroad mismanagement, Thomas W. Lawson attacked stock market manipulators, and David Graham Philipps indicted what he called the "treason" of the United States Senate. Scores of such writers were at work during most of the Progressive Era, invariably calling for a public crusade against the evil at hand. These "muckrakers," as Theodore Roosevelt dubbed them in 1906 (after a passage in John Bunyan's *Pilgrim's Progress* about one "who could look no way but downward"), helped sensitize their largely urban middle-class readers to the injustices of the period and contributed significantly to the swelling tide of reform.

With reform in the air, the emphasis among many artists was increasingly upon the injustices of contemporary urban and industrial society. Notable painters such as Thomas Eakins and Winslow Homer had made a concern for accuracy and detail fashionable by 1900. Robert Henry, John Sloan, William Glackens, and George Luks, among others, selected such subjects as alleys, tenements, and saloons. Art, they argued, should reflect facts and bear social messages. After a New York exhibition in 1908, conservative critics labeled these painters the "Ashcan School" and the "Revolutionary Black Gang." Despite the sneers, these innovative individuals enhanced the art of the new century and intensified the reform spirit.

Pragmatism

Charles Darwin's scientific findings and the appearance of disturbing and often radical critiques of the Bible had produced considerable turmoil in the late nineteenth century among the thoughtful. In 1878 the brilliant philosopher Charles Sanders Pierce introduced what he called pragmatism as a way of defining truth. The value of ideas, he declared, should be weighed solely by their consequences. This was a sharp departure from the traditional norms of revelation and reason.

Pragmatism was developed and popularized by the great Harvard psychologist and philosopher William James. James argued that human beings had free will and were not simply slaves of natural or physical laws. Nothing was predetermined, he asserted. All absolutes and systems were illusory and served to paralyze human will. Ideas, he said, should be tested strictly by experience: they were true if they worked satisfactorily and untrue if they did not. Historian Henry Steele Commager observed of James that he "confronted all dogma with skepticism and made skepticism itself a dogma."

This new philosophical method reinforced the strong American belief in individualism and practicality and greatly influenced the Progressive Era. It encouraged reformers to seek facts; challenge prevailing social, political, and economic theories; and work for change. Progressives tended to believe that the world could be reshaped through human intelligence and good will. This faith, at the heart of twentieth-century liberalism, owed much to pragmatism.

The Scholarly Disciplines

The burgeoning universities of the Gilded Age provided many of the ideas that fueled progressivism. Younger professors often took their doctorates in Germany and were impressed by the emergence of the German welfare state.

Informed Americans would also be attracted to the advanced social legislation of the Liberal governments in Great Britain after 1900. Social scientists
were especially interested in reform.

In 1885 a number of young economists (including 29-year-old Woodrow
Wilson, a graduate student in government) organized the American Economic
Association. They proclaimed their rejection of laissez faire, their belief in
the necessity of state intervention in the economy, and their appreciation of
the importance of ethics in economic affairs. Richard T. Ely of Johns Hopkins University wrote, "We regard the state as an educational and ethical
agency whose positive aid is an indispensable condition of human progress."
Simon Nelson Patten of the University of Pennsylvania, a cofounder of the
association, became a prominent spokesman for state planning and public
works programs. John R. Commons, a student of Ely's and a labor expert at
the University of Wisconsin, would be an important scholar-reformer of the
Progressive Era.

Thorstein Veblen's sardonic *Theory of the Leisure Class* (1899) would appeal to reform-minded economists for decades. Veblen sharply criticized what
he saw as a wasteful and irrational economic system, and he condemned the
captains of industry and finance for their "conspicuous consumption." He advocated control of the economy by technicians and engineers.

Lester Frank Ward, an obscure federal bureaucrat and one of the most
learned men in America, was a major influence upon the social scientists in
the universities who were grappling with ways to expand human happiness.
His pathbreaking *Dynamic Sociology* (1883) was the most effective attack on
laissez faire and Social Darwinism of the late nineteenth century. Ward believed that humanity's power over nature was unlimited. He called for public education and careful social planning. He thought that government was
the most effective mechanism for helping the weak against the strong, and
he urged legislators to become experts in "the science of society."

In the 1880s political scientists, led by Woodrow Wilson, began to ignore
the abstractions that had long dominated the study of government in favor
of careful studies of actual political institutions. In place of lofty tomes on
natural law and states rights, for example, scholars became increasingly anxious to investigate such topics as the congressional committee system, lobbying, and the spoils system. They relied on statistics and facts drawn from
a variety of sources, such as the federal census and state agency reports.

Historians, under the influence of the distinguished German scholar Leopold
Von Ranke, also sought to discard theoretical models and ground their con-
clusions on painstaking research. Objective truth, historians increasingly contended, could best be discovered by the study of primary sources—the man-
uscripts and other materials from the past itself. Much traditional history was
soon rewritten and reinterpreted.

As the clamor for reform grew louder, a number of historians focused their
attention on modern history and became involved in the campaigns for
change. Their well-documented books and articles stressed conflict and struggle in the recent past, condemned social and economic privilege, and trum-

peted the glories of democracy. One of the most influential of the "progressive historians" was Frederick Jackson Turner of the University of Wisconsin. His lifelong stress upon the environmental and economic factors in history (the "Turner Thesis" argued that the frontier gave Americans distinctive characteristics) helped shape the thinking of many intellectuals and reformers who were busily challenging the "iron laws" dear to conservatives. Charles Beard's *An Economic Interpretation of the Constitution* (1913) grew directly out of the frustrations of progressives at the way conservative courts and legislators used the Constitution to block reforms.

The science of law, it was widely thought, consisted of an unchanging body of information, grounded in natural law and found within books on jurisprudence. The dramatic changes of the nineteenth century made this rigid system increasingly divorced from reality and hostile to the public welfare. Courts became instruments of reaction at the same time that reform was capturing national attention. Still, a few legal scholars were able to step beyond the boundaries of their profession. As early as the 1870s the brilliant Boston patrician Oliver Wendell Holmes, Jr., was contending that law was rooted in human experience and should not be viewed as a lifeless, hidebound science. "It is revolting," he would later write, "to have no better reason for a rule of law than that so it was laid down in the time of Henry IV." In his influential book *Common Law* (1891) and in lengthy service on the Massachusetts Supreme Court (1883–1902) and the United States Supreme Court (1902–32), Holmes argued that law should respond to the "felt necessities of the time."

The great legal scholar Roscoe Pound called this new approach "sociological jurisprudence," by which he meant that law should become an active and pragmatic social science, existing to serve the needs of society. Jurisprudence, he said, "must be judged by the results it achieves, not by the niceties of its internal structure; it must be valued by the extent to which it meets its ends, not by the beauty of its logical process." This blend of law and pragmatism was introduced to the United States Supreme Court in 1908 by Louis Brandeis in *Muller* v. *Oregon*, a case involving a ten-hour-day law for women laundry workers. In addition to legal precedents, Brandeis used evidence in his argument about the sociological effects of long working hours. The case was won, but it would be thirty years before the Court would be entirely comfortable with this approach.

Religion and Reform

In the 1880s some liberal Protestant seminaries, such as Union in New York, began to teach reform as a religious duty. Younger ministers in the cities often threw open their churches to the disadvantaged and entered the battle against the suffering that surrounded them. In 1887, for example, Episcopalians created the Church Association for the Advancement of the Interests of Labor, which supported unions and worked for the elimination of sweatshops, child labor, and slums. Congregationalists soon joined the effort, and Methodists were not far behind. The Federal Council of Churches, organized in 1908, frequently injected itself into a variety of reform movements. Roman Catholics slowly lent their support after the appearance of *Rerum novarum* (1891), Pope Leo XIII's dramatic encyclical criticizing the excesses of capitalism and defending the existence of labor unions.

A vital part of this surge for reform was a body of literature promoting what came to be called the Social Gospel. This involved a modification of the traditional emphasis on individual sin and salvation that stressed good works through the improvement of society. Washington Gladden's influential *Applied Christianity* (1886) attacked speculators and monopolists, maintained the right of labor to organize, and urged profit sharing. Charles M. Sheldon's best-selling novel *In His Steps* (1896) contended that true Christians would lead reform efforts and transform their communities into models of virtue. Walter Rauschenbusch, in *Christianity and the Social Crisis* (1907) and other books, condemned the industrial revolution on religious grounds, labeled capitalism "essential atheism," and advocated the communism of early Christianity (not of Marx).

Most supporters of the Social Gospel limited their criticisms of capitalism to its abuses. They wanted "Christian capitalism" instead of laissez faire, an economic system in which wages were fair, working conditions decent, and competition restrained by brotherly love. The application of Christian ethics in all areas of life, they believed, would lead to happiness and plenty.

Urban Reformers

In the 1880s and 1890s a number of young, idealistic, middle-class social workers, mostly women, put the concepts of the Social Gospel to work in the form of "settlement houses." Patterned after London's Toynbee Hall and privately financed, these houses were situated in urban slums and were designed to improve the lives of slum dwellers physically, morally, socially, and intellectually. Reformers established restaurants, club rooms, recreational facilities, public baths, libraries, day nurseries, and kindergartens, and offered classes in a wide range of practical and cultural subjects. By 1900 there were almost a hundred settlement houses in the nation's large cities—more than four hundred by 1911. The most prominent were Jane Addams' Hull House in Chicago (1889) and Lillian D. Wald's Henry Street Settlement in New York (1893). Mary Simkhovitch opened Greenwich House in 1901 and served her west Manhattan working people for forty-five years. These humanitarian leaders wanted to live with the poor, to understand and share their suffering, and, in Addams' words, to make social service "express the spirit of Christ."

The firsthand experience of life in the slums convinced settlement house workers of the need for government to provide the poor with such necessities as tenement regulation, consumer protection, educational opportunity, child labor restrictions, and maximum working hours for women. These reformers became ardent backers of social welfare legislation, and they supported a variety of organizations dedicated to the cause of good government.

Every major city during the late nineteenth century contained nonpartisan clubs, committees, leagues, and commissions devoted to municipal reform. Some such organizations became national in scale. The National Civil Service Reform League (1881) fought the spoils system at all levels of government. Membership in organizations affiliated with the reform-minded General Federation of Women's Clubs (1889) grew from fifty thousand in 1898 to more than a million in 1912. The National Municipal League, a nationwide clearing house promoting better government, had two-hundred branches within two years of its founding in 1894. Municipal Ownership leagues, Direct Legislation leagues, and similar beacons of reform were commonplace as progressivism began to dominate American politics.

Urban political machines, frequent targets of the good-government groups, also gave their important backing to selective reform proposals that would directly benefit their working-class constituents and ensure their own authority. From New York to California bosses supported welfare legislation of all types, business regulations, taxes that threw the heaviest burdens on those able to pay, and such political reforms as primaries, the initiative and referendum, and the direct election of senators. This activity was sometimes idealistic as well as self-serving. Bowery Boss "Big Tim" Sullivan worked in Albany on behalf of a fifty-four-hour-per-week bill for women because he "had seen me sister go out to work when she was only fourteen and I know we ought to help these gals by giving 'em a law which will prevent 'em from being broken down while they're still young." Tammany Hall, the powerful Democratic machine in New York City, backed a series of tough factory safety laws following the death of 146 workers (all but 15, girls and young women) who could not escape the building during a fire at the Triangle Shirtwaist Company in 1911.

Municipal Reform

Progressivism started in the cities during the 1890s and spread to the state and federal levels. Municipal reformers, such as mayors Tom Johnson of Cleveland and Samuel M. "Golden Rule" Jones of Toledo, fought corruption, special interests, and political machines, and sought a wide range of legislation to improve the quality of urban life. Jones, for example, tried to stamp his golden rule philosophy on city government by setting a minimum wage of $1.50 a day for common laborers; by establishing free kindergartens, playgrounds, night schools, and a lodging for tramps; and by creating an open-air church for people of all faiths.

By the turn of the century cities began to obtain "home rule" charters from state legislatures, enabling them to deal in novel ways with their problems. In 1901 Galveston, Texas, pioneered the commission system of government, a plan for achieving nonpartisan, effective administration by placing the powers of the mayor and council in the hands of an elected commission. Des Moines, Iowa, adopted a version of the plan in 1907, and by 1921 about five hundred cities had some form of commission. In 1908 Staunton, Virginia, initiated the city-manager form of government, whereby a professional expert was appointed to administer urban affairs. This too proved popular throughout the nation. Despite all of this activity, however, the three largest cities—New York, Chicago, and Philadelphia—would continue for many decades to be controlled by corrupt political machines.

Many cities fought special interest groups by controlling public utilities. By 1915 almost two-thirds of the nation's waterworks were owned and operated by municipalities. More limited experiments were undertaken in the fields of gas, electricity, and public transportation. Cities also passed or inspired passage of the first laws regulating labor, housing, and public health. Historian George Mowry has reminded us that the American city was "the inspirer of social democracy" and "the originator of social regulation."

Progressivism in the States

In the late nineteenth century many state legislatures had become tools of political bosses and unscrupulous corporations. A map of the United States published in France in 1905 showed twenty-five of the forty-five states as wholly corrupt and thirteen as partially corrupt. Municipal reformers learned that their effectiveness would be limited unless efforts were made to clean up state politics.

Wisconsin led the way after the election of Robert M. La Follette as governor in 1900. La Follette, an ambitious, energetic, charismatic, articulate reformer, had worked within the regular Republican machine during three terms in Congress. As governor, however, he became the zealous champion of the small farmer and factory worker, and built a personal faction within the GOP that defied party regulars and their corporate friends. From 1901 until he went to the Senate in 1906, La Follette led the often bitter fight for a sweeping series of reforms that prompted Theodore Roosevelt to call Wisconsin "the laboratory of democracy."

The legislature's achievements during this period included a workmen's compensation law, restrictions on lobbying activities and campaign expenditures, the increased taxation of railroads, a railroad-rate commission, laws limiting the work hours of women and children, a state civil service, and the creation of a state forest reserve. Wisconsin also boasted such innovations for public participation in government as the direct primary system for nominating candidates, the initiative (which enabled voters to propose a law and submit it to the electorate or to the legislature for approval), the referendum (permitting voters to approve or reject a measure passed or proposed by a legislative body or by popular initiative), and the recall

Fighting Bob La Follette, champion of the Progressive Movement. Source: Reproduced from the Collections of the Library of Congress

of public officials at the ballot box. Moreover, the groundwork was laid for the nation's first income tax, passed soon after La Follette left office.

Several of the governor's advisers during these years of the "Wisconsin Idea" were professors at the University of Wisconsin, including economists Richard T. Ely and John R. Commons. The use of progressive scholars by reformers would become widely followed on the state and federal levels.

With Wisconsin as a model, many states throughout the nation elected reformers, Democrats and Republicans, and enacted progressive legislation. Many of the new laws proved extremely popular. The direct primary, for example, an attempt to prevent political machines from selecting candidates, was adopted by thirty-seven states by 1915. Workmen's compensation laws were on the books of forty-three states by 1920. Most states created commissions to regulate their public utilities, adopted civil service rules, passed restrictions on lobbying and corrupt practices in elections, and obtained laws limiting the exploitation of women and children in industry. (The United States Supreme Court voided two federal child labor laws. In 1923 it also nullified a District of Columbia statute establishing a ten-hour day for women.)

The Progressive Amendments

State progressives soon realized that several reforms, to be truly effective, would have to take the form of constitutional amendments. In the span of eight years, 1913–20, four amendments were ratified. This unprecedented achievement revealed the intensity of the nation's quest for reform and the degree to which Americans were willing to discard some of the assumptions of the Gilded Age.

The Sixteenth Amendment (1913) gave Congress the authority to collect an income tax. This was a tax, declared unconstitutional by the Supreme Court in 1895, on economic success; it was a public acknowledgment of the fact that wealth was not necessarily the product of virtue. While the initial rates were extremely low—only 1 person in 270 had to pay the first year, and a 6-percent ceiling was placed on incomes above $500,000—an important principle was established that fundamentally altered the nation's tax structure and enabled later reformers to fund the social service state.

The Seventeenth Amendment (1913) required the direct election of senators. It was an attempt to bring democracy to the upper house and to cleanse it of its corruption and opposition to reform. When senators were chosen by state legislatures, the victor often simply purchased the office and felt no obligation toward the public.

The prohibition movement, which was triumphant when the Eighteenth Amendment became part of the constitution in January 1919, had roots in the mid-nineteenth century. In part, prohibitionists were responding to the genuine evils associated with the saloon and alcoholism. The movement was also a reaction by rural Americans, especially in the South and Midwest, against the city, with its Catholics, Jews, bankers, intellectuals, radicals, agnostics, and lovers of vice. "Prohibition," wrote Andrew Sinclair, "was the final victory of the defenders of the American past. On the rock of the Eighteenth Amendment, village America made its last stand. . . ."

Five states adopted prohibition by 1900, and by 1907 two-thirds of the counties in the South were dry. Carry Nation was a tireless crusader of this era. She specialized in leading groups of followers into saloons, where they smashed the fixtures and stock with hatchets, a Nation trademark. Paintings of naked or scantily clad women, common in barrooms, were special targets. Nation was frequently jailed, shot at, and beaten up, but her zeal, born in part from an alcoholic first husband, was undaunted when she died in 1911.

A constitutional amendment to bring about prohibition was first submitted to Congress in 1913. The national emphasis on moral exhortation and self-denial during World War I prompted Congress to respond favorably, and all but two states—Connecticut and Rhode Island—ratified the amendment. The Volstead Act defined "intoxicating liquors" as anything containing more than 0.5 percent alcohol by volume. National prohibition went into effect on January 16, 1920.

The Nineteenth Amendment (1920) gave women the right to vote. Although the first woman suffrage association had been founded in 1869, it was only after 1900, when significant numbers of women were in college, were independent wage earners, and were active in social reform, that the movement began to make headway. In 1910, for example, eight million women were gainfully employed. Having a firsthand knowledge of sweatshops, long hours, and child labor, many of them understood the importance of reform legislation and desired access to the ballot to hasten change. In the West, pioneering conditions blurred sexual stereotypes to such a degree that by 1914 a dozen states west of the Mississippi adopted woman suffrage. Two years later Montana sent the first woman, Jeannette Rankin, to Congress. (She would be the only member of Congress to vote against American entry into both world wars.)

After intensive nationwide campaigns led by Carrie Chapman Catt, Dr. Anna Howard Shaw, the militant Alice Paul, and others, an amendment reached Congress in 1914. Its defeat only accelerated efforts by suffragists, who lobbied, paraded, picketed, lectured, signed petitions, went on hunger strikes, and chained themselves to the White House fence. World War I, with its demand for female war workers and its democratic rhetoric, weakened resistance, as did President Woodrow Wilson's reluctant endorsement. Ratification of the amendment followed in August 1920. As Hilda L. Smith has observed, the woman suffrage movement was the most important democratic movement in American history, for it brought the vote to more people than any other drive to expand the franchise.

THEODORE ROOSEVELT

When President William McKinley died from an assassin's bullets on September 14, 1901, Theodore Roosevelt became the chief executive. Progressivism came to the White House with Roosevelt, and the 42-year-old New Yorker quickly became the nation's foremost spokesman for reform.

Roosevelt had been born into a fairly wealthy upper-class family of Dutch origins. He was a sickly child who suffered from asthma and poor eyesight. When he was 12 his strong-willed father ordered him to build up his body by rigorous exercise. He took up boxing and track and became an enthusiastic horseman and hunter. For the rest of his life Roosevelt would glorify the "strenuous life" and be an outspoken advocate of manliness and courage. He seemed always obligated to compensate for his childhood weaknesses.

Aggressive, hyperactive, highly intelligent, gregarious, shrewd, and extremely ambitious, Roosevelt graduated from Harvard in 1880 and two years later won election to the first of three terms in the New York State Assembly. By 1900, barely into middle age, he had distinguished himself as an intellectual, a naturalist, and a prolific author (ten books, including five volumes of history). He had also been a rancher in the Dakota Territory, an unsuccessful Republican candidate for mayor of New York City, a member

Theodore Roosevelt returning from a bear hunt in Colorado. Source: Reproduced from the Collections of the Library of Congress

of the federal government's Civil Service Commission, New York City's police commissioner, assistant secretary of the navy, a colorful leader of the "Rough Riders" in the Spanish-American War, and the governor of New York. New York State's Republican boss, Tom Platt, helped place Roosevelt on the national ticket with McKinley out of fear that the Governor's firm convictions might endanger the local GOP machine.

Roosevelt's strict moral code prompted him to insist on honesty and efficiency in public office and to champion civil service reform. He accepted the Social Gospel and backed numerous efforts to narrow the gap between rich and poor. While fundamentally conservative, he had no love for the big businessmen whose unprincipled behavior, he thought, threatened the capitalist system.

Roosevelt believed in dynamic presidential leadership and a strong state, and he was the first president since the Civil War to declare the supremacy of government over business. Roosevelt's complex personal creed also embraced a faith in the superiority of Anglo-Americans, an intense nationalism, and a penchant for militarism and imperialism.

Trust Busting

In his first annual message to Congress in December 1901, Roosevelt called for steps to be taken against big corporations. He was not in fact opposed to the existence of industrial giants; he thought them inevitable and more efficient than their predecessors. In general, he believed in government regulation rather than the dissolution of corporations. Still, he knew that some business leaders were using their vast powers to destroy all competition, and he was convinced that this was wrong.

Roosevelt's initial requests of Congress resulted in a law expediting antitrust suits, and in the Elkins Act, a law forbidding railroads to grant rebates to large corporations. (Weary of granting these expensive breaks to big shippers, railroad executives had actually backed the bill.) Congress also gave Roosevelt a law creating a new Department of Commerce and Labor with a Bureau of Corporations which was to supply the president with information about interstate corporate activity and have the power to subpoena witnesses and compel testimony.

In early 1902 the president stunned Wall Street by announcing a suit, using the long-moribund Sherman Act, to dissolve the Northern Securities Company. This was the first important holding company, created a year earlier by J. P. Morgan and a number of other multimillionaires for the purpose of controlling transportation in the Northwest. Within a year a federal court dissolved Northern Securities, and the Supreme Court, by a vote of 5 to 4, soon concurred. The principle was established that the federal government had the constitutional authority to break up monopolies. During Roosevelt's administration the government started forty-four more suits against corporations, including such combines as the American Tobacco Company, the Du Pont Corporation, and the Standard Oil Company. The president's actions earned him the popular title "trust-buster."

The Labor Question

Roosevelt, like most progressives, was more sympathetic toward labor unions than the majority of businessmen and conservative politicians. He believed in the right to join unions, thought that they contributed to the general welfare, and assumed that big labor was as natural a development as big business. As police commissioner, governor, and then president, he met with labor leaders and listened to their views. On the other hand, Roosevelt rejected all efforts to coerce workers to join unions, including the union shop, and he opposed labor boycotts and the use of force during strikes.

In early October 1902 the president took a hand in a five-month-old coal strike by 150,000 miners in Pennsylvania that threatened the fuel needs of the eastern seaboard from Boston to Washington. The United Mine Workers had struck in May seeking a 20-percent wage hike, an eight-hour day, union recognition, and other benefits. The owners of the coal fields, in large part six regional railroads, refused to bargain with union leaders and closed down the mines.

Roosevelt, who lacked any legal authority to intervene in the matter, summoned Reading Railroad president George F. Baer and his colleagues to the White House, along with union chief John Mitchell, to work things out. A compromise settlement was soon worked out, but only after Roosevelt threatened to send ten thousand federal troops to open and operate the mines, and after J. P. Morgan was quietly recruited by the administration to put pressure on the railroad officials. A five-man arbitration commission, appointed by the president, gave the miners a 10-percent raise and reduced their working hours. The owners were permitted to increase the price of coal 10 percent, however, and the union failed to achieve recognition.

The president's conduct in the crisis differed sharply from the way chief executives had responded to strikes in the late nineteenth century. The White House conference, the presidentially appointed commission, and the threat to take over the coal fields all set important precedents. Roosevelt said that he had tried to give both labor and capital a "square deal." The phrase caught on and soon became the label to describe the entire administration.

The Election of 1904

Roosevelt was a professional politician. He had long had what historian John Blum called "an incurable case of Potomac fever," and once fate had thrust him into the presidency he used his incredible energy at almost every opportunity to retain the office. In 1904, he carefully planned the Republican national convention, which handed him the nomination by unanimous vote.

Roosevelt easily defeated Democrat Alton B. Parker of New York, a conservative judge virtually unknown outside his home state. Republicans also won the largest majority in the Senate and House since the Civil War. On election night Roosevelt, eager to dismiss the charge that he was power hungry and sincerely convinced that no one should hold the presidency too long, declared: "Under no circumstances will I be a candidate for or accept another nomination." He would later regret that statement.

Railroad Regulation

Roosevelt used his election mandate to call for more effective reform legislation. High on his agenda was interstate railroad regulation, the goal of farmers and small businesspeople throughout the country. Earlier the Supreme Court had stripped the Interstate Commerce Commission of any real authority over rates and rebates.

After a vigorous struggle between the president, the railroads, and GOP conservatives, Congress passed the Hepburn Act of 1906, a compromise measure widely recognized as a victory for Roosevelt. It gave the ICC power to investigate the books of interstate utilities and to set rates, subject to judicial review. Railroad owners thought that the courts would side with them, but as it turned out judges worked in harmony with the commission. Congress increased the body's authority in 1910, 1911, and 1913, and by World War I effective federal regulation of the railroad industry was a reality. The Hepburn Act marked the first step in the later development of a variety of federal regulatory agencies, staffed by experts and designed to protect the public's welfare.

Pure Food and Drugs

In 1906, with Roosevelt leading the fight, Congress passed the Meat Inspection Act and the Pure Food and Drug Act. Experts had known for years that the meat and patent medicine industries were guilty of scandalous misrepresentation and carelessness. Harvey W. Wiley, the Department of Agriculture's chief chemist, had appealed in vain for corrective legislation. In 1905 Samuel Hopkins Adams stirred public opinion with a series of articles on the dangers of patent medicine. Muckraker Samuel Merwyn condemned packers for deliberately selling diseased meat. In 1906 Upton Sinclair's *The Jungle* revealed disgusting abuses by meat packers and prompted a storm of indignation throughout the country.

While the legislation that emerged from a number of battles in Congress fell short of everything progressives wanted, it was a step in the right direction. The Meat Inspection Act banned the use of unhealthy dyes, chemical preservatives, or adulterants and provided $3 million for an improved government inspection system. The Pure Food and Drug Act prohibited the sale of harmful foods and required the correct labeling of foods and medicines.

The Public Domain

Roosevelt's first message to Congress revealed his desire to protect the nation's natural resources from exploitation by private interests. His passionate concern for conservation reflected his love of the outdoors but was primarily part of his campaign to combat the "malefactors of great wealth." Beginning with the Harrison administration, some 45 million acres had already been reserved by the federal government. Not until Roosevelt, however, would the nation have a comprehensive conservation policy. The president's principal adviser on the topic was famed Gifford Pinchot, a zealous conservationist who was trained in European forestry techniques and had been active in federal projects since 1896. Preservationist John Muir, founder of the Sierra Club, also gained Roosevelt's attention. (Conservationists, unlike preservationists, seek carefully managed use of public lands.) The muckrakers gave added impetus to action by exposing the theft of thousands of acres of government land.

As early as 1902, by supporting the Newlands Act, Roosevelt proved his concern for western flood problems and irrigation needs. This legislation established a federal Reclamation Bureau to set aside a portion of funds from the sale of public land for dams and reclamation projects.

The president's overall record on conservation was extremely impressive. He enriched the public domain by about 230 million acres; quadrupled the existing forest reserves (from 43 million to 194 million acres); set aside the first federal wildlife refuges (50 of them); doubled the number of national parks; proclaimed the first eighteen national monuments; strictly enforced existing land laws; backed the reorganization of the federal bureaucracy supervising the nation's forest, mineral, and water resources; and vetoed a bill permitting a private company to build a dam at Muscle Shoals on the Tennessee River. In 1908 Roosevelt created the National Conservation Congress, chaired by Pinchot and attended by forty-four governors and some five hundred other dignitaries and experts. It conducted the first inventory of the nation's remaining natural resources. Within eighteen months some forty-one states had created conservation commissions of their own, and the governors were committed to holding annual meetings.

Western cattlemen, mine operators, lumber barons, and power companies frequently used their influence in Congress to obstruct the president's efforts. Roosevelt usually got his way, however. His conservation crusade succeeded for the first time in alerting the American people to the importance of preserving and planning the use of their natural resources. It must be considered among the most valuable contributions of the Progressive Era.

The Panic of 1907

In his second term Roosevelt lashed out against big business as he never had before. When a financial panic struck in late October 1907, he thundered against unscrupulous bankers and financiers and charged them with attempting to undermine his administration. In fact, the collapse had largely been triggered by the careless speculations of several New York trust companies. It worsened because of the inelasticity of the nation's currency. The total amount of paper currency in circulation was set by law, preventing the federal government and the national banks from enlarging the supply when special demands were made by depositors. The panic started runs on financial institutions, and the tight supply of money threatened the nation's entire financial structure. Four trust companies and a national bank were forced to close their doors.

Financier J. P. Morgan, with the aid of the Treasury Department, pooled sufficient funds within a few weeks to curb the crisis. A brief depression followed, nevertheless, driving up unemployment in the manufacturing and transportation industries from 3.5 percent in 1907 to 12 percent in 1908.

The need for financial reform was apparent. With the support of Roosevelt and big business, Congress passed the Aldrich-Vreeland Act in 1908, increasing the elasticity of the currency and creating a National Monetary Commission to study the country's fiscal operations. The commission's voluminous reports led to the creation of the Federal Reserve System in 1913.

Roosevelt's increasingly radical proposals during his last two years in office contributed to a growing schism within the GOP between a bitterly conservative majority and a growing progressive minority that enjoyed the support of the most popular president since Lincoln.

ROOSEVELT AND FOREIGN AFFAIRS

Flushed with victory in the Spanish-American War, and with an empire in their possession, many Americans, including progressives, were convinced that the United States should be a bold, vigorous force in international affairs. Roosevelt was a strident advocate of this view. His imperialist tendencies were in part grounded in the widely held belief in Anglo-Saxon superiority. He told Congress in his first message that it was the duty of the "civilized powers" to be international policemen. Keenly aware of the growing naval might of Germany and Japan, he also contended that national dignity, even self-preservation, demanded military prowess in a world of competing powers. The president's closest advisers on world affairs, Senator Henry Cabot Lodge of Massachusetts and Secretary of War (after mid-1905 Secretary of State) Elihu Root, shared his passion for a militant foreign policy.

One of the first actions of the Roosevelt Administration was the creation of the Army War College, set up by Root. In 1902 Congress passed the army reform bill containing proposals by Root to create a general staff and to modernize the army's administrative machinery. Roosevelt's repeated pleas for a modern navy resulted by 1906 in a fleet second only to that of Great Britain.

The Panama Canal

A vital link in the Roosevelt foreign policy was the construction of a canal across Central America to enable the navy to move swiftly from ocean to ocean. In 1850 the United States and Great Britain had agreed to share control of a proposed waterway. The second Hay-Paunceforte Treaty of 1901, backed by Roosevelt, gave America the right to build, control, and fortify a canal, provided that ships of all nations could use it on equal terms.

On the advice of experts, Roosevelt selected a site on the isthmus of Panama, in Colombia, where the famed French engineer Ferdinand de Lesseps had tried unsuccessfully to dig a waterway in the 1880s. After a series of frustrating and at times questionable dealings with the New Panama Canal Company, a French corporation, and the government of Colombia, Roosevelt supported a political rebellion against the government that was swift and successful. Two hours after word of the coup reached Washington, the United States recognized the independent state of Panama. A treaty was signed granting America a zone 10 miles wide in perpetuity. Work on the canal began in 1904, and the first ships passed through the locks a decade later.

The Panama affair, shrouded in secrecy and involving millions of dollars, the Republican party, and J. P. Morgan, revealed limits to the president's integrity. Roosevelt was sensitive to charges against him and repeatedly denied participation in inciting the revolution against Columbia. At the same time, he continually boasted about his conduct toward Panama. In 1911 he told a University of California audience, "I stole the canal."

Caribbean Policy

America's renewed interest in national security after the Spanish-American War prompted Washington to take an aggressive posture toward the Caribbean. In the Platt Amendment of 1901 Congress declared that the United States had the right to intervene in Cuba whenever it was necessary to maintain order and preserve the nation's independence. Cuba was also obliged to sell or lease to the United States sites that became the naval base at Guantanamo Bay (still in American possession).

In 1904, with the canal zone taken, Roosevelt made the nation's policy clear in what became known as the Roosevelt Corollary to the Monroe Doctrine. (The nationalistic pronouncement by President James Monroe in 1823 had warned Europe not to extend their political systems "to any portion of this hemisphere," presumed to be controlled by the United Sates.) This bellicose statement declared that the United States could intervene in Latin America wherever it saw "chronic wrongdoing, or an impotence which results in a general loosening of the ties of civilized society." The Corollary was greatly disliked by Latin Americans, of course, and was generally ignored by the European powers.

A year later, the president intervened in the Dominican Republic when European nations threatened to attack in order to enforce payment of debts. He had the Dominican government sign a treaty turning over collection of its customs duties to an American, who would see that the country met its foreign obligations. The marines were sent in for two years to put the affairs of the nation in order.

In 1906, the President sent American troops into Cuba, using the Platt Amendment, to prevent civil war. A provisional government was created and the island remained in American control until 1909.

America's new role as the policeman of the Western Hemisphere was well established by the end of Roosevelt's administration. As a variety of American interests in the Caribbean increased—some selfish, others altruistic—future presidents would make intervention a habit. Sugar-rich Cuba, for example, which became autonomous in 1902, would again be partially controlled by the United States in 1912 and from 1917 to 1922. America would occupy the Dominican Republican from 1916 to 1924, Haiti from 1915 to 1934, and Nicaragua from 1912 to 1925 and 1926 to 1933.

Roosevelt and the World

Roosevelt believed that the great powers should supervise their own areas of the world. Where the superior nations had conflicting interests, he advocated a "balance of powers." In practice this meant that the United States would support the weaker of two nations in order to maintain an equilibrium. Roosevelt also believed that his increasingly powerful nation had an obligation to further world peace. During his administration American diplomats played an active role in international conferences for the first time. The president himself was an enthusiastic participant in world affairs.

In 1905, Roosevelt intervened in the Russo-Japanese War, persuading both sides to attend a peace conference at Portsmouth, New Hampshire. The treaty that emerged recognized Japan's territorial gains, guaranteed the Open Door in Manchuria, and earned Roosevelt the Nobel Peace Prize.

In December 1907, Roosevelt sent the nation's sixteen battleships, the "Great White Fleet," on an unprecedented, fifteen-month, 45,000 mile voyage around the world. This show of force appeared to be a message that the president was not to be bullied. (Roosevelt said later that he was principally trying to impress the American people, who were less than enthusiastic about playing a strong role in world affairs.) The fleet's reception in Japan was friendly, and relations between the two nations improved. This seemed to confirm one of the president's favorite adages: "Speak softly and carry a big stick, you will go far."

In the Root-Takhira Agreement of 1908, the United States and Japan agreed to maintain the status quo in the Pacific, to respect each other's territory, and to retain the Open Door (equal privileges among nations trading with China). It would not be long, however, before America would learn that Japanese imperialism in Asia could not be restrained by agreements.

Roosevelt's concern for international stability and the Open Door also led him to accept an invitation from the kaiser to become involved in a Moroccan dispute between France and Germany that threatened to become a war. The president supervised the delicate negotiations in the matter and persuaded both sides to attend a conference in Algeciras, Spain, in early 1906, to which the United States would be a party. American delegates supported French claims in Morocco, and the talks resulted in a diplomatic victory for France.

America's presence at Algeciras angered isolationists in Congress and in the press. They argued that intervention in European politics was as much a violation of the Monroe Doctrine as Europe's encroachments in Latin America. Typically, Roosevelt shrugged off his critics. He had again served the cause of peace and demonstrated his understanding that America was now an international power whose security was unavoidably entangled with events taking place all over the world.

SUGGESTED READING

John D. Buenker, *Urban Liberalism and Progressive Reform* (1973); Steven J. Diner, *A Very Different Age: Americans of the Progressive Era* (1997); Lewis L. Gould, *The Presidency of Theodore Roosevelt* (1992); Samuel P. Hays, *The Response to Industrialism, 1885–1914* (1957); Richard Hofstadter, *The Age of Reform: From Bryan to F.D.R.* (1955); James Kloppenberg, *Uncertain Victory: Social Democracy and Progressivism: European and American Thought, 1870–1920* (1988); Aileen S. Kraditor, *The Ideas of the Woman Suffrage Movement, 1890–1920* (1965); Henry F. May, *Protestant Churches and Industrial America* (1949); Daniel R. Rodgers, *Atlantic Crossings: Social Politics in a Progressive Age* (1998); David P. Thelen, *The New Citizenship: Origins of Progressivism in Wisconsin* (1972).

Chapter Three

THE TRIALS AND TRIUMPHS OF PROGRESSIVISM

Roosevelt was only 50 when he left office on March 4, 1909. He believed that a president should serve only two terms, and he had announced in 1904 that he would not seek reelection. During his last two years in the White House he had sponsored several far-reaching reform measures, including federal income and inheritance taxes, stricter railroad regulation, and downward revision of the tariff. The proposals alienated Congress and drove a deep wedge within the GOP between conservatives, headed by Senator Nelson W. Aldrich of Rhode Island and Congressman Joseph G. Cannon of Illinois, and progressive "insurgents," led by Senator La Follette and Congressman George W. Norris of Nebraska. It would take a highly skilled chief executive to heal the wounds left by Roosevelt and get on with the business of expanding progressive legislation. The task fell to Roosevelt's hand-picked successor, William Howard Taft.

Fifty-one-year-old Taft was a native of Cincinnati, Ohio, whose father had served as President Grant's secretary of war and attorney general. Following graduation from Yale Law School and admission to the Ohio bar, Taft had been a state judge, solicitor general of the United States, a United States circuit judge, and civil governor of the Philippines. In 1904 Roosevelt chose him to be secretary of war, and he became a sort of executive assistant to the president and general troubleshooter. He was highly regarded in Washington as an affable and intelligent gentleman, an effective administrator, and a loyal supporter of the Square Deal. His antilabor record as a judge also elevated him in the eyes of conservatives.

The Election of 1908

The Republican convention nominated Taft on the first ballot. It defied Roosevelt and the progressives, however, by placing conservative Congressman James S. Sherman of New York on the ticket and by adopting a highly conservative platform. The Democrats nominated William Jennings Bryan, their candidate in 1896 and 1900. Bryan, whose evangelical oratory had long championed the common man, saw himself as Roosevelt's true heir.

The campaign proved rather dull. Taft disliked partisan politics (he had been elected to public office only once), and he failed to inspire the electorate. Bryan's appeal faded quickly outside the South, and the Democrats were so short of funds that their effort was called the "barefoot campaign." Taft carried the election by more than a million votes and defeated Bryan in the electoral college 321 to 162. Eugene V. Debs, the saintly founder and perennial candidate of the Socialist Party, received just over 400,000 votes, about what he had won four years earlier and less than 3 percent of the total.

Troubled Taft

It was quickly apparent that Taft was not cut out to be an effective chief executive. Some observers blamed his obesity and apparent physical sluggishness. (He at times weighed more than 300 pounds and once became stuck in the White House bathtub.) In fact, Taft's problems stemmed mainly from his penchant for conservatism in an age of reform. Although he had backed numerous progressive proposals over the years, Taft did not welcome change, and was hostile toward zealous reformers. He believed in the strict separation of powers and was content to let Congress handle legislative matters. He was not committed to a strong, interventionist state; indeed, he had great respect for laissez-faire economics. Roosevelt rapidly became disillusioned with his successor, and Capitol Hill progressives were soon completely alienated.

The split between Taft and the insurgents became public in early 1909 when the president redeemed a campaign pledge by calling a special session of Congress to lower the tariff. Taft soon sided with those attempting to protect eastern industry, however, and when the generally high-tariff Payne-Aldrich bill was passed, he further angered progressives by failing to veto it. Then, in a transcontinental speaking tour that fall, Taft called the act "the best tariff bill that the Republican party ever passed," and he snubbed the progressives who had opposed it. Many reformers were now thinking wistfully of Roosevelt.

Taft's appointment of Richard A. Ballinger as secretary of the interior set the stage for another bitter clash with progressives. Ballinger was a one-time corporation lawyer and ex-commissioner of the General Land Office who was known to have associates eager for federal lands. He replaced James R.

Garfield, an ardent conservationist close to Roosevelt and Gifford Pinchot. When the new secretary invalidated Roosevelt's effort to set aside certain waterpower sites as federal land, and returned more than a million acres to public entry, Pinchot spoke out publicly against the action. When a General Land Office investigator named Louis R. Glavis told Pinchot of what seemed to be a plot by Ballinger and some friends to claim national domain in Alaska and secretly sell part of its coal fields to a Morgan-Guggenheim syndicate, the nation's chief forester appealed directly to the president.

Taft did not like Pinchot; he thought of him privately as "a radical and a crank." Following an investigation, the president rejected the charges made by Glavis and contended that Ballinger was "in full sympathy with the attitude of this administration." Pinchot responded angrily by publishing two magazine articles critical of the secretary, writing numerous letters opposing him, and leaking confidential information to the press. When progressive Jonathan P. Dolliver of Iowa read one of Pinchot's heated letters on the Senate floor, Taft had no choice but to dismiss the nation's chief forester for insubordination.

Although a joint congressional committee cleared Ballinger of all charges, many progressives continued to have serious qualms about his role in the shady Alaska land deal and about his overall commitment to conservation. When Ballinger resigned a short time after the congressional investigation, Taft replaced him with a friend of Pinchot's. Moreover, the president proceeded to take major steps to expand the federal domain. The political damage to the administration, however, was irreparable. The Ballinger-Pinchot fray further convinced progressives that Taft had abandoned Roosevelt's high principles and become a tool of special interests.

Cannon, Roosevelt, and the Elections of 1910

During his election campaign Taft had criticized House Speaker Joseph G. "Uncle Joe" Cannon, a dictatorial arch-conservative who had blocked reforms for years. He had also let it be known that if elected he would support progressive efforts to curb Cannon's power. In 1909, however, the desire for tariff reform forced Taft to bow out of a struggle to unseat Cannon. When a new fight broke out a year later, Taft, bitter over progressive opposition to the Payne-Aldrich tariff and Secretary Ballinger, refused to lend a hand. Even without White House support, a coalition of Democrats and insurgents managed to limit Cannon's authority over legislation.

Progressives emerged from the battle further convinced that Taft had become an enemy. Taft, by this time, thought that his former friends were bent on the destruction of his administration. He denied them patronage, refused to meet them socially, and began working for the election of "orthodox Republicans" in the 1910 primaries. "Taft Republican" clubs and "Progressive Republican" clubs were created during the spring, revealing what was becoming a full-scale split within the GOP. By June, "Roosevelt

Republican" clubs were advocating the former president's nomination in 1912.

Roosevelt was keenly aware of the turmoil during his travels abroad. Pinchot had hurried to Europe to inform him of events, and friends had sent letters full of details. When Roosevelt returned to the United States in June 1910, his friendship with Taft was badly shaken. During the summer and fall he campaigned across the country for both conservative and progressive candidates, attempting to heal the breach. His relations with the White House, however, became increasingly strained. In a speech at Osawatomie, Kansas, in September his call for a sweeping set of reforms labeled the "New Nationalism" greatly irritated Taft and the conservatives.

As Taft had moved to the right during the past two years, Roosevelt had continued to move to the left, along with progressives generally. He had been strongly influenced by Herbert Croly's important book *The Promise Of American Life*, which had appeared a year earlier. The New Nationalism advocated a highly active federal government and the full agenda of progressive proposals, including such political reforms as the initiative and referendum, direct primaries, the recall of elected officials, and the recall of judicial decisions. Roosevelt was especially critical of the conservative judiciary, arguing that human rights should never be subordinate to property rights, and adding that the community should have the power to regulate property "to whatever degree the public welfare may require." Taft and his allies were appalled by Roosevelt's views, just as progressives cheered him.

Progressives trounced conservatives in the primaries, repudiating the efforts by Taft to purge the party of troublemakers. In the general elections, however, the newly revived Democratic party captured most of the headlines. Democrats won control of the House for the first time in sixteen years and elected twenty-six governors, including Woodrow Wilson of New Jersey. Republicans continued to hold a majority in the Senate, but the balance of power was precarious due to the presence of several progressives who might vote with Democrats on any given issue. Reform was at fever pitch in America in 1910, and Democrats and progressives were clearly in step with public opinion. Taft, with two more years to serve, had been severely damaged politically.

Dollar Diplomacy

Taft's foreign policy also had its critics. Both the president and Secretary of State Philander C. Knox, a domineering corporation lawyer, actively encouraged and supported American overseas investments, convinced that whatever profited our bankers and industrialists was beneficial to the United States. (Ideally, at least, foreign nations were to prosper along with American investors.) This union between foreign policy and commercial interests, which had roots in the earliest years of the republic, was called "dollar diplomacy."

In Latin America dollar diplomacy seemed to be but another excuse to expand the power of the United States, and it proved highly unpopular. When American mining firms helped foment a revolution in Nicaragua in 1909 against the uncooperative President Jose S. Zelaya, Knox quickly recognized the revolutionary government. An American warship helped persuade the new leaders to take out a large loan from New York bankers, and by 1911 Americans were in control of the nation's finances. The following year 2,500 marines were sent in to quell widespread disorder, and a number of them remained until 1925. Other efforts to increase Wall Street's financial authority in the Caribbean were made in Honduras, Guatemala, and Haiti.

Taft's Achievements

Despite his penchant for conservatism, Taft could boast of a number of significant reforms enacted during his administration. The Mann-Elkins Act of 1910 strengthened the Interstate Commerce Commission by giving it the power to revise railroad rates without waiting for complaints by shippers. The ICC also received the authority to regulate the increasingly important telephone and telegraph companies. The president supported the Sixteenth Amendment, creation of the Federal Children's Bureau, safety laws for mines and railroads, and the Mann White Slave Traffic Act. His antitrust campaign obtained far more indictments in four years than Roosevelt's had in seven.

These achievements did not improve Taft's political position, however, for he continued to war with progressives while at the same time alienating conservatives. He struggled mightily with reformers over railroad legislation and creation of the nation's first postal-savings bank system. His zealous use of the Sherman Antitrust Law irritated business leaders. A Canadian reciprocity treaty angered eastern and western farmers, who sought low tariffs, as well as Republicans in the industrial states who were devoted to the protective principle. The veto of the proposed constitution of Arizona, because it permitted the recall of judges, persuaded people from all areas and walks of life that their president opposed democracy.

The Reemergence of Roosevelt

On January 21, 1911, several progressives created the National Progressive Republican League, intending to take over the GOP and prevent Taft's nomination for a second term. Senator La Follette, one of the league's founders, was the early favorite, but it soon became clear that Roosevelt was the choice of most reformers. The former president stayed aloof from the contest until late October, when the administration filed an antitrust suit against the United States Steel Corporation. Roosevelt no longer thought it sensible to break up the huge corporations. In his New Nationalism speech at Osawatomie he had said, "The effort at prohibiting all combinations has substantially failed. The way out lies . . . in completely controlling them." More troubling was the fact that the U.S. Steel suit emphasized the corporation's acquisition of the Tennessee Coal and Iron Company in 1907, a deal approved unofficially by Roosevelt and discussed repeatedly with Taft. This affront by the president infuriated Roosevelt, and in February 1912 he declared, "My hat is in the ring."

Roosevelt won several major primary contests, including one in Ohio, Taft's native state, and was no doubt the popular choice of the Republican rank and file. Nevertheless, as the GOP national convention neared, it became obvious that the president, in control of party machinery, was going to be nominated.

The Election of 1912

When the Republicans gathered in Chicago in mid-June, Taft won the nomination easily on the first ballot. Roosevelt and his backers cried "foul" and soon laid plans for running an independent campaign. With financial assistance from such wealthy supporters as publisher Frank Munsey and George W. Perkins of the House of Morgan, the Progressive party was created. Ten thousand of its partisans sang "Onward Christian Soldiers" at an emotional convention in Chicago in early August. In a lengthy address he called a "Confession of Faith," the exuberant candidate said that he felt "as strong as a bull moose," thus providing the nickname "Bull Moose" party. Roosevelt called for a sweeping number of reforms, including the strict regulation of corporations, minimum wage and workmen's compensation laws, the eighthour day for all workers, the elimination of child labor, and woman suffrage.

Meanwhile, the Democrats had convened in Baltimore, exhilarated by the Republican schism and optimistic about capturing the White House for the first time in sixteen years. On the forty-sixth ballot the convention selected 55-year-old Woodrow Wilson, the reform-minded governor of New Jersey. Wilson, strongly influenced by the well-known "people's lawyer" Louis D. Brandeis, offered progressive voters an alternative to Roosevelt's New Nationalism. His "New Freedom" program called upon the federal government to break up the large trusts and restore competition and individual initiative. Whereas Roosevelt had become convinced that huge corporations were inevitable and, with proper government supervision, beneficial, Wilson believed that industrial bigness was a curse, the enemy of the free-enterprise system that had made America great. In the Jeffersonian tradition of his native Virginia, Wilson also defended states' rights and thought that the power of centralized government should be strictly limited. Thus voters not only had their choice between conservatism and progressivism but between two different brands of reform.

However attractive and distinctive the candidates appeared on the campaign trail (Roosevelt was shot in the chest by a would-be assassin in Milwaukee but bravely shook off the incident and continued to orate for more than an hour before receiving medical attention), voters appeared to remain loyal to their parties in November. Wilson received the regular Democratic vote and Republicans divided between Roosevelt and Taft. Wilson captured forty states and won handily in the electoral college, receiving 435 votes to Roosevelt's 88 and Taft's 8. (The president carried only Vermont and Utah.) The popular vote was Wilson, 6,286,214; Roosevelt, 4,126,020; Taft, 3,484,922. Eugene V. Debs had 897,011 votes, the largest total enjoyed to date by a Socialist candidate. By any interpretation of the data, the nation clearly sought reform.

The Bull Moose campaign was clearly a political blunder. A monument to Roosevelt's ego, the Progressive party was soon abandoned by the candidate and disappeared. It had not only handed the presidency to the Democrats but had virtually driven reform out of the Republican party.

Socialism in America

The sizable vote won by the Socialist Party of America in 1912 called attention to the popularity of radical alternatives to the capitalist system during the years 1900 to 1914. By October 1912 the Socialist party, founded eleven years earlier, had 127,966 members. In New York, Chicago, and Milwaukee, among other places, Socialists were scoring impressively at the polls. Milwaukee had sent Victor Berger to Congress in 1910, and by 1911 Socialists were running thirty-three cities and towns. In 1912 party members won election to more than a thousand state and local offices. Socialism was strongest in urban areas among immigrants, particularly the Germans and Jews. It had a special appeal for New York intellectuals. Its greatest relative voting strength, however, lay west of the Mississippi, particular in Oklahoma.

Most Socialists sought peaceful reform through political action. A more radical tradition existed within the party, however. Daniel De Leon, founder of the older Socialist Labor party, was a passionate advocate of the extreme left who tried in the late nineteenth century to create a trade union movement to oppose the American Federation of Labor. With his help, the Industrial Workers of the World was founded in 1905. Led by William D. "Big Bill" Haywood, the "Wobblies" abandoned political activity and turned to industrial violence and sabotage to unify the working class and "take possession of the earth and the machinery of production and abolish the wage system." A violent strike in Lowell, Massachusetts, in early 1912 gained nationwide attention and earned the wrath of progressives, conservatives, and AFL trade unionists alike.

The socialism of both Debs and Haywood steadily declined in popularity during the prosperous and reform-conscious years of the Wilson administration and would never again regain its turn-of-the-century appeal. Both the Socialist party and the IWW were to oppose America's involvement in World War I and suffer persecution by government officials and private organizations. The party would waste much of its energy on internal ideological struggles, and it split into hostile camps in 1919 with the exit of the Communists.

Above all, socialism lost out to the American Dream. It was a casualty of the high degree of prosperity, class mobility (both real and imagined), and individualism enjoyed by the great majority of the nation's people. Within the first decade of the twentieth century alone, the gross national product rose by 50 percent, per capita income rose about 20 percent to over $600, and the number of automobiles registered throughout the nation rose from 8,000 to 458,000. Socialism could not thrive among a people with the deeply ingrained conviction that anyone, with enough hard work and character, could strike it rich in a land of plenty.

The Birth Control Movement

In 1912 Margaret Sanger, founder of the birth control movement in America, was a radical Socialist and militant feminist. A 29-year-old nurse in the Lower East Side of New York City, she was horrified by the death of a slum dweller from an attempted abortion and, by her own account, dedicated her life thereafter to helping women avoid unwanted pregnancy. Even before this incident, however, Mrs. Sanger, one of eleven children and the mother of three, had personally discarded the Victorian view of marriage, sex, and the family accepted by the vast majority of Americans. Her radicalism stemmed in part from childhood experiences and the challenging new literature on sexual psychology by Sigmund Freud and Havelock Ellis.

Sanger was also greatly influenced by the budding science of eugenics. She saw birth control as "the process of weeding out the unfit" aimed at "the creation of a superman." Sanger sought the sterilization of "genetically inferior races," singling out Asians in particular, and called for the segregation of "morons, misfits, and the maladjusted."

Contraception had been practiced among the better educated for decades; the national birthrate and average family size had been declining since 1867. Nevertheless, Mrs. Sanger's efforts to collect and widely distribute contraceptive information were widely and often militantly resisted. She was indicted in 1914 for sending a birth control periodical in the mail. Two years later she opened the nation's first birth control clinic and was arrested and sent to a workhouse for thirty days.

In time, however, Mrs. Sanger's tireless crusade increased in popularity, especially among middle-class women. In 1921 she organized the American Birth Control League, which five years later had a membership of over 37,000. In the 1930s several major Protestant denominations endorsed birth control as an instrumentality for enhancing family life. In 1936 the United States Court of Appeals affirmed the right of physicians to prescribe contraceptives. Two years later *Fortune* magazine reported that American women spent $210 million annually on contraceptive materials. By 1942, with the appearance of the Planned Parenthood Federation of America, birth control had been endorsed by the American Medical Association and was supported by the federal government. While the Roman Catholic church continued its strong opposition, Margaret Sanger's "shocking" reform, announced in the magazine *Woman Rebel* in 1914, had become respectable and widely accepted.

Progressive Education

The philosopher and psychologist John Dewey was one of Mrs. Sanger's ardent supporters. A professor at the University of Chicago and, after 1905, Columbia University, Dewey wrote a steady stream of immensely influential books and articles calling for educational reforms that reflected his commitment to pragmatism, democracy, and progress.

Dewey denounced traditional educational requirements and authoritarian teaching methods as firmly as he rejected fixed moral codes. He argued that education should be practical and contribute to what he saw as the improvement of society. Instead of the rote memorization of Latin verbs and Greek myths, schooling ought to be based on "learning by doing" and contain such subjects as recent history, geography, and citizenship, supplemented by group activity in such useful pursuits as cooking and carpentry. This education for modern life would be taught in a classroom that stressed flexibility and democratic participation.

Dewey's followers were still in a minority in 1912 but their influence was beginning to spread rapidly. As early as 1913 a committee of the National Education Association called for open admission into high schools and colleges, and for a curriculum that developed good personal traits. Dewey's magnum opus, *Democracy and Education* (1916), attracted nationwide interest. In the decades that followed, public education would be dominated by the "progressive" educators. Many of these teachers and administrators distorted Dewey's ideas and offered courses and programs devoid of mental rigor and knowledge. American education sometimes seemed to critics to be little more than babysitting or vocational training. Nevertheless, the public embraced the progressive innovations, and as educational opportunities expanded and school and college enrollments increased, these principles grew more popular than ever.

WOODROW WILSON

The new president was born in Staunton, Virginia, the son of a Presbyterian minister and an English-born mother whose father and brother were Presbyterian clergymen. Thomas Woodrow Wilson, as he was christened, was an extremely intelligent, self-confident, pious, idealistic, and ambitious young man. As a teenager he cultivated the art of oratory and dreamed of being a great statesman. He graduated from Princeton, took a law degree at the University of Virginia, practiced law briefly until bored, and then completed a doctorate degree at the new Johns Hopkins University in Baltimore. His dissertation, published in 1885 as *Congressional Government*, and a large number of subsequent books and articles, earned him a national reputation as a keen observer of American history and politics. In these days Wilson greatly admired the British cabinet system and believed fervently in free trade, the gold standard, clean government, and the Democratic party.

In 1902, following several years as an inspiring and popular college teacher, Wilson became president of Princeton. He proved to be an outstanding educational reformer, eager to have his institution follow standards and patterns set by Oxford and Cambridge. He was a haughty, tenaciously self-righteous leader, however, and bitter feuds with men of equal sternness on the campus led to his resignation in 1910.

By this time several New Jersey politicians and businessmen were promoting Wilson's considerable political ambitions. Democratic machine chieftains admired his national prominence and thought they could profit from his election to high office. A number of men in business and finance approved of his conservative attitudes toward labor unions and governmental regulations. Wilson appeared friendly to both the bosses and bankers and won the gubernatorial nomination on the first ballot. During the campaign, however, Wilson sensed the reform mood of the electorate and jolted many of his backers by running as an ardent progressive. He was elected by a 50,000 majority, and in his two years as governor, New Jersey became a model for reformers.

A bipartisan progressive majority in the legislature, prodded by the forceful governor, reformed the state's primary and election practices, created a Public Service Commission with the power to set rates, passed a corrupt-practices act, and permitted municipalities to adopt the initiative, the referendum, the recall, and the commission form of government. By mid-1911 Wilson was campaigning all across the country for the presidential nomination, and by the end of the year his selection appeared certain. Biographer Arthur S. Link has observed, "No man in the history of American politics had such a spectacular rise to political prominence."

New Freedom Legislation

Wilson had long lamented what he termed "the clumsy misrule of Congress" and had called for a bold, vigorous chief executive who would use the full powers of his office to carry out the public will. Once in the White House, he played a direct role in creating a record he and his party could be proud of. Wilson helped formulate legislation, he revived Jefferson's tradition of addressing Congress in person, he invented the regular press conference, and he cajoled and cracked the whip over Democrats, who held majorities in both houses of Congress. The result was passage of a number of major progressive proposals.

The Underwood-Simmons tariff, signed in October 1913, contained the first genuine rate reductions since the Civil War. The new law placed more than one hundred articles on the free list, including food and such products of

President Woodrow Wilson in 1918. Source: Reproduced from the Collections of the Library of Congress.

the trusts as iron and steel. It dropped the average duty almost 11 points. To compensate for the government's loss of revenue, a modest graduated income tax was inserted, authorized by the new Sixteenth Amendment. This stunning victory over powerful special interest groups prompted Agriculture Secretary David F. Houston to gasp, "I did not much think we should live to see these things."

The Federal Reserve Act of December 1913 reflected the widespread belief that something was seriously wrong with the nation's banking and currency system. After the Panic of 1907 (a brief financial crisis triggered by the irresponsible speculations of several New York trust companies), businessmen, farmers, progressives, economists, political leaders of both parties, and bankers themselves agreed that the regulations created during the Civil War were inadequate to meet the needs of industrialized America. For one thing, the money supply was tied to the amount of government bonds held by banks, and there was rarely enough currency in circulation. Moreover, there was no central control over the nation's approximately 30,000 banks, and consequently no system for shifting bank reserves around the country to save particular institutions during a financial crisis. Bankers were now calling for a great central bank, authorized by the government but controlled exclusively by themselves. Farmers and progressives, on the other hand, were seeking public control and even ownership of banks. They were particularly sensitive to the findings of a House investigating committee headed by Louisiana Democrat Arsene Pujo that supported suspicions about a "money trust" led by the Morgan-Rockefeller empire. Wilson's proposal, a Federal Reserve System, was a compromise, developed after consultation with Louis D. Brandeis. (In 1914 Brandeis would publish *Other People's Money*, which popularized Pujo Committee findings.) Congress accepted it, but only after several months of heated debate and intensive activity by the president.

The Federal Reserve Act established twelve regional Reserve banks across the country, privately controlled but regulated and supervised by a presidentially appointed Board of Governors. All of the national banks were required to become part of the new system, and state banks were invited to join. (Within a year the system would control nearly half of the nation's banking resources, and the figure would jump to 80 percent by 1928.) The inelastic currency issue was tackled by giving the Reserve banks the authority to issue the nation's currency in the form of new Federal Reserve notes, backed by the government. By manipulating the "discount rate" of these notes—the interest rate the board charged member banks for borrowing from Federal Reserve banks—the board had the ability to control the money supply and thereby make needed adjustments to counteract inflationary and deflationary movements. The board could also buy and sell government bonds to affect the money supply and influence national interest rates. The question of bank reserves was met by requiring the twelve regional banks to hold the reserves of its members and by providing devices for the transferral of needed funds from one area of the country to another.

The Federal Reserve System was not at first as radical a departure from tradition as many reformers had hoped. It did not function as a central bank, it did not prevent bank failures, and it did not wrest control of the money supply from powerful private bankers. Still, a reasonably efficient banking system had been created for the first time since Andrew Jackson, one that would help the nation meet the financial demands imposed by World War I.

Moreover, the vital principle of public supervision over the banking and currency system was established. The Federal Reserve Act was the most important piece of domestic legislation passed during the Wilson Administration, and the president surely deserved the public applause that accompanied its signing.

By mid-1914 Wilson was having second thoughts about the New Freedom. A depression had gripped the country during the preceding fall, and Republicans were blaming the new tariff and the president's antitrust policies. Moreover, Louis D. Brandeis and a number of other progressives were persuading Wilson to move in the direction of Roosevelt's New Nationalism. Instead of attempting to break up the corporate giants in order to unleash the public's competitive instincts, they argued, the president should embrace the conceivably more effective policy of governmental regulation.

The Federal Trade Commission Act of September 1914 marked the beginning of Wilson's shift in philosophy. The FTC had originally been planned as a mere clearinghouse for information about big business. As the legislation ground through Congress, Wilson endorsed the Brandeis idea and worked successfully to make the commission a regulatory agency.

The FTC consisted of five members, appointed by the president and confirmed by the Senate, who would have seven-year terms. The commission had the authority to investigate corporate behavior, to hear complaints of unfair methods of competition, and to issue "cease and desist" orders that were subject to court review. The new law outlawed several practices designed to prevent competition, including price discrimination and interlocking directorates in large industrial corporations which had once been competitive. But the language of the legislation was fuzzy, and Wilson himself admitted that the Senate had made the bill "so weak that you cannot tell it from water." Mild provisions in the Act favoring labor were crippled by the courts after World War I. The administration, having largely abandoned the New Freedom solution to restraints of trade, did not pursue trust busting vigorously.

Retreat and Renewal

By the fall of 1914 Wilson was persuaded that the Progressive movement had come to an end. To the dismay of reformers, the president refused to support woman suffrage and dismissed all proposals for new social legislation. Moreover, he began cultivating the friendship of the business community. Disturbed by the depression, Wilson sought advice from J. P. Morgan and Henry Ford, he assured the financial community that he had never been an enemy, and he appointed conservatives to the Federal Reserve Board and the Federal Trade Commission. Some disappointed observers wondered if, in fact, Wilson had ever been a zealous reformer.

The administration's increasingly passive attitude toward social justice was nowhere better revealed than in the area of race relations. Black leaders, who had responded to Wilson's encouraging campaign appeals and worked for his election, were stunned to observe the Democrats reimpose racial segregation throughout the federal government. As early as the summer of 1913 the Treasury Department had segregated toilets, lunchroom facilities, and working areas. The practice spread, and those who complained were dismissed. Wilson and no doubt every member of his cabinet believed in racial segregation. (The president, along with many other Americans, would greatly enjoy the 1915 movie "Birth of a Nation," which championed the Ku Klux Klan.) Booker T. Washington wrote to a friend, "I have recently spent several days in Washington, and I have never seen the colored people so discouraged and bitter as they are at the present time." The government made token efforts to reverse its segregation policy only after outcries from the progressive leadership of the North and the Midwest.

The elections of 1914 jolted Wilson from his complacency. Democrats lost forty-eight seats in the House of Representatives, lowering their majority to twenty-five votes, and suffered a number of setbacks on the state level. Voters were disturbed about the depression and the outbreak of war in Europe. It was also apparent that former members of the Progressive party were returning to the GOP. Wilson needed these one-time Roosevelt partisans to win reelection in 1916. To appeal to them, and to regain the confidence of restless elements within his own party, the president realized that he would have to reverse his course and prove that his administration was committed to meaningful reform. The transformation was complete by late 1915.

The president's new stance became public in January 1916 when he nominated his liberal adviser Louis D. Brandeis to the United States Supreme Court. Businessmen and their allies were enraged at the selection, and a grueling battle broke out. The president publicly defended his nominee and threw the full weight of his office into the fray. Progressives were elated by Wilson's courage and praised him highly when Brandeis was confirmed. The first Jewish member of the Court, Brandeis began what would become a quarter century of highly distinguished service.

Wilson wooed farmers by reversing an earlier pronouncement and supporting the Federal Farm Loan Act. This law created twelve Federal Land banks that sold bonds to the public and made loans to farm associations. These associations, controlled by farmers, then made long-term mortgage loans to members at low interest rates. By 1930 farmers had received a total of $1.6 billion through these channels.

Within a single month the president signed three important pieces of legislation that revealed his new determination to use the federal government as an instrument of social justice and public welfare. The Kern-McGillicuddy bill provided workmen's compensation for federal employees. The Keating-Owen child labor bill prohibited the shipment in interstate commerce of goods produced in whole or in part by underage children. The Adamson Act established the eight-hour day, without a reduction of wages, for employees of interstate railroads. (The Supreme Court later struck down the child labor law, and the eight-hour day law survived by a vote of 5 to 4.)

As the election of 1916 neared, Wilson could boast that the Democratic party, for the first time, held a firm grip on the banner of reform. He could portray himself, with much justice, as a forceful and energetic leader and boast that his administration had "come very near to carrying out the platform of the Progressive party."

The Twilight of Reform

Wilson could not know that he had brought the Progressive movement to a climax. While there would be flickers of reform after the 1916 elections and indeed into the 1920s, the widespread drive for a more equitable, humane, honest, and democratic nation was largely spent. Americans increasingly devoted their attentions to developments overseas.

Later generations of reformers would often belittle progressivism, noting that it had failed to curb the massive power of corporations and banks, end racism, protect the rights of labor, and solve the plight of farmers and immigrants. While much can be said about the inadequacies of La Follette, Roosevelt, Wilson, and other progressive leaders, especially when their actions are taken out of historical context, their many achievements should not be minimized.

From the turn of the century until America's serious involvement in World War I, ideas were developed, precedents were set, and mechanisms were created for wrestling with some of the thorniest problems of industrial society. In particular, Wilson's move toward the New Nationalism, with its vision of a dynamic federal government, would help pave the way for bolder efforts in the 1930s and beyond.

MISSIONARY DIPLOMACY

Wilson took office declaring that American international relations would henceforth operate in accordance with eternal verities. He and Secretary of State William Jennings Bryan denounced self-interest and interventionism and expressed their desire to use American power in the service of morality. Neither man had more than a rudimentary knowledge of foreign policy or, indeed, foreign countries. Shortly before assuming the presidency, Wilson confided to a friend, "It would be the irony of fate if my administration had to deal chiefly with foreign affairs." Both men, however, were deeply religious and firmly believed that they could be instruments of God's will across the globe, bringing Christianity, peace, stability, and democracy to millions. More often than not during the next eight years, they failed. And in the course of attempting to be missionaries for a "superior" way of life, they antagonized peoples in many nations, who were unable to tell the difference between Wilsonian diplomacy and old-fashioned Yankee imperialism.

The Far East

Relations between Japan and the United States were strained throughout 1913 and into the following spring because of racist laws passed in California prohibiting Japanese ownership of land. In the spring of 1915 new tensions arose. Japan, an ally of Great Britain in World War I, had seized Germany's islands in the North Pacific and had moved into the Shantung province of China. Tokyo then presented Peking with twenty-one demands, seeking complete control of Shantung and Manchuria and threatening China's independence. It seemed that Japan was determined to slam shut the Open Door, which had given nations equal trading rights in China.

Wilson and Bryan applied quiet pressure to resolve the crisis. The secretary of state declared publicly that his government would not recognize any agreement that impaired the treaty rights of the United States, or the political and territorial integrity of China, or the Open Door. This doctrine of nonrecognition would later be used in the futile attempt to halt Japanese expansion into China's Manchuria and would be a cause of war with the Japanese Empire. For the time being, however, America's firm stand prompted Japan to drop her most objectionable demands. The Ishii-Lansing Agreement of late 1917 recognized Japan's "special interests" in China but affirmed the Open Door and the territorial integrity of the Chinese nation.

The Caribbean

Wilson denounced dollar diplomacy in Latin America only a week after taking office. Bryan and his successor Robert Lansing often advocated nonintervention and asserted the equality of all states in the Western Hemisphere. Nevertheless, the Wilson administration was responsible for more armed interventions in Latin America than any of its predecessors. The president and his secretaries of state had what to them were honorable intentions: They sought to preserve stability in the Caribbean, to check foreign control, and to lend a helping hand to the unfortunate. Their involvement in the affairs of their southern neighbors, however, often produced extreme hostility.

Wilson ordered marines and sailors into Haiti during the summer of 1915 after a series of bloody revolutions had reduced the country to anarchy. A pro-American was quickly elected president and pressured to sign a treaty making his country virtually a United States protectorate. Despite the return of peace and prosperity, many Haitians detested the rule of white foreigners. In a rebellion of 1918, more than 2,000 natives were killed by American forces.

Insurrection and chaos brought the marines into the Dominican Republic in 1916 and into Cuba a year later. The American dictatorships that followed produced fiscal stability and improved roads, schools, and sanitation. Many local citizens, however, preferred disorder and backwardness to rule by bayonet.

The administration took other actions in the Caribbean that were based exclusively on self-interest. The fierce fighting of World War I prompted fear that Germany would subdue Denmark, grab the Danish-owned Virgin Islands, and use them as a submarine base against the United States and the Panama Canal. In 1916 the government purchased the islands for $25 million.

Mexico

Missionary diplomacy's greatest challenge occurred in Mexico, where Wilson attempted to impose his own design upon the revolution of a sovereign neighbor. The president again had a sincere desire to help a nearby people gain peace, liberty, and land. His policies, however, resulted in the very sort of intervention he had repeatedly deplored and once more produced bitterness and hatred toward the United States.

American businessmen had been dabbling in Mexican politics for years when Wilson took office. In 1911 they had supported an insurrection by reformer Francisco Madero, who overthrew the aged and pro-British president Porfirio Diaz. When Madero became unsympathetic to their financial interests less than two years later, they backed a coup led by Victoriano Huerta and a number of right-wing generals. Huerta proved to be corrupt and dictatorial, and by early 1913 he was opposed by a number of reform-minded Constitutionalists, who saw themselves as Madero's true successors. The country was plunged into civil war.

Wilson despised Huerta and refused to extend diplomatic recognition. "I will not recognize a government of butchers," he said privately. The president imposed an arms embargo on Mexico and tried to pressure Huerta into resigning and permitting free elections. When Huerta refused to budge and appeared to be in league with the British, Wilson used diplomatic channels to force him from power. He also encouraged the Constitutionalists and lifted the arms embargo for them.

When all else seemed to fail, the president resorted to force. In April 1914 he used a trivial incident at Tampico involving a point of honor, along with a rumor about a German weapon shipment, to justify the seizure of Vera Cruz by the marines. This action, which took the lives of 19 Americans and 126 Mexicans, was condemned by both sides in the civil war as a violation of national sovereignty and was unpopular everywhere, including the United States. It sparked anti-American demonstrations throughout Latin America.

Military victories by the Constitutionalists (who rejected direct American assistance) forced Huerta into exile in July, and his place was taken by Venustiano Carranza. The marines left Vera Cruz in November, and Wilson looked forward to the return of peace in Mexico. This was not to be, however, for factions within the Constitutionalists, led by the dashing ex-bandit Francisco "Pancho" Villa, rebelled against Carranza in late 1914, and the civil war resumed.

At first, Wilson and Bryan favored Villa over the more independent Carranza. This proved to be a blunder, as Carranza soon demonstrated that he enjoyed more public popularity and military prowess than his opponent. Lacking alternatives, the United States extended de facto recognition to the Carranza government in October 1915. Villa then tried to provoke American intervention as a way of embarrassing the government and regaining his power. On January 11, 1916, he stopped a train at Santa Ysabel, in northern Mexico, and shot sixteen Americans. In March he raided Columbus, New Mexico, killing nineteen Americans and burning the town. The administration could no longer resist demands for military intervention. With the approval of several Mexican diplomats, Wilson sent General John J. Pershing and a force that ultimately numbered about 12,000 men into Mexico to capture Villa.

The so-called Punitive Expedition traveled more than 300 miles into Mexico, triggering fears of a Yankee takeover in the north. Following a skirmish in the town of Parral in which two American soldiers and forty Mexicans died, Carranza, who had not personally approved of the entry, demanded withdrawal. By the spring of 1916 the United States and Mexico were on the brink of war.

Tensions soon eased, largely because neither Wilson nor Carranza wanted war. (A lesser man than Wilson might have yielded to powerful demands for intervention and used a war to aid his reelection campaign.) Details of a settlement were turned over to an international commission, Pershing's troops left Mexico—without the elusive Villa—in early 1917, and Wilson extended de jure recognition to the Carranza government. After four years of effort, Wilson had gained nothing but the Mexican people's lasting enmity toward the United States. Mexico was now free to get on with its own business. Wilson and the American people faced far graver dangers in Europe.

The End of an Era

For some two decades, a wide variety of progressives had been hard at work altering the intellectual and moral foundations of the nation and influencing

Women flock to the polls thanks to the Nineteenth Amendment. Source: Reproduced from the Collections of the Library of Congress

the course of virtually every American institution. The sixteenth through nineteenth amendments to the Constitution—the income tax, the direct election of senators, prohibition, and women's right to vote—illustrate the significance of the reform movement. If the progressive measures as a whole seem to us modest (women's rights), naive (prohibition), and incomplete (race relations), it is wise to place the movement in its historical context, recalling how far the nation had traveled since Mark Twain was cursing the Gilded Age in his novel of 1873.

Reform had occurred in conjunction with dramatic advances in science and technology, the growth of urbanization, the acceleration of educational levels, and increasing socioeconomic mobility. Few lamented this often profound change. To be modern, even intellectually respectable, one was expected to have absorbed at least a good measure of the progressive spirit. It was no accident that all three major presidential candidates in 1912 were progressives.

But American reform movements do not last long, especially when the nation is faced with the threat of war. The energy and passion required to clean up slums, fight corruption in government, and create legislation to ensure the safety of medicine and food are greatly dissipated by one of history's most common features: the call to arms.

SUGGESTED READINGS

Paolo Coletta, *The Presidency of William Howard Taft* (1973); John Milton Cooper, *The Warrior and the Priest: Woodrow Wilson and Theodore Roosevelt* (1983); Herbert Croly, *The Promise of American Life* (1909); Stephen R. Fox, *The American Conservation Movement: John Muir and His Legacy* (1986); David M. Kennedy, *Birth Control in America: The Career of Margaret Sanger* (1970); Arthur S. Link, *Woodrow Wilson and the Progressive Era, 1910–1917* (1954); Richard Leopold, *Elihu Root and the Conservative Tradition* (1954); Alpheus T. Mason, *Brandeis, A Free Man's Life* (1956); David M. Southern, *The Malignant Heritage: Yankee Progressives and the Negro Question, 1901–1914* (1968); Robert B. Westbrook, *John Dewey and American Democracy* (1991).

Chapter Four

THE FIRST WORLD WAR

In August 1914, Americans were stunned to learn that almost all of Europe was at war. Two great coalitions, the Allies (chiefly Great Britain, France, and Russia) and the Central Powers (mainly Germany and Austria-Hungary) had been competing for power and prestige since the late nineteenth century but had always managed to resolve their differences peaceably. Indeed, many people thought that war had become a barbaric relic of the past, and that peace and progress would be the hallmarks of the twentieth century. Instead, the first general European war since the defeat of Napoleon in 1815 was at hand. And before it was over thirty sovereign states would become involved, four empires would be overthrown, and seven new nations would be born. Some 30 million lives—half of them noncombatant—would be lost in this unprecedented slaughter.

On the western front during that first awful summer the German drive toward Paris was stopped at the first Battle of the Marne. Thereafter, the war settled down into a relatively static and agonizing war of attrition. Trenches were dug across northern France and Belgium from Switzerland to the English Channel, some 470 miles away. During the next four years they became the graves of an entire generation of Englishmen, Frenchmen, and Germans. Americans were shocked by reports of the carnage; as many men died at the ancient fortress city of Verdun in 1916 as on all the battlefields of the American Civil War combined.

Initial Reactions

Virtually all Americans wanted to keep the United States out of the conflict. The president proclaimed the nation's neutrality almost immediately and soon appealed for impartiality "in thought as well as in action." Public sympathies, however, were largely with the Allies. A majority of Americans were of British descent, and the cultural, political, economic, and historical ties between the

United States and Great Britain remained strong. The French similarly commanded respect and admiration. Wilson and his top advisers were quietly pro-Allied, the exception being the near-pacifist Secretary of State William Jennings Bryan.

Germany, in contrast, was associated in many American minds with autocracy, militarism, and international expansionism. The spiked helmet was a common symbol of the German nation. The much-publicized violation of Belgium's neutrality as the war commenced contributed to a widespread belief that the Central Powers had initiated the conflict. Still, there were eight million German-Americans and more than four million Irish-Americans, many of whom were openly hostile to the British. Many American Jews supported the Central Powers because of their hatred of Russian anti-Semitism.

Both sides in the war mounted extensive propaganda campaigns within the United States. Germany would spend some $35 million to glorify its history and culture and assure Americans of its highest intentions. The British spread Belgium atrocity stories and flooded the country with literature and lecturers. These efforts seem to have had little impact, however; public perceptions were formed early in the struggle. Throughout the two-and-a-half years of neutrality most Americans continued to be pro-Allied. They were also firmly determined to avoid intervention.

Economic Involvement

The industrial and financial strength of the United States made involvement in a world war inevitable. All parties to the conflict sought access to America's rich resources. Exports to the Allies quickly began to soar—from almost $825 million annually in 1914 to more than $3.2 billion by 1916. Munitions sales alone amounted to $1.7 billion between January 1916 and March 1917. All segments of the economy, including agriculture, enjoyed the burgeoning prosperity.

In August 1915, when the British ran short of funds to continue their massive purchases, the president permitted Wall Street bankers to make loans to the Allies. During the next year and a half Great Britain borrowed more than a billion dollars, Canada $400 million, France $300 million, and Russia $50 million. Germany, at the same time, was able to raise only about $20 million in the United States.

Trade between the Central Powers and the United States was severely curtailed by a British blockade of Germany declared soon after the start of the war. The blockade was gradually extended to include almost all commodities, including foodstuffs, entering and leaving Germany. This violated international law. In 1916 Great Britain "blacklisted" neutral firms, including some eighty-seven owned by Americans, suspected of trading with Germany; seized and searched American ships; and examined mail passing between the United States and Germany. Wilson fumed and the government protested, but no severe action ensued.

When Germany called for an embargo on munitions sales and complained about war loans, American officials stated that any steps taken against the Allies would be unneutral. It was not America's fault, they said, that the British navy controlled the seas and prevented U.S. products from reaching German shores. Neither could the government be blamed for the reluctance of private bankers to lend the Central Powers great sums of money. Washington officials repeatedly contended that their policies were strictly neutral. In fact, the United States had become the arsenal of the Allies, and the Wilson administration chose not to alter that mutually advantageous relationship.

Submarine Warfare

On February 4, 1915, Germany retaliated by declaring a submarine blockade of the British Isles. The German Admiralty owned only twenty-eight of the new weapons, called U-boats, but was busily building more. (While 140 U-boats were available by October 1917, only about 60 were on duty at any one time.) All Allied merchant and warships found within the war zone, it was announced, would be destroyed. Neutral vessels were warned to stay out of the area because the British often disguised their ships with neutral flags.

Germany made it clear from the start that its submarines would not follow international law by formally warning a vessel of an impending attack and permitting crews and passengers to disembark on lifeboats. The traditional courtesy would be suicidal, for the British armed their merchantmen with cannons and the U-boats lacked protective armor. British vessels often tried to ram as well as blow up submarines when they surfaced. Wilson quickly expressed "grave concern" over this announcement and warned the German government that it would be held to "a strict accountability" for the loss of American lives and vessels. He did not mention, however, the rights of Americans working and traveling on Allied ships.

That issue came to a head on May 7, 1915, when a U-boat sank the British liner *Lusitania* off the Irish coast. Of the 1,959 persons on board, 1,198 drowned, including 128 Americans. The *Lusitania*, although an unarmed passenger ship, was carrying munitions to the English, and the German Embassy had warned Americans in newspaper advertisements that they traveled at their own risk. Nevertheless, the killing of defenseless citizens without warning, including hundreds of women and children, caused an uproar in the United States. A small group of enraged citizens, including Theodore Roosevelt, was ready to go to war against the kaiser. Wilson stayed calm but sent protests to the Imperial government strong enough to cause Secretary of State Bryan to resign and work for peace as a private citizen.

Bryan contended that Americans, to be truly neutral, should avoid traveling on belligerent ships: "A ship carrying contraband should not rely upon passengers to protect her from attack—it would be like putting women and children in front of an army." The president and his advisers disagreed, taking the position that neutrals had every right to travel on the nonmilitary ships of belligerents. Wilson saw national honor at stake on this issue and ruled out any concession or compromise. Repetitions of ruthless conduct, he warned, would be seen as "deliberately unfriendly," raising the possibility of a break in diplomatic relations.

When two Americans lost their lives in the sinking of a liner in August, Germany retreated somewhat and promised not to sink passenger ships "without warning and without safety of the noncombatants." This pledge was violated on March 24, 1916, when the unarmed French steamer *Sussex* was sunk with eighty casualties, including several Americans. Wilson threatened to break relations and demanded that Germany agree not to attack merchant or passenger ships, armed or unarmed, without warning. On May 4 the German government agreed. This was a major step in helping the Allies, but the ultimatum placed the United States in the position of being forced into the war should Germany resume unlimited submarine warfare.

National Preparedness

Throughout the first year of the war a number of prominent individuals and organizations clamored for increases in American military strength. These demands were intensified by the *Lusitania* tragedy, when public attention began to focus upon America's military impotence. Wilson resisted the pressure until the summer of 1915, when he reluctantly reversed his earlier position of seeking to cut military budgets. That November he announced his own preparedness program, "not for war, but only for defense."

After heated and prolonged debate, the president got most of what he wanted. Congress more than doubled the size of the regular army, federalized the National Guard and gave it an authorized strength of 440,000, appropriated $313 million to strengthen the navy, and agreed to spend $50 million to build merchant ships—marking the birth of the modern American merchant marine.

The preparedness program was designed for the postwar era and was not intended to hasten American entrance into the European conflict. Most Americans, including the president, remained committed to neutrality.

Wilson the Mediator

From the outset of the war Wilson had offered his services as a mediator and actively pursued a negotiated settlement. Two efforts at peace-making proved futile, and by the autumn of 1916 Wilson was bitterly disillusioned with both the Allies and the Central Powers.

The peace issue played a prominent role in the presidential election of 1916. The Democratic platform promised a neutral foreign policy and backed a postwar League of Nations. Democrats cheered all references to peace during their national convention, and during the campaign they extolled the president as the champion of peace and progressivism. Their favorite slogan was, "He kept us out of war."

The Republican candidate, Supreme Court Justice Charles Evans Hughes, was a New York progressive with a reputation for independence, integrity, and intellectual depth. He was handicapped during the campaign, however, by being widely thought to be pro-German. Wilson won a narrow victory in the fall but gained more than three million votes over his 1912 total.

With the election over, the president's thoughts again turned overseas, where conditions were rapidly developing that made American neutrality almost impossible. Germany had greatly stepped up its submarine warfare; from June 1916 to February 1917, U-boats and raiders sank more than 2 million tons. No one could predict how long the Imperial government would honor its *Sussex* pledge.

Wilson's personal friend and adviser Colonel Edward M. House and Secretary of State Robert Lansing were convinced that the United States should join the Allies to crush German militarism. At the same time, Anglo-American affairs were increasingly tense. This stemmed not only from incidents at sea but from the brutal British suppression of the Irish Rebellion.

On January 22, 1917, in a speech before the Senate, Wilson outlined his terms for a just settlement. He called for a "peace without victory," a peace based on the right of all nationalities to self-government, freedom of the seas, massive disarmament, the equality of all nations, and an end to entangling alliances. He sought a "league of peace" to enforce the settlement. "I am speaking for the silent mass of mankind everywhere," he said. Neither side in the war was moved by such noble idealism, however. German military leaders, in fact, had decided two weeks earlier to unleash their U-boats and declare war on American shipping.

The Road to War

On January 31, 1917, the German government declared a war zone around Great Britain, France, and Italy and in the eastern Mediterranean. It further announced that vessels entering the zone, neutral and belligerent, would be destroyed without warning. German officials knew that this repudiation of the *Sussex* pledge would probably bring America into the war. The military situation currently favored them, however, and they were confident of starving the British into submission before the United States could have an impact on the conflict.

Shocked and saddened, Wilson hesitated for a short while, agonizing over his choices. After consulting with House and Lansing, he broke diplomatic relations with Germany. His February 3 message to a joint session of Congress continued to call for peace.

During the next few weeks Wilson came to realize that war was unavoidable. On February 25 the British sent him an intercepted and decoded message from the German foreign secretary to the German minister in Mexico City. In case the United States should declare war, the "Zimmermann Telegram" read, the minister would propose an alliance with the Mexican government by which Mexico would receive the territories of Texas, New Mexico, and Arizona, taken by Americans in 1848. The Mexican president was also to ask Japan (one of the Allies) to join the scheme. A few days later Wilson gave the telegram to the press, and the nation was stunned and outraged to learn of Germany's hostile designs.

The day after receiving the telegram, Wilson asked Congress for authority to arm American merchant ships. When the proposal was filibustered to death in the Senate by several noninterventionists and pacifists, the President exclaimed, "A little group of willful men, representing no opinion but their own, have rendered the great Government of the United States helpless and contemptible." On March 9, with Congress adjourned, Wilson took it upon himself to order guns and sailors on merchant vessels and to issue instructions to shoot at enemy submarines in the war zone. Within a few days U-boats began sinking American merchantmen. Four unarmed ships soon went down, with a heavy loss of life.

On March 20 Wilson discovered that his cabinet was unanimously in favor of declaring war. The following day he summoned Congress into special session, to begin on April 2. He had decided to prepare a war message. The president continued to suffer, however, and search for a way out. He expressed fear of public intolerance unleashed by war, and was afraid that the Constitution might not survive.

The next day Wilson went before a joint session of Congress and read his war message. Armed neutrality was no longer possible, he said. Germany had "thrust" war upon the United States. Rather than fighting for conquest or plunder, however, Americans would be asked to shed their blood for peace and justice. All wars must be ended, Wilson declared, and autocracies like the Imperial government must be crushed. "The world must be made safe for democracy." In the end, then, Wilson had succeeded in quieting his conscience only with a heavy dose of idealism.

The Senate passed the resolution of war by a vote of 82 to 6, and the House soon concurred, 373 to 50. Resistance came largely from the Midwest, where many people of German ancestry lived. Most Americans, however, no doubt for the first time, were prepared to fight. On April 6, 1917, the United States was officially at war.

Those who voted against the resolution claimed that bankers, munitions makers, and propagandists were responsible for dragging America into the conflict. While the evidence does not sustain the charge, a second argument by the isolationists rings true. The United States had not been genuinely neutral prior to entering the war. Public and official sympathies were pro-Allied from the start, and Americans enjoyed highly profitable economic ties with the Allies. The United States permitted Great Britain to violate international law with its blockade but expected Germany to obey it with its submarines.

Moreover, the president failed to keep Americans off belligerent ships and keep American ships out of the German war zone.

Still, Wilson would not have written his war message had not Germany broken the *Sussex* pledge and begun killing Americans. His sense of national honor compelled him to take action, and most Americans sanctioned that decision. The president was correct in saying that the Imperial government had "thrust" war upon the United States. As historian Thomas A. Bailey concluded, "The decision that we should fight was made in Germany, not in America." From a hatred of the German government it was but a short step in Wilson's mind to seek to rid the world of all such governments—to call for an American crusade to create a new world order.

It is also wise to consider what would have befallen Western Europe, and perhaps the world, had Wilson elected to swallow his pride and stay out of the war. The Allies were in desperate economic shape by April 1917, and morale was low. U-boats soon began massive assaults upon Allied shipping, bringing England near starvation. With Nikolai Lenin and the Bolsheviks making peace with the Central Powers in November, freeing about a million German veterans to leave the Eastern Front for France, it is likely that the Allies would have collapsed in 1918. The strikingly powerful presence of the United States changed the course of the Great War and no doubt prevented Germany from dictating the peace.

MOBILIZATION

Confusion, inefficiency, and waste were rampant for several months after the declaration of war as government officials grappled with a number of highly complex problems. An effective military effort had to be planned and carried out. The war had to be financed. The economy had to be geared to wartime production. Efforts had to be designed to enlist overwhelming public support. Modern warfare was not just a struggle between rival soldiers and sailors; it involved economic systems and entire populations. In the twentieth century whole societies were at war against each other.

One important truth soon became apparent: the notion of laissez-faire government was obsolete. Significant participation in the war required unprecedented centralized authority. Many progressives, of course, had long dreamed of a powerful federal government. The war was to teach them, however, that such authority could have unintended results.

The Draft

The president soon learned from the Allies of the urgent need for a large contingent of American troops overseas. Following recommendations by his military advisers, he rejected proposals to raise volunteer units and endorsed conscription as the only way to obtain the necessary manpower. Congress debated for six weeks before approving a national draft, the first since the Civil War. The Selective Service Act became law on May 18, 1917.

Altogether, 4,649 local draft boards, staffed by civilians, registered some 24 million men between the ages of 18 and 45 and provided nearly 3 million to the armed forces—all but some 8,000 to the army. During the eighteen months America was at war, another 2 million men joined the armed services voluntarily.

Financing the War

Not counting postwar expenses, World War I cost Americans about $32 billion. About $7 billion of this was loaned to the Allies, and most of that sum was spent in the United States, increasing national prosperity. The federal government borrowed about two-thirds of the war costs from the public. Four massive drives to sell "Liberty Bonds" plus a "Victory Loan" in April 1919 proved highly successful. Patriotic advertisements, parades, and appeals, and even threats by some employers, rallied Americans to the cause. The fourth bond drive alone attracted 21 million subscribers. By 1920 these efforts had produced $23 billion.

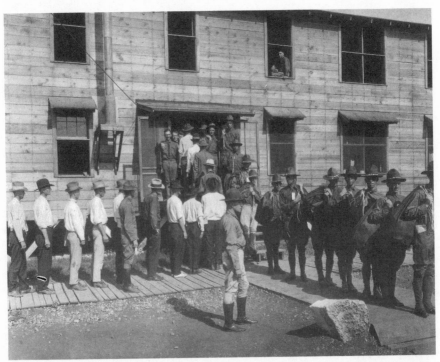

Draftees reporting for service at Camp Travis, San Antonio, Texas. Source: National Archives

The government also raised almost $10 billion in taxes. Much of this came from new graduated income taxes, backed by Wilson and congressional progressives, which rose as high as 70 percent for the very wealthy. Corporate income taxes also went up, special excess profits taxes yielded more than $2 billion in 1918, and a 25-percent inheritance tax was passed.

On the whole, the cost of the war was distributed widely and equitably. Moreover, wartime economics proved that high taxes and heavy government spending did not damage the economy, as business had long claimed. The gross national product soared from an average of $40 billion between 1912 and 1916 to more than $80 billion between 1917 and 1921.

The War Boards

War forced the federal government to exercise unprecedented power over the nation's economy. Trade, industry, and labor vital to the military effort had to be supervised and coordinated. At first, Wilson appointed a Council for National Defense to handle this gigantic task. The council, in turn, created a number of agencies, led chiefly by dollar-a-year businessmen, to deal with vital areas.

The Food Administration, authorized by the Lever Act of August 1917, was headed by Herbert Hoover, a wealthy, 43-year-old mining engineer who had gained international fame by leading the Belgian relief effort early in the war. Hoover encouraged production, supervised food exports and imports, organized government corporations to purchase the nation's wheat and sugar crops, and urged Americans to conserve food supplies. Millions observed "Wheatless Mondays" and "Meatless Tuesdays" and planted backyard gardens. Largely through voluntary efforts, and without rationing, the nation's total agricultural production increased, farmers enjoyed a 25-percent increase in real income, and exports to the Allies soared. Between July 1, 1918, and July 1, 1919, the Food Administration sent 18.5 million tons of food overseas, more than three times the normal amount.

The Fuel Administration, headed by Harry A. Garfield, son of the twentieth president, stimulated the production of coal by raising its price. Under the Railroad Administration, led by Secretary of the Treasury William G. McAdoo, the government leased the nation's railroads and operated them as a single system in order to promote efficiency. The War Trade Board controlled all imports and exports, prohibiting trade with neutral countries that might aid Germany.

The War Industries Board was the most important of the new agencies because it was designed to oversee all industrial production and distribution. In March 1918 Wilson reorganized the board and placed it under the authority of Bernard M. Baruch, a wealthy and knowledgeable Wall Street speculator. Through persuasion and an ability to "look any man in the eye and tell him to go to hell," Baruch became the virtual dictator of American industry. He controlled government purchases, allocated raw materials, coordinated the manufacture of war goods, standardized industrial production, and fixed prices. Baruch was openly sympathetic to businessmen and consistently helped them reap high profits.

Workers also benefited from wartime conditions and enjoyed the friendship of federal authorities. The National War Labor Board, designed to arbitrate labor disputes, consistently pressured businessmen to avoid strikes by granting such concessions as the eight-hour day, better working conditions, and collective bargaining. The War Labor Policies Board, headed by Harvard law professor Felix Frankfurter, created wages-and-hours standards for war industries and helped accelerate unionization.

With the encouragement of the Wilson administration, union membership rose by 2.3 million during the war. In 1920 Samuel Gompers, a member of the National War Labor Board, could boast that his AFL had 3.26 million members. Wartime wage increases amounted to a 20-percent hike in the average real income of blue-collar workers. While impressive, this was less than the gains made by business and agriculture.

Several efforts in the drive to plan the nation's economy proved disappointing. The shipbuilding program suffered from mismanagement and, despite huge expenditures, new vessels began to be completed only months before the end of the war. The government had to rely upon ships confiscated from Germany, purchased from neutrals and private industry, and obtained from the British. Programs to construct heavy artillery, tanks, and airplanes started slowly and did not affect the war. Much weaponry had to be purchased from the British and French, and American aviators flew British and French planes throughout the conflict. Still, genuine progress was made in the shipping and aircraft fields, and had the war lasted longer American production would have been substantial.

On the whole, the administration's record in the uncharted area of economic mobilization was impressive. While some programs were flawed and overly ambitious, most were effective and all were free of scandal. Wilson, who worked feverishly throughout this period, deserves much of the credit.

Shaping Public Opinion

Wilson and his advisers were keenly aware of the doubts many people had about the nation's participation in the war. The president had conquered his own at the last minute. But once in the struggle, Wilson was determined that all Americans should see the war as he did—a holy crusade to alter the future for the benefit of the human race. A week after war was declared, he created the Committee on Public Information to mobilize public opinion. As its chairman, Wilson selected George Creel, a zealous and colorful newspaper editor from Denver with a reputation as a progressive.

The "Creel Committee" undertook the greatest propaganda effort in American history. It hired thousands of artists and writers, distributed 75 million pieces of literature, sent out 75,000 volunteers to give speeches, filled magazines with advertisements, and plastered walls everywhere with posters. In all of this Americans were said to be fighting only for freedom and democracy, while Germans ("Huns") were portrayed as evil beasts eager to conquer the world. The propaganda grew increasingly shrill as the months wore on and American casualty lists grew lengthy. In 1918 Committee literature suggested that hordes of German spies were loose in the land and urged citizens to report neighbors who seemed in any way unpatriotic.

Creel and his committee undoubtedly contributed in a major way to the public hysteria that gripped the nation during these years. Patriotic groups created such organizations as the American Vigilante Patrol, the Sedition Slammers, and the Boy Spies of America. The 250,000-member American Protective League enforced loyalty and conformity on the local level. Meetings were spied on, telephones were tapped, mail was opened. Radicals, strikers, labor organizers, and conscientious objectors were often reviled and assaulted. A jury in Indiana took two minutes to acquit a man who had shot and killed a person for yelling "To hell with the United States." Americans abandoned instruction in the German language, yanked German books out of libraries, refused to listen to German music, renamed sauerkraut "liberty cabbage," and subjected people of German descent to cruel harassments and beatings.

With the president's blessing, Congress also contributed to this outburst of hatred. The Espionage Act of 1917 imposed stiff fines and jail sentences on persons who interfered with recruiting or made false statements obstructing the war effort. It also authorized the postmaster general to ban printed materials he considered treasonable from the mails. The Sedition Act of 1918 went much farther, making it a crime to "utter, print, write, or publish any disloyal, profane, scurrilous, or abusive language" about the government, the Constitution, the armed forces, or the flag. Government officials used these statutes to close the mails to several publications of the Socialist party (which opposed the war), to prosecute almost two thousand people, and to send a sizable number of antiwar radicals to prison, including Socialists Victor Berger and Eugene V. Debs, and IWW leader Bill Haywood. Debs got ten years for making a speech. One woman received the same sentence for writing, "I am for the people, and the government is for the profiteers."

Women and Work During the War

Women found new employment opportunities during the war because of a labor shortage. As many men went into the military and the war reduced the flow of new immigrants, increased demands for domestic production were difficult to meet. Some women worked in jobs usually held by men, including streetcar conducting, police work, and factory work. Wages for women increased by 20 percent between 1914 and 1918. Most women working for pay, however, remained in traditionally female jobs, and their numbers were not great; the percentage employed outside the home stayed at roughly 25

percent from 1910 through 1920. After the war, many women in traditionally male positions lost their jobs.

African Americans and the War

High wages and full employment in northern cities prompted half a million
African Americans to leave the South between 1914 and 1919. This first great
exodus of blacks sparked violence in the South, where whites lamented the
loss of cheap labor. In the North whites often responded with fear and anger.
Segregation and subjugation were commonplace, and in 1917 race riots broke
out in twenty-six cities. That August, forty-nine people were killed in East
St. Louis, thirty-nine of them black.

Black leaders strongly endorsed America's war effort, and more than
400,000 African Americans served in the army. They were frequently assigned
to segregated areas of camps, and three of every four served as laborers. The
army created a single Negro division for overseas duty and placed whites in
all the vital positions. When some 200,000 blacks were sent to France in
1918, army officials tried to persuade the French to segregate them.

There were some encouraging developments, however. The army accepted blacks for officer training and commissioned some 1,200. African
Americans fought with considerable distinction in France, although two battalions of one regiment were widely condemned by white army officials
for retreating under fire in the Argonne Forest. Blacks also held several
high posts in government agencies during the war and were welcomed as
Red Cross nurses.

The War at Sea

America's participation in the war first had an effect in the crucial battle
against the U-boats. In late April Secretary of the Navy Josephus Daniels ordered six destroyers to head for European waters, and twenty-nine others
were dispatched that summer to patrol for submarines. The following year
the navy planted 56,571 mines across the 250-mile North Sea strait between
Norway and Scotland, and a small fleet of wooden subchasers, manned with
listening devices and depth charges, joined the fray.

Of more significance was the decision in May 1917 to use American and
British warships to escort merchant and troop ships across the Atlantic in
convoys. This "bridge of ships" proved to be a lifeline for the Allies. By
December 1917 sinkings declined to 350,000 tons; by October 1918 they
had dropped to 112,000 tons. Some two million Americans were transported
across the 3,000 miles to France without the loss of a single life. By the
time of the Armistice the American navy was using 200,000 men and 834
ships either in patrolling or convoying. Germany's gamble that the Allies
would be crushed before America could make a difference in the war proved
incorrect.

The Western Front

Cheering crowds greeted the first American troops who reached Paris on July 4, 1917. An American colonel uttered the stirring words, "Lafayette, we are here!" This token force numbered only some 14,000 men, however, and additional soldiers were slow in coming. By March 1918 there were fewer than 300,000 Americans in France, all inadequately equipped. Thereafter, reinforcements began to arrive in huge numbers, and by July 1 a million American troops were on the Western Front. Slightly more than four months later the war was over.

Wilson appointed General John J. Pershing commander-in-chief of what was called the American Expeditionary Force. Both men insisted that the AEF eventually be a separate force. Pershing wanted his troops trained for attack and victory and did not relish the thought of having British and French generals send Americans into the trenches as replacements. Reflecting America's isolationist tradition and historic distrust of entangling alliances, the President went so far as to label the United States an "associate" power rather than one of the Allies. This aloof attitude irritated the British and French and would later cause problems at home when Wilson tried to persuade Americans to join the Allies in a League of Nations.

General John Pershing arrives in France. Source: Reproduced from the Collections of the Library of Congress

In March 1918 the Germans launched a massive spring offensive that by June 1 left them only 50 miles from Paris. AEF troops fought valiantly in bloody battles at Chateau Thierry and Belleau Wood and helped the French halt the German advance. On July 18 the Allied armies launched a counter-attack that turned the tide in the war. On September 12 at the St. Mihiel salient, north of Verdun, some 550,000 Americans joined 110,000 French soldiers in an impressive two-day victory that was planned entirely by American commanders and staff officers. (The battle featured the daring exploits of some 1,481 Allied airplanes, under the command of Colonel Billy Mitchell.) On September 26 1.2 million American soldiers participated in a grisly and often chaotic drive along a 200-mile front into the region of the Argonne Forest and the Meuse River. "The most impressive fact about the Americans, as far as the Germans were concerned," historian Edward M. Coffman has written, "was that there were so many of them." The AEF suffered 26,277 dead and 95,786 wounded during the fierce fighting.

In late September, facing an invasion of their own country, the German high command began to press for an armistice. On October 6 it contacted President Wilson and requested an immediate suspension of hostilities. The fighting ground on for weeks, however, during discussions of agreeable terms. In one of the most celebrated feats of the war, Corporal Alvin C. York captured 132 prisoners and thirty-five machine guns, leaving behind perhaps as many as 28 Germans he had killed. During one twenty-four-hour period two units of Allied planes dropped 79 tons of bombs behind German lines, a forecast of what war would be like in the future.

Finally, faced with the dissolution of the Central Powers, mutinies at home, and defeat on the battlefield, the kaiser abdicated and a new German government agreed to an armistice. On November 11 the Great War, as it was called, came to an end.

American losses included 112,432 dead (more than half from disease) and 230,074 wounded. European casualties, of course, were far greater. Germany suffered 1.8 million deaths, Russia 1.7 million, France 1.38 million, Austria-Hungary 1.2 million, the British Commonwealth 947,000, and Italy 460,000. Some 20 million men were wounded. The first modern war, with its powerful artillery, tanks, machine guns, submarines, airplanes, and poison gas, had been the most destructive in history.

MAKING THE PEACE

By late 1918 much of European civilization had been destroyed or badly shaken. A mysterious flu epidemic during the year added to the war's woes, killing up to 40 million people worldwide, including 548,452 Americans. (Scientists got their first direct look at the flu virus in 1997, concluding that it originated from American pigs and was unique.) It was the worst infectious disease episode in history. People staggered into the future confused, disillusioned, hungry, angry, and afraid.

Many put their trust in Woodrow Wilson and the United States to heal their wounds, create a just peace, and put an end to all war. Wilson had brought America into the conflict declaring the highest principles, and throughout 1918 he had won the hearts of millions in a series of speeches laden with lofty idealism about the peace that was to follow. Indeed, this oratory was instrumental in persuading the German people to seek an armistice.

Wilsonian Idealism

If Wilson had consulted with the Allies before writing his war message he would have discovered that they did not accept much of his idealistic rhetoric. This important truth became apparent in late 1917 when the Bolshevik government of Russia began disclosing secret treaties among the Allies for dividing the colonies of their enemies after the war. Wilson was determined to prevent such traditional statecraft and to create a peace in line with his own goals.

After attempting unsuccessfully to work out a joint statement with the Allies, he took the initiative and became the self-appointed spokesman of the war aims. With the British and French relatively silent on the issue, people assumed that the president was speaking for them as well as the United States. Wilson assumed his new role confident that he could control the British and French after the war and with a certainty that he represented the aspirations of most men and women everywhere.

On January 8, 1918, in a speech before Congress, Wilson outlined what he said were America's war aims. These Fourteen Points contained several guidelines for the future handling of international affairs, including open covenants instead of secret treaties, freedom of the seas in peace and war, the removal of economic barriers between nations, a reduction of national armaments, and an impartial adjustment of colonial claims. The most important point of all, to Wilson, was the fourteenth: the call for a "general association of nations" to guarantee world peace.

The British and French were delighted that Wilson's pronouncements helped bring an end to the war. Even before the combat stopped, however, they were quietly preparing to resist the peace plans of their American "associate." Having suffered mightily for four years, they were eager to wring as much out of their enemies as possible. At no time were the Allied leaders genuinely committed to Wilsonian idealism.

Republican Opposition

In the spring of 1918 the GOP launched an intensive campaign to win the fall congressional elections. Despite a general reluctance to attack the chief executive during wartime, several leading Republicans, including Theodore Roosevelt, former President Taft, and Senator Henry Cabot Lodge, made angry speeches against the president. In late October Wilson fired back with a

personal appeal to the American people to vote for Democrats as an expression of confidence in his leadership "at home and abroad." Republicans,
who had loyally supported the administration's wartime programs, were infuriated by this partisan tactic and stepped up their attacks. The Fourteen
Points and the League of Nations were favorite targets.

On election day Republicans captured the Senate by a two-seat margin,
making Senator Lodge chairman of the Foreign Relations Committee. They
gained twenty-five seats in the House and now outnumbered Democrats 237
to 190. The returns largely reflected unhappiness about big government, high
taxes, low wheat prices, the Eighteenth Amendment, and violations of civil
liberties. The election was widely interpreted throughout the country and
overseas, however, as a public repudiation of the president.

When Wilson made the stunning announcement on November 18 that he
would personally attend the Peace Conference at Paris, many observers
thought he would be an ineffective spokesman in light of his rebuke by the
electorate. Theodore Roosevelt roared, "Our allies and Mr. Wilson himself
should all understand that Mr. Wilson has no authority whatever to speak
for the American people at this time." Republican leaders in general agreed,
declaring their firm opposition to Wilson's postwar aims and activities.

No president had ever traveled to Europe while in office, and even some
Democrats were opposed to this innovation in American foreign policy. Allied leaders, moreover, subtly objected to Wilson's presence at the peace
table because they feared he would demand a "soft peace" and block their
efforts to grab the spoils of war. But Wilson dismissed all objections. Always
a rather rigid and self-righteous man, he now saw himself as an apostle of
a new world order, a prophet with a burning moral mission to create a just
peace and end war forever. This supremely important task, he believed, required his personal presence at Paris.

Republican hostility toward the president intensified when he selected four
men to join him on the Peace Commission. Only one, career diplomat Henry
White, was a Republican, and he was a minor figure in the party. It was undoubtedly a mistake not to appoint at least one distinguished Republican to
the commission in order to create bipartisan support for the momentous decisions that lay ahead. But Wilson had long disliked and distrusted the opposition party and had deeply resented the recent campaign attacks. The logical choice would have been Senator Lodge, but he and the president were
personal as well as political enemies. On December 3, 1918, Wilson sailed
for Europe convinced that he alone represented the millions in the world
crying for peace and justice.

The Paris Peace Conference

After spending two weeks in France, Wilson made brief visits to England and
Italy. Wherever he appeared crowds cheered and wept. In Rome people cried
"Viva Wilson, god of peace," and in Milan wounded soldiers attempted to

kiss his clothes. The tumultuous ovations further convinced Wilson that the common people of Europe backed his high-minded principles. In fact, the very people who cheered the president were as eager as their leaders to punish Germany severely and to gain as much as possible from the peace talks.

The Peace Conference began its deliberations in mid-January. Hundreds of delegates and experts from twenty-seven nations were on hand (the American contingent alone numbered about 1,300), and some sixty different commissions were created to handle a mountain of largely technical issues. At first, a Council of Ten, including the United States and the major Allied powers, handled the important decisions. Before long this task was assumed by the Council of Four: Wilson, George Clemenceau of France, David Lloyd George of Great Britain, and Vitorrio Orlando of Italy. Orlando represented the weakest of the four powers and had little influence. In April he left the conference in a huff. This meant that three men, often meeting in private, bore the responsibility of restructuring much of the world. It was an ironic ending to a war fought in the name of democracy, and was inconsistent with the goal of the Fourteen Points to put an end to secret diplomacy.

Wilson worked extremely hard at Paris to master every detail of the complex issues brought to the peace table and was the best prepared of the Big Four. Although he did not dominate the talks as he had hoped, he was able within the first five weeks to score two important victories: adoption of the mandate principle and the incorporation of the League of Nations Covenant in the peace treaty.

The mandate plan was a compromise. Germany was stripped of all its colonies in Africa and the Far East. Rather than being parceled out among the victors, however, these territories were to be held as mandates by certain nations under the supervision of the League of Nations. This arrangement was more in harmony with the Fourteen Points than naked annexation, it offered eventual self-rule to the people of the colonies, and it provided the league with some immediate duties. Still, critics later noted that the major powers wound up possessing most of what they had sought to own and that the mandates bore a close relation to the terms of the dozen or so secret treaties the Allied powers had made among themselves during the war.

During April the Council of Four hammered out the specifics of the treaty. Wilson fought bitterly with Clemenceau, who was determined to defend French security and was committed to the return of balance-of-power politics. Compromises were soon reached, however, forced in large part by deteriorating economic and political conditions throughout the world. Germans were starving, for example, central Europe was in chaos, and Bolsheviks were winning the civil war in Russia and communism was spreading into the West.

Article 231 of the Treaty of Versailles, the "war guilt clause," declared that Germany and its allies were responsible for the war and all the losses suffered by the Allied and associated nations. Germany was required to sign a "blank check" by agreeing to pay whatever reparation figure an expert commission would later arrive at, a sum that would include all civilian damages and future Allied war pensions. (The final tally, established in 1921, was $33 billion, far beyond anything Germany could pay.) Among other penalties, Germany also lost its colonies, was stripped of Alsace-Lorraine in the west and Polish territories in the east, and was virtually disarmed.

The treaty fell far short of guaranteeing the "self-determination" of peoples. Italy, for example, was given a section of the Austrian South Tyrol containing more than 200,000 Austrian-Germans. The four new states of central Europe—Poland, Czechoslovakia, Rumania, and Yugoslavia—incorporated an assortment of nationalities. Mandates ignored the wishes of those inhabiting the former German colonies. The treaty also saddened Wilsonians by omitting references to free trade, freedom of the seas, "open covenants openly arrived at," and disarmament.

Only a threat to renew the war forced Germany to sign what it considered a slave treaty. When Germans laid down their arms, they had been promised a peace based on the Fourteen Points. Instead, they were handed what German diplomat Philipp Scheidemann called "the vilest crime in history." Historian A. J. P. Taylor has observed, "All Germans intended to repudiate the treaty at some time in the future, if it did not first fall to pieces of its own absurdity."

It must be repeated, however, that public opinion within the victorious nations demanded stern treatment of the Germans. Clemenceau and Lloyd George were assailed repeatedly by critics at home for alleged leniency. In February 1919 the United States Congress specifically excluded Germany and its allies from receiving any part of a $100 million appropriation to feed starving Europeans. Moreover, while self-determination was not fully achieved, territorial readjustments were on the whole reasonable, and fewer people found themselves living under alien domination after the war than ever before.

In fact, considering the passions of those first months after the armistice, the Treaty of Versailles was an extraordinarily moderate document. Wilson's presence among the peacemakers undoubtedly kept the terms of the agreement from being far more vengeful than they were.

Wilson was keenly aware of the discrepancies between the Fourteen Points and the treaty but was confident that the document's inadequacies would be ironed out by the new League of Nations. He returned home certain that the American people would back his efforts at the peace table and embrace their new international responsibilities.

The president was physically and mentally exhausted, and often moody and irritable. He had been forced to compromise on numerous issues during the past several months in order to create the League and was unwilling to give further ground. "Anyone who opposes me . . . I'll crush!," he told a Democratic Senator. "I shall consent to nothing. *The Senate must take its medicine.*" Wilson biographer Arthur Link later revealed that Wilson suffered from serious arterial disease at the time. "In his normal, healthy state, Wilson would have found compromise with the large group of moderate Republicans."

The Ratification Struggle

Among other things, Article X of the League of Nations Covenant was certain to face stiff opposition. By it each member nation promised to protect "the territorial integrity and existing political independence" of all other members. Collective security was to replace balance of power, and the United States would be committed to a fully active participation in international affairs for the first time.

There were many other reasons for opposing the treaty and the Covenant. At the core of much of the opposition, however, was political partisanship. Republicans, looking ahead to the 1920 elections, were determined to discredit the President.

At the same time, Lodge realized that Wilson had a great deal of support across the country. Thirty-three governors and thirty-two state legislatures had endorsed the League. A poll of newspaper editors revealed an overwhelming majority in favor of American membership in the international body. To give the antiratification forces more time to mobilize public opinion against the treaty, Lodge used the Foreign Relations Committee to stall consideration of the document. After nearly two months had passed, and efforts to win over GOP senators had failed, Wilson announced that he would take his case directly to the American people.

On September 3, 1919, the President embarked on a speaking tour through the Midwest and Far West. In twenty-two days he traveled more than 8,000 miles and delivered thirty-seven addresses to cheering crowds that grew larger and more enthusiastic the farther west he went. Now 63, Wilson had begun this exhausting journey against the advice of his physician. The strains of the presidency and a severe case of influenza suffered while he was in France had severely taxed his strength.

What drove him on was the belief that he could rally the public and force senators to accept the treaty as he had handed it to them. On September 25, in Pueblo, Colorado, his health gave out and the remainder of the tour was canceled. Back in Washington, on October 2, he suffered a near fatal stroke that paralyzed his left side.

Wilson was totally disabled for almost two months, and he would never again be able to fulfill all of his presidential duties. His mind was undamaged, but the illness permanently upset his emotional balance. Cabinet members ran the government. The First Lady, Edith Galt Wilson, covered up the extent of her husband's illness and thwarted suggestions that he resign. As he slowly regained his strength, Wilson grew increasingly certain that he was locked in combat with the forces of evil.

In early November Senator Lodge presented for his committee a series of fourteen reservations to the treaty—a number designed to match Wilson's Fourteen Points. The second reservation was the most significant, declaring that the United States would not assume obligations under Article X of the Covenant without a joint resolution of Congress. From his sickbed, Wilson rejected numerous appeals to compromise and demanded that Democrats oppose all reservations. On November 19, following a bitterly partisan struggle, the Senate defeated the treaty with and without reservations. Still, the votes revealed that nearly four-fifths of the senators favored the league in some form.

Pleas for compromise poured into the White House, and the British government said publicly that the Allies would be willing to accept the reservations if that was the price for bringing the United States into the league. But Wilson, like the haughty Senator Lodge, refused to budge. On July 21, 1921, a joint resolution of Congress simply declared the war at an end.

The failure by the president, Senator Lodge, and a number of senators from both parties to place the welfare of the nation and the world ahead of their political goals and personality conflicts blocked what was undoubtedly a desire by the majority of Americans to join the league. The tragic course of events that followed might have been altered had America assumed the international leadership Wilson envisioned. We can never be certain. Without the United States, however, the league proved ineffective, and the ghastly specter of the Second World War was not far away.

The election of 1920 did not turn out to be the "great and solemn referendum" on the treaty Wilson had hoped for. The Democratic candidate, Governor James M. Cox of Ohio, won the nomination in large part because he was not identified with Wilson. He supported the league, but sometimes with hesitation. The GOP platform was vague about the nation's international duties, as was the party candidate, Senator Warren G. Harding of Ohio, a strong reservationist. Although Harding had the endorsement of more than fifty internationalists during the campaign, he interpreted his smashing victory at the polls (winning 37 states with an unprecedented 404 electoral votes) as a repudiation of the treaty.

After Harding's inauguration the Covenant was forgotten. Before long, the nation began to accept the new president's views on foreign affairs. Exhausted by the war, troubled by peacetime readjustments, weary of reform, the American people chose to go it alone in the world. They eagerly sought what Harding called "normalcy." Woodrow Wilson died in 1924, an embittered shell of a man who believed to the end in his vision of a world body devoted to freedom and peace.

SUGGESTED READING

Edward M. Coffman, *The War to End All Wars: The American Military Experience in World War I* (1968); Robert Ferrell, *Woodrow Wilson and the World War, 1917–1921* (1985); Florette Henri, *Black Migration: Movement North, 1900–1920* (1975); Herbert Hoover, *The Ordeal of Woodrow Wilson* (1958); John Keegan, *The First World War* (1999); Henry Cabot Lodge, *The Senate and the League of Nations* (1925); David M. Kennedy, *Over Here: The First World War and American Society* (1980); Erich Maria Remarque, *All Quiet on the Western Front* (1929); Ronald Schaffer, *America in the Great War: The Rise of the Welfare State* (1994); Edith B. Wilson, *My Memoir* (1938).

Chapter Five

THE TWENTIES

The war persuaded many Americans to abandon all forms of the idealism that had been expanding for more than a generation. They rejected not only lofty-sounding foreign entanglements but the spirit of progressivism itself. While not all reform activity was spurned, the rhetoric of laissez faire was again in style. A new America was dawning, a nation of huge cities, massive industries, exciting inventions, and sweeping changes in traditional social and moral standards. People were eager to get in on the prosperity and fun they thought was within everyone's grasp.

Postwar Tensions

Demobilization was hasty and unplanned. The government simply dropped wartime controls, canceled war contracts, and discharged military personnel. Temporary unemployment and inflation resulted. By 1920 the cost of living was more than twice what it had been before the war. That summer the country began to suffer a sharp recession that lasted almost two years.

A wave of labor disturbances broke out in 1919: 3,600 strikes involving more than four million workers. General strikes in Seattle and Boston paralyzed both cities and badly frightened the middle class. In Boston the police joined strikers, and Governor Calvin Coolidge gained national attention by calling out the National Guard to restore order. State and federal troops helped break a violent strike in the steel industry. Wilson's Attorney General A. Mitchell Palmer obtained an injunction against the bituminous coal miners when they walked off the job. Many leaders of industry, government, patriotic societies, and the sensationalistic press blamed labor trouble on foreigners, Socialists, and Communists.

The confusion and stress of the time triggered other disturbances as well. The hundreds of thousands of African Americans who had migrated to the

North during the war in search of jobs were often seen in 1919 as economic competitors and invaders of white neighborhoods. Increasing demands by black leaders for equal rights and higher wages intensified hostilities. Twenty-five race riots broke out during the year, resulting in hundreds of deaths and injuries and millions of dollars in property damage. In Chicago, where the black population had doubled in a decade, a battle went on for thirteen days, killing fifteen whites and twenty-three blacks and leaving a thousand people homeless. More than seventy blacks were lynched in the South.

The First Red Scare

There were about 70,000 Communists in the United States in 1919—less than one-tenth of 1 percent of the nation's adult population. They were largely foreign-born and had practically no influence on the labor scene. Still, "the Reds"—as the Communists and a variety of others on the left were loosely labeled—became scapegoats for much of the postwar turmoil. An emotional wave of hostility broke out in 1919–20 that reached hysterical levels. Much of the hatred that wartime propaganda had directed toward Germans and nonconformists was now transferred to the Reds.

There were good reasons for distrusting Bolsheviks. Few Americans had forgiven them for pulling Russia out of the war and calling for the dissolution of all capitalistic governments. In March 1919, Soviet leaders organized the Third International, an agency dedicated to world revolution that was actively subverting governments in eastern Europe. Moreover, Red flags and literature had appeared in some postwar strikes, a rash of bombings were linked to radicals, and there were highly publicized May Day riots in several cities. All of this was little justification, however, for the irrational hatred focused upon the tiny handful of American Communists and those said to be allies.

The Red Scare affected many areas of American life. Labor unions were widely thought to be infested with subversives. Schools and colleges were said to be filled with Reds; scores of teachers were fired and thousands were required to sign loyalty oaths. Clergymen and church organizations were condemned. The patriotism of progressives was questioned. The newly created American Civil Liberties Union was called a "Bolshevist front." At least fifty mobs attacked allegedly radical individuals and groups during 1919. The million-member American Legion, founded in May 1919, called for the immediate deportation of all individuals who defamed the American way of life.

The federal government, under the direction of Attorney General A. Mitchell Palmer, was a major agent fostering this witch hunt. Palmer, a Quaker and progressive Democrat, was enraged when his house was bombed by an anarchist. Continued pressure from the press and Congress to take action against such people helped persuade him of the existence of a Red menace. Then too, Palmer had presidential aspirations and thought that a dramatic pursuit of Reds would help him capture his party's nomination.

In November 1919, the attorney general launched a nationwide hunt for radicals led by young Justice Department official J. Edgar Hoover. Agents raided the Union of Russian Workers headquarters in New York City, and in a short time 249 aliens were deported to Russia, the vast majority being innocent of any crime. On January 2, 1920, some six thousand suspected radicals were rounded up in thirty-three cities, covering twenty-three states. Many of the arrests were made without warrants, and many of the captives were beaten, forced to sign confessions, and held in deplorable jails. By mid-year, 591 aliens were awaiting deportation. Even though the Palmer raids failed to reveal any actual threat to the nation, most Americans cheered the attorney general. State governments were also in pursuit of Reds. Under state legislation, some 1,400 people, citizens and aliens, were arrested in 1919–20, and some 300 were ultimately convicted and sent to prison.

The Red Scare subsided almost as quickly as it had developed. The expulsion by the New York state legislature of five legally elected Socialists in April 1920 shocked people of all political persuasions concerned with the principle of representative government. Furthermore, Palmer's excesses began to become evident. When the attorney general's prediction of a massive radical upheaval on May 1, 1920, proved inaccurate, the public began to scoff at his persistent anti-Red propaganda. Neither party used the Red issue in the presidential campaign of 1920. The victory by businesspeople over most strikers, the gradual return of prosperity, the increase of a Communist threat in Europe, and the election of the affable Harding also contributed to the restoration of calm and sanity.

The Communist party in the United States was badly damaged by the scare. In 1924 its presidential candidate received only 36,000 votes. Three years later the party had only eight thousand members. But hard times and war were to rejuvenate the party, and its membership would reach about 75,000 in 1947.

The New Era

Business leaders were fond of labeling the 1920s the New Era, calling attention to its productivity and wealth. There was much to boast about. American industrial output nearly doubled between 1922 and 1929, and the gross national product rose by 40 percent. In 1928, the Dow Jones industrial average hit 381, up from the century mark in 1906. The national per capita income increased by 30 percent during the decade. By 1928 real wages were about one-third higher than they had been in 1914. In 1920 the six-day, sixty-hour week was normal for industrial workers. By the end of the decade the standard was a five-and-one-half-day, forty-eight to fifty-four hour week. Medical plans, paid vacations, and similar benefits were often available.

Not everybody shared in this unprecedented prosperity; by 1929 almost half of the nation's families still earned less than $1,500 a year. Still, millions of Americans were able to enjoy a standard of living that was barely imaginable only a generation earlier. Between 1922 and 1932, consumer prices declined by an average of 2.8 percent each year. People purchased automobiles, radios, and household appliances; shopped at chain stores; went to movies; enrolled in colleges; stocked personal libraries; invested in the stock market and Florida real estate; and enjoyed the delights of the nation's booming cities.

Business leaders were eager to take credit for all of this, and most Americans were willing to oblige. In no other era were they so widely venerated. Colleges and universities scrambled over each other to offer business courses. Clergymen routinely linked capitalism with Christianity. Bruce Barton's best-selling *The Man Nobody Knows* called Jesus "the founder of modern business." Politicians seemed eager to grant almost any favor business requested. Calvin Coolidge declared solemnly that "the chief business of the American people is business," and millions agreed.

The Mass-Production–Consumption Society

Giant corporations, which began to dominate the American economy in the late nineteenth century, grew steadily larger during the 1920s. Eight thousand mergers took place within the decade, and by 1930 the two hundred largest nonfinancial corporations owned almost half of the nation's corporate wealth. Of foremost importance was the new emphasis on standardization, division of labor, and mass production. World War I had called attention to the effectiveness of these concepts, and throughout the 1920s manufacturers hastily applied them to nearly every industry.

Henry Ford, who had founded the Ford Motor Company in 1903 and had introduced the popular Model T five years later, brought mass production to his Highland, Michigan, plant in 1913 and became its most effective pioneer. In the twenties he further refined the system in a sprawling industrial complex at River Rouge, southeast of Detroit, that was the talk of the industrial world. Ford sought to improve efficiency, increase output, reduce prices, and boost sales. By mid-decade the company had produced more than 15 million Model Ts and had lowered the price from $950 per unit in 1909 to $260. Ford was pushing a new car out the factory door every thirty seconds. In one year alone the company enjoyed a surplus balance of $700 million.

By 1927, when Ford introduced the more luxurious Model A, the new system of industrial production had reduced the number of major automobile manufacturers from close to twenty before the war to three: William C. Durant's General Motors (the decade's most spectacular money-maker), Ford, and Chrysler. By 1929 the "big three" produced 83 percent of the cars made in the United States.

There were similar stories throughout industry. The Maytag Company manufactured 105,000 washing machines in 1924, twice as many as just four years earlier, and was the world's largest manufacturer of washers. Employing improved machine technology, the Maytag worker in 1926 made 48 percent more washers than his 1923 counterpart (and earned 32 percent more money, when adjusted for inflation). By 1929 a majority of American factories were using electric motor-driven machinery in the race against competitors.

Mass consumption was vital to mass production, and during the decade a gigantic advertising industry sprouted, determined to persuade, cajole, and intimidate the public into buying more and more of everything. The nation's advertising bill doubled during the twenties, rising to $1.5 billion by 1927.

Installment buying became an integral part of sales promotion. People were urged to abandon old taboos about debt and purchase on time payments the hundreds of labor-saving devices and luxuries now pouring from the factories. They flocked to the new chain stores, such as A&P, Rexall, and Woolworth, to load up on the wristwatches, mouthwashes, cigarettes, and rayon stockings advertisers convinced them were essential to the "good life." Between 1923 and 1929 installment buying amounted to an estimated $5 billion a year. By the end of the decade about 75 percent of the automobiles and more than half of the major household appliances were purchased on credit.

The new levels of prosperity and technological change had profound effects on American life. The automobile, for example, contributed significantly to the rise of cities and suburbs, fostered homogeneity between sections of the country, and freed young people from the constraints of parents and chaperons. Labor-saving devices such as the washing machine, range, refrigerator, and vacuum cleaner lightened the load of the domestic chores that had always dominated the lives of women.

Movies and radio programs altered traditional values and life styles. (One not atypical producer attracted film-goers by advertising "neckers, petters, white kisses, red kisses, pleasure-mad daughters, sensation-craving mothers . . . the truth—bold, naked, sensational.") Almost everyone admired movie superstars Mary Pickford, Douglas Fairbanks, Charlie Chaplin, and Rudolph Valentino. By 1929, two years after the appearance of sound pictures, 95 million people went to the movies each week. Radio caught on in the early part of the decade. By 1923 there were more than five hundred stations; by 1930 40 percent of all American families owned sets. More than any other development in communications, radio linked the nation together, providing its millions of daily listeners the latest news and popular entertainment.

The Urban Nation

The census of 1920 revealed that for the first time the nation had become predominantly urban. A majority of Americans (51.4 percent of the 106 million population) lived in urban areas of 2,500 or more inhabitants, and one in four lived in the sixty-eight cities with 100,000 or more. The long-established trend from rural to urban accelerated during the 1920s as manufacturing continued to replace agriculture in importance. More than 19 million people moved to the cities during the decade.

Soaring land prices forced buildings upward, and soon the skyscraper became the most distinctive feature of America's big cities. By 1929 there were
377 buildings more than twenty stories tall. New York City's Empire State
Building, completed in 1931, rose to 1,248 feet and contained over 2 million
square feet of office space. The construction of suburbs outside the urban
centers was under way at the same time.

Those living in and around the nation's cities became part of an urban culture that amazed and angered many Americans still in small towns and on the
farm. Movies, plays, books, and tabloids taught a new sexual freedom that
scoffed at Victorian inhibitions. Prohibition prompted the rise of speakeasies,
bootleggers, racketeers, and gang warfare. Cities were the home of intellectuals, learned men and women whose disdain for the common sense of most
Americans often provoked suspicion and envy. Cities also housed a growing
number of blacks and the swarm of immigrants who continued to pour into
the United States. To many Americans, still no doubt a majority in 1920, there
was something sinful and unhealthy about the urban areas. To others, the city
meant learning, entertainment, prosperity, excitement, and tolerance. Advocates of both views realized during the course of the decade that urbanization
was to become an increasingly significant force in American life.

The New Woman

Many urban women, strongly influenced by the cultural and technological
innovations of the era, began to take jobs outside the home; by 1928 five
times as many women were employed as in 1918. They also began to assume an unprecedented and controversial independence. Youthful "flappers,"
who led the way, shortened their skirts above the knee, abandoned their
corsets and petticoats, flattened their breasts and bobbed their hair to achieve
the new boyish look, wore rouge and lipstick, smoked cigarettes, drank cock-
tails, read racy novels, and danced the fox trot and Charleston. They also
experimented with sex and talked freely about the fashionable theories of
Sigmund Freud. The new freedom led to a sharp rise in the divorce rate.
While at the turn of the century there had been 8.8 divorces for every one
hundred marriages, in 1928 there were 16.5 divorces—almost one divorce
for every six marriages. Five books on the so-called marriage crisis appeared
in 1929.

And yet for all of the publicity about the "New Woman," most women remained at home, and marriage and the family continued to be the feminine
ideal. The husband was still the head of the house. While the widespread
accessibility of birth control information meant smaller families, a married
woman still put in an average fifty-six-hour work week. Millions of women
devoted their spare time to religious and civic organizations. For every
Chicago flapper whose prattle about kissing and petting made the tabloids,
there was more than one mother of five in Evanston who labored at church
suppers when the family dishes were put away.

Silent screen star Clara Bow, the "It Girl," personified the flapper. Source: Reproduced from the Collections of the Library of Congress

Education for the Masses

The prosperity of the era enabled millions of young people, especially city dwellers, to stay in school during and even after adolescence. All forty-eight states had enacted compulsory education laws by 1918, ensuring access of all to at least a rudimentary education and dropping the national illiteracy rate from 11 percent in 1900 to 4.3 percent in 1930. In the 1920s the emphasis was on the secondary school and higher education. State laws began to require school attendance for all youngsters up to 16 or 18 years of age. Higher education started to expand as never before. Student enrollment climbed from approximately 240,000 in 1900 to more than a million.

A college education had always been a social and economic advantage in American life. Now, more than ever before, the great impetus for continued schooling was the desire for money. Business was interested in people with diplomas, and young people flocked to take "practical" classes. Critics made fun of the advertising courses, football fever, and fraternity hijinx that often characterized the expanding college and university. But they did little to change the direction of life on campus. Higher education in this country began to be transformed in the Twenties, becoming increasingly accessible, democratic, secular, job oriented, and popular.

The Ballyhoo Years

The cities of the New Era were filled with excitement about crime, sports, sex, styles, fads, and an assortment of tragedies and heroics. The mass media focused the entire nation's attention on what Frederick Lewis Allen called "tremendous trifles." One day it was the story of a Chicago gangland killing or of a man trapped in a Kentucky mine. The next morning's news might be about a flag pole sitter, a six-day bicycle race, the latest automobile model, crossword puzzles, the Mah Jong craze, goldfish swallowing, an errant evangelist, or a celebrity divorce. "The country had bread," Allen wrote, "but it wanted circuses—and now it could go to them a hundred million strong."

Everyone seemed crazy for sports. Millions followed the two heavyweight championship fights between Jack Dempsey and Gene Tunney in 1926–27. Babe Ruth became a national hero in 1927 when he hit sixty home runs. Bobby Jones was the darling of golf. Bill Tilden was a tennis celebrity. Every schoolboy knew that Red Grange was a great football player. Women cheered when Gertrude Ederle became the first mother to swim the English Channel. The world series drew record crowds. Universities built football stadiums seating fifty and sixty thousand. Two million people spent half a billion dollars annually on golf. More people could identify Knute Rockne, Notre Dame's football coach, than could tell who was the presiding officer of the United States Senate.

The most celebrated man of the decade was Charles Lindbergh, the first person to make a nonstop flight in a heavier-than-air craft between New York and Paris. Lindbergh, a former air mail pilot, made the trip alone in a small, single-engine plane, the Spirit of St. Louis. Even before his plane took off, in a contest to win a $25,000 prize, the slim, attractive, 25-year-old had attracted the attention of the media and won the favor of millions in America and abroad.

The young national idol filled a public need in an era brimming over with cynicism, materialism, and stories of human depravity. In his simple modesty, quiet dignity, bravery, and individualism, he seemed to personify traditional American values. Then too, the Spirit of St. Louis was a symbol of the nation's technological progress.

The Culture of Disenchantment

The cities were also the scene of one of the most fertile periods in American culture. Scores of often extremely talented intellectuals, disillusioned by the war and alienated by the materialism, greed, conformity, and general silliness of the decade, retreated to arty enclaves such as New York's Greenwich Village or fled to Europe to find fulfillment. Their contempt for the val-

Charles A. Lindbergh, an international hero of the 1920s. Source: Reproduced from the Collections of the Library of Congress

ues of the new business society found expression in a number of major books, articles, and poems. The emphasis of the era's most influential writers was on criticism and often savage satire. No sensitive, humane, creative person, they assumed, could or should be happy in modern America.

The most popular of these writers was Sinclair Lewis, the first American to win a Nobel Prize in literature. His best-selling novel *Main Street*, published in 1920, mercilessly ridiculed life in small-town America. The powerful *Babbitt*, which appeared two years later, satirized the narrow-minded businessman and "booster" who thought the twenties the best of times. *Arrowsmith* (1925) took on the medical profession. *Elmer Gantry* (1927) savaged evangelical Christianity. *Dodsworth* (1929) contrasted European and American values.

In 1923 the brilliant and cynical H. L. Mencken founded the *American Mercury*. This monthly magazine quickly became the favorite of people who despised majority values. The perceptive Walter Lippmann called Mencken "the most powerful personal influence on this whole generation of educated people." Nothing seemed to please the Baltimore journalist and linguistic scholar. He jeered at "homo boobiens" and sneered at everything from democracy, organized religion, and prohibition to boy scouts, hillbillies, and home cooking. When asked why he remained in a society he despised, Mencken replied, "Why do people go to the zoo?"

People who enjoyed Mencken were also attracted by the novels and short stories of F. Scott Fitzgerald. His popular *This Side of Paradise*, published in 1920, described the despair and excesses of rebellious youth. *The Great Gatsby* (1925) contained vivid descriptions of the booze-happy party-goers of the twenties, along with a bitter condemnation of the American dream of material success.

Ernest Hemingway, who had been in a U.S. ambulance unit in Italy during the war, supported himself as a journalist while living in Europe during the 1920s. His *The Sun Also Rises* (1926) described the amoral emptiness of American expatriates. In *A Farewell to Arms* (1929) he used his sparse, direct style of writing to condemn war. Poets Ezra Pound and T. S. Eliot also lived in exile and produced influential works stressing the theme of postwar disillusionment. Edna St. Vincent Millay, a poet who epitomized the Jazz Age literati, won the Pulitzer Prize.

The scope of this outburst of cultural energy was broad. Sherwood Anderson's novels and short stories described the psychological maladies of small-town midwesterners. Anderson's friend William Faulkner experimented with a complex stream-of-consciousness style. Journalist Ring Lardner earned a national reputation as a short story writer. Thomas Wolfe published the powerful *Look Homeward Angel* in 1929. Edith Wharton won the Pulitzer Prize for *The Age of Innocence* (1920) and Willa Cather was presented with the same award two years later. Ellen Glascow published *Barren Ground* in 1925. Playwright Eugene O'Neill won three Pulitzer prizes, and Maxwell Anderson brought *What Price Glory?* to the stage in 1924.

The world of art flourished as well. Artists and pioneering photographers Edward J. Steichen and Alfred Steiglitz presented highly influential avant-garde art exhibits in New York. Georgia O'Keeffe, married to Steiglitz, was a major painter. One of her great flower paintings sold for $25,000 in 1928.

New York City's Harlem district enjoyed a golden age of culture in the 1920s. James Weldon Johnson, Countee Cullen, and Langston Hughes were scholars and distinguished poets who celebrated their blackness and demanded racial justice. W. E. B. Du Bois, editor of the militant magazine *Crisis*, published by the National Association for the Advancement of Colored People, was a major intellectual force behind the Harlem Renaissance. Trumpeter Louis Armstrong and bandleader-composer Edward Kennedy "Duke" Ellington performed regularly in Harlem's thriving nightclubs and theaters.

Armstrong and Ellington were also major pioneers in the development of jazz, which had come out of turn-of-the-century New Orleans. The rhythms and improvisations of this uniquely American contribution to culture proved popular in the 1920s. Composer-pianist George Gershwin won fame in 1924 for his "Rhapsody in Blue," a type of symphonic jazz.

Immigration Quotas

The increasingly sophisticated and secular culture of the cities did not dominate the whole of America, of course. Millions in rural areas and small towns clung to traditional values and customs and were convinced that the cities were bleeding the nation of its moral virtue.

Of principal concern to many Americans after the war were the newcomers from southern and eastern Europe—the Jews, Slavs, and Catholics who were thought to be somehow subversive and dangerous. Organized labor, eager to minimize competition for jobs, joined the drive to curb immigration. In 1920 810,000 people entered the country. Congress took action the following year.

The Emergency Quota Act of 1921 restricted immigration from any country in one year to 3 percent of the number of persons of that nationality living in the United States in 1910. This strategy proved ineffective: the total exceeded 700,000 in 1924. Congress then passed the National Origins Quota Act. This lowered the quota to 2 percent and based it, at first, on the census of 1890, a year in which there had been relatively few southern and eastern Europeans in the country. The law banned all Asian immigration.

The new policy produced the desired results. Immigration dropped to an annual average of about 300,000 during the rest of the decade and fell to 50,000 a year with the aid of the depression. People from northwestern Europe were favored at the expense of the Italians, Poles, and other "less desirables." Italian immigration fell about nine-tenths. President Coolidge exclaimed on signing the bill, "America must be kept American."

The nation's hostility toward southern European immigrants surfaced in the famous case of Nicola Sacco and Bartolomeo Vanzetti. These two Italian immigrants and anarchists were convicted in 1920 of the murder of a paymaster and guard in South Braintree, Massachusetts. The evidence against the two was shaky, and the trial judge was clearly prejudiced against the accused. For seven years the case was debated in the press and in the courts. Radicals demonstrated, intellectuals anguished; in Europe, bombs went off, and there were general strikes and boycotts. Those who detested radicals and southern Europeans on general principles cried for revenge. Others, seeking to protect the rights of minorities, thought the entire case a matter of prejudice.

Recent studies reveal that Sacco, at least, was guilty. At the time, however, the facts of the crime were secondary in people's minds. Angry crowds demonstrated all over the world when Sacco and Vanzetti were executed in August 1927.

The Ku Klux Klan

The Ku Klux Klan was revived in 1915 and began to flourish after the war. As in Reconstruction days, men dressed in white robes and hoods, conducted weird rituals, burned crosses, held parades and demonstrations, organized boycotts, and harassed and attacked blacks. In the twenties, however, the socioeconomic level of the membership was somewhat higher and the organization more respectable. By 1923 there were some 4.5 million Klansmen throughout the country, and they controlled the legislatures of Texas, Oklahoma, Indiana, and Oregon.

The Klan's targets expanded to include Jews, Catholics, immigrants, liberals, intellectuals, and advocates of the new urban morality. Its principal purpose was the enforcement of conformity: the standard, in their view, was "100 percent Americanism." Imperial Wizard Hiram Wesley Evans declared that the Klan demanded "a return of power into the hands of the everyday, not highly cultured, not overly intellectualized, but entirely unspoiled and not de-Americanized, average citizen of the old stock." Its object, he said, was to recreate a "native, white, Protestant America."

Revelations about immoral and illegal activities by Klan leaders and a national revulsion against several acts of Klan violence prompted the organization's rapid decline. It was still a factor in the 1928 presidential election, however, when Alfred E. Smith, the first Catholic to head a major party ticket, went down to defeat.

Prohibition

When the Volstead Act implemented the Eighteenth Amendment in January 1920, the country was supposed to go completely dry. In large part, as we have seen, prohibition was an attack by rural dwellers against the urban-immigrant-Catholics, who loved their beer and wine, and against the new morality of the cities. It was a popular cause in 1919 when it swept through the state legislatures. Herbert Hoover called prohibition "an experiment noble in purpose." Indeed, alcohol consumption was cut by perhaps as much as half during the decade, many being unable to afford the high prices for illegal liquor. The death rate for cirrhosis of the liver dropped by two-thirds. It was also apparent, however, particularly in the cities, that this attempt to legislate morality was a costly flop.

Smuggling became a major industry; the Department of Commerce estimated that $40 million worth of liquor entered the country in 1924 alone. Illegal commercial stills and breweries flourished, sometimes producing lethal products. Countless Americans manufactured their own beverages. Bootlegging was a highly profitable business that quickly became entangled with organized crime. Al Capone controlled most of Chicago's 10,000 speakeasies and ran a criminal empire that brought in $60 million a year. Big city mobs fought each other ferociously to gain control of the liquor trade; there were five hundred gangland murders in Chicago alone. Law enforcement, by Congress and the states, proved futile, and governments, court systems, and police forces at all levels frequently wallowed in corruption.

Ironically, prohibition undermined rather than elevated public morals. It fostered hypocrisy and disrespect for the law, it made criminals wealthy, and it strengthened the public's appreciation of hard liquor. In early 1930, the *Outlook and Independent* magazine editorialized,

The Metropolitan Life Insurance Company has published the fact that the alcoholic death rate among their nineteen million policy holders has increased nearly six hundred percent in the last ten years—double what it was in 1918, and approximately the same as in the years preceding. This removes the last doubt from the mind of any reasonable person that the time has come to move for the repeal of the Eighteenth Amendment.

In 1933, to the relief of millions, two-thirds of the states voted to repeal the amendment and abandon the thirteen-year national experiment. By 1937 only seven states were still dry.

There was a similar drive to make cigarettes illegal. This was led by Lucy Page Gaston, a zealous member of the Women's Christian Temperance Union who started her antismoking crusade in 1899 and had helped temporarily outlaw cigarettes in sixteen states. But the effort was doomed, as cigarettes became closely identified with urban sophistication and female emancipation. Between 1918 and 1928, American cigarette sales quadrupled, and the drive to ban them ended.

Fundamentalism

The hostility between the cities and the countryside could also be seen within Protestantism. By the early 1920s there was a profound split between the denominations that appealed to urban, middle-class Americans and those that attracted their rural and small-town counterparts. (The split involved socioeconomic levels as well as geography. Many who held rural and small-town views lived and worked in cities, where fundamentalist churches often flourished.) The controversy centered on the nature of the Bible. The more sophisticated Christians tended to accept the Scriptures as vital and inspired by God but containing human errors and explanations of nature that had to be rejected in light of scientific findings. Their opponents took the older view that the Bible came directly from God and was infallible. These "fundamentalists" abhorred much of modern life. They were especially critical of the "higher criticism" of the Scriptures taught in the seminaries of the larger denominations, and they passionately opposed Charles Darwin's theory of evolution. The Book of Genesis, they argued, contained a literal and inerrant account of God's creation of man, and all other explanations were to be rejected and condemned.

Fundamentalist evangelists were especially effective in the South and parts of the West. Billy Sunday, a one-time professional baseball player and YMCA worker, conducted more than three hundred revivals during his career, preaching to an estimated 100 million people. Aimee Semple McPherson, an attractive ex-missionary with a flair for theatrics, won a large following in Los Angeles. The successors of Dwight Moody had a highly effective ministry in Chicago. Still, the fundamentalist outlook was declining within Protestantism. Large numbers of Methodists, Baptists, Presbyterians, and Episcopalians, especially in the North, welcomed modern life and accepted a

Christianity that stressed reasonableness, tolerance, and good works. Fundamentalists knew they were losing ground in the New Era, and this fear intensified their efforts.

In 1925 the Tennessee legislature outlawed the teaching of evolution in the state's schools and colleges. The American Civil Liberties Union decided to make this a test case, and supported 24-year-old high-school teacher John T. Scopes when he challenged the law. The ACLU hired the celebrated Chicago attorney Clarence Darrow to defend Scopes. William Jennings Bryan, the elderly politician and orator, offered his services to the state. With over a hundred newspaper reporters on the scene, along with radio microphones and movie cameras, the "monkey trial" became one of the decade's foremost "media events."

The contrast between Darrow's skeptical rationalism and Bryan's simple fundamentalism revealed to millions the difference between modern America and its provincial critics. For example, a zoologist summoned by Darrow drew gasps from locals by estimating that life had begun about 600 million years earlier. Bryan, on the other hand, dated creation at 4004 BC and the Flood at about 2348 BC, estimates made before the flowering of modern science. In the end, Scopes was convicted, fined $100, and released by the state Supreme Court on a technicality. The teaching of evolution remained illegal in Tennessee until 1968. Still, the ACLU emerged victorious in the Scopes trial, for all over the country sophisticated and influential people ridiculed fundamentalism and those who espoused it.

The Politics of Retreat

The GOP dominated the era, controlling the White House and enjoying majorities in Congress. Many Republicans seemed primarily interested in returning to the values of the Gilded Age. The outlook of the Democrats was similar. The party was split between urban and rural factions and suffered from the public's lingering dislike of Woodrow Wilson. Its national ticket in 1920 was headed by James M. Cox, the successful governor of Ohio, whose bland personality and fuzzy convictions stirred little enthusiasm.

Harding

Warren G. Harding of Ohio won the presidential election of 1920 by a landslide. He was a handsome, dignified, and affable machine politician of limited intellect and weak character. He had been a newspaper owner and editor in Marion, Ohio, before becoming a state senator, lieutenant governor, and, in 1914, a United States senator. A standpat Republican, Harding had a bleak political record, and his qualifications for the presidency were virtually nonexistent. This did not matter, however, to the party leaders and businessmen who guided his career. At the insistence of his counselors, Harding stayed at home during the campaign, offering visitors folksy charm and empty platitudes. His slogan "back to normalcy" proved to be just what voters wanted to hear.

Harding made several widely admired cabinet appointments, notably Charles Evans Hughes as secretary of state, Andrew Mellon as secretary of the treasury, Herbert Hoover as secretary of commerce, and Henry C. Wallace as secretary of agriculture. In addition, he named William Howard Taft chief justice of the United States Supreme Court. Unfortunately, Harding also appointed several corrupt cronies to high office who brought disgrace upon the administration.

Secretary of State Hughes led the negotiations at the Washington Armament Conference of 1921, summoned to reduce tensions in the Far East. The major naval powers agreed to limit certain naval armament, freeze fortifications on Pacific island possessions, and recognize America's Open Door policy. While the agreements in fact solved little and failed to restrain Japanese ambitions, they were popular and helped restore America's international credibility after the failure to join the League of Nations. Congress, largely uninterested in foreign affairs, approved the treaties and proceeded to let the American military deteriorate seriously. Between 1922 and 1929 the United States navy built eleven ships. Japan constructed 125.

Andrew Mellon, a multimillionaire banker and secretary of the treasury during all three Republican administrations of the 1920s, was a commanding figure in Washington. To stimulate business activity, he got Congress to reduce taxes for the wealthy. He succeeded in slashing government expenditures, balancing the budget, and reducing the national debt. With his blessing, Congress raised the tariff in 1922. Business leaders applauded Mellon's policies and agreed with Harding when he exclaimed, "We want less government in business and more business in government."

In fact, government expanded its role in the economy during the 1920s. Secretary of Commerce Hoover, for example, helped promote industrial efficiency and assist corporations with their labor problems. Attorney General Harry M. Daugherty refused to enforce the antitrust laws and issued an injunction that broke a major railroad strike. The Agriculture Department worked closely with agribusiness. The major federal regulatory agencies, packed with conservatives, helped businessmen in numerous ways. The government gave massive gifts and loans to the shipping industry. For all of the rhetoric about a return to laissez faire, the Republicans of the New Era were actually developing what historian Robert K. Murray called "a wedding of government and business in what amounted to a joint enterprise."

Republican defeat at the polls in 1922 and private evidence of widespread corruption within his administration persuaded Harding to escape Washington for a while and make a cross-country speaking tour that would includ ed a visit to Alaska. In low spirits and in poor health, the President died of an apparent heart attack in San Francisco on August 2, 1923. The nation mourned the loss of its still highly popular leader. Three million people viewed the coffin on its return by train to Washington.

A few months later the public began to learn about the extent of the corruption during Harding's 882 days in office. Bribery and influence peddling in the Justice Department and thievery and waste in the Veterans' Bureau made headlines for years. Attorney General Daugherty, a presidential chum, was shown to be morally unfit for public office. The Teapot Dome scandal was the worst of the lot. It involved, among others, Secretary of the Interior Albert B. Fall, who accepted nearly $400,000 in bribes from two oil promoters in return for secret leases on government oil fields in Elk Hills, California, and Teapot Dome, Wyoming. Fall was eventually fined $100,000 and sentenced to a year in prison. The oil fields were restored to government control in 1927.

Harding's reputation was damaged further by his long-time mistress Nan Britton, whose book *The President's Daughter* described alleged sex episodes in cheap hotels, the Senate Office Building, and even a White House closet. Similar activities earlier in the Ohioan's life came to light later. Scholars have often rated Harding the worst president in the nation's history.

Coolidge

When word of Harding's death reached the vice president in his native Vermont, his father, a notary public, administered the presidential oath of office in "the sitting room by the light of the kerosene lamp." Calvin Coolidge's personal integrity and association with small-town, old-fashioned virtues proved highly popular in an era of rapid change and daily stories about gangsters and corrupt public officials. His comforting presence in the White House helped save the Republican party's reputation and restore confidence in government.

Coolidge had been a public servant since 1899 and was governor of Massachusetts when nominated for the vice presidency. He was a bland, reserved, taciturn man. His philosophy of government was simple and clear: the smaller the government, the freer and more prosperous the people. His faith in hard work and free enterprise was unlimited.

Coolidge had once been an ambitious workaholic. But his limited view of the presidency was compounded by personal depression, caused by the accidental death of his 16-year-old son in 1924. He added a daily nap to his ten or eleven hours of sleep each night. He worked about four hours a day, declaring that one of the important duties of the chief executive "consists of never doing anything that someone can do for you." Coolidge once declared that "Four-fifths of all our troubles in this life would disappear if we would only sit down and keep still."

In 1924 most Americans were happy to "keep cool with Coolidge," and the dour Yankee easily won election to a full term over conservative New York corporation lawyer John W. Davis. Robert M. La Follette, running as a Progressive, received 17 percent of the vote and carried only his home state of Wisconsin.

Coolidge's record was largely negative, a fact in which he took pride. He vetoed a veterans' bonus bill because of its cost. He pocket-vetoed a progressive bill to create a public power corporation at Muscle Shoals in Alabama. He twice vetoed legislation that would have used government controls to help farmers fight overproduction and falling prices. Coolidge also cut taxes four times, and presided over what Ronald Reagan would later call "the greatest growth and prosperity we've ever known."

Despite the prevailing passion for isolationism, the Coolidge administration took several steps toward improving international relations. American banker Charles G. Dawes was appointed to work out what became known as the Dawes Plan of 1924, an international agreement to help Germany stabilize its economy and make its staggering reparation payments. In 1928 Secretary of State Frank B. Kellogg signed the Kellogg-Briand Peace Pact, by which sixty-two nations eventually agreed to outlaw war forever. Coolidge eased tensions in Latin America. He withdrew troops from the Dominican Republic and personally opened the Pan-American Congress in Havana in 1928. His appointees helped arrange free elections in Nicaragua and soothe a serious crisis with Mexico.

The American people enjoyed peace and unprecedented prosperity under Coolidge. While there were soft spots in the economy, business boomed, and opportunity seemed unlimited. The number of millionaires in the country rose from 4,500 in 1914 to 11,000 in 1926. By the end of the president's full term, 98 percent of Americans paid no taxes at all, and 93 percent of all taxes were paid by the wealthiest Americans. When the president announced in August 1927 that he would not run for reelection, millions were profoundly disappointed. "Silent Cal" had seemed to many, especially in the business world, to be the ideal chief executive.

The Election of 1928

The GOP chose Herbert Hoover on the first ballot to succeed Coolidge. The secretary of commerce in many ways embodied the virtues most admired at the time. He had been born of poor Quaker parents in rural Iowa and was a believer in hard work and self-reliance. He graduated from Stanford University as a mining engineer and not long afterward was a self-made millionaire. Hoover shared his party's faith in economic orthodoxy, limited government, isolationism, and prohibition. His devotion to free enterprise was tempered, however, by a sense of civic responsibility and commitment to public service. He was a progressive. Aloof, tactless, and intellectually inclined, Hoover had never run for public office. Still, his relief work during and after World War I, his service as Wilson's U.S. food administrator, and his record as a cabinet member were greatly admired.

If Hoover represented the old-stock, Anglo-Saxon, Protestant, upper-middle-class type that had always dominated American life, his Democratic opponent symbolized a powerful new force in politics: the melting pot in the large eastern cities. Alfred E. Smith, the grandchild of Irish immigrants, had been born in a tenement house on the East Side of New York City. He was a Roman Catholic, a wet (meaning he favored repeal of prohibition), and a long-time functionary of Tammany Hall. Despite a minimum of formal education and a lifetime of associating with machine politicians, Smith was an able and efficient public official. He served four terms as governor of New York and proved to be popular and somewhat reform minded.

Al Smith was unashamedly a city man. He wore a derby, smoked cigars, had a pronounced East Side accent, and made "The Sidewalks of New York" his campaign theme song. This imagery, as well as the candidate's opposition to prohibition, alienated a great many rural and small-town Americans. Of even greater significance was Smith's religion: he was the first Roman Catholic to head a major party ticket. Millions feared that he would turn the White House over to the pope.

The candidates were not far apart ideologically, but issues mattered little in the campaign. Anti-Catholicism was rampant, especially among fundamentalists, and Coolidge prosperity would probably have defeated any Democrat. Hoover buried Smith in the electoral college 444 to 87, although the popular vote was much closer: 21,391,000 to 15,016,000. In fact, Smith won more votes than any Democratic candidate ever had.

The election returns revealed a major political realignment in the making. Urban voters, largely immigrant and Catholic, became attracted to the Democratic party for the first time. Smith carried the twelve largest cities; four years earlier they had gone Republican. Many midwestern farmers, unhappy with GOP agricultural policies, began to drift toward the Democrats. Liberal intellectuals strongly backed Smith. If the South could be returned to the fold with a Protestant candidate, the Democrats could be in a powerful position in 1932.

The Promise of Prosperity

Prosperity, more than anything else, accounted for the GOP's victory in 1928, and few entertained doubts about the continued growth of wealth. In his acceptance speech, Herbert Hoover declared, "We in America today are nearer to the final triumph over poverty than ever before in the history of any land." On leaving office, Coolidge assured Americans that their prosperity was "absolutely sound."

Perhaps as many as nine million Americans—some 7 or 8 percent of the population—and hundreds of corporations were pouring funds into the "Hoover bull market." Here you could purchase stocks "on margin," with the broker (who borrowed his money from banks and corporations) lending a buyer from 50 to 75 percent of the price. When the stock advanced, the buyer sold, pocketing the profit. The steadily rising market during the late 1920s turned hundreds of thousands of normally conservative investors, here and abroad, into madcap gamblers. Radio Corporation of America soared from under $100 to $400 per share in nine months. The market value of all shares listed on the New York Stock Exchange almost tripled between January 1, 1925, and January 1, 1929. The number of shares listed increased from over 433 million to over 757 million. By September 1929 stocks had reached fantastic levels.

Billions of dollars were being poured into speculation, driving stock values far beyond their capacity for earning dividends. And there were other largely unseen dangers. Holding companies flooded the market with securities of dubious value. Merging corporations issued new securities based on little more than optimism. "Stock splitting" produced yet more doubtful issues.

On every side one heard: "Prosperity due for a decline? Why, man, we've scarcely started," and "Never sell the United States short." Bank salesmen combed the country in search of ever more investors. The Federal Reserve System blessed the market with an "easy money policy"; by September 1929 bank loans to brokers totaled $8.5 billion. Millionaire John J. Raskob published an article in the *Ladies Home Journal* entitled "Everybody Ought to Be Rich," and that outlook became increasingly contagious. As the New Era came to a close, people from all walks of life were convinced that prosperity was limitless.

SUGGESTED READING

Frederick Lewis Allen, *Only Yesterday: An Informal History of the 1920s* (1931); David M. Chalmers, *Hooded Americanism: The History of the Ku Klux Klan* (1965); Stanley Coben, *A. Mitchell Palmer* (1963); Robert H. Ferrell, *The Strange Death of President Harding* (1996); Oscar Handlin, *Al Smith and His America* (1958); Paula Fass, *The Damned and the Beautiful: American Youth in the 1920s* (1977); William E. Leuchtenburg, *The Perils of Prosperity, 1914–1932* (1958); William R. Manchester, *Disturber of the Peace: The Life of H. L. Mencken* (1951); George E. Mowry, *The Urban Nation, 1920–1960* (1965); Robert Sobel, *Coolidge: An American Enigma* (1998).

Chapter Six

THE DEPRESSION DECADE

On October 24, 1929, "Black Thursday," prices on the New York Stock Exchange dropped sharply. Investors were shaken by the sudden and unprecedented decline, even after six powerful banks took steps to stabilize the market and President Hoover gave assurances that all was well. On October 29 panic selling drove prices to drastically low levels, and the public soon realized that the market had crashed. The dreams of millions in all walks of life were shattered. The tragedy soon reached the markets in Western Europe and throughout the world.

The stock market crash triggered the Great Depression of the 1930s. Investments declined, businesses failed, stores and factories closed, banks collapsed, unemployment soared—from 5 million in 1930 to 13 million in 1932. One laborer later recalled seeing a thousand men outside a sugar refinery "fight like a pack of Alaskan dogs" for three or four jobs.

People lost their homes and savings, panhandlers roamed the streets, the jobless slept on park benches, hospitals treated people who passed out due to hunger, soup kitchens and bread lines were commonplace. "Brother Can You Spare a Dime?" was a top song of 1932–33.

In Chicago, one observer reported, "We saw a crowd of some fifty men fighting over a barrel of garbage which had been set outside the back door of a restaurant. American citizens fighting for scraps of food like animals!" Another remembered seeing "thousands of men, rolled up in their overcoats, just on the pavement" under the Michigan Avenue Bridge. Cynicism and despair accompanied the hard times. The Roaring Twenties were ancient history.

Causes of the Depression

While experts continue to debate about the precise causes of the cataclysm, several major weaknesses in the economy appear to have contributed sig-

101

nificantly. Unequal income distribution, for one thing, limited the number of customers for the products pouring out of the nation's factories. While individual prosperity increased significantly during the decade, in 1929 5 percent of the population received 26.1 percent of the income. Wages and salaries did not keep pace with the sharp rise in industrial productivity, corporate profits, and dividends.

The corporate structure, moreover, contained serious deficiencies. The holding-company device enabled unscrupulous businesspeople to create corporate pyramids of little actual value and reap huge profits with investors' money. By the beginning of 1929, twenty-one of the nation's ninety-seven largest corporations were holding companies. Investment trusts, designed to assist investors with expert knowledge, were often operated by people interested solely in their own gain. Speculators created pools and syndicates to manipulate stock prices and make fast profits. One millionaire later recalled, "In 1929, it was strictly a gambling casino with loaded dice. The few sharks taking advantage of a multitude of suckers." Banking practices were often irresponsible, and failures were common. In the first six months of 1929, 346 banks closed their doors. The federal government chose to look the other way and to continue to assure the public that all was well.

An unfavorable balance of trade was also a factor. With World War I the United States had become a creditor nation. During the 1920s Americans sold more to the war-torn European nations than they purchased. A high U.S. tariff intensified the imbalance. Moreover, the United States was determined to collect its war debts from the Allies. European and Latin American governments borrowed funds from American investors to meet their international obligations. With the stock market crash, the subsequent drying up of American loans, and the appearance of an even higher tariff, war debts went into default and American exports fell. This increased the distress of the nation's farmers, already suffering from the effects of unrestrained overproduction.

Hoover's Response

The economy deteriorated disastrously throughout the remainder of the Hoover administration. Between 1929 and 1932 the national income dropped from over $82 billion to $40 billion. Corporate profits plummeted; by 1932 369,000 companies reported deficits. Industrial production declined by 48 percent. Industrial construction dropped from $949 million to $74 million. Five thousand banks went under in three years, wiping out nine million savings accounts.

The unemployed and destitute were everywhere. By 1932 about 25 percent of the work force lacked jobs. Industrial cities suffered acutely: the unemployment rate in Cleveland was 50 percent, in Toledo 80 percent. Between one and two million people, including some 200,000 children, roamed the country, often by freight train, in search of a better life. As many as a million of the homeless lived in makeshift communities of boxes and scrap metal bitterly called "Hoovervilles."

City treasuries could not begin to meet the cries for relief. New York offered families an average of $2.39 a week. In Detroit, where the closing of the Ford plants in 1931 cost some 75,000 men their jobs, assistance was limited to 7½ cents a day per individual. Private charities and churches were overwhelmed with pleas for help.

In January 1932, Wisconsin became the first state to approve unemployment compensation. Progressives had fought for decades to overcome America's laissez-faire tradition. (Great Britain established a national compulsory system in 1911.) While the legislation set an example for other states, in 1932 three-fourths of the unemployed throughout the nation were without public aid.

Rural America felt the full force of the depression. Between 1929 and 1932 farm incomes dropped from almost $13 billion to $5.56 billion. As many as a third of all farmers lost their land through foreclosure or eviction. And nature made things worse. Beginning in 1933 and lasting for as long as a decade, the farm belt experienced one of the worst droughts in the nation's history. On the Great Plains hundreds of dust storms known as "black blizzards" blew away the soil. Intense heat killed livestock. Grasshoppers moved in huge waves, devouring crops and even fence posts. Hundreds of thousands of families fled the "Dust Bowl" in the thirties, often winding up in California in the quest for prosperity. The plight of these "Okies," so-called because many came from Oklahoma, was vividly portrayed in John Steinbeck's 1939 novel *The Grapes of Wrath*.

President Hoover was by no means insensitive to the suffering that surrounded him. He rejected the advice of wealthy advisers who urged him to do nothing and let the economy heal itself. During the first two years of the depression he tried to restore public confidence by exuding optimism and encouraging business and labor leaders to forego production cuts, layoffs, and wage demands. He encouraged the Federal Reserve Board to adopt a policy of easy credit. He urged Congress to spend unprecedented sums on public works, and federal expenditures in this area rose from $275 million before the Great Crash to $575 million in 1931. In the hope of protecting farmers from overseas competition, the president signed the Hawley-Smoot Act of 1930, which drastically raised the tariff. He also approved of efforts by a federally sponsored Farm Board to loan money to farmers and purchase agricultural surpluses. Calvin Coolidge sighed, "I am no longer fit with the times. These socialistic notions of government are not of my day."

The condition of the economy continued to worse, however. By mid-1931 the president's optimism had worn thin. His reliance on voluntary agreements had proved futile. His penchant for balanced budgets and his belief in limited federal authority had restricted the effectiveness of public funds. The new tariff, moreover, contributed to an international financial panic by making it impossible for European nations to make payments on their World War I debts. Now blaming the depression on international developments and stung by mounting criticisms, Hoover proceeded to call for a more vigorous approach toward economic recovery.

In January 1932 Congress established the Reconstruction Finance Corporation, a federal agency with unprecedented authority to lend money to troubled banks, railroads, and other corporations. The RFC's scope was soon expanded to include loans to state and local governments for public works and to assist states with their relief needs. By March 1933 the RFC had loaned $1.78 billion to corporations, most of it to large banks.

The RFC restored some public confidence and eased the financial crisis, but it was not as effective as many had hoped. The agency was authorized only to provide loans, which meant that none but the healthiest institutions could qualify. Its financial resources were insufficient in light of the crisis. And the agency failed to spend all that it had; it released only 20 percent of its public works budget. This was in line with the president's cautious philosophy. "The sole function of government," he declared, "is to bring about a condition of affairs favorable to the beneficial development of private enterprise." A healthy business community, he believed, meant national prosperity. He consistently opposed and vetoed measures aimed at providing direct, large-scale federal assistance to the needy.

No one worked harder than the president to end the depression. Indeed, some national Democratic party leaders condemned him for doing and spending too much. Hoover's chief handicap was his rigid outlook. These desperate years called for boldness, imagination, and a willingness to experiment, and Hoover could not meet the challenge. As a result, millions of Americans unfairly thought of the man in the White House as a heartless, unfeeling aristocrat.

Popular Unrest

However severe the depression, the vast majority of Americans continued to have faith in the nation's political and economic institutions. The nation's strong tradition of optimism and self-confidence, born of unprecedented abundance and the dream of individual economic and social mobility, remained intact. In 1932 the Socialist party was weaker than it had been in 1912. Communism appealed largely to a handful of urban intellectuals and immigrants. Fascist sympathies were barely visible.

There were several instances of violence during the depths of the depression. Desperate people seized the county-city building in Seattle, for example. Wisconsin dairy farmers dumped their milk and fought battles with police. A brief farmers' strike in Iowa made headlines. But the national mood was far from revolutionary.

The most incendiary struggle of the Hoover years occurred in June and July 1932 when some 20,000 unemployed veterans marched on Washington demanding all of a bonus payment due them in 1945. The president vetoed one such congressional proposal and the Senate killed another. Most of the veterans returned home after the defeat, but several thousand settled down in crude shacks and tents at Anacostia Flats, outside the Capitol, to continue their appeal. No administration official expressed sympathy with the veterans and their families. Hoover, who had surrounded the White House with guards, contended incorrectly that the Bonus army was filled with criminals and Communists. On July 28, folllowing a disturbance in which two veterans were killed, troops under the command of General Douglas MacArthur drove the marchers out of their encampments and burned them. One Washington newspaper commented, "What a pitiful spectacle is that of the great American government, mightiest in the world, chasing unarmed men, women and children with army tanks." Millions saw the incident in movie newsreels and condemned the president for his lack of compassion. Almost no one thought that Hoover could be reelected.

Election of 1932

Despite misgivings, Republicans renominated Hoover and Vice President Charles Curtis in 1932. Democrats, on the fourth ballot, nominated New York governor Franklin D. Roosevelt and chose House Speaker John N. Garner of Texas as his running mate. Accepting the nomination in person, FDR promised "a new deal for the American people."

Born in 1882, Roosevelt was an only child raised in wealth on an estate in Hyde Park, New York. A doting and imperious mother instilled in him an unshakable self-confidence, and FDR would always believe that no one could resist his charm. He ambled through Groton, Harvard, and Columbia, and after becoming an attorney entered public service. His distant cousin Theodore Roosevelt was a career model. In 1905 he married the former president's niece, reform-minded Anna Eleanor Roosevelt.

FDR was a complex man—intelligent, articulate, personable, humane, pragmatic, tough, ambitious, and aggressive. At times he could be inscrutable and insensitive. Never a deep thinker or an ideologue, he accepted most of the conventional principles of his time, place, and class. Roosevelt thrived in politics. After serving as a state senator in New York, he went into the Wilson administration for seven years as assistant secretary of the navy. In large part because of his last name, he was the vice presidential candidate in 1920.

Roosevelt was stricken with polio in 1921 and lost the use of his legs. But he labored valiantly to recover his strength and in 1928 was elected governor of New York. In two highly successful terms, he created the first comprehensive system of unemployment relief, aided business, and favored conservation and public power programs. In 1932, FDR's ability to get along with a variety of Democrats, from big city bosses to southern patricians and western populists, served him well.

During the campaign, with the help of a small group of intellectuals known popularly as the "brains trust," FDR called for active federal involvement to aid the American people. He advocated emergency relief and suggested a variety of projects to provide large-scale temporary employment. At the same time, he portrayed himself as a fiscal conservative, which pleased business.

Perhaps the sharpest contrast between the two presidential aspirants was the public image they presented. FDR was ebullient, hopeful, and committed to action. Hoover seemed defensive, weary, and negative. When the ballots were counted, Roosevelt won 57 percent of the votes, and carried the electoral college 472 to 59. Democrats also won large majorities in both houses of Congress. The landslide proved that the American people were hungry for a "new deal."

New Deal Thought

The depression deepened sharply between election day and the inauguration. By March 4, 1933, some 13 million were unemployed, industrial production had slumped to 56 percent of its 1929 level, and most of the nation's banks were closed.

Roosevelt lacked a coherent plan to end the crisis; indeed, no one had such a plan. But he and those around him approached the task in a general way that reflected the reform tradition. The populists formed their thinking about agriculture and Wall Street. Their concern for the poor in the cities rested upon the Social Gospel and the experiences of urban reformers. (Numerous top-level appointees, including Harry Hopkins and Francis Perkins, the first woman to serve in a cabinet, had labored in settlement houses.) Their confidence in the power of the federal government stemmed from the WWI experiences. And their faith in the ability of intelligence to right wrongs came from decades of progressive ruminations.

Still, FDR was supremely pragmatic. Enjoying the clash of ideas, he surrounded himself with people of differing views and listened carefully before making his own decisions. Braintruster Rexford Tugwell, for example, was a strong believer in central planning; his conservative colleague Raymond Moley was not. Agriculture Secretary Henry A. Wallace of Iowa was a dreamy, idealistic sort of progressive. Director of the Budget Lewis W. Douglas was a hard-nosed, laissez-faire Democrat.

On the whole, New Dealers sought both economic recovery and reform. Their chief concern was the immediate crisis, but they were also mindful of conditions and policies that had brought the country to its knees and were determined to correct them.

The Hundred Days

Within the first one hundred days of his administration, FDR and Congress made a number of bold moves. The president sent fifteen major requests to Capitol Hill and received fifteen pieces of legislation in return. The public responded enthusiastically. The legalization of beer in April intensified the growing belief that new and better times were at hand. (The Twenty-first

Amendment, ratified in December, ended the failed and unpopular experiment with prohibition after nearly fourteen years.) Confidence was also restored by FDR's "fireside chats" on the radio and his frequent press conferences assuring the American people that he was doing his best on their behalf.

The president, for example, closed all the banks, and banking reform legislation and federal loans soon strengthened the surviving institutions. The Federal Deposit Insurance Corporation (FDIC) would hereafter guarantee deposits, as high as $5,000 in 1934. The president stunned many conservatives by heeding calls for inflation and taking the country off the gold standard to pave the way for price-raising ventures.

The relief of farmers was a top priority in Washington, and the Agricultural Adjustment Administration (AAA) tackled the age-old problem of overproduction. Farmers were paid to keep land out of production; millions of acres under cultivation were plowed up. The goal was to provide a level of prosperity, "parity," that farmers had enjoyed in the prewar years of 1909–14. The AAA gradually helped at least the most efficient and financially stable farmers. Productivity was curbed and farm income rose to 90 percent of parity by 1936. Still, prosperity was evasive, and the relatively unsatisfactory farm income of 1929 would not be reached until 1941. The Farm Credit Administration (FCA) aided farmers by refinancing a fifth of all their mortgages.

An FDR fireside chat in 1941. Source: Courtesy of the Franklin D. Roosevelt Library

A cornerstone of the Hundred Days, the National Recovery Administration (NRA) was designed to administer voluntary fair-competition codes in major industries. Created by business and labor, the codes set production limits and price guidelines and protected workers with maximum hours, minimum wages, and the guarantee, in the famous section 7a of the Recovery Act, of collective bargaining by unions. This was a conservative and somewhat naive approach to the economic crisis that did not, on the whole, prove effective. The codes had minimal effect on business profits, and employers often chafed at the benefits extended to workers. Some cheating and much squabbling went on. Newspaper mogul William Randolph Hearst called the NRA "a measure of absolute state socialism" and "a menace to political rights and constitutional liberties." Auto workers said that the NRA stood for "National Run Around."

The agreements were largely abandoned before being declared unconstitutional by the Supreme Court in 1935. Still, the NRA effort, symbolized by the Blue Eagle in a frenzy of patriotic parades, rallies, signs, and buttons, raised national morale and made significant improvements in working conditions.

The Public Works Administration (PWA), conservatively administered by Secretary of the Interior Harold Ickes, put people to work building, among other things, schools, city halls, hospitals, bridges, libraries, and the nation's first public housing. (By 1939, when it was discontinued, the PWA had completed over 34,000 construction projects at a cost of over $6 billion.)

The Civilian Conservation Corps (CCC) passed swiftly through Congress and proved popular and effective. Run by the army, the Corps eventually sent some two and a half million young men into the countryside all across the nation to plant trees, fight fires, stock fish, control insects, and build wildlife shelters, lookout towers, roads, and trails. Workers were paid $30 a month, of which $25 was sent home, and provided with all of their basic necessities.

In 1932 a quarter of a million families had lost their homes, and in the first half of the following year a thousand homes a day were being foreclosed. The Home Owners' Loan Corporation (HOLC) assisted both real estate interests and homeowners, eventually helping to refinance one of every five mortgaged urban private dwellings in the country.

The Tennessee Valley Authority (TVA) built and operated dams in seven states that controlled floods and generated cheap electricity. TVA officials also improved area recreation, health, and education. An entire region, filled with impoverished whites commonly known as "hillbillies," was aided by this bold exercise in federal authority. Equally desperate blacks in the area were largely ignored by administrators.

The Federal Emergency Relief Administration, headed by Harry Hopkins, was given a half billion dollars in relief funds to be channeled through state and local agencies. Social worker Hopkins, knowing well how desperately people needed help, spent more than $5 million in his first two hours in office.

The Civilian Conservation Corps in action. Source: Courtesy of the Franklin D. Roosevelt Library

That winter, as millions faced increased hardship, FDR authorized Hopkins to set up the Civil Works Administration (CWA), which hired construction workers, teachers, artists, writers, and others. By mid-January 1934, the CWA employed 4.2 million people. Appalled at the financial cost of the CWA, FDR soon shut it down. But during its brief existence it pumped a billion dollars into the nation's economy.

New Directions

The congressional elections in the fall of 1934 strengthened the administration's hand, reducing the GOP to a shadow of its former self. But the key to national prosperity remained elusive. By year's end, for example, the federal government had spent over $2 billion on relief and had little to show for it. Ten million were still unemployed, 20 million were receiving public assistance, and the gross national product remained $30 billion less than it had been before the crash.

In 1935 the New Deal appeared to be in trouble. The Supreme Court killed the NRA and threatened to limit drastically the powers of Congress over the economy. Critics on the right, like the American Liberty League, howled about government waste and excessive government authority. On the left, demagogic Governor Huey Long of Louisiana was gaining widespread attention for his "Share Our Wealth" proposals, which advocated, among other things, stringent taxes on the rich, generous benefits for the poor, a national minimum wage, and a shortened work week. By early 1935, Long claimed to have a mailing list of more than 7.5 million persons, and "The Kingfish" was threatening to become a presidential candidate.

Father Charles E. Coughlin of Royal Oak, Michigan, a "radio priest" whose audience was estimated as high as 40 million, shared the anti-New Deal sentiments of both the right and left. Interested principally in the money question (he sought to inflate the currency by making it silver based), and often engaging in anti-Semitism, he created an organization that proposed replacing capitalism with a system of "social justice." At the same time, Long Beach, California, physician Francis Townsend won the sympathies of millions by calling for a pension of $200 a month for every citizen over age 60.

To defuse critics and better reach those to whom they appealed, the president and the Democratic-controlled Congress stepped up their reforms in 1935. The Emergency Relief Appropriation Act authorized the president to spend nearly $5 billion to give people jobs. Historian William E. Leuchtenburg has noted that this was "the greatest single appropriation in the history of the United States or any other nation." The Works Progress Administration (WPA), under the guidance of Harry Hopkins, spent over a billion of these dollars, eventually hiring some three million men, including construction workers, actors, artists, musicians, and writers. The National Youth Administration provided part-time employment for more than 600,000 college students, over 1.5 million high-schoolers, and over 2.6 million jobless youth.

The federal jobs, as critics noted, were often make-work, and the pay was low, averaging only $52 a month and sinking as low as $19 a month in the rural south. The programs failed to reach even a third of the nation's unemployed at any one time. Those citizens deemed unemployable were left in the care of state governments that were often indifferent to their plight. Still, the federal efforts were generally popular and useful. Jobs helped people keep their self-respect and their faith in the political and economic system. Participants contributed to the national welfare in a wide assortment of ways, including the construction of parks, hospitals, and school buildings; the creation of art works that embellished public buildings across the country; the performance of plays, circuses, and concerts (the WPA maintained 36 symphony orchestras); and the publication of guides to cities, states, and territories.

The Social Security Act of 1935 created a national system of old-age insurance. At age 65, most Americans were eligible to receive a monthly check from the federal government, the amount being based on their past earnings. In addition, the act provided funds to states to help the elderly who were unable to take part in the system, and to assist an assortment of others in need. It also created a federal-state unemployment insurance program.

Critics on the right mourned the financial cost, the loss of traditional American self-reliance, and the growing power of the federal government. Their counterparts on the left complained that the legislation was overly conservative in that benefits were small (from $10 to $85 a month in 1942), that many Americans such as farmers and domestic workers were excluded, and that workers, already strapped for cash, were required along with their employers to contribute to the funding of the program. But the Social Security Act was the best that could be achieved at the time, and it proved popular. Americans now had social rights that their government must respect. This marked the beginning of a permanent system of public welfare in the United States. It also helped cement the growing belief that the Democrats were the party of compassion.

The National Labor Relations Act, often called the Wagner Act, was another major landmark, placing the authority of the federal government squarely behind collective bargaining. When a majority of a company's workers wanted a union, management was required to recognize it and negotiate on all matters. Unfair labor practices were spelled out, and the list included the firing or blacklisting of employees engaged in union activities. A National Labor Relations Board was created to enforce the legislation.

The Wagner Act rejuvenated organized labor. In 1935 several union leaders created the Committee for Industrial Organization (CIO), designed to organize the mass production workers of entire industries. Three years later, under the leadership of United Mine Workers president John L. Lewis, the Committee became officially independent of the AFL, calling itself the Congress of Industrial Organizations. Among its distinctive features was the policy of welcoming women, immigrants, and blacks.

The CIO found that organizing the steel and automobile industries was especially difficult and dangerous. In 1937 ten workers died in a clash with police outside Republic Steel. "Sit down strikes," in which workers refused to move from their machines until they won collective bargaining, brought General Motors around. But fiercely independent Henry Ford held out for a time, employing company guards and strikebreakers to stop the United Auto Workers. (Union activist and future CIO head Walter Reuther was beaten up in 1937.) By 1941 contracts were signed with both industries. The CIO, with some five million members, was now larger than the AFL. A record 23 percent of the nonagricultural work force in America belonged to unions.

The Wealth Tax Act of 1935 elevated a variety of taxes paid by the affluent and big corporations to record levels. It did not redistribute wealth significantly and enraged business leaders. But it was politically popular. During the depression people sometimes threw stones and insults at limousines as they passed by. The "soak the rich" act was a similar gesture against an entire class by a Congress that stood politically to the left of the chief executive.

Several efforts were made to help farmers in 1935, the most effective being the creation of the Rural Electrification Administration (REA). Midway through the decade, about nine out of ten farms were without power-line electric service. The REA transformed rural America by loaning funds to nonprofit cooperatives and enabling farmers to string wires throughout the countryside.

The First Lady

The president's wife was also popular on farms and in towns and cities all across the nation. Sometimes naive, always deeply concerned about the welfare of others, Eleanor Roosevelt was the most active first lady in American history. While serving as a gracious White House hostess and a mother of five, she found the time and energy to crusade for a number of reforms, particularly those that aided women and African Americans. She held news conferences (only women reporters were invited), wrote a syndicated newspaper column, made speeches, traveled extensively (40,000 miles in her first year), and quietly badgered her husband to do more for the downtrodden and neglected.

Although Franklin and Eleanor did not enjoy a happy marriage (she had discovered an extramarital affair many years earlier), they respected each other and worked in harmony. On her much-publicized travels, Eleanor served as FDR's "eyes and ears," bringing him information about Americans and their needs that might otherwise have escaped him and pleading with him to do what she thought was right, even if it was politically imprudent.

The Election of 1936

With his record of achievement and tireless campaigning, FDR created in 1936 a coalition of supporters that made his party the largest in the country. A majority of urban and ethnic voters, western and southern farmers, union members (the CIO contributed nearly half a million dollars), reform-minded intellectuals, African Americans, and much of the middle class wanted four more years of Roosevelt and reform.

On the whole, blacks were new to the Democratic Party, having clung to the GOP since the Civil War. They were attracted to the New Deal in large part by the benefits they received, including public relief, low-cost housing, and jobs. More than a million blacks worked for the WPA by 1939. (In Milwaukee, unskilled African American women were paid $60 a month to make dolls. The WPA's Handicraft Project was for many the only place in town where wages could be earned.) The New Deal assisted some 40 percent of the nation's African Americans. Moreover, FDR appointed more blacks to important government positions than any president ever had. He also condemned lynching, although the political realities of the time prohibited him from backing a proposal to make it a federal crime.

To be sure, New Deal programs frequently discriminated against blacks, and no civil rights legislation emerged during the first term. Moreover, the Democratic party contained powerful southerners who were actively hostile

to blacks. (The Scottsboro trial of 1931, an outrageous case of injustice per-
petrated in Alabama against nine blacks accused of raping two white women,
illustrated the prejudice harbored by millions of whites in the South.) Jim
Crow segregation continued to prevail throughout the United States. Still,
most African American voters were convinced that the president and first
lady were friends and overwhelmingly backed the Roosevelt-Garner ticket.

Republicans were left largely with support from the wealthy, many of whom
were angrily labeling the New Deal Fascist and Communist, and rural and
small-town Americans of native stock. The GOP nominated Governor Alfred
M. Landon of Kansas and named Chicago newspaper publisher Frank Knox
his running mate. Landon, a friendly, bland, independent oil producer and
former Bull Mooser, disappointed many backers by failing to condemn the
whole of the New Deal.

Followers of Long, Coughlin, and Townsend formed the Union party and
nominated North Dakota Congressman William Lemke. The Socialists and
Communists also fielded candidates.

The election was a stunning endorsement of the New Deal. Roosevelt carried every state except Maine and Vermont, an unprecedented achievement.
The margin in the electoral college was 523 to 8. Democrats now controlled
Congress by a wide margin, 331 to 89 in the House and 76 to 16 in the Senate (four senators being independents).

The Supreme Court Battle

The only hope conservatives had of curtailing the course of federal authority was the Supreme Court. By the end of its 1936 term, a majority of the
Court had declared New Deal legislation unconstitutional in nine of the eleven
cases set before it. Never before in American history had judicial authority
been employed so effectively to thwart reform. Even after Roosevelt's triumph at the polls, it appeared that the Social Security Act and the Wagner
Act were in danger of being nullified. And what about future legislation? FDR
in his inaugural address called for bold steps to help the "one-third of a nation ill-housed, ill-clad, ill-nourished."

Roosevelt decided to attack the Court indirectly. In February 1937 he proposed a reorganization of the federal judiciary. The legislation proposed to
give the president authority to name new federal judges, no more than six
to the Supreme Court and forty-four to the lower courts, whenever an incumbent failed to retire or resign six months after his seventieth birthday.
The ostensible purpose was to enable the courts to keep up with a heavy
work load. When that argument fell flat, Roosevelt made it plain that the
Supreme Court was obstructing publicly supported efforts to end the depression. The memory of FDR's smashing reelection victory gave weight to
his appeal.

The "court-packing scheme" triggered a serious national debate, led initially by conservative Democrats. Suddenly, the Court made a hasty retreat,

approving both the Wagner and Social Security acts. Moreover, FDR soon had opportunities to name new justices. (Hugo Black, William O. Douglas, and Felix Frankfurter would become major figures in the history of the Court.) After 1937 all New Deal legislation was upheld. Even though the president's proposal to reorganize the judiciary was defeated, he could contend correctly that he won the war with the Court.

The struggle was costly, however, for it helped lead to a conservative coalition of Republicans and southern Democrats that by the end of the following year brought the New Deal to a virtual halt.

The End of the New Deal

Other factors also weakened the impetus for reform. Labor violence involving the CIO in the spring of 1937 was widely blamed on FDR, the Wagner Act, and Democrats in general. In August a severe recession began, in part caused by cutbacks in federal spending. (FDR always had hopes of balancing the budget.) Profits fell 78 percent and payrolls slid 35 percent, prompting widespread criticism of New Deal policies.

The major legislative achievements of 1938 included a new and largely ineffective AAA law, large-scale public works appropriations to help fight the recession, and the Fair Labor Standards Act, which prohibited the employment of child labor in interstate commerce and, despite many exemptions, set minimum wage and maximum hour standards for millions of Americans.

The New Deal did not end the Great Depression. A decade after the stock market crash, there were still some 10 million unemployed out of a labor supply of 40 million, billions of federal dollars were being spent to create jobs, millions of Americans earned less than the 40 cents per hour Congress supported, farmers continued to suffer from the effects of overproduction, many businesses and entire industries such as steel continued to lag behind earlier economic levels. As late as 1942 the Dow Jones industrial average languished below 100.

In 1940 most Americans were renters; most households had neither a refrigerator nor central heating; a third lacked inside running water. More than 20 percent of Americans lived on farms, less than a third of which had electric lights, and only a tenth had flush toilets.

Between 1930 and 1940, the national debt nearly doubled, from $28 billion to $51 billion. Federal spending as a share of national output tripled from 3.4 to 10.4 percent. And still, America was in a depression.

By 1938 the Democrats were in turmoil. Fed up with party conservatives who worked against his reforms, FDR tried unsuccessfully to "purge" them from the party by backing others in elections. That fall Republicans gained eighty-one seats in the House and eight in the Senate. Congress proceeded to slash and kill New Deal programs in 1939, and Roosevelt was widely thought to be ready to retire.

And yet the New Deal was successful in many ways and earned the gratitude and admiration of most Americans. By helping the recovery of business; by encouraging the rise of organized labor; by providing Americans with unemployment insurance, old-age pensions, price supports, jobs, homes, mortgage protections, better working conditions, electricity, and new and improved educational and recreational facilities; by protecting investments and savings; by giving millions hope, the New Deal kept the depression from getting worse and helped save America from the extremes of laissez faire and socialism.

By reaching out in small but meaningful ways to women, ethnic groups, and minorities, the New Deal contributed to a growing sense of equality and justice. In 1939, when the Daughters of the American Revolution refused to let black contralto Marian Anderson sing in Constitution Hall, the first lady and Interior Secretary Harold Ickes arranged an Easter Sunday concert at the Lincoln Memorial that attracted 75,000 people.

Under Roosevelt and his allies, most Americans had recovered from the despair of the last Hoover years and were persuaded as never before of the value of a responsive, humane, moderate, and active federal government.

The New Deal made the Democratic party the major force in American politics. Even in 1938 Democrats won twenty-four of the thirty-two Senate contests. And FDR remained the most popular and powerful American. With his mind increasingly on foreign affairs, he would soon prove again his value to the nation and the world.

Everyday Life in the 1930s

The depression altered the lives of most Americans in many ways. On all socioeconomic levels, and in all corners of the nation, people scrambled to cope with the economic realities. And as they adjusted, new values, visions, heroes, fashions, and fads quickly followed.

Family life was profoundly affected by the hard times. Marriages were delayed, birth rates dropped, contraceptive sales soared, and divorce rates were down. Much of the cynicism and flippancy about sex faded, and marriage and the family seemed to be taken more seriously than in the previous decade. But this did not reflect a return to Victorian morals. One national magazine poll of 1936 reported 63 percent of men and women favoring the teaching and practice of birth control. A study of college juniors and seniors showed that half of the men and a quarter of the women had premarital sex.

Women's fashions revealed the penchant for change characteristic of the thirties. Women opted for a more feminine and practical image than in the days of the flapper. Skirt length fell well below the knee, busts and waists reappeared, hair styles became softer and more graceful. Ruffles and bows, and hats of all sizes and descriptions were seen again. Still, women often smoked cigarettes, drank and gambled with men in public, wore slacks and revealing bathing suits, and participated in such fashionable sports as soft-

ball, rollerskating, and bicycling. Actress Katharine Hepburn defied stereotypes in her many films, showing that a woman could be brainy, athletic, independent, and efficient as well as vulnerable, compassionate, cultured, and
romantic.

Movies were a common source of escape for people plagued by the Depression. Some 85 million Americans went to the nation's 17,000 movie theaters each week. Admission prices were as low as a nickel. Musicals, like
Forty-Second Street, were especially popular, the screen being filled with
beautiful young women, luxurious sets, extravagant choreography, songs,
comedy, and simple stories of people who found romance, wealth, and fame,
often in show business.

Hollywood, in the "Golden Age" of movies that began in the early 1930s
and lasted for about twenty years, was largely controlled by five major studios, led by Metro-Goldwyn-Mayer. They commanded the services of such
superstars as Hepburn, Clark Gable, Myrna Loy, James Cagney, Fred Astaire,
Ginger Rogers, William Powell, Jean Harlow, Spencer Tracy, Cary Grant, Bette
Davis, and John Wayne. (Wayne made 13 movies in 1933 and would appear
in more films during his long career than any other star.) Animator Walt Disney was a major figure in Hollywood, producing the first three-color tech-
nicolor film in 1932 and *Snow White and the Seven Dwarfs* in 1937, the first
full-length cartoon.

Some 150 studios made "race movies" during the 1930s through the 1950s.
Their films, starring blacks and often shot on extremely low budgets, served
the six hundred theaters that catered to African Americans.

Radio was extremely popular in the thirties. The living room console was
often the family gathering place. Comedians Amos n' Andy were heard widely,
as were Jack Benny, Fred Allen, Edgar Bergen, and George Burns and Gra-
cie Allen. The western adventure series *The Lone Ranger* reached some 20
million people a week in 1939.

Popular music was a major feature of radio broadcasting, and the decade
was rich in composers. The list included Cole Porter, Irving Berlin, Harold
Arlen, Hoagy Carmichael, and George Gershwin, whose powerful opera *Porgy
and Bess* made its debut in 1935. Classical music could be heard regularly
on the radio. In 1938–39 the combined audiences for the Metropolitan Opera
broadcasts on Saturday afternoons (still the longest-running radio series in
history) and three programs offering symphonic music attracted 10.2 million
families each week.

The phonograph continued to be a staple in American homes. Recordings
of classical music sold especially well, as did songs by crooner Bing Crosby.
Singer Ella Fitzgerald was becoming widely appreciated by the end of the
decade. "King of Swing" bandleader Benny Goodman, who reached fame in
1935 and performed in New York's Carnegie Hall in 1938, had a huge following. The Duke Ellington, Count Basie, Artie Shaw, and Tommy Dorsey
bands were making memorable recordings. The scores of many "sweet" bands
that played strictly for dancing, like those of Guy Lombardo and Jan Garber,
were popular with record buyers.

Sports continued to win the hearts of millions of Americans. The New York Yankees won four straight world series from 1936–39 (they would win 16 world series and 18 American league pennants between 1923 and 1953), and fans were learning to venerate the "Yankee Clipper," Joe DiMaggio. Boston Red Sox backers were being impressed by young slugger Ted Williams at the end of the decade. In 1941, he would hit 406, a batting average unequaled by a major leaguer to this day. Black pitcher Satchel Paige, playing year-round in segregated baseball leagues, pitched 153 games in 1935, starting twenty-nine times in one month. African Americans were especially proud of Joe Louis, who won the heavyweight championship of the world in 1937 and would reign for almost twelve years.

Books also provided diversion, and the advent of inexpensive paperbacks hiked sales. Hervey Allen's *Anthony Adverse*, Pearl Buck's *The Good Earth*, Kenneth Roberts's *Northwest Passage*, Willa Cather's *Shadows on the Rock*, and Margaret Mitchell's *Gone With The Wind* (made into a classic film in 1939) were best-sellers. "For a time," Frederick Lewis Allen commented, "the likeliest recipe for publishing profits was to produce an 800-page romance in old-time costume."

Some notable volumes directly confronted the economic and political problems of the era. John Gunther's *Inside Europe* and *Inside Asia* discussed the looming crises abroad. Sinclair Lewis's *It Can't Happen Here*, published in 1935, showed how fascism could come to the United States. Erskine Caldwell's *Tobacco Road*, a story of hardship and depravity in the rural south, became a popular Broadway play in the late 1930s. John Steinbeck's *The Grapes of Wrath* appeared in 1939, when defense contracts and a large measure of economic recovery made the painful tale of the migrant Okies more palatable.

SUGGESTED READING

Frederick Lewis Allen, *Since Yesterday, The Nineteen-Thirties in America* (1939); Michael A. Bernstein, *The Great Depression* (1987); Alan Brinkley, *Voice of Protest: Huey Long, Father Coughlin, and the Great Depression* (1982); James M. Burns, *Roosevelt: The Lion and the Fox* (1956); Otis L. Graham, Jr., *An Encore for Reform* (1967); Joseph Lash, *Eleanor and Franklin* (1971); William E. Leuchtenburg, *Franklin D. Roosevelt and the New Deal, 1932–1940* (1963); John Salmond, *The Civilian Conservation Corps, 1933–1942* (1967); Studs Terkel, *Hard Times: An Oral History of the Great Depression* (1970); Rexford G. Tugwell, *The Democratic Roosevelt* (1957).

Chapter Seven

THE WORLD AT WAR AGAIN

F aced with unparalleled economic woes in 1933, the Roosevelt administration did not place foreign affairs high on its agenda. Moreover, there was a strong enthusiasm for isolationism left over from the twenties. This viewpoint was bolstered in the mid-1930s by books, articles, and a congressional investigation headed by Senator Gerald P. Nye of North Dakota charging that America had been duped into World War I by bankers, munitions makers, and reckless visionaries. Americans were also upset by the failure of economically exhausted allies to pay their war debts.

Roosevelt's "Good Neighbor" policy was a repudiation of efforts in the past to intercede in Latin American affairs. In late 1933, for example, FDR renounced the policy of armed intervention. A year later the marines were withdrawn from Haiti. In 1936 America relinquished its right to intercede in Panama. Mutually beneficial trade agreements also helped make Roosevelt popular in Latin America.

Responding to developments in Germany was more difficult. The day after FDR entered the White House, Adolf Hitler came to power, promising to fix the severe economic problems of the Weimar Republic and restore the national pride that had been battered by the First World War and the Treaty of Versailles. FDR and administration officials immediately recognized the fanaticism, aggressiveness, and racism inherent in fascism. Hitler's persecution of the Jews, scapegoats in many countries over many centuries, was widely deplored. But isolationism was so popular in Congress and across the country in the early 1930s that little could be done to curb the Nazis.

Japanese aggression was also a concern. In the late 1920s militarists took control of the nation and pursued a policy of aggression that dated from 1895. In 1931 Japan invaded Manchuria, then Chinese territory, and seemed poised to expand further in East Asia. In November 1936 Japan signed an anticommunist pact with Germany and fascist Italy, led by Benito Mussolini.

Secretary of State Cordell Hull fumed, but no action was taken. The United States was determined to stay neutral.

In 1935, while helping defeat a presidential proposal to join the World Court, Senator Thomas Schall of Minnesota shouted, "To hell with Europe and the rest of those nations." That same year, with Germany rearming, authoritarian regimes growing in southern and eastern Europe, and Italy conquering the independent African nation of Ethiopia, Congress swiftly passed a law keeping America free of foreign entanglements. The first neutrality act authorized the president, after declaring a state of war, to prohibit arms shipments and withhold protection from American citizens traveling on belligerent ships.

In 1936 Congress added a ban on loans or credits to belligerents. A year later, with Hitler and Mussolini actively supporting fascist dictator Francisco Franco in the Spanish Civil War, legislators banned travel by Americans on belligerent ships. While sales of raw materials were continued, under the "cash and carry" principle, belligerents would have to pay for them on delivery and ship them in their own vessels or in ships owned by a nation other than the United States.

Despite personal misgivings, Roosevelt bowed to prevailing public opinion and signed the neutrality acts. By 1937, 94 percent of the American people favored isolationism, no matter who the combatants were.

That October, following further Japanese incursions into China, the president proposed a "quarantine" of aggressor nations. Isolationists in Congress threatened impeachment, and FDR quickly backed down. When the Japanese sank the American gunboat *U.S.S. Panay* in Chinese waters, public opinion remained firmly isolationist. (Japan apologized and took steps that appeared to signal a desire for peace.) Against the wishes of the White House, the House of Representatives came within twenty-one votes of passing the Ludlow amendment to the Constitution providing that, short of invasion, the United States could declare war only with the approval of a majority of American voters.

In 1938 the prospects for peace dimmed sharply. Hitler annexed Austria and demanded a large part of Czechoslovakia, a nation formed in 1918 out of the former Austro-Hungarian Empire. Hitler claimed merely to be creating a "Greater Germany," and the Sudentenland contained millions of Germans. In September, at a peace conference in Munich, leaders of war-weary England and France voted to support Hitler's demand. British Prime Minister Neville Chamberlain announced "peace in our time."

But appeasement was not the solution. In November Hitler stepped up his persecution of Jews. (During the decade the United States welcomed a large number of Jewish refugees, including scientist Albert Einstein and composer Paul Hindemith. Writer Thomas Mann, whose wife was Jewish, also came to America.) In March 1939 Hitler invaded the rest of Czechoslovakia, confirming his ruthlessness and making war virtually inevitable. Franco, Mussolini, and the Japanese were also on the march. In May Germany and Italy concluded a military alliance. In August Hitler signed a nonaggression pact with

Soviet leader Joseph Stalin, a cynical deal between ideological enemies that enabled both powers to expand. On the first day of September Germany invaded Poland. Britain and France, having pledged their support to Poland, declared war two days later.

FDR was saddened but not surprised by the outbreak of World War II. For months he had been beefing up American military strength and expressing his opposition to the designs of Axis dictators. Still, when General George C. Marshall took up his duties as U.S. Army chief of staff, on the day that Hitler invaded Poland, the American army had 174,000 troops and was ranked seventeenth in the world, behind Bulgaria and Portugal.

In a fireside chat on September 3, the president promised to do everything in his power to avoid American involvement in the conflict. But he acknowledged that people did not have to remain neutral in their thoughts about the war. In fact, a Gallup poll revealed that 84 percent wanted an Allied victory, 2 percent favored the Nazis, and 14 percent had no opinion.

France and England were soon desperate for help, and in late September Roosevelt called for a special session of Congress to repeal the arms embargo. Later that fall Congress reluctantly agreed, but attached a "cash and carry" provision in order to keep the United States from direct involvement. The Neutrality Act of 1939 also gave the president the authority to define combat zones, areas that American ships and citizens were forbidden to enter. Roosevelt soon declared the entire Baltic Sea and the Atlantic Ocean from southern Norway to the northern coast of Spain such a zone. This major effort to keep the United States neutral actually helped Hitler by taking American ships out of the action and making the German blockade of Britain more effective.

In the spring of 1940 Nazi troops rolled through Denmark, Norway, the Low Countries, and France. This six week *blitzkrieg* (lightning war) terrified millions. Great Britain, the next target, was soon fighting for its life. In the United States, war fever gripped much of the nation, and a group of eastern intellectuals organized the Committee to Defend America by Aiding the Allies. Roosevelt called for a greater military buildup. America was not prepared to fight. The army remained small and was extremely short of weapons. During maneuvers in August, soldiers had to pretend that beer cans were ammunition and trucks were tanks.

From early August through October 1940 the Nazis bombed English cities and wreaked havoc on the nation's fleet in advance of a planned invasion. Americans were saddened by the daily accounts in the media of suffering and destruction, and polls showed that a majority of Americans now preferred all-out war to Britain's defeat.

Responding to appeals from Prime Minister Winston Churchill, FDR traded fifty World War I destroyers to the British in return for the rights to build defense bases on an assortment of British possessions in the Western Hemisphere, including the Bahamas, Jamaica, and Trinidad. The president made the deal on his own, avoiding a fight with congressional isolationists, and justified it on the grounds of national security. Critics howled, for they knew that Roosevelt had abandoned the policy of neutrality.

Buoyed by Nazi triumphs, the Japanese moved into strategic portions of northern French Indo-China in September and soon signed a treaty of alliance with Germany and Italy. FDR, who had banned the sale of aviation fuel to the Japanese in July, now stopped all shipments of iron and steel scrap to Japan. The administration hoped that economic sanctions could contain the Japanese in Southeast Asia while the United States focused on the plight of the English.

Congress too responded to the international crisis. In September the nation got its first peacetime draft, affecting 16.5 million men between the ages of 21 and 36. By October legislators had authorized more than $17 billion for defense.

Still, isolationism remained strong, especially among German and Irish ethnic groups, college students, and Republicans. Their ranks were augmented by Communists, eager to back their Nazi allies, and an assortment of others on the left, like John L. Lewis and Socialist Norman Thomas, who opposed FDR in general. In September 1940 the America First Committee became a major platform for those convinced that the United States should shun what GOP Senator William Borah of Idaho called "European power politics."

The Election of 1940

In late May 1940, Roosevelt, 58, apparently decided to run for an unprecedented third term. But he would do nothing on his own behalf, preferring to be "drafted" by the Democratic party convention. He won the nomination on the first ballot and selected Agriculture Secretary Henry Wallace for his running mate. Wallace was strongly antifascist and was popular in the Midwest.

The GOP convention selected 48-year-old Wendell Willkie on the sixth ballot. Willkie, a wealthy Wall Street lawyer and president of a utilities holding company that had feuded with the Tennessee Valley Authority, was an amiable and moderate internationalist. Republicans chose Senator Charles McNary, an Oregon isolationist, to balance the ticket.

During the campaign Willkie hammered at Roosevelt for the failure of the New Deal to end the depression and for the president's alleged inattention to national defense. A former Democrat, he also tended to favor many of FDR's policies. When Willkie's campaign began to falter, he portrayed Roosevelt as a warmonger. In reply, FDR resorted to wishful thinking by declaring, "I have said this before, but I shall say it again and again and again: Our boys are not going to be sent into any foreign wars."

Roosevelt won by five million votes and carried the electoral college 449 to 82. But Willkie made important gains in Democratic strongholds, especially among voters who opposed American involvement overseas.

Prelude to War

By the end of 1940, despite American assistance, the British were in desperate shape. Churchill, warning of the dangers to the whole world of fascist victory, pleaded for more help. FDR echoed this warning in a fireside chat, contending that "the Nazi masters of Germany" intended to enslave Europe and dominate the rest of the world. In his third inaugural address, he declared: "We would rather die on our feet than live on our knees."

In January 1941 Roosevelt asked for the authority to lend and lease $7 billion worth of war supplies to any country whose defense he deemed necessary for the defense of the United States. He sought, he said, to make America "the arsenal of democracy." After a furious battle in Congress, the aid began flowing to Britain. The United States was now unmistakably on the side of the Allies. The president quickly promised increased aid to enable a total Allied victory. (In the course of the war, total lend-lease aid would amount to more than $50 billion.)

During the first three months of 1941 British and American military leaders conducted private talks about steps to take should the United States become a belligerent. They agreed that Hitler posed the greatest danger to the world (Japan was only fighting in China to this point) and must be stopped first.

That spring, as German military efforts proved increasingly effective, America inched closer to direct involvement. With German submarines sinking 500,000 tons of shipping a month, Roosevelt sent American "patrol" ships to help the British avoid the enemy. In April he expanded the range of patrols as far as Greenland, a Danish colony, which he agreed to place under American protection. In May he declared an unlimited national emergency and increased his authority over the economy. In June he froze Axis assets in the United States.

Still, Roosevelt acted cautiously. While he believed that Hitler's defeat was imperative and realized that America could probably not avoid an open clash with Germany, he was keenly mindful of public opinion and the isolationists in Congress. In FDR's mind, the führer would have to take the first step to drag the United States directly into the war.

On June 22, 1941, Hitler violated his alliance with Stalin and attacked the Soviet Union. Both the British and American governments promised to help resist the aggression, and a billion dollars in lend-lease aid was soon on its way. While Roosevelt and Churchill were staunchly anticommunist, they knew that Russia would be a highly valuable ally. Indeed, until the Allied invasion of France in mid-1944, the great bulk of the fighting in Europe was between Russians and Germans.

In July 1941 FDR sent troops to Iceland and announced that American ships would hereafter extend their search and patrol efforts to that strategic point. In August, Roosevelt and Churchill met secretly at sea off Newfoundland, a meeting that produced the Atlantic Charter. This joint statement of postwar goals was filled with Wilsonian principles about self-determination, freedom, and the desire to improve the economic and social conditions of the peoples of the world. War aims included "the final destruction of Nazi tyranny." While neither an official alliance nor a contract, the document again revealed the close relationship between Britain and the United States. Within a few weeks fifteen anti-Axis nations, including the Soviet Union, endorsed the charter.

Still, millions of Americans, from all walks of life, were determined to stay out of Europe's great war. They argued that the United States could successfully remain free of the conflict and warned that war would bring about, among other things, depression, socialism, and fascism. In August a bill to extend the draft for eighteen months passed the House of Representatives by a single vote.

By year's end the America First Committee had 450 units and at least a quarter of a million members. Historian Justus Doenecke has called the AFC, "one of the most vigorous action groups ever to appear in the United States." Aviation hero Charles Lindbergh, who had been wined and dined by Nazi leaders in Germany, joined the America First national committee in April. He made numerous speeches and radio broadcasts urging America to stay out of the war. Lindbergh's effectiveness ended when he publicly expressed anti-Semitism.

Events continued to push America closer to the war. On September 4 the destroyer *U.S.S. Greer* was attacked by a German submarine it was tracking off the coast of Iceland. FDR angrily declared that American ships would "shoot on sight" all German submarines found between Iceland and North America. In October he asked Congress to alter the Neutrality Act by allowing the arming of American merchant ships and permitting them to carry cargoes to belligerent ports. Following submarine attacks on two destroyers, one incident costing the lives of more than one hundred Americans, Congress complied. The votes were close, 50 to 37 in the Senate and 212 to 194 in the House. Still, by mid-November 1941, Germans and Americans were shooting at each other and the United States was a full participant in the Battle of the Atlantic.

Pearl Harbor

The German conquest of the Netherlands and France left the colonies of these two nations in the East Indies and Indochina highly vulnerable. Needing foreign sources of raw materials to remain a world power, the Japanese were determined to exploit these areas. In July 1941 they moved into southern Indochina. Continuing to hope that economic pressure would restrain Japan, FDR ordered all Japanese assets in the United States frozen, virtually ending trade between the two nations.

When the Dutch governor of the East Indies cut off Dutch oil to Japan, the Japanese military and government moderates waged a heated debate about the nation's future foreign policy. The admirals favored a massive surprise attack against the United States in the Pacific, hoping to gain a free hand in Asia that would begin with grabbing rich and much-needed supplies of oil and rubber. In October the moderate Prince Fumimaro Kenoye and his cabinet resigned. Militant General Hideki Tojo headed the new government, and within a month Ambassador Joseph Grew was privately warning Washington of a sudden Japanese attack.

Japanese negotiators in Washington wanted the United States to get out of China, to free frozen Japanese assets and normalize trade relations, to help secure oil supplies from the East Indies, and to halt American naval expansion in the Pacific. The Roosevelt administration countered with proposals that included the withdrawal of Japanese troops from China and Indochina and a nonaggression pact.

Americans had broken the top-secret Japanese diplomatic code and learned that fall that their diplomatic efforts were futile. Some sort of Japanese eruption was feared, but confusion reigned about the time and place. On Sunday morning, December 7, Chief of Staff General George C. Marshall sent a warning, based on intercepted code, to Hawaii and several other strategic locations. The telegram to Hawaii was delayed after its arrival and did not reach the military until the bombs were already dropping on Pearl Harbor, home of the Pacific Fleet.

Numerous subsequent investigations of the tragedy have blamed local military leaders for failing to provide adequate precautions against attack. They have also faulted Washington officials for misreading signs of Japanese intentions and underestimating that nation's daring and might. Historians have rejected the charge that FDR led a conspiracy to bring America into the war. Scholar Thomas C. Schelling has observed, "Our stupendous unreadiness at Pearl Harbor . . . was just a dramatic failure of a remarkably well-informed government to call the next enemy move in a cold-war crisis."

The surprise attack, by nearly two hundred planes launched from aircraft carriers, lasted just under two hours. It sank 21 American warships, destroyed 165 planes, and killed 2,338 military and civilian personnel. The sinking of the *Arizona* (left on the site as a memorial to the attack) took the lives of 1,177 crewmen. The Japanese, in contrast, lost only twenty-nine planes, five midget submarines, and fewer than one hundred men. The naval task force escaped without being attacked.

The next day, President Roosevelt called December 7 "a date which will live in infamy" and asked Congress for a declaration of war against Japan. Congress, with only a single dissent, quickly complied. Germany and Italy declared war on America three days later.

In retrospect the assault on Pearl Harbor was a serious blunder. The "sneak attack" united the American people as perhaps nothing else could have and provided them with a firm determination to win the war. The huge oil reserves on Hawaii, which were unscathed, would have been a better target than the Pacific Fleet. Moreover, some of the battleships (no aircraft carriers were present) hit in the raid were later restored to active duty. At the time, however, it was widely thought that Japan had taken a major step in winning the war for the Axis powers. The Japanese also launched attacks on the Philippines, Guam, and Midway Island, as well as on the British forces in Hong Kong and in the Malay Peninsula.

The Home Front

Even before Pearl Harbor, the federal government was strongly influencing the economy in the interest of the war effort. The Office of Price Administration, for example, imposed a number of controversial price controls soon after its creation by the president in April 1940. Throughout 1941 the government made numerous efforts to convert industry to military production. Munitions production increased by 235 percent during the year.

Facing an all-out war effort in early 1942, federal agencies began to sprout, frequently led by "dollar-a-year" business executives. The National War Labor Board, for example, was designed to prevent labor disputes and keep production at a maximum. The War Production Board directed industrial mobilization and exercised "general responsibility" over the nation's economy. The War Food Administration led the nation's all-important food program. The Office of Defense Transportation helped keep the nation's railroads efficient.

On the whole, the federal agencies made impressive contributions. By mid-1943, after a rocky start, the OPA was able to maintain a reasonable level of price stability. Consumer prices rose only 8.7 percent between October 1942 and the end of the war.

Sugar, gasoline, meat, shoes, and tires were rationed, and the production of automobiles ceased. But people got by with a minimum of grumbling, and contributed toothpaste tubes, cans, and rubber boots to the war effort. Historian Richard Polenberg has observed, "If the mood of the 1930s had been expressed by an old jalopy filled with migrant workers on their way west, that of the war was conveyed by an old jalopy on its way to the scrap pile with a sign reading 'Praise the Lord, I'll Soon Be Ammunition.'" Many people turned to the thriving black market to obtain scarce commodities.

There were numerous labor disturbances during the war. At one point the federal government seized and operated mines when truculent union leader John L. Lewis threatened to strike for higher wages. Still, industrial peace was the general rule, productivity was high, and millions enjoyed a level of prosperity only dreamed of in the preceding decade. Weekly earnings grew by 70 percent during the war. A manpower shortage, hastened by the draft and the need for defense workers, led to the expiration of New Deal relief agencies including the Civilian Conservation Corps, the Works Progress Administration, and the National Youth Administration. In 1943, when wartime employment peaked, more than 12.5 million people worked in basic war industries.

Under the guidance of the War Production Board, headed by Donald M. Nelson, the nation's factories quickly expanded America's military arsenal.

Between 1940 and 1945 they turned out some 300,000 aircraft, 5,425 merchant ships, 72,000 naval vessels, 87,000 tanks, and 2.5 million trucks. By 1944 a huge Ford factory in Willow Run, Michigan, was producing a new plane every hour. Henry J. Kaiser's plant in Richmond, California, could build a merchant ship in two weeks. America's factories played a major role in the Allied victory, turning out twice as many military goods as the Germans and Japanese combined.

The armed forces preferred to do business with large manufacturers known for dependability, and two-thirds of all military contracts went to one hundred firms. Government purchases of goods and services reached $89 billion in 1944, and government guarantees helped corporate profits rise from $6.4 billion in 1940 to $10.8 billion in 1944. About half of the nation's annual production went to the war effort.

Congress hiked taxes on corporations and individuals significantly in 1942, forcing most Americans for the first time to pay federal income taxes. (In 1939, only 5 percent of the population filed returns.) A year later the Treasury Department began withholding the sums due from paychecks. Still, taxes paid for only about 46 percent of the war effort; the rest was borrowed. Numerous war bond campaigns, often promoted by movie stars, were successful in raising $135 billion. Government spending soared from $9 billion in 1940 to an unprecedented $100 billion in 1945. The war was far more effective than decades of reform in creating big government.

Some nine million defense workers and their families moved to areas, notably in the South and West, offering defense jobs. California alone grew by nearly 2 million people in less than five years. Housing was often in short supply, and family life was often disrupted by tensions stemming from moving, cramped quarters, overcrowded schools, the absence of working parents, and the overall violence bred by war. Juvenile delinquency increased dramatically during the war, the divorce rate soared, and there was much concern about teenage sex and venereal disease. It was an unsettling period, best illustrated by the changing role of women.

The number of women working outside the home swelled from 14 million to 19 million. By war's end, 36 percent of all women were in the work force, up from 28 percent in 1940. There was truth in the stereotype of "Rosie the Riveter," for some women labored alongside men in steel mills and shipyards, and worked at jobs like cab driving that had been open almost exclusively to men. Barbara Heningburg traded 35 cents an hour at a Georgia laundry for the "big money" of $1.35 an hour riveting rudders and elevators for B-17 bombers in Detroit. Still, few women challenged traditional sex roles; femininity remained a positive concept, and full-time homemakers were in the majority. There was nothing masculine about movie star Betty Grable, the nation's favorite wartime "pin-up girl."

Millions of young women, called "bobby-soxers" because of their short white stockings, screamed in delight at singer Frank Sinatra. Sinatra began his phenomenally successful career in 1939 with one of the first-rate swing bands, led by trumpeter Harry James, that continued to be popular during

the war. The Glenn Miller band had a unique sound that many would always associate with World War II.

African Americans continued to be discriminated against in virtually all occupations and suffered high levels of unemployment and poverty. The irony
of the continuation of Jim Crow in a war against fascist racism and bigotry
did not escape civil rights leaders. In mid-1941, President Roosevelt prevented
a march on Washington by blacks with Executive Order 8802, which prohibited discrimination in defense industries. It also created a Fair Employment Practices Committee to monitor complaints and enforce the ruling. The
FEPC, lacking legal authority to enforce its orders and weakened by hostility in Congress, made slight gains. But most Americans were not yet ready
to embrace racial equality. Rigid discrimination in labor unions, fierce antiblack rhetoric in the South, and race riots in northern cities during the summer of 1943 underscored this fact. Twenty-five blacks and nine whites lost
their lives and nearly seven hundred were injured in the riot in Detroit.

Civil liberties, on the other hand, were respected to a far greater degree
during this war than in the last. The shrinking number of immigrants had
been largely assimilated by this time and were no longer feared. Few believed that Americans of German or Italian descent had divided loyalties. The
Federal Bureau of Investigation, given new authority by the president, seemed
entirely capable of thwarting espionage and sedition. Most conscientious objectors, whose largest estimated number amounted to only a third of 1 percent of the 34 million registrants in the draft, were assigned an assortment
of noncombatant duties.

The government harassed several right-wing extremists, Federal employees submitted to loyalty tests, newscasts were mildly censured, and the
Office of War Information engaged in a limited amount of wartime propaganda. But public support of the war was such that these efforts faced little
resistance.

The glaring exception to the general harmony on the home front involved
the Japanese Americans on the Pacific Coast. In early 1942, more than 110,000
of them, two-thirds born in the United States (Nisei), were rounded up and
placed in ten hastily constructed camps located in the interior of seven western states. The evacuees suffered income and property losses amounting to
some $350 million. Army officials justified the removal on military grounds;
all Japanese, in this view, were by definition potential traitors. (A small percentage of the evacuees refused to give up allegiance to the emperor, and
some 8,000 eventually chose to go to Japan.) This action, later widely
lamented, was also a response to public anger over the Pearl Harbor invasion and the outbreak of war.

In the Service

After Pearl Harbor, millions of young men joined the armed services, while
still other millions were drafted. By the end of the war, some 8.3 million

were in the army, 3.4 million were in the navy, nearly half a million were marines, and some 170,000 served in the Coast Guard. The air force was part of the army.

About a quarter of a million women donned military uniforms, working as secretaries, technicians, nurses, jeep drivers, and having an assortment of other duties. About 100,000 women served in the Women's Army Auxiliary Corps (Wacs), and smaller numbers belonged to the Waves (navy), Spars (Coast Guard), and Marine Corps.

In 1940, African Americans were kept out of the Marine Corps and Air Corps, and could join the navy only as messmen. The army was rigidly segregated. White officers commanded black units, and black officers in those units could not exercise authority over the white officers. It was widely believed in top military circles that blacks could neither lead nor fight effectively. Of the 1.7 million African Americans who served, not a single one received one of the 432 Medals of Honor awarded. (Acknowledging racism at the time, the army awarded Medals of Honor to seven black World War II veterans in 1997.) The situation changed somewhat as the war progressed and manpower shortages developed. But segregation continued, even on the battlefield. Blood plasma from black donors was not given to others.

The War in Europe

Even before America's direct entry into the war, military planners agreed that Germany should be the primary target. Hitler was attacking Great Britain and the Soviet Union simultaneously and threatened to take over the whole of Europe. His outpost on the Atlantic posed a danger to the Western Hemisphere. Moreover, there was the possibility of a German technological breakthrough that might tilt the war in Germany's favor. Roosevelt argued in 1942, "Defeat of Germany means defeat of Japan, probably without firing a shot or losing a life."

The American Joint Chiefs of Staff, under the inspired leadership of General George C. Marshall, favored an invasion of France. British military leaders argued, however, that German forces should be encountered elsewhere while the necessary resources were amassed to wage a cross-Channel attack. Russia was pleading for immediate action that would divert Hitler from the Eastern Front. And Roosevelt was anxious to get Americans into the fighting. In July 1942 the President agreed to confront the Nazis first in North Africa, where General Erwin Rommel, the "Desert Fox," had made dramatic gains and was threatening Egypt and the Suez Canal. General Dwight D. Eisenhower was placed in command of the operation.

In November 1942, Anglo-American troops landed in Morocco and Algeria. Vichy French controlled the area, and General Mark Clark made a quiet and controversial agreement with the collaborationist French leaders to join the fight against the Axis powers. In Tripoli, to the east, British troops under General Bernard C. Montgomery were advancing westward, and it was hoped that the Axis forces would be caught in an Allied vice. After five months of often fierce fighting, the efforts of American and British ground, air, and naval forces proved successful. German troops were driven out of North Africa, the Italian army was decimated, over a quarter million enemy troops were captured, and the Mediterranean was opened to the Allies. Two American generals, Omar Bradley and George S. Patton, Jr., played distinguished roles in the North African victory.

In January 1943, Roosevelt and Churchill met in Casablanca to determine future strategy. They agreed to demand "unconditional surrender" from the Axis powers and to attack Sicily. The idea was to keep pressure on Hitler while preparations were made for an eventual invasion across the English channel. The Allies pushed northward in July. The collapse of the Italian Army in Sicily drove Mussolini from power, and Italy surrendered on September 3. Allied troops quickly moved into Italy, facing powerful German forces. The struggle proved extraordinarily difficult and destructive. Nazi resistance and blunders by the Allied command at Anzio, just south of Rome, for example, resulted in costly losses. German forces did not surrender until May 1945.

Beginning in August 1942, American and British air forces bombarded German-occupied territory. In January 1943 the attacks began on Germany itself, knocking out numerous military installations, destroying whole cities,

D-Day invasion, June 6, 1944, "Into the Jaws of Death." Source: Courtesy of the Franklin D. Roosevelt Library

African American WACS hold an "open house" for black soldiers in Rouen, France in 1945. Source: National Archives

and doing great damage to the nation's industries. By the end of that year, more than 2,100 bombers a day were being dispatched from British air fields. In early 1944, a single raid against aircraft factories in central Germany contained one thousand bombers; in one week Allied bombers dropped 10,000 tons of bombs. Berlin was first hit in March 1944. The Germans bitterly resisted the raids, and losses in air battles were often heavy. In one six-day period, the Eighth Air Force lost 148 bombers and crews.

The Allies were in control of the air by the time they were ready for the cross-Channel invasion. D-Day, June 6, 1944, "the longest day," was the largest military operation in history. The surprise attack on the beaches of Normandy involved nearly 3 million men, 4,000 landing craft, 600 warships, and some 11,000 aircraft. Allied losses were often horrendous, especially among the Americans at Omaha Beach. But solid planning by Supreme Commander Dwight D. Eisenhower and the courage and skill of untold numbers of troops proved successful.

During June and July, the Allies swarmed into France, moving slowly against fierce Nazi resistance. On July 25, following devastating air bombardment, the First Army broke through German lines. An invasion on the French Mediterranean coast in mid-August struck the Germans from behind. Paris was liberated on August 25, and the Allies headed toward the Rhine. By October Americans were on German soil.

The Pacific War

Japanese forces struck quickly after Pearl Harbor, taking Guam, Wake Island, and Hong Kong in December and Singapore and Java in early 1942. Following heroic American resistance at Bataan, the Philippines fell in May. Japan hoped eventually to control all of East Asia.

Although concentrating on the war in Europe, the Allies made several determined efforts to block Japanese aggression. This was largely an American effort; General Douglas MacArthur served as the supreme commander of the southwest Pacific area, and Admiral Chester W. Nimitz headed naval forces in the central Pacific.

In May 1942, at the Battle of the Coral Sea, planes aboard American aircraft carriers blocked the Japanese drive toward Australia. This was the first naval battle in history fought entirely from the air, with the contending surface craft never seeing each other. The Battle of Midway, in June, was a major victory for Nimitz, stopping the Japanese advance and permitting the start of a limited and costly Allied offensive.

American marines landed in Guadalcanal in August 1942, and a fierce struggle lasted six months before the Japanese conceded defeat. In 1943, the Allies scored major victories in New Guinea, New Georgia, and the Solomon Islands and at Tarawa in the Gilbert Islands. Casualties at Bougainville, the largest of the Solomons, and at heavily defended Tarawa, were high. But both victories gave the Allies valuable air bases.

In 1944 the Allies invaded the Marshall Islands, the Admiralty Islands, Hollandia in Dutch New Guinea, the Marianas Islands, the Palaus Islands, and the Philippines. In October the massive Battle of Leyte Gulf, in the Philippines, gave control of the Pacific to the Allies.

Japanese losses were particularly severe. Over 50,000 Japanese died in the effort to retain the Marianas. In two days of the "Battle of the Philippine Sea," Japan lost three carriers and about four hundred planes. At Leyte, the Allies destroyed much of what was left of Japan's air and sea power. So desperate were the Japanese that in October they began *kamikaze* attacks, suicide missions by pilots against enemy targets.

Successful island hopping gave the Allies the means to launch large-scale air invasions of Japan, which commenced from Saipan in November 1944. At the same time, American submarines were greatly damaging the Japanese economy, sinking 776 ships in 1943–44. Military planners envisioned a land invasion of Japan in 1947–48. Having experienced the ferocity of Japanese troops, they feared that victory alone might cost a million American casualties.

The Election of 1944

Roosevelt, exhausted and ill, accepted the Democratic nomination for a fourth term "as a good soldier." After some confusion about his preference for a running mate, liberal Henry Wallace was replaced by Senate insider Harry Truman of Missouri, whose support of postwar peace treaties could prove crucial. The GOP selected 42-year-old Thomas E. Dewey, the governor of New York. As Dewey was an internationalist with some liberal leanings, Republicans balanced the ticket geographically and ideologically with John W. Bricker of Ohio.

FDR spoke out for internationalism and postwar liberal reform, proving on several occasions that he remained an effective campaigner. In October, to demonstrate his physical stamina, he rode through New York all day in an open car through pouring rain. The consequences to his health were probably severe. Organized labor, in particular the CIO, gave the president strong and unprecedented support. Dewey proved largely ineffective on the stump, generally endorsing the New Deal and the nation's foreign policy. At times he resorted to linking the president with communism.

Roosevelt won at the polls by a margin of 3.6 million (down from 5 million in 1940), carried thirty-six states, and took the electoral college 462–99. Democrats picked up twenty-two seats in the House and lost one in the Senate. America had decided to stick with its commander in chief.

Wartime Diplomacy

Roosevelt wanted the four great powers—the United States, the United Kingdom, the Soviet Union, and China—to work in harmony to achieve the lofty Allied war aims expressed in the Atlantic Charter. His relations with English Prime Minister Churchill were generally good. Joseph Stalin, being a Communist and having an intense desire to gain control of territories on his nation's western border, posed difficulties. But Roosevelt thought that he and the Russian dictator could work things out face to face. FDR had an unshakable confidence in his own ability to charm.

China was a world power largely because Roosevelt thought it necessary. The Nationalist government led by Chiang Kai-shek was exhausted, unpopular, corrupt, and deeply concerned about the growing strength of Chinese communists. Driven into the interior by the Japanese, the Chinese government relied on American aid transported from India through Burma and by air. During 1943–44, while Chinese troops struggled against the Japanese in Burma, top American military advisers lost confidence in Chiang and his government. General Joseph W. Stilwell was recalled after bitter quarrels with the Chinese leader.

Chiang was present at the Cairo conference in November 1943 with Roosevelt and Churchill. A few days later at Tehran, Stalin met with Roosevelt and Churchill for the first time. Military strategy dominated these discussions, and at Tehran Stalin was promised a cross-channel invasion within six months. The Big Three seemed united and confident.

During 1944 the Allies discussed postwar territorial settlements and loans, and laid plans for a United Nations. The major wartime conference of the

Big Three occurred at Yalta in the Crimea, February 4–12, 1945. By then George Patton's Third Army had repelled a German counteroffensive at the fearsome Battle of the Bulge, and the Allies were headed for the Rhine. Russian armies had been fighting their way across central Europe and the Balkans, suffering tremendous losses but doing great damage to the Nazi war machine. Moving with unexpected speed, the Russians reached the Oder River, well within Germany, in late January 1945.

At Yalta, participants squabbled at length about the future of Poland. Stalin was unyielding in his demands to expand Russian authority, but he promised prompt and free elections throughout liberated eastern Europe. General principles of German reparations were established, and separate zones of German occupation were confirmed. In a secret agreement, Stalin endorsed a voting formula for the United Nations and won three seats in the United Nations Assembly. To secure Russian participation in the attack on Japan, Roosevelt and Churchill made secret concessions including the restoration of properties lost in the Russo-Japanese War of 1904–5. Stalin promised to enter the Pacific war two or three months after Germany's surrender.

Critics later would complain of a "sell-out" to the Soviets at Yalta, some noting FDR's ill health and presumed incompetence, some claiming that he was duped by procommunist advisers. Historians have generally dismissed this interpretation. While FDR's penchant for secrecy is debatable, the major decisions at the conference were based solidly on military realities of the time. Only a war with the Soviets, then unthinkable, could have freed Poland from Stalin's grip. Moreover, it was not FDR's fault that Stalin later ignored his commitment to free elections in eastern Europe. Roosevelt and Churchill came away from Yalta optimistic about Allied unity and of their ability to end the war as quickly as possible.

Victory in Europe

By March, Americans were on the Rhine, and Soviet troops closing in from the east continued to wreak destruction on Nazi forces. The hope that flowed from the Yalta conference soon dissipated, however, as Stalin began to make an assortment of charges against the United States and Great Britain and install procommunist governments in eastern Europe. Shortly before his death, on April 12, Roosevelt told Churchill of his deep concern about the Soviet attitude toward world peace.

Churchill worried about the postwar implications of Soviet gains in Europe. But Supreme Commander Eisenhower rejected the British Prime Minister's pleas to outrace the Russians to Berlin and Prague, preferring to concentrate on the destruction of the Nazi war machine. President Harry Truman, inexperienced and uninformed by Roosevelt about international developments, declined to overrule this strategy. He shared the desire of millions to end the war as swiftly as possible. The unspeakable horrors of the Holocaust, discovered by advancing Allied troops as they encountered German concentration camps, strengthened this resolve.

Pounded from the air ("terror" bombing in Dresden leveled the once beautiful city and killed 60,000 or more), encircled by Allied troops, and guided by self-destructive orders issued by Hitler, the Nazis collapsed in mid-April. American and Russian armies met at Torgau on the Elbe on the twenty-fifth. Five days later, Hitler committed suicide in his Berlin bunker. His globe, discovered by the Soviets, was emblazoned with a huge swastika. Over Russia were the words, "I am coming." Over North America, Hitler had written, "I will be there soon." Germany formally signed an unconditional surrender on May 8.

The fledgling United Nations got under way even before the war in Europe officially concluded. On April 25 delegates from fifty nations gathered in San Francisco to endorse a charter. President Truman signed the document on June 26 and two days later it sailed through the Senate with only two dissenting votes. The United States had now made a strong commitment to participate fully in international affairs.

In mid-July, President Truman and Secretary of State James F. Byrnes flew to Potsdam, a suburb of Berlin, to attend the last great wartime conference. (Winston Churchill was defeated at the polls during the meetings and was replaced by Clement R. Attlee.) At Potsdam the Allies sparred for control of the Pacific war, set Poland's boundaries (which necessitated the resettlement of millions of Germans), and established the four postwar occupation zones of Germany, Berlin, Vienna, and Austria conceived at Yalta. Each Allied power was permitted to seize reparations from its occupation zone. Controversy later erupted over a concession to the Soviet Union permitting it to strip much industrial equipment in the western zones of Germany in exchange for agricultural and natural products from its own zone.

At Potsdam, it was becoming clear that the Soviets and the Allies were prepared to disagree on a great many things after the shooting stopped. Stalin staunchly refused, for example, to let the Allies meddle in the affairs of Eastern Europe, which he now controlled. Still, leaders expressed optimism that the Allies would stick together and work things out amicably.

During the conference, Truman learned of the successful explosion of an atomic bomb at Alamogordo, New Mexico. Since late 1941 the United States had quietly spent some $2 billion to develop an atomic bomb. The top secret (not even Vice President Truman knew) Manhattan Project was led by the brilliant physicist J. Robert Oppenheimer. On June 1, as the theoretical seemed increasingly possible, a special committee of civilians close to the Manhattan Project had advised the president to use the bomb against Japan as soon as possible.

At Potsdam, Truman mentioned the atomic bomb in general terms to Stalin. The Soviet leader said little in response and did not ask for details. We now know that Stalin had spies in the Manhattan Project and was well informed about developments in New Mexico. Indeed, the Russians were developing a bomb of their own.

On July 26, Truman, Churchill, and Chiang Kai-shek (reached by telephone) issued the Potsdam Declaration, which again demanded Japan's unconditional surrender, promised reprisals against "war criminals," but added that Japan would not be "enslaved as a race nor destroyed as a nation." The Japanese premier ignored the ultimatum, calling it "unworthy of public notice." Convinced that Japanese militarists were in control and would fight to the end, Truman chose to proceed with plans to drop atomic bombs without warning on Japan. Some presidential advisers, including Byrnes, were persuaded that this course of action would also help the United States in postwar negotiations with the Soviet Union. But this consideration was not foremost in Truman's mind.

Victory in Asia

The savage fighting on the tiny Pacific islands of Iwo Jima and Okinawa in the winter and spring of 1945 foretold how bloody the invasion of Japan would be. The marines suffered 20,000 casualties at Iwo Jima before four marines (a scene captured in the war's most famous photograph) raised the American flag on Mount Suribachi. There were 39,000 American casualties at Okinawa, and thirty-four ships went down. The Japanese lost 110,000 men on Okinawa and sacrificed some 3,500 kamikaze planes. Military strategists could only shudder at the magnitude of the death and destruction that lay ahead.

Raising the flag at Iwo Jima, February 23, 1945. Source: National Archives

In early 1945 every major American military leader thought that Russian troops would be needed to conquer Japan. By June and July, however, some changed their mind. Bombing raids over Japan had been devastating, prompting some army air force leaders to conclude that the war might be won without a land invasion. Raids over Tokyo during a single night, March 9–10, had destroyed a quarter of the city's buildings and killed perhaps 100,000 people. During July, B-29 Superfortresses flew 1,200 sorties a week over Japan. Submarine attacks were also proving highly effective. But Truman and his advisers were convinced that the atomic bomb was needed to bring the war to a rapid halt.

In early August only enough material was available to assemble two atomic bombs. On August 6 the B-29 *Enola Gay* dropped the first of them on Hiroshima. Having the power of 20,000 tons of TNT, the bomb killed between 70,000 and 80,000 people and injured as many more. About 4.4 square miles of the city were turned to rubble. Two days later, Russia entered the war against Japan.

Threatening further devastation from the air, President Truman called on Japanese leaders to surrender. When a positive response did not appear, a second bomb was dropped on August 9 on Nagasaki. Casualties included some 35,000 dead, 5,000 missing, and 60,000 injured. The next day, on a direct order from the emperor, the Japanese government sued for peace. On August 14 both sides agreed on the terms of surrender. The Japanese formally surrendered on September 2, 1945, in a memorable ceremony aboard the battleship *Missouri.* The Second World War was over.

Then and since, the decision to drop atomic bombs has been challenged. Some have thought it unnecessary, excessively cruel, even politically motivated. It is, of course, a terrible burden to be the first and only nation to have used such weapons in battle. At the time, however, Harry Truman justified the action in words that were cheered by war-weary Americans:

> having found the bomb we have used it. We have used it against those who attacked us without warning at Pearl Harbor, against those who have starved and beaten and executed American prisoners of war, against those who have abandoned the pretense of obeying international laws of warfare. We have used it in order to shorten the agony of war, in order to save the lives of thousands and thousands of young Americans.

The world war killed 322,000 Americans and injured another 800,000. These figures pale, however, when compared with the untold tens of millions of soldiers and civilians who died in Europe and Asia. Russia lost perhaps 26 million people; Poland, nearly 6 million; Germany, 4.2 million; Japan, almost 2 million. More than 15 million died in the deliberate and well-calculated genocide called the Holocaust. About 6 million out of an estimated 8.3 million Jews living in German-occupied territory were exterminated after 1939. It has been estimated that at Auschwitz-Birkenau alone the total number of victims was 2.5 million Jews and 500,000 others gassed and incinerated.

The destruction and devastation greatly exceeded that of World War I. Direct military costs were estimated at a trillion dollars; property damage reached perhaps $800 billion. The United States treasury spent $625 billion. No one can even guess at the costs throughout the world in human suffering. The bitter fruits of both world wars stood in sharp contrast to earlier views of human goodness and inevitable progress.

From the ashes, however, grew a firm determination by millions to rebuild cities and nations, to resist evil ideologies and tyrants, and to do whatever was necessary to restore peace and prosperity to one of the darkest centuries in history. True, many now worried about nuclear conflagration, for the ingredients of the atomic bomb could not be kept secret forever. But there were still optimists who believed that thoughtful men and women of good will could control the use of such weapons. Indeed, there was no positive alternative.

SUGGESTED READING

Karen Anderson, *Wartime Women* (1981); A. Russell Buchanan, *The United States and World War II*, 2 vols (1964); James M. Burns, *Roosevelt: The Soldier of Freedom* (1970); Justus D. Doenecke, *The Battle Against Intervention, 1939–1941* (1997); Dwight D. Eisenhower, *Crusade in Europe* (1948); Richard Polenberg, *War and Society: The United States, 1941–1945* (1972); Robert Jan van Pelt and Deborah Dwork, *Auschwitz: 1270 to the Present* (1996); J. Samuel Walker, *Prompt and Utter Destruction: President Truman and the Use of Atomic Bombs Against Japan* (1997); Roberta Wohlstetter, *Pearl Harbor: Warning and Decision* (1962); Neil A. Wynn, *The Afro-Americans and the Second World War* (1976).

Chapter Eight

POSTWAR CHALLENGES

A
t war's end some 12 million GIs were eager to return home, get a job, raise a family, and begin buying the things that all Americans had done without for years. Some critics predicted depression-like conditions in 1946 as industry weaned itself from government contracts and attempted to meet the demand for goods and services. But it was soon evident that the economy was strong and that business could make the necessary adjustments. In the five years that followed the war, the gross national product climbed from $213 billion to $284 billion, and national income rose from $181 billion to $241 billion.

Automobiles were snapped up as quickly as they came off the assembly lines. Electrical appliances, including refrigerators and garbage disposals, proved extremely popular. A million television sets were produced in 1948. Massive housing developments sprang up in the suburbs, providing single-family dwellings at affordable prices. In 1948, developer William Levitt opened Levittown on Long Island, which set the pattern. Levitt offered mass-produced two-bedroom homes, complete with kitchen appliances and a washing machine, for under $7,000 apiece. Critics sneered at the look-alike, "ticky tack" houses, but they proved popular. Three years later, Levittown contained over 17,000 homes.

Marriage and the family were high priorities in the postwar years. In 1940 only 42 percent of all 18- to 24-year-old women were married. By 1950 the figure had risen to nearly 60 percent. Birthrates soared, starting a generation labeled the "baby boomers." In 1945 the birthrate per 1,000 women ages 15 to 44 was 20.4. The following year it rose to 24.1, with a total of 3.4 million births. Total births would average more than 4 million annually for the next seventeen years.

Liberals and conservatives differed greatly about the role of government in the postwar period. The GI Bill of Rights set an example to millions of the positive force government could be. Passed in 1944, this legislation provided veterans with educational expenses, loans, and unemployment compensation. Nearly eight million GIs pursued some form of schooling, at a cost to taxpayers of $14.5 billion. The college population soared from 1.4 million in 1940 to 3.2 million in 1960. This program had profound effects on higher education, expanding its facilities and moving it steadily toward more practical and occupational goals.

President Truman

Harry Truman, 62, had come from a Missouri farm family. Lacking a college education, he was known to be intelligent and well read as well as hard working, honest, religious, and self-confident. Critics were quick to point out that he lacked the Roosevelt charm, style, and public relations expertise. On both the left and right there were sneers at "that little piano player in the White House."

Truman had entered politics in 1921 after the failure of a clothing store. He had become an efficient public official, despite serving the notorious Pendergast machine in Kansas City. He entered the Senate in 1934 as a committed New Dealer and won distinction during the war chairing a special Senate investigating committee that exposed graft and waste. Now chief executive, Truman had ambitious plans for using government to meet the many postwar needs of the American people.

On September 16, 1945, the president submitted to Congress a progressive twenty-one-point program. He soon made additions to his requests. Among other things, Truman sought to raise the minimum wage from 40 to 65 cents an hour, ensure full employment, expand social security, retain price and wage controls, continue price controls for farmers, clear slums, extend federal aid to education, and eventually create a national health insurance program.

Congress, weary of big government and increasingly conservative, was not prepared for such venturesome projects. Moreover, soaring inflation (prices jumped 25 percent in two years) and massive labor unrest eroded public confidence in the president. In 1946 there were 4,985 work stoppages involving 4.6 million workers. When John L. Lewis led his United Mine Workers out on strike that spring, badly crippling the economy, Truman ordered government seizure of the mines. When two railway unions went out, Truman threatened to draft strikers into the army.

Truman supporters could point to the Full Employment Act of 1946. This landmark legislation committed the federal government to the maintenance of maximum employment and created a Council of Economic Advisers to assist the president. Truman's Civil Rights Commission placed the issue of race on the national agenda.

Still, by mid-1946 millions of Americans thought Truman confused, inconsistent, and ineffective. The President's quick temper, blunt speech, and often poor choice of advisers contributed to this negative image. "Too err is

Truman," said Republicans. That fall, they asked "Had Enough?" and won majorities in the Senate and House for the first time since 1930.

For the next two years Truman called repeatedly for liberal reforms, stressing housing and anti-inflation legislation. When little was achieved, he blamed the Eightieth "do-nothing" Congress. In mid-1947, the president vetoed the conservative Taft-Hartley bill, which he called the "slave-labor" bill. The legislation, among other things, outlawed the closed shop (a contract requiring union membership as a precondition for employment), banned secondary boycotts, required unions to make annual statements of their finances, compelled union leaders to take an oath that they were not Communists, and permitted the president to invoke an eighty-day "cooling off" period to delay strikes that might endanger the nation. Congress overrode the veto, but Truman's action earned him the support of organized labor and millions of average Americans who were persuaded that the plainspoken man in the White House was on their side.

Truman also won friends among African Americans. In early 1948, he advocated the most ambitious civil rights program ever proposed by a president. Among other things, the president sought voting protections, protections against lynchings, a permanent Commission on Civil Rights, and a permanent Federal Employment Protections Commission. The conservative Democrat-Republican coalition in Congress rejected the proposals. That July Truman ordered the desegregation of the military and established a committee charged with ending discrimination in the federal civil service.

THE COLD WAR

The cordiality that existed between the United States and the Soviet Union during the war was short-lived. The two nations had long been at odds. American leaders, for example, had not forgiven the Communists for pulling Russia out of World War I, attacking capitalism during the depression, and forging the cynical pact with Hitler in 1938. Soviet leaders contended that America had tried to subvert the Bolshevik Revolution in 1918 by sending troops into Russian territory. They resented their long exclusion from international affairs. (The United States did not extend diplomatic recognition until 1933.) The Soviets harbored strong doubts about the length of time the Allies took to mount a second front against the Nazis. And they boiled over American reluctance to extend aid and loans in 1945.

But at the heart of the clash was an irreconcilable issue: The Soviet Union was committed to the Marxist-Leninist dream of a world under communism. Permanent coexistence with democracy and capitalism was impossible. Moreover, Josef Stalin, one of history's greatest murderers, was determined to be the ruler of this global empire. Historian John Lewis Gaddis has argued that as long as Stalin was running the Soviet Union, the Cold War was inevitable.

Predictably, the two nations disagreed strongly about the future of postwar Europe. The United States expressed the desire to let Europeans choose their own leaders, hoping they would be allies. The Soviets were determined to control lands they had conquered, both to exploit their economic resources and to seal off avenues for future Western invasions. Throughout 1946 and 1947, the Soviets installed Communist governments in Poland, Hungary, Rumania, and Bulgaria. Winston Churchill, in a speech in Fulton, Missouri, on March 5, 1946, declared, "From Stettin in the Baltic to Trieste in the Adriatic, an iron curtain has descended across the [European] Continent." These words officially marked the beginning of the Cold War.

The Truman Doctrine

Harry Truman, who accompanied Churchill to Missouri, was persuaded by this time that the Soviets were as ruthless as the Nazis. As he wrestled with the enormously complex problems facing Europe, he reversed his initially favorable impression of Stalin, and became convinced that the Russian dictator was merely out to grab what he could. The United States had a moral duty, Truman believed, to protect a war-weary world from atheistic, imperialistic communism.

Truman was soon aided in formulating his views by three extraordinary public servants. General George C. Marshall, a major figure in the recent Allied victory and a man of strength and integrity, became secretary of state in January 1947. Two of his subordinates, diplomat and scholar George F. Kennan and the brilliant attorney and bureaucrat Dean Acheson, were highly informed critics of the Soviets. In the spring of 1947, the United States launched a policy of *containment*, a term coined by Kennan in a historic article in the journal *Foreign Affairs*. This meant steady, firm resistance to communist expansion.

The initial step in this direction was taken in February 1947 when the British informed Washington they could no longer afford to protect Greece and Turkey. Greece was threatened by communist insurgents. Turkey was under pressure from the Soviets who were eager for joint sovereignty over the Turkish straits. Truman requested $400 million from Congress and declared what became known as the Truman Doctrine. "I believe," he said, "that it must be the policy of the United States to support free peoples who are resisting attempted subjugation by armed minorities or by outside pressures." Congress, warned that communism might spread throughout the world if it failed to act, quickly approved. American action proved successful in both Greece and Turkey.

Initially, the Truman Doctrine was designed to apply only to the two countries in question and perhaps Eastern Europe in general. But as the Cold War heated up, the policy would be expanded to apply to the entire globe. Anywhere pro-American governments found themselves under communist attack, the United States might be obligated to come to the rescue, regardless of local circumstances and even if the government under siege was not committed to democracy.

The Marshall Plan

Economic aid was a vital part of the containment policy. On June 5, 1947, Secretary Marshall announced a plan to help all European nations, including the Soviet Union, recover from the war. (The Soviets and their satellites, as Truman and Marshall no doubt expected, refused to participate.) The proposal was idealistic; Marshall declared, "Our policy is not directed against any country or doctrine, but against hunger, poverty, desperation and chaos." In fact, it was also designed to halt the spread of communism and to provide markets for American goods. The communist seizure of power in Czechoslovakia in March 1948 helped persuade Congress to endorse the Marshall Plan. From 1948 to 1951, the United States gave $13 billion worth of money, services, and goods—an amount equivalent to at least $88 billion in 1997.

This spending contributed greatly to the rapid economic recovery of Western Europe. Two other free-market economic reforms were also vital: the liberalization of commerce under the General Agreement on Tariffs and Trade, and the stabilization of currencies established in 1945 and fully implemented in 1948. Five countries that both received significant aid and joined GATT had annual average GNP growth of 8.3 percent from 1947 through 1955 and average unemployment of 2.6 percent. Europe's per capita GNP rose by a third between 1948 and 1951.

The Marshall Plan also helped fulfill America's political objectives in Western Europe. France and Italy ejected the Communists from their coalition governments, and Austria soon freed itself from Soviet influence.

In 1949 Truman proposed a Point Four Program for the world's underdeveloped nations, struggling to combat poverty and communist insurgency. In the early 1950s Congress appropriated modest funding that helped thirty Latin America, African, and Asian nations improve their economies, largely through scientific and technological assistance.

North Atlantic Treaty Organization

The third step in the policy of containment was the creation of the North Atlantic Treaty Organization (NATO). This grew out of fears by Western Europeans of a possible Soviet attack. The NATO treaty, signed on April 4, 1949, by ten European nations, Canada, and the United States, stated that "an armed attack against one or more shall be considered an attack against them all." American membership in NATO marked the first formal departure from the nation's tradition of refusing to enter into entangling alliances with foreign nations. In 1950 Truman named General Eisenhower to be supreme commander of NATO and sent four American divisions to Europe to serve as the body's major force.

Greece and Turkey joined NATO in 1952, and when West Germany was granted full membership in 1955 the Soviet Union and seven satellite states in Eastern Europe formed a similar alliance called the Warsaw Pact. Both sides were fully prepared for combat.

THE COLD WAR AT HOME

Anticommunism dominated much of the activity in Washington during the Truman administration. The National Security Act of 1947 created a new Department of Defense, the National Security Council (NSC), and the Central Intelligence Agency (CIA). The civilian secretary of defense, who had cabinet rank, would now supervise all military operations. The NSC, which included the secretary of state, the secretary of defense, and the service secretaries, advised the president on national security matters. The CIA was a top-secret intelligence-gathering agency. These innovations increased the power of the White House and made the president the key player in the nation's anticommunist efforts.

An Executive Order of March 21, 1947, created a tough new loyalty security program for the executive branch designed to weed out Communists and their sympathizers. The FBI and a variety of loyalty boards hunted diligently for evidence of disloyalty. Grounds for denying employment or dismissal from office were at times vague and included "sympathetic association with" an organization or group declared by the Attorney General to be totalitarian, fascist, communist, or subversive. The accused were denied basic legal rights. Historian Henry Steele Commager called the Truman program "an invitation to precisely that kind of witch-hunting which is repugnant to our constitutional system."

The loyalty-security program was in part a reaction to well-grounded fears of communism. Charges of domestic subversion were gaining widespread attention in 1947. FBI Director J. Edgar Hoover branded the (still legal) Communist party a "fifth column" and waged a campaign against members and fellow travelers. The House Committee on Un-American Activities (HUAC) made sensational headlines with charges of communist propaganda in the movie industry. Labor unions were actively purging their leadership of Reds and their allies.

The hunt for subversives also had to do with politics. Politicians of both parties were eager to ward off charges that they were "soft" on the Reds. The loyalty-security program was a way of proving that Truman and the Democrats were vigilant as well as patriotic. The higher the number of employees fired, the more the administration could boast. By 1951, more than 2,000 government employees had resigned and 212 were dismissed. None of those removed was found guilty of overt actions against the government; all were judged on the future likelihood of disloyal activity based on past associations, attitudes, even their "basic philosophy."

However inadvertently, and despite much rhetoric to the contrary, the Truman administration and its allies in Congress helped lay the foundation for the Second Red Scare and the excesses of Joe McCarthy.

THE BERLIN BLOCKADE

In mid-1948 Stalin made a move in Germany that intensified anticommunism throughout the West. After the war, Germany had been divided into zones. The United States, England, and France now planned to merge their zones to create the West German Republic. This merger included the zones allocated in the important city of Berlin, located 100 miles within the Soviet zone and linked to the West by a highway. On June 24 the Soviets blockaded the western sectors of Berlin, shutting off traffic by land and water. Stalin was intent on humiliating the Western powers and preventing the creation of West Germany.

Truman responded with a round-the-clock airlift, bringing food, fuel, and supplies to the more than two million West Berliners. To send Stalin a further message, he moved sixty B-29s, planes capable of dropping atomic bombs, to London. (They were not armed with nuclear weapons, but Stalin presumably did not know this.) After a tense fifteen months and 278,228 flights—an average of 599 per day, 25 an hour—by U.S., British, and French planes, the Soviets backed down. This was Stalin's first defeat of the Cold War, and it convinced Truman and many other Americans of the importance of fortitude in the face of Soviet aggression. The scare helped lead to the creation of NATO.

THE ELECTION OF 1948

Truman captured his party's nomination only after a struggle. One group of prominent liberals appealed unsuccessfully to Dwight Eisenhower to be the standard bearer. The president had to threaten and woo many other Democrats. He was not without support. Jewish leaders, for example, were enthusiastic because in May the president had recognized the new state of Israel—eleven minutes after independence was declared. Civil rights leaders were on the whole positive, as were union leaders. But Truman was not able fully to revive the coalition that Roosevelt had forged.

After the convention, defections soon decreased Truman's chances for victory. Some Democrats on the far left went for Henry Wallace, who ran as a third-party candidate. They were disappointed with Truman's promotion of domestic programs and opposed his hard-line approach toward the Soviet Union. On the right, "Dixiecrats," angry about advances in civil rights and the strong civil rights plank adopted by Democrats, backed the States' Rights ticket headed by South Carolina governor Strom Thurmond.

Republicans again nominated Thomas E. Dewey, the moderate and popular governor of New York. A GOP landslide was widely predicted, and in late September pollsters stopped taking surveys. Undaunted, Truman hit the campaign trail by train, traveling nearly 32,000 miles and giving 356 speeches. He blamed Congress and the Republicans for the nation's ills and called for an assortment of government programs to help the "common man." He took

a bold position on civil rights and was the first president to campaign in
Harlem. Truman's message and his rather awkward earnestness proved popular. Before long, cries could be heard from crowds, "Give 'em hell, Harry."

On election day, Truman stunned the experts by defeating Dewey handily, 49.5 percent to 45 percent, and carrying the electoral college 303 to 189.
It was the greatest upset in the history of presidential elections. Democrats
also won both houses of Congress.

Republicans, reeling from their fifth consecutive losing bid for the White
House, vowed to do whatever was necessary to regain power. A major
weapon in their assault would be the charge that the Truman administration
and the Democratic party were loaded with Communists and Communist
sympathizers. (Some conservative and fearful Democrats joined this effort.)
Developments, at home and abroad, soon persuaded millions that the allegation was true.

POSTELECTION SHOCKS

Several days after the election, Whittaker Chambers accused Alger Hiss, president of the Carnegie Endowment, of espionage. Both men became interna-
tionally known in August during HUAC hearings. Chambers, a senior editor
of *Time* magazine, had been a Communist spy in the federal government
during the 1930s, and he accused Hiss of belonging to the Communist party
at the same time. Chambers now claimed that Hiss, a former State Department official and the embodiment of New Deal, liberal establishment re-
spectability, had been a spy. President Truman and many prominent liberals, including Eleanor Roosevelt, Dean Acheson, and Adlai Stevenson, sided
with Hiss. HUAC member Richard Nixon and a large number of conservatives championed Chambers. Hiss sued Chambers for slander.

In mid-November, Chambers produced typed and microfilmed copies of
State Department documents he said Hiss had turned over to him. There
were also items written in Hiss's own hand. The statute of limitations had
expired on spying charges, but a federal grand jury indicted Hiss on two
counts of perjury on the basis of statements he made under oath in August.
A national uproar ensued.

While the Hiss case ground through the courts in 1949, the public was
jolted by the arrest, in March, of Judith Coplon, a Department of Justice employee charged with being a Soviet spy. In September, Russia exploded its
first atomic bomb, prompting charges that spies had provided Stalin with vital information. In October, eleven top leaders of the American Communist
party were convicted of violating the Smith Act, the first peacetime sedition
law since 1798. In December, communists took over China, and Chiang Kai-
shek and his government fled China to Formosa. Conservative critics claimed
that this was the result of subversive activity within the State Department.
(In fact, the United States had given the corrupt and inept Chiang govern-

ment more than $2 billion since the war in order to prop up resistance to the popular Chinese communists.)

"The shocks of 1949," historian Eric Goldman wrote later, "loosed within American life a vast impatience, a turbulent bitterness, a rancor akin to revolt. It was a strange rebelliousness, quite without parallel in the history of the United States." By November 1949, 68 percent of the American people wanted to outlaw the Communist party.

When Alger Hiss was convicted of perjury in January 1950, most understood that the real crime involved was espionage. Hiss and the Ivy League New Dealers he represented were dealt a severe blow. This impression was compounded when Dean Acheson, now secretary of state, said that he would not turn his back on his old friend. Despite Hiss's assertion of innocence until his death in late 1996, solid studies by Allen Weinstein in 1978 and Sam Tanenhaus in 1997 left little doubt that he had been a spy.

Soon after the Hiss conviction, President Truman announced work on the hydrogen bomb, a weapon far more powerful than its nuclear predecessor. Three days later, Dr. Klaus Fuchs, a British physicist who had worked on the Manhattan Project, was arrested as a Soviet spy. Further investigations led to David Greenglass, another employee in New Mexico, and his sister and brother-in-law, Julius and Ethel Rosenberg. The Rosenbergs were executed in 1953. (In 1997 it was learned for the first time that Theodore Alvin Hall, a young Harvard-trained physicist with the Manhattan Project, had been the major culprit in the espionage effort.) In March, Judith Coplon and So-

Alger Hiss gives sworn testimony before the HUAC. Source: Archive Photos

viet agent Valentin Gubitchev were convicted of spying. FBI Director J. Edgar Hoover warned that the United States contained 540,000 Communists and fellow travelers. Screaming headlines warned daily of Red subversion and world conquest.

THE FAIR DEAL

In January 1949, the president announced a package of progressive proposals he labeled the "Fair Deal." Congress, controlled by conservative southern Democrats and Republicans, was less than enthusiastic. In the first two years of Truman's second term, Congress passed a hike in the minimum wage from 40 to 75 cents an hour, an increase in Social Security benefits and coverage, and a major public housing law. The president failed to win passage of proposals in the areas of health, education, agriculture, and civil rights.

THE KOREAN WAR

The Fair Deal was effectively shut down in June 1950 by the invasion of pro-Western South Korea by communist North Korea. Suddenly American boys were being sent to Asia, under the United Nations flag, to fight what Truman called "a police action." It was an undeclared war that we apparently could not win. Many on the right again blamed Reds in high places.

Soviet troops had entered strategically located Korea soon after declaring war against Japan at the end of World War II. The Soviets agreed to accept the surrender of Japanese forces north of the thirty-eighth parallel of latitude, while the United States accepted the surrender south of the line. The industrialized north contained 9 million people, while the largely agrarian south had a population of some 21 million.

In 1948, the United Nations called for free elections in Korea. The Soviets refused, installing a heavily armed communist government. Elections were held in the South, under U.N. supervision, and Syngman Rhee headed the Republic of Korea. The Soviets withdrew in 1948, and America pulled out in the following year. The sudden invasion by the North, on June 24, 1950, was an effort to conquer the entire peninsula. The Soviets attempted to conceal their backing of the North Koreans, but American leaders were not fooled. (The approval by Stalin and China's Mao Zedung was confirmed by North Korean officials in 1990. In 1995, scholars learned that Stalin had urged China to send troops into North Korea in early October 1950, a week before they were dispatched. In 1997, it became known that Soviet interrogators got valuable information out of the more than 200 captured American fliers.)

Truman quickly sent assistance and appealed to the United Nations to restore peace. Because the Soviet Union was boycotting the Security Council at the time over another matter, American delegates were able to secure a resolution to aid Rhee. The resolution meant that aid from other countries would help the United States resist communist aggression, and it would forestall allegations of imperialistic motivation.

U.N. troops, sent from sixteen nations but largely American, were led by General Douglas MacArthur. At first they were pushed back to the southernmost tip of the peninsula. On September 15 a successful invasion at Inchon forced North Korean forces to return to the thirty-eighth parallel. Truman then gave MacArthur permission to move north, a daring attempt to unify the country. The Chinese stepped in, pouring waves of troops into North Korea. United Nations forces were again driven back, with heavy losses, deep into southern territory. In early 1951, the Chinese were back across the thirty-eighth parallel, and the war turned into a deadly stalemate.

MacArthur wanted to invade China, and when he made his intentions public, Truman, eager for a negotiated settlement, relieved him of his command. A firestorm of outrage against the president ensued. When MacArthur returned in triumph to the United States, eager himself for the White House, many Republicans gleefully amplified the General's intimations of Communist sympathies at the highest levels in Washington.

THE SECOND RED SCARE

The public's fear of spies, communist aggression, and nuclear war, combined with the willingness of politicians and their allies in the media and elsewhere to exploit these fears, produced the Second Red Scare. It can be dated from 1948 to 1957. From the upset presidential election and the most startling charges of the Hiss case to the calm that followed the reelection of Eisenhower, much of the country was embroiled in an anticommunist hysteria that surpassed the similar outbreak following World War I.

The Great Fear was felt in virtually all walks of American life. Untold numbers of Americans lost their jobs, their reputations, their freedoms, even their citizenship. In Hollywood, for example, actors and actresses suspected of Communist sympathies or actions were "blacklisted," made unemployable, in a few cases permanently. Loyalty oaths were required of millions. "Subversive" literature was banned and destroyed in untold numbers of local libraries. In 1949, thirty-eight states had general sedition laws and twenty-two states required oaths of allegiance for teachers. Several states had their own "un-American" activities committee. HUAC continued its probes.

In 1950, over Truman's veto, Congress passed the McCarran Act, designed to cripple the Communist party and all "Communist front" organizations. The law contained an emergency detention measure authorizing the attorney general to round up and detain those "he had reason to believe" might engage in subversive activities during a presidentially declared "internal security emergency." The "concentration-camp" proposal was made by liberals, frantic to prove their anticommunism.

Senator Joseph R. McCarthy of Wisconsin was the most visible proponent of the Red Scare. He gained national prominence in February 1950 from an irresponsible speech in Wheeling, West Virginia, in which he claimed that the State Department contained 205 Communists and that he and Secretary of State Dean Acheson knew their names. McCarthy had entered the Senate in 1946, and after much searching for an issue that would bring him fame, stumbled upon the Reds-in-high-places theme. Liberal political cartoonist Herbert Block (Herblock) labeled the Senator's reckless tactics "McCarthyism," and the term quickly caught on.

Joe McCarthy was a complex man, much beloved by those who knew him, much hated by those who stood in his way. At times this one-time farm boy could be generous, playful, loyal, and compassionate. He was highly intelligent (although undisciplined and poorly read), extroverted, hyperactive, and extraordinarily ambitious. The ambition brought out the dark side of his character, for McCarthy would lie, slander, cheat, bluff, and bully to gain popularity and win elections. At first, McCarthy saw the Red Scare as a ticket to the front pages. Soon, under the tutelage of an assortment of Red hunters, some zealous and some corrupt, he became a True Believer, making him all the more dangerous.

McCarthy fought carefully documented rebuttals of his charges by making more irresponsible allegations. He knew how to manipulate the media and

President Truman and fellow admirers seeing Secretary of State Dean Acheson off to a diplomatic conference. Source: National Park Service photograph courtesy of the Harry S. Truman Library

stay one step ahead of his critics. Far East expert and State Department adviser Owen Lattimore became the "top Soviet espionage agent" in America. General George Marshall and Dean Acheson were part of "a conspiracy on a scale so immense as to dwarf any previous such venture in the history of man." McCarthy also threatened opponents with political reprisals, illustrating his power by helping defeat a reelection bid by a major critic, veteran Democratic Senator Millard Tydings of Maryland.

From 1950 well into 1952, McCarthy was a formidable demagogue, enjoying national popularity. Truman and an assortment of liberals condemned him, but few others dared his wrath. Many Republicans thought that McCarthy and anticommunism would help them win the White House.

THE ELECTION OF 1952

At the conclusion of a bitter convention battle, the GOP nominated General Dwight D. Eisenhower on the first ballot to head the ticket. The 62-year-old war hero was a social conservative and an internationalist, much admired for his leadership ability, integrity, and powers of persuasion. Born in Denison, Texas, and raised in Abilene, Kansas, "Ike" had entered the U.S. Military Academy at West Point in 1911 and had served in the military all his life except for a brief stint as president of Columbia University. He was commander of NATO forces when moderate Republicans began to urge him to run for the White House. To please McCarthyites, Republicans nominated 39-year-old Richard Nixon as vice president.

The Korean stalemate, the Red Scare, and corruption in the administration lowered Truman's popularity to the point that he dropped out of the contest. After a wide-open contest for the nomination, Democrats nominated Governor Adlai Stevenson of Illinois. Stevenson was a witty and eloquent intellectual with strong ties to the liberal community. The ticket was balanced with Senator John J. Sparkman of Alabama as the vice presidential nominee.

During a nasty campaign in which Republicans stressed the theme "Korea, Communism, and Corruption," McCarthy and his allies took delight in painting Stevenson and the Democrats with a red brush. To Richard Nixon, Stevenson became "Adlai the appeaser" who "carries a Ph.D. from Dean Acheson's Cowardly College of Communist Containment." The vice presidential candidate endorsed both McCarthy and his methods. Eisenhower, on the other hand, abhorred the Wisconsin senator. Still, he did not challenge him publicly, and at one point, in Wisconsin, chose not to read prepared remarks critical of him.

Nixon was almost dumped from the ticket when it became known that he had benefited illegally from an $18,000 "slush fund" raised by supporters. Nixon defended himself in the "Checkers" speech on national television, a mawkish and carefully staged performance that millions found moving and persuasive. To save his political career, Nixon declared his innocence of the charge against him, portrayed himself as a man of extremely modest financial means, and decried his critics—so heartless, he said, that they wanted him to return the gift of the family dog, Checkers. The speech, followed by some quiet and shrewd political moves, returned Nixon to Eisenhower's good graces.

Eisenhower won in a landslide, carrying thirty-nine states and taking nearly 55 percent of the popular vote. Thus ended two decades of Democratic control of the White House. The GOP also won both houses of Congress by narrow margins. Still, few Republicans seriously sought to repeal the New Deal, and even fewer wanted to abandon the Truman Doctrine. The election of 1952 did not alter the basic commitments and functions of government. Historian Arthur Schlesinger, Jr., has said that "Conservatives can be defined, in American history, as men who stand firmly on the liberal position of the preceding generation." That would be largely true in the 1950s.

THE END OF THE RED SCARE

Republican victory meant that the Red Scare should have spent its course. Intensified security probes could weed out all the Reds and fellow travelers in government talked about during the campaign. In April, Eisenhower greatly expanded the Truman loyalty-security program by executive order. By October a White House official boasted that 1,456 "subversives" had been kicked out of government. (By 1956, the administration counted 9,700 departed federal employees.)

Moreover, in July 1953, following the death of Stalin in March and a quiet threat by Eisenhower to use the atomic bomb, the North Koreans signed a truce with the United Nations. The war in Korea had caused 140,000 American casualties and some 850,000 South Korean combat casualties. In the United States it had increased draft calls and prompted highly unpopular economic controls.

The tensions that had propelled the Red Scare had now largely dissipated. Republican leaders expected McCarthy and his minions to devote their time and energy to the support of the administration. Many McCarthyites did just that, including Nixon. But Joe McCarthy, believing himself in a holy crusade, hooked on headlines, and fighting alcoholism, refused. He continued making charges and holding investigations. The senator focused on Reds in government, but no institution in American life was safe from his often sensational allegations.

The president seethed, letting it be known, both privately and (albeit subtly) in public, that he did not approve of the Wisconsin demagogue. McCarthy responded by talking about "twenty-one years of treason," adding the first year of the Eisenhower presidency to the Roosevelt and Truman administrations.

McCarthy's downfall occurred in 1954. During a heated investigation of the army, the senator charged that army leaders had been soft on the Communists by promoting leftist dentist Irving Peress. This celebrated case, actually stemming from bureaucratic inefficiency, became an attack on the administration as well as the Pentagon. The army, backed by the White House, responded by charging correctly that hyperaggressive Roy Cohn, McCarthy's chief assistant, had tried to gain preferential treatment for another McCarthy employee G. David Schine, who had been drafted. A mountain of charges and countercharges resulted in a full-scale congressional investigation on television, the first of its kind.

The "Army-McCarthy" hearings began on April 22, 1954, and lasted thirty-six days. As millions watched, the brilliant army special counsel Joseph Welch and others revealed the arrogant and scowling senator to be a liar, a bluffer, and a character assassin. At one point, in a bitter confrontation over a Welch assistant who played no part in the investigation, Welch cried out, "Have you no sense of decency, sir, at long last? Have you no sense of decency?" (The documentary film "Point of Order" features this dramatic confrontation.)

McCarthy's popularity dropped sharply after the hearings, and the media grew increasingly hostile. Even many close friends and political allies thought the senator had gone too far. But McCarthy defied all efforts at compromise and swore to continue his wide-ranging investigations. In December he was formally condemned by the Senate, 67 to 22, for abusive conduct toward colleagues. The censure bore no penalty, but McCarthy took it extremely hard. Falling from the spotlight and shunned by colleagues and reporters, McCarthy turned increasingly to alcohol and died, at age 48, in 1957. He had not in fact discovered a single Communist.

The Second Red Scare died at about the same time. The internal subversion issue began to drop out of the headlines in the mid-1950s, and it played almost no role in the presidential election of 1956. Supreme Court decisions of the following year acknowledged that the frenzy was over.

The Cold War, nevertheless, would remain a top priority in the United States. The defense budget soared from $13 billion in 1950, when it represented a third of the nation's budget, to $46 billion in 1960, when it amounted to half. Stalin's successors went all out to achieve superior destructive capabilities.

In November 1952, the United States exploded the first H-Bomb at Eniwetok, in the Marshall Islands. It took the Soviets only ten months to make their own such test. Famed scientist Albert Einstein warned that all life on earth could be destroyed by such weapons. But for the next few years, both sides in the Cold War continued to explode hydrogen bombs in the race to be the most powerful.

SUGGESTED READING

Dean Acheson, *Present at the Creation: My Years in the State Department* (1969); Joseph Albright and Marcia Kunstel, *Bombshell: The Secret Story of America's Unknown Atomic Spy Conspiracy* (1997); John L. Gaddis, *We Now Know: Rethinking Cold War History* (1997); Joseph C. Goulden, *The Best Years, 1945–1950* (1976); Alonzo Hamby,

Beyond the New Deal: Harry S. Truman and American Liberalism (1973); Burton I. Kaufman, *The Korean War: Challenges in Crisis, Credibility, and Command* (1986); Richard Gid Powers, *Not Without Honor: The History of American Anticommunism* (1995); Thomas C. Reeves, *The Life and Times of Joe McCarthy: A Biography* (1982); Irwin Ross, *The Loneliest Campaign* (1968); Sam Tanenhaus, *Whittaker Chambers* (1997).

Chapter Nine

THE "BEST YEARS"

To a great many Americans who lived through them, the years 1953 to 1963 were an especially pleasant time in this country's history. Millions enjoyed peace, opportunity, and prosperity under Eisenhower and Kennedy. Journalist Alan Ehrenhalt has called stability and confidence the major themes of this period. He observed in 1995, "If you visit middle-class American suburbs today, and talk to the elderly women who have lived out their adult years in these places, they do not tell you how constricted and demeaning their lives in the 1950s were. They tell you those were the best years they can remember."

In general, however, historians have been critical of this period. Cold War tensions were dangerous and McCarthyism roamed the land. Minorities continued to suffer from discrimination. Some women chafed at the "full-time mother" stereotype that reigned. The gap between rich and poor remained large. Many intellectuals derided the conformity and respect for authority that most Americans appeared to relish. The emphasis upon large families, religion, and what most considered wholesome values have particularly irritated those who prefer the very different outlook of the explosive era that was to follow.

GROWTH AND PROSPERITY

The postwar emphasis on earlier marriages and larger families continued throughout this period. And advances in nutrition and medicine kept people alive longer; the number of people over age 75 jumped from 2.6 million in 1940 to 5.5 million in 1960. The population of the United States climbed from 150.6 million to 179.3 million during the 1950s. The number of households grew from 37.5 million in 1945 to nearly 53 million in 1960.

Increasingly, people moved into the West and Southwest. The population of the Pacific states increased by 110 percent from 1940 to 1960, and by 1963

California was the most populous state. Cities such as Phoenix, Houston, Dallas, and Atlanta grew at a phenomenal pace. Florida's population soared from 2.7 million in 1950 to 4.9 million in 1960. Air conditioning and massive government spending on interstate highways (over $100 billion starting in 1956) accelerated the emigration.

The gross national product climbed from $213.6 million in 1945 to $503.7 million in 1960. Unemployment was in the 5-percent range in the 1950s and inflation was about 3 percent or less a year. Between 1945 and 1960, per capita disposable income went from $500 to $1,845 for every man, woman, and child. By the mid-1950s, almost 60 percent of the American people enjoyed a "middle class" standard of living, compared with 31 percent in 1928. By 1960 the great majority of families owned their own automobile, television set, and washing machine. The population of the suburbs soared 47 percent in the 1950s.

Still, there was no redistribution of wealth after the war. In 1960 between one-fifth and one-fourth of the American people could not survive on their earned income. The bottom 20 percent owned less than half of 1 percent of the nation's wealth. In 1958, 30 percent of industrial workers earned under $3,000 a year.

Government spending, spurred on by military expenditures during the Korean War, contributed significantly to the economic boom. In 1962, federal, state, and local government expenditures amounted to about $170 billion, or almost one-third of the total GNP. One in ten working Americans was employed by government in 1965.

Big government aided the rise of huge corporations. As early as 1941, 45 percent of all defense contracts were going to just six corporations. By 1960 approximately five hundred corporations accounted for two-thirds of all industrial production. By 1967, two hundred firms owned 60 percent of all corporate assets in the United States.

"Automation" was widely discussed at the time. Labor-saving devices increased productivity while decreasing the need for factory workers. In 1956 America became a "postindustrial society" when white-collar workers outnumbered blue-collar workers for the first time. Union membership slumped, and to maximize their strength, the American Federation of Labor and the Congress of Industrial Organizations merged in 1955 to create the AFL-CIO. Job requirements grew increasingly technical, specialized, and service related.

A highly trained "managerial class" emerged to lead corporations. On the upper levels of business and government there was an emphasis on personal conformity in thought, word, deed, and even clothing as a requisite for success. William H. Whyte's *The Organization Man* (1956) brilliantly described the rigid and often subtle rules.

THE FAMILY

During these years, Americans celebrated the family. The popular image, often drawn by Norman Rockwell (the most popular American artist of the century) on *Saturday Evening Post* covers and seen on television in such popular programs as "Father Knows Best," included the bread-winning father, the domestic-minded mother, and three or four happy children living in a single-family home in the suburbs. Family members experienced "togetherness," sharing activities at home and in the community, and taking trips in the large station wagons that were symbols of the "good life" for the middle-class suburban family. Drive-in movies (more than 4,000 of them at their peak in 1958) attracted millions of car-borne families.

While families enjoyed the abundance of postwar life, they also tended to heed a set of traditional moral standards that stressed religious faith, integrity, and personal responsibility. Many children experienced the parental kindness and consideration taught in Dr. Benjamin Spock's 1946 best-seller *Baby and Child Care.*

Still, the number of mothers with children who worked outside the home climbed from 4.1 million in 1948 to 7.5 million in 1958. (This labor was less for "personal fulfillment" than the need for extra family income.) Illegitimate births by white and black mothers climbed significantly in this period. The birth control pill, first available in 1960, paved the way for a revolution in the lives of women.

Television and Movies

By the mid-1950s, two-thirds of all American homes owned at least one television set. The "boob toob" altered American culture. Many nightclubs, dance halls, and skating rinks closed, attendance at movies and lectures plummeted, music lessons and schoolwork went undone. Millions enjoyed the antics of comedian Milton Berle ("Mr. Television"), the variety show hosted by journalist Ed Sullivan, and such favorites as "Kukla, Fran and Ollie," "I Love Lucy," "The Honeymooners," "I Remember Mama," and "Your Show of Shows." Professional wrestling and baseball's world series attracted huge audiences. Network news became the primary source of information for a large percentage of the population. With the debut of TV dinners in 1954, families could watch even while eating.

Television programs, like movies, were severely censured. This policy was enforced by the three networks that dominated the industry, and they had the widespread backing of religious and civic organizations. When rock-and-roller Elvis Presley made his debut in 1956, cameras filmed him from the waist up, shielding audiences from his swaying pelvis. Violence levels in westerns and crime programs were restrained. Profanity was prohibited. The emphasis during these years was on wholesome entertainment for the whole family.

There were strict rules even for television advertising: no American flags, no toilets in cleaning ads, no athlete's foot commercials during the dinner hour.

At first, viewers could find thoughtful plays and serious music on television, interrupted by a minimum of commercials. That soon changed as advertisers realized the massive sales potential of television and programmers catered increasingly to popular taste.

While the "golden age" of movies was rapidly waning in this period, the musical, often based on a successful stage production, reached its greatest heights. The list includes *Annie Get Your Gun* (1950), *American in Paris* (1951), *Showboat* (1951), *Singin' in the Rain* (1952), *The Band Wagon* (1953), *Call Me Madam* (1953), *Brigadoon* (1954), *There's No Business Like Show Business* (1954), *Oklahoma* (1955), *Guys and Dolls* (1955), *The King and I* (1956), *Silk Stockings* (1957), *South Pacific* (1958), *Gigi* (1958), and *West Side Story* (1961). Sexy Marilyn Monroe, an idol of millions, showed that she could sing in *Gentlemen Prefer Blondes* (1953). The Hollywood musical was a major cultural contribution of the United States.

Lavish biblical epics were also in fashion during this period, including *David and Bathsheba* (1951), *Quo Vadis* (1951), *The Ten Commandments* (1956), and *Ben-Hur* (1959). *A Man Called Peter* (1955) praised a Protestant minister and Senate chaplain who died in 1949.

The Golden Age of American Churches

The nation experienced a religious revival in this era. Church construction rose from $76 million in 1946 to $409 million in 1950, to more than a $1 billion by the end of the decade. Between 1945 and 1955 church membership soared from about 70 million to over 100 million. In 1955 and 1958, a record 49 percent of Americans reported having attended a church or synagogue in the past week.

The Roman Catholic church, the nation's largest, flourished and expanded. Between 1945 and 1965, the number of seminarians grew from 21,523 to 48,992. Between the end of the war and 1966, the number of sisters climbed from 138,079 to 181,421. The number of priests increased from 38,451 in 1945 to 59,803 in 1968. Between 1948 and 1958, the Archdiocese of Chicago, the nation's largest, opened an average of six new parishes every year.

Public opinion polls further documented the public's spiritual concern. In 1952, 75 percent of Americans said that religion was "very important" in their lives. Five years later, 69 percent thought that religion was increasing its influence on national life. At the same time, 81 percent of Americans expressed the belief that religion could answer all or most of life's problems.

In 1957, Yale University introduced religion as a new undergraduate major. Two thousand students attended Easter services at Stanford. Educated Christians of all denominations read, or at least were familiar with, the important writings of American theologians Reinhold and H. Richard Niebuhr, and the German refugee Paul Tillich. Reinhold Niebuhr, a professor at New York's Union Theological Seminary, had a great influence on political and theological liberalism, emphasizing man's penchant for sin and the folly of utopianism. Political scientist Hans J. Morgenthau called him "the greatest living political philosopher of America." Niebuhr's "Christian Realism" persuaded many intellectuals of the relevance and wisdom of the faith.

Evangelist Billy Graham and Roman Catholic Bishop Fulton J. Sheen appeared regularly on prime-time television, attracting huge audiences. (Sheen drew more viewers than Milton Berle and singer-actor Frank Sinatra, whose programs were scheduled at the same time.) Six major Protestant clergymen appeared on the cover of *Time* magazine between 1951 and 1961. Christian book sales soared, and in 1953 six of the top eight best-sellers in nonfiction had religious themes. The song "I Believe" was a big hit, inspiring, he said, even the president.

Eisenhower inaugurated the White House Prayer Breakfast, sought to establish a national day of prayer, and opened his cabinet meetings with prayer. Secretary of State John Foster Dulles proudly declared his Christian principles. The words "under God" were soon added to the pledge of allegiance. "In God We Trust" became the nation's official motto. The president of the newly created National Council of Churches declared, "Together the Churches can move forward to the goal—a Christian America in a Christian world."

Much of this revival was no doubt fashion. Going to church was some-

Bishop Fulton J. Sheen on television, 1952. Source: Reproduced from the Collections of the Library of Congress

thing proper families were supposed to do, and membership in certain main-line Protestant churches bestowed status. Polls showed that the public's knowledge of basic Christianity was minimal. Only 35 percent, for example, could name all four New Testament Gospels. Another explanation for the national turn to religion was fear, based on the Cold War, the Red Scare, and the Korean War. But the churches themselves were also responsible, as their missionary efforts, at home and overseas, reached new heights during this period.

MODERATE CONSERVATISM

The Eisenhower administration's approach to domestic issues reflected policies that had dominated the GOP since the 1920s. The president was a fiscal conservative who wanted to balance the budget, curb inflation, and limit the power of the federal government. Unlike his two predecessors, he did not seek social and economic change. On the other hand, Eisenhower was

Eisenhower on the golf course exhibiting his winning smile. Source: Courtesy of the Dwight D. Eisenhower Library

reasonably responsive to social needs and did not intend to repeal the major New Deal programs.

The first Republican cabinet in two decades was composed almost exclusively of affluent business leaders. Conservative Ohio industrialist George Humphrey was named treasury secretary and had a major influence on Eisenhower. General Motors president Charles E. Wilson, appointed secretary of defense, told senators at his confirmation hearings that "what was good for our country was good for General Motors, and vice versa."

Eisenhower, shrewder and more knowledgeable than his liberal critics realized, was not a hard-working chief executive. After a major heart attack in 1955, he turned over even more of his responsibilities to others. White House Chief of Staff Sherman Adams, a former governor of New Hampshire, was given extraordinary authority from the start, including the handling of congressional relations. Republicans lost control of Congress in 1954, and Democrats retained authority in both houses for the rest of Eisenhower's tenure in office. This awkward relationship contributed to the modest record of legislative achievement.

The president signed bills to extend Social Security benefits to an additional ten million people and unemployment compensation to four million more workers. He approved a significant tax cut. The minimum wage went from 75 cents to a dollar an hour. Several housing acts made home buying easier. The Air Force Academy was established in 1954, and Alaska (1958) and Hawaii (1959) became states. The Highway Act of 1956 authorized the creation of a 41,000-mile interstate highway system linking the nation's major cities. The president approved the creation of the Department of Health, Education, and Welfare in 1953 and named a woman, Oveta Culp Hobby, to the cabinet post.

After easily defeating Adlai Stevenson again in 1956, Eisenhower abandoned his determination to balance the budget and used federal spending to combat a recession. Despite his fiscal prudence, the president was able to balance the budget in only three of his eight years in office. But he contributed to a billion dollar surplus in both 1959 and 1960.

CIVIL RIGHTS

Hitler's barbarous actions resulted in a decrease in anti-Semitism after the war. Anti-Catholic bias was down. The Japanese were no longer persecuted. But African Americans in large part failed to benefit from the growing tolerance of the period. They remained segregated in housing, schools, and jobs, and occupied the bottom rung of the socioeconomic scale. Few Americans thought them equal in any way.

In the South, where even water fountains were labeled "black" and "white" to keep the races apart, African Americans were often subject to intimidation and violence. A variety of tactics kept them from the polls. A government study in 1959 found that only 5 percent of eligible blacks in Mississippi were registered to vote.

In Chicago, neighborhoods were segregated, black and white policemen were not allowed to work together, and only six of the seventy-seven hospitals in the metropolitan area would accept black patients.

Eisenhower, like Truman, was not personally committed to the complete desegregation of American life. But the president was sensitive to the direction in which the country was moving and took major steps along that path. By 1953 segregation was virtually eliminated in the armed forces. The following year all federal contracts contained clauses banning discrimination and segregation by employers. The administration led a successful campaign to eliminate segregation in movie theaters, hotels, restaurants, and buses in the nation's capital.

On May 17, 1954, the United States Supreme Court, presided over by Eisenhower appointee Earl Warren, issued a path-breaking civil rights decision. In *Brown* v. *Board of Education*, the Court ruled that the segregation of American public schools was unconstitutional. Agreeing with the NAACP position advocated by its legal chief Thurgood Marshall, the Warren Court declared unanimously that "Separate educational facilities are inherently unequal" because of the psychological damage done to black children by segregation. Communities were ordered to desegregate their schools "with all deliberate speed."

The Brown decision angered a great many, who complained of "judge-made law." There was open hostility in the deep South, and even the president fumed privately. But the ugliness and cruelty inherent in racial segregation was becoming increasingly apparent to millions. The case of Emmett Till in 1955 illustrated the injustice haunting the nation. Till, a brash, 14-year-old Chicago black, made slight advances toward a white woman during a visit to rural Mississippi and was brutally murdered by the woman's husband and half-brother. An all-white, all-male jury acquitted the killers.

In December 1955, Rosa Parks, a black seamstress, weary afters a day's work, refused to give up her seat in the segregated section of a crowded bus to a white passenger. She was arrested and fined $10 for violating a city segregation law. The incident led to a black boycott of city buses that lasted for more than a year and resulted in a Supreme Court decision in 1956 ordering the desegregation of Montgomery's buses.

The boycott was led by Martin Luther King, Jr., a youthful Baptist minister in Montgomery. King was a graduate of Morehouse College in Atlanta, Crozer Theological Seminary in Pennsylvania, and Boston University, where he earned a doctorate in theology. Attracted by the teachings of India's Mahatma Gandhi as well as basic Christianity, he preached passive resistance and love in the face of persecution. To segregationists he declared, "We will soon wear you down by pure capacity to suffer." King attracted international attention during the boycott as an eloquent and effective spokesman for the budding civil rights movement. After the victory in Montgomery, he founded the Southern Christian Leadership Conference (SCLC) to lead the crusade against segregation.

In September 1957, Arkansas Governor Orval Faubus, a militant segregationist, defied a federal court order integrating Little Rock's Central High School and surrounded the campus with state troopers to keep nine young blacks from entering. When mob violence flared up, President Eisenhower sent army paratroopers to the scene. This display of federal authority led by year's end to the admission of the nine students. But tension in the Little Rock school system remained high for several years.

Throughout the South the *Brown* decision was obeyed with great reluctance, resulting in much legal wrestling between federal and state and local officials. By the fall of 1957, only 684 of the 3,000 affected southern school districts had even begun to integrate. By the end of the decade, fewer than 1 percent of black students in the deep South attended integrated schools.

During the volatile events at Central High School, Congress passed and the president signed the first civil rights bill since 1875. The Civil Rights Act of 1957 established a permanent Civil Rights Commission and a Civil Rights Division of the Justice Department. The six-member commission collected data and investigated complaints that state and local officials were denying citizens the right to vote. The Justice Department had the authority to issue injunctions. The Civil Rights Act of 1960 strengthened the federal government's hand by giving it the authority in some circumstances to place qualified blacks on the voting rolls. Still, a great many southern blacks continued to be denied access to the ballot box.

In early 1960, four black college students in Greensboro, North Carolina, began a "sit-in" in a restaurant to protest being denied service. This led to widespread demonstrations by young blacks throughout the South that resulted in the desegregation of public facilities in over a hundred cities. In April 1960, the influential Student Nonviolent Coordinating Committee (SNCC) was formed.

Racial change could be seen on many fronts. In 1947, baseball great Jackie Robinson had been the first black to play in the major leagues, and by the mid-1950s blacks were prominent in almost all professional sports. Wilt Chamberlain, Bill Russell, and Elgin Baylor were dominant players in professional basketball. Hank Aaron became one of baseball's greatest hitters. Sugar Ray Robinson and Archie Moore were among the best boxers of all time.

In show business, African Americans were stepping beyond the subservient and clownish roles that had long been their lot. The film *The Jackie Robinson Story*, starring Robinson himself and Ruby Dee, appeared in 1950. Actors Sidney Poitier and Harry Belafonte starred in highly acclaimed movies during this period. Films such as *Pinky* (1949) and *Show Boat* (1951) were sympathetic toward blacks. Singers Nat "King" Cole, Sarah Vaughan, and Billy Eckstine made hit records. Rock-and-roll stars Little Richard, Chuck Berry, Sam Cooke, and Fats Domino had millions of fans.

Numerous jazz artists, including saxophonist Charlie Parker, trumpeters Dizzy Gillespie and Miles Davis, and pianist Oscar Peterson, enjoyed large audiences and critical acclaim. In 1955 contralto Marian Anderson became

Baseball hero Jackie Robinson, civil rights leader Roy Wilkins, and musician-composer Duke Ellington in 1956. Source: Reproduced from the Collections of the Library of Congress

the first African American to sing at the Metropolitan Opera. Soprano Leontyne Price made her debut in 1961, and mezzosoprano Grace Bumbry followed four years later.

SCIENCE IN ACTION

Innovations in medicine, agriculture, air travel, nutrition, computer technology, and an assortment of other fields during these years changed the lives of most Americans. The release in 1955 of the polio vaccine developed by Dr. Jonas Salk seemed to confirm the direct relationship between science and progress. In 1950 there were 33,344 cases of poliomyelitis in the United States, and two years later severe epidemics occurred in Europe. By 1967 there were only forty-seven cases reported in the United States and Canada.

On October 5, 1957, the world was stunned to learn that the Russians had launched the first satellite—the 184-pound *Sputnik*—into orbit around the earth. On November 3, *Sputnik II*, weighing a then incredible 1,100 pounds and carrying a dog, was sent aloft. Soviet leader Nikita Khrushchev's boastful speeches about his nation's missile superiority now seemed terribly true. "We will bury you," he told the Western democracies.

After an initial failure, America launched its first satellite, *Explorer I*, on January 31, 1958. Later that year, in a fervent bid to win the space race, Congress created the National Aeronautics and Space Administration (NASA). Congress also passed the National Defense Education Act (NDEA) to fund scientific and foreign language studies in the nation's schools and colleges.

On October 26, 1958, a Boeing 707 made the first commercial jet flight across the Atlantic. Flying time for the 111 passengers was eight hours and forty-one minutes, with a one-hour fueling stop at Newfoundland. This was a striking improvement over the five-day trip by ocean liner and the fifteen-hour flight by propeller double-deckers.

In May 1961, astronaut Alan Shepard became the first American to be launched into space. In February 1962, John Glenn orbited the globe. (Both achievements had been pioneered a short time earlier by Soviet cosmonaut Yuri Gagarin.)

Science played a crucial role in the arms race. Soon after the war, American and Soviet scientists began work on rocket-powered missiles. Both sides were assisted by Germans who had developed the fearsome V-2 rockets that had pounded England during the Second World War. The most famous of the Germans was Wernher von Braun, whose talents greatly aided the United States.

By the mid-1950s substantial progress had been made by both Cold War powers. In 1958 the United States set up the first missiles in Germany capable of delivering nuclear warheads. Later that year, Jupiter intermediate-range (1,600 miles) missiles were placed in Turkey and Italy. All of these weapons were aimed at the Soviet Union as part of the overall American policy of containment.

By 1960 intercontinental ballistic missiles were developed that could reach targets 7,000 miles away. By the early Kennedy years, nearly three hundred huge ICBMs were deployed underground in various sites across the United States.

The United States also developed a nuclear-powered submarine program. The first such vessel, the *U.S.S. Nautilus*, was launched in 1954. In 1960 the submarine *George Washington* launched its first polaris missile. Soon a fleet of such submarines would be deployed carrying missiles capable of reaching targets at distances of up to 2,900 miles. Few informed observers doubted that the world had become a very dangerous place.

EISENHOWER AND FOREIGN AFFAIRS

Secretary of State John Foster Dulles, a veteran lawyer and diplomat, was the dominant figure in American foreign relations during this period. Knowledgeable, aristocratic, religious, and fervently anticommunist, he commanded the respect of the president, who gave him extraordinary leeway in making foreign policy decisions. During the election Dulles had talked of abandoning the containment policy and "liberating" peoples ruled by Communist dic-

tatorships. Once in office, however, Dulles followed general Cold War guidelines established by Truman.

Dulles put much stock in the threat of using nuclear weapons, warning
the communist world of "massive retaliation" to counter aggression. The secretary of state was inclined to force the Soviets into tense situations to test
their resolve, a policy known as "brinkmanship." But recognizing the extreme
danger of a direct confrontation with the world's other superpower, the United
States failed to take action when anti-Soviet uprisings occurred in East Germany in 1953 and Hungary in 1956.

Eisenhower and Dulles made special use of the Central Intelligence Agency,
headed by the secretary's brother, Allen W. Dulles. Steps were taken by this
largely clandestine organization in several nations across the world to overthrow unfriendly governments and install pro-Western authorities. In 1954,
Operation Success, initially approved by Truman, toppled the freely elected
president of Guatemala, Jacobo Arbenz Guzman, and installed a right-wing
leader favorable to the United States.

The most notorious example of CIA intervention occurred in Cuba, where
Fidel Castro replaced a corrupt dictator, Fulgencio Batista, on the first day of
1959. After Castro began expropriating foreign-owned businesses and accepting aid from the Soviets, the CIA secretly employed American gangsters,
eager to reopen their local gambling casinos and nightclubs, to assassinate
the Cuban leader. Plans were also laid to mount an invasion of Cuba led by
expatriates, trained and supported by the United States. The decision to proceed with or abort this invasion would face Eisenhower's successor, John F.
Kennedy. As one of its last acts in 1961, the administration severed diplomatic relations with Cuba.

TROUBLE IN ASIA

After the Second World War, France attempted to reassert authority over its
one-time colony Vietnam. The Vietnamese, who had bitterly fought the Japanese during the war, sought independence. The struggle became part of the
Cold War because of Ho Chi Minh, the popular Vietnamese leader who combined nationalism with communism. By 1954, Ho was accepting aid from the
Soviets and Communist China. The Eisenhower administration believed that
a communist takeover in Vietnam would lead to the conquest of all Southeast Asia, like a "row of dominoes."

By 1954, the United States was paying nearly 80 percent of the cost of
France's war in Vietnam. The administration considered sending troops and
using atomic weapons to preserve French authority. But these moves lacked
support from Congress and the nation's allies, and the president chose not
to intervene directly. On May 7, 1954, the French were defeated after a prolonged battle at the city of Dienbienphu.

A peace conference in Geneva that summer, in which the United States
did not officially participate, produced the Geneva Accords. Vietnam was to

be divided temporarily at the seventeenth parallel, Ho Chi Minh ruling in the north and a pro-Western government in the south. Elections held in 1956 were to determine the country's future. The Eisenhower administration, fearful of a communist victory, responded by creating the Southeast Asia Treaty Organization. SEATO was an anticommunist alliance of three Asian nations (Thailand, Pakistan, and the Philippines), the United States, and American allies France, Britain, Australia, and New Zealand. A special protocol extended its protection to South Vietnam, Laos, and Cambodia.

The administration then began building support in South Vietnam for the government of Ngo Dinh Diem. (A similar noncommunist strongman was backed in Laos.) Diem was a haughty, rigid, and corrupt anti-French nationalist who belonged to the area's Catholic minority. In 1955 Diem rejected the idea of elections promised by the Geneva Accords and took steps to extend his control over what had now become a separate, officially pro-Western nation. The alliance between Diem and the United States, unpopular in South as well as North Vietnam, would yield bitter fruit.

By the end of the Eisenhower years, Laos was falling to the communists and South Vietnam was in civil war. Between 1955 and 1961 the United States poured more than a billion dollars into South Vietnam, most of it in military aid. American leaders were determined to prevent the falling dominoes. Senator John F. Kennedy used different metaphors in 1956 with the same meaning: "Vietnam represents the cornerstone of the Free World in Southeast Asia, the keystone in the arch, the finger in the dike."

THE MIDDLE EAST

The Middle East was especially volatile during this period, in large part due to the creation of Israel in 1948, nationalist tensions, and the world's need for the area's vast oil reserves. Oil was the major issue in Iran where, in the summer of 1953, the CIA helped engineer a coup that replaced a pro-Soviet prime minister, Mohammed Mossadegh, with the friendly but despotic shah of Iran, Mohammed Reza Pahlevi. American, British, French, and Dutch oil companies benefited handsomely from the change in leadership.

In Egypt, nationalist leader General Gamal Abdel Nasser flirted with the Soviets to such an extent that Dulles canceled American plans to help build the huge Aswan dam on the Nile. Nasser then seized control from the British of the strategically vital Suez Canal, saying he would finance the project himself. In late October and early November 1956, armed forces from Israel, Britain, and France attacked the Egyptians at Suez. The Eisenhower administration, which had not been consulted, deplored this move because it smacked of colonialism and might push the Arab world closer to the Soviet Union. The president pressured the three attackers by withholding American oil and financial assistance. The crisis was largely over by Christmas. The United States was widely admired, especially in the Third World, for its peace-making efforts. But eventually the Egyptians accepted Russian financial assistance in building the Aswan dam, enhancing Soviet authority in the area.

On March 9, 1957, the president signed into law the Eisenhower Doctrine, which declared that the chief executive could swiftly offer economic and military assistance to those Middle Eastern governments threatened by "overt armed aggression from any nation controlled by International Communism."

The administration also hoped to block efforts by Nasser, whom Eisenhower said publicly was a Communist, to unite all Arab states under his authority. Both the Americans and Soviets busily supplied weapons to Middle East governments. In July 1958, Eisenhower sent five thousand marines to Lebanon to show Nasser that the United States would fight to protect its interests in the region. It was the only time the president unleashed the military while in office. Soviet leader Nikita Khrushchev made threats, and much of the Arab world was in an uproar. But little came of the intervention, and the crisis was over in less than four months.

THE U-2 AFFAIR

After the death of Dulles in 1959, Eisenhower became in fact his own secretary of state. His principal goal was a test ban treaty with the Soviets to slow down the extremely dangerous nuclear arms race. In biographer Stephen Ambrose's words, "It would be the capstone to his half century of public service, his greatest memorial, his final and most lasting gift to his country." The Soviets agreed in principle, and negotiations were scheduled to be discussed, along with other vital issues, at a summit meeting in Paris in mid-May 1960.

On May 1 the Soviets shot down a CIA spy plane, the U-2, over Russia. Such flights had been made since 1956, and Soviet leaders, along with their British and French counterparts, were well aware of them. Congress and the American people, however, had been kept in the dark. Assuming the pilot was dead, Eisenhower, who had personally authorized the flight, attempted a cover-up. On May 7 Khrushchev produced the pilot, Francis Gary Powers, and the wreckage of his plane. The Soviet leader (who had satellites flying over the United States and other parts of the world daily taking photographs) made much of the president's embarrassing lies. For reasons that are not entirely clear, he chose to ruin the summit meeting. The U-2 incident and Khrushchev's walk-out in Paris escalated Cold War tensions and the arms race. It also drew the NATO forces closer together.

THE MILITARY-INDUSTRIAL COMPLEX

President Eisenhower's farewell address in January 1961 contained warnings about the union of the federal government and the permanent arms industry that had developed during the Cold War. "In the councils of government, we must guard against the acquisition of an unwarranted influence, whether sought or unsought, by the military-industrial complex." Public policy, he warned, "could itself become the captive of a scientific-technological elite."

Eisenhower noted that the United States spent more on military security than the net income of all American corporations. Between 1950 and 1960, the portion of the federal budget allocated to the military jumped from one-third to one-half. And 3.5 million men and women were directly engaged in the defense establishment.

THE ALIENATED

A small group of poets and writers on the far left became famous for attacking the conformity, prosperity, Christianity, anticommunism, and popular culture of the 1950s. To "beat generation" poets and writers virtually everything in postwar middle-class America reeked of hypocrisy and meaninglessness. Allen Ginsberg's poem "Howl" (1955), Jack Kerouac's best-selling novel *On The Road* (1957), and William Burroughs' novel *Naked Lunch* reflected the scorn "beatniks" (as critics called them) had for conventional values.

By the end of the decade, especially in San Francisco's North Beach, in Venice West (near Los Angeles), and in New York's Greenwich Village, a few thousand full-time beats had developed a subculture that emphasized alienation (being "cool"), sexual license, long hair, bizarre clothing, and drugs. Ginsberg composed "Howl" with the assistance of a cocktail of peyote, amphetamine, and Dexedrine; Keruoac was on Benzedrine when he wrote the first draft of his novel; Burroughs was a heroin addict for about fifteen years. The "counterculture" of the 1960s was in the making.

"Howl" and *Naked Lunch* were the objects of obscenity trials, and the latter was not published in the United States until 1962. The media and the academic literary establishment lionized the authors as artistic pioneers. Others were less flattering. In 1997, when Burroughs died, conservative Roger Kimball wrote, "In fact, Burroughs helped open the door on the public acceptance and academic adulation of violent, dehumanizing pornography as a protected form of free speech."

Some contemporary scholars had joined the attack earlier. David Riesman's *The Lonely Crowd* (1950) decried the change from traditional "inner-directed" behavior, grounded on individual values, to "other-directed" conduct, based on conformity to social and economic pressures. C. Wright Mills, in *White Collar* (1951), railed against the corporate powers that allegedly dehumanized the work place. In *The Power Elite* (1956) he warned of a cabal of business executives, government bureaucrats, and military leaders that dominated American life.

The far right also experienced alienation. After the demise of the Second Red Scare, many of the fears that had fueled it remained powerful in the minds of a few. In 1958 Massachusetts candy-maker Robert Welch founded the John Birch Society, an extremist organization that saw Communist conspiracy almost everywhere (including in the Eisenhower Administration). Fundamentalist preacher Billy James Hargis and his Christian Crusade, and Australian evangelist Fred Schwartz and the Christian Anti-Communist Crusade were in the same ideological camp.

Most Americans, however, paid little attention to the extremists of the right or left. Indeed, the basic agreement on national and local values and issues was so strong in the fifties that a "consensus school" of historical interpretation appeared. Clinton Rossiter's *Seedtime of the Republic* (1953), Daniel Boorstin's *The Genius of American Politics* (1953), David M. Potter's *People of Plenty* (1954), and Seymour Martin Lipset's *Political Man* (1960) were thoughtful examples. Potter and Boorstin argued that economic abundance was the key to understanding the high level of consensus that could be traced throughout the nation's history. The latter exclaimed, "Much of what passes for public debate in the United States is . . . less an attempt to tell people what to think than to state what everybody already thinks."

THE ELECTION OF 1960

Vice President Richard Nixon easily won the GOP nomination, receiving only tepid support from Eisenhower. Nixon had received much attention two years earlier when, on a goodwill tour of South America, he was the target of violent anti-American demonstrations. Shifty, aggressive, and highly intelligent, Nixon was a skilled campaigner and fund-raiser. Henry Cabot Lodge of Massachusetts was the GOP vice presidential choice.

The Democrats chose 43-year-old Massachusetts senator John F. Kennedy on the first ballot. Kennedy, under the strict supervision of his father, wealthy and cynical multimillionaire Joseph P. Kennedy, had been running for the White House since entering politics in 1946. The formidable Kennedy public relations machine portrayed JFK as heroic, brilliant, and cultured. In fact, he was reasonably intelligent, sickly from birth, often feckless, and given to a ferocious appetite for sexual adventure. Above all, he was a skilled politician with a firm determination to be worthy of his father's ambitions. Kennedy's attractive and shrewd wife, Jacqueline, was a strong political asset, as were speech writer Theodore Sorensen and young Robert "Bobby" Kennedy, the candidate's whip-cracking campaign manager. JFK selected Senate majority leader Lyndon B. Johnson as his running mate.

The hard-fought and often bitter campaign featured allegations against Kennedy's Roman Catholic faith, charges by both sides of the opposition being "soft on the Reds," and a telephone call by Kennedy to the wife of jailed Martin Luther King, Jr., that won many African American votes for the Democrat. There were four nationally televised debates between the two presidential candidates, the first such encounters. While weak in substance, the debates helped Kennedy, contrasting his good looks, studied charm, and self-confidence with Nixon's tense manner and somewhat unappealing demeanor. Pollster Samuel Lubell quoted a Detroit auto worker who said, "It's all phony. This has become an actor's election."

On election day, Kennedy won 49.7 percent of the vote to Nixon's 49.6 percent. A mere 112,803 votes separated the two candidates, making this the closest election of the century. Blacks tipped the scales for Kennedy in several states. Illinois went for Kennedy because of the margin produced in Chicago by the powerful political machine led by autocratic Richard M. Daley, a long-time friend of the candidate's father.

THE KENNEDY STYLE

The handsome young couple in the White House made a tremendous impression on the American people. The president seemed eloquent, vigorous, and courageous. He promised to get America moving again, and he filled his administration with people of high intelligence and lofty academic credentials—"the best and the brightest." The first lady, Jacqueline "Jackie" Kennedy, was a woman of considerable learning and good taste. Her wardrobe set international standards. She redecorated the White House and skillfully presented the finished product on television. Great musicians performed at the White House, and scholars, writers, and artists were unusually welcome. It was a far cry from Eisenhower and the Republicans, who often dismissed intellectuals as "eggheads." Historian Arthur Schlesinger, Jr., a special assistant to the president, would spend the rest of his long life praising what he called this "golden interlude." Liberal journalist Theodore H. White would label the Kennedy administration "Camelot."

There was an underside to this administration, however, that did not appear in the press and would be concealed by partisans. The president intimidated and bullied media people to get sympathetic coverage. He in fact had little personal interest in culture. His extramarital affairs continued on a grand scale (Secret Service agents later told of their astonishment to see the parade of young women secretly ushered into the White House), and he cavorted with a group of "swinging" entertainers known as the "Rat Pack."

Though he always denied it, the president was in poor physical health. He suffered from Addison's disease (failure of the adrenal gland) and lifelong chronic back pain. He took massive doses of amphetamines, administered by a medical quack, to ease his pain and stimulate activity. He had a fierce temper and was easily rattled.

Kennedy's obsession with anticommunism abroad would prove dangerous. At home, despite all the lofty rhetoric, political advantage, more often than not, was the guiding motive in his presidential actions. The gap between the public image and the reality was larger in the case of Kennedy than was true of any other chief executive to that time.

THE BAY OF PIGS INVASION

In his eloquent inaugural address, Kennedy declared, "Let every nation know, whether it wishes us well or ill, that we shall pay any price, bear any burden, meet any hardship, support any friend, oppose any foe to assure the survival and the success of liberty." JFK and his father had always been militantly anticommunist, and both were personal friends of Joe McCarthy. From the beginning, the young president let it be known that he was an uncompromising disciple of the containment policy.

The first test of the president's effectiveness as a diplomatic and military leader appeared in his approach to the invasion of Cuba secretly planned by the CIA and approved by the Eisenhower administration. An army of Cuban exiles was trained in Guatemala. It was thought that when those troops landed, with American air support, they would be greeted by an anti-Castro civilian uprising. Efforts were continued to assassinate the Cuban dictator.

Kennedy was enthusiastic about the overall invasion plan but took a cautious approach. To please him, the CIA changed the landing site from Trinidad to the Bay of Pigs, a move later discovered to be a serious mistake. The president also banned direct American military intervention in case the effort failed. When Operation Pluto got under way on April 15, 1961, Kennedy canceled a second and crucial air strike by Cuban pilots in disguised American planes. He also denied major American air cover for the 1,400 invaders, an act that the chairman of the Joint Chiefs later called "absolutely reprehensible, almost criminal." The result was disaster: nearly five hundred killed and the rest of the exiles captured within forty-eight hours. After lying repeatedly about American involvement, Kennedy was forced to take personal blame for the Bay of Pigs fiasco.

The president and his brother, Attorney General Bobby Kennedy, were soon planning other secret operations against Cuba. One, Operation Mongoose, run by the CIA, cost $50 million a year and included intelligence gathering, propaganda, minor sabotage, and continued efforts to assassinate Castro. Congressional investigators in 1975 would count a total of eight CIA attempts to kill the Cuban dictator in the early 1960s. Castro bragged that the number was two dozen.

THE BERLIN CRISIS

In June 1961 Kennedy met in Vienna with Soviet Premier Khrushchev. The 67-year-old Russian leader wanted to get to know his American counterpart, sensing after the Bay of Pigs that he might be weak and easily bullied. The talks, focusing largely on the future of Berlin, confirmed Khrushchev's suspicions. In mid-August, the Soviets began building a wall around the Eastern zone of Berlin. More than 100,000 refugees had fled to the West in the first six months of 1961. Kennedy responded by sending a 1,500-man battle group along the route to West Berlin, deep in the Soviet zone, making the point that America would defend its legal rights in the German capital. That fall Soviet and American tanks confronted one another across the East-West border of Berlin. Diplomatic talks soon eased the situation. JFK's determination, accompanied by some tough and eloquent rhetoric, improved American-Soviet relations and enhanced his popularity at home and abroad.

THE NEW FRONTIER

The president was mostly uninterested in domestic reforms, and he tended to ignore long-range national goals. The Congress elected in 1960, while controlled by Democrats, was conservative. Kennedy acknowledged privately that few of the hundreds of promises he made during the campaign would become reality.

The chief executive pleased civil rights advocates by naming more blacks to important government posts than any of his predecessors. Robert C. Weaver, president of the NAACP, was named administrator of the Housing and Home Finance Agency. The Justice Department worked to ensure voting rights. The Interstate Commerce Commission took steps to stop segregation in all interstate travel. Still, early in his administration Kennedy was not personally committed to civil rights and did not, as promised, end discrimination in the federal government. He feared that new civil rights legislation would anger southern Democrats, who were powerful in Congress.

The administration was largely unsympathetic to civil rights demonstrators. In 1961, the president was extremely unhappy about having to send federal marshals into Montgomery, Alabama, to restore peace when touring civil rights activists known as Freedom Riders prompted a racial backlash. In 1962, Kennedy was forced to send in troops to quell riots over the court-ordered admission of James Meredith, an African American, to the University of Mississippi.

The following year, after demonstrations and riots broke out in more than a thousand cities across the nation, the president and attorney general realized that the civil rights issue required strong federal action. Both worked hard to push a civil rights bill through Congress, and the president publicly justified the legislation on moral grounds. Bobby Kennedy carefully controlled the March on Washington, which attracted 230,000 people and featured Martin Luther King's electrifying "I Have a Dream" speech, out of fear it would harm the proposal. The bill was in trouble in Congress at the time of the president's death.

While generally unsympathetic to presidential proposals, Congress responded positively to several. The Peace Corps sent trained volunteers overseas to live in primitive conditions and help developing nations with their economic and social problems. The Alliance for Progress (with an eye on Castro) backed economic development and domestic reform in Latin America. The United States Arms Control and Disarmament Agency was created in September 1961. At the same time, the United States embarked on the largest and most rapid military buildup in the nation's peacetime history (America's arsenal of nuclear weapons increased by 150 percent) and created an ambitious space program.

The economy during the Kennedy years performed admirably: economic growth averaged 5.6 percent a year, unemployment dropped to 5 percent, and inflation held at 1.3 percent. Kennedy was almost as pro-business as his predecessor. Historian Allen J. Matusow concluded that the administration's economic policies were based on the theme "What was good for the corporate system would be good for the country."

THE CUBAN MISSILE CRISIS

During the summer of 1962 the Soviets began sending troops, technicians, and weapons into Cuba. It was later revealed that more than 40,000 Russian troops and 270,000 armed Cubans were on hand at the peak of the crisis. Shortly after the administration discovered the military buildup in late August, the Soviet government assured Kennedy that the weapons were strictly defensive and designed to protect Cuba from invasion.

The Soviets were lying, and before long they quietly began constructing medium-range and intercontinental ballistic missile sites. The latter missiles could reach all of the United States except the Pacific Northwest, southeastern Canada, all of Mexico and Central America, and much of South America. If armed with a nuclear weapon, each missile could deliver a blow twenty to thirty times the force of the explosion at Hiroshima. (In 1998, researchers learned that Soviet premier Khrushchev had sneaked about one hundred small nuclear weapons into Cuba in addition to the strategic missiles. Most of these short-range rockets and airplane bombs were as powerful as the Hiroshima bomb. The Kennedy administration was unaware of the presence of these tactical weapons. The crisis was even more dangerous than was thought at the time.)

Khrushchev had a dual motive. Knowing about Operation Mongoose, he was indeed interested in defending Cuba from attack. Castro had asked him for military assistance. But he also wanted to intimidate Kennedy, whom he thought weak and ineffective, and enhance Russia's first-strike capability.

In early October, newspapers carried stories of the missile sites. When they were photographed by a U-2 plane on October 15, the Cuban missile crisis began. For the security of the country, the future of the Cold War, and his reputation as a tough anticommunist, the president could not let Khrushchev's aggressive and deceitful act go unchecked. Kennedy was also mindful of the forthcoming 1962 congressional elections. Some Republicans were already charging him with appeasement.

Appointing an ad hoc committee of administration hard-liners ("ExCom") to advise him, Kennedy chose to blockade Cuba (the action was called a "quarantine" to prevent it from being considered an act of war) in order to stop further shipments of offensive weapons. On October 21 the president went on television to describe the crisis and pledged to rid the Western Hemisphere of the missiles at all cost.

The public and the nation's allies strongly backed the quarantine. The Soviets howled, calling the action "piracy" and vowing not to be intimidated. Rapid construction of the missile sites continued; the weapons were only days away from being capable of launching. The possibility of World War III raised fears throughout the world.

The Soviets chose not to cross the quarantine line. But the missiles in Cuba remained a threat to world peace. Kennedy and his advisers thought long and hard about a military invasion of the island. When a Soviet SAM missile shot down an American U-2 plane, killing the pilot, American forces were on the edge of attack.

The tension abated on October 27 when Kennedy accepted a quiet Soviet proposal: He pledged to end the quarantine and promise that the United States would never invade Cuba in return for the Soviet promise to dismantle the missiles and never reintroduce them in Cuba. The president also secretly agreed to a Soviet demand to remove American missiles in Turkey pointed at the Soviet Union.

Even though Khrushchev took the major steps to end the crisis (which he had started), most observers gave Kennedy the credit, noting his restraint and decisiveness. The president emerged from the struggle, which Secretary of State Dean Rusk called "the most dangerous crisis the world has ever seen," more popular and more highly respected than ever.

Following the crisis, Kennedy and Khrushchev agreed to install a telephone "hot line" between Washington and Moscow to provide speedy and direct communication in an emergency. An unfortunate product of the crisis was the acceleration of the arms race. The Soviets, eager to gain military superiority, engaged in a crash program that in five years yielded an impressive naval force and superiority over the United States in ICBMs.

INVOLVEMENT IN SOUTHEAST ASIA

The president inherited crises in Laos and Vietnam, where communists were rapidly expanding their territorial authority. Kennedy, committed to the nation's containment policy and eager to show his "toughness," responded in the same way that Truman and Eisenhower had. Only he went a step further.

Under Eisenhower, the CIA had secretly spent nearly $300 million to bolster the Royal Laotian Army against communist attack, and the president had privately talked about unilateral intervention by the United States. The communist Pathet Lao, enjoying aid from Moscow and Hanoi, seemed to be on the brink of a takeover soon after Kennedy took office.

Kennedy amassed a military force and was about to intervene in Laos when the Bay of Pigs fiasco persuaded him to change his plans. He was shaken by the military's ineptitude and was fearful of getting bogged down in a jungle war thousands of miles away. Congressional leaders were also opposed to a military action. A neutralist government was formed in 1962, but Kennedy was unhappy about the settlement and did not trust the nation's rulers. The Pathet Lao continued its aggression, and North Vietnam continued to send troops into South Vietnam through Laos.

Kennedy responded with a secret CIA counterinsurgency program that cost close to a half billion dollars a year and involved bombing operations and guerrilla raids into North Vietnam and China. This effort came to light in 1975, when it was labeled "the largest paramilitary effort in post-war history."

Kennedy decided that Vietnam was the major battleground for the United States to take a firm stance against communist aggression. Early in 1961 he sent a secret military mission to South Vietnam that encouraged troops loyal to Diem to conduct a clandestine war against Hanoi. That fall, with advisers eager for action and Republicans charging the administration with worldwide appeasement, the president approved a massive increase in American aid and the dispatch of "military advisers." He declined requests to send combat forces. Kennedy committed the United States to helping Diem defend himself.

By the end of 1962, 11,000 American "advisers" were in South Vietnam. An elite special forces unit, known as the Green Berets, trained government troops to engage in guerrilla warfare. The increase in manpower was accompanied by a huge military buildup directed by Secretary of Defense Robert McNamara. Some of the Americans were directly involved in military actions, on land and in the air. Both sides in the increasingly bloody struggle used napalm and chemical defoliants. Despite all efforts, Communist Viet Cong expansion continued. In early 1963 Diem grew increasingly critical of both his army and his American supporters. American reporters in Vietnam often portrayed Diem as a corrupt and unpopular strongman.

That spring violence broke out in South Vietnam between Buddhists and the largely Catholic government. Several Buddhist monks and nuns set themselves afire to protest government persecution. Tensions escalated during the summer, much to the embarrassment of Kennedy and his advisers. Following much debate and uncertainty, the administration quietly and clumsily backed a military coup. On November 1, Diem and his brother, Ngo Dinh Nhu, were murdered. Bobby Kennedy later admitted that the entire situation was poorly handled by his brother.

Some Kennedy partisans later contended that the president would have pulled out of Vietnam had he lived. This seems highly unlikely. By October 1963 there were 16,732 American military advisers in Vietnam. Aid to Diem had reached $400 million per year. The president's speeches bristled with anticommunism right to the end. Secretary of State Rusk later denied that evacuation was discussed. Bobby said later that his brother was firmly committed to victory in Vietnam. Moreover, it was Kennedy's advisers, the "best and the brightest," who would later encourage Lyndon Johnson to escalate the war to new heights.

THE KENNEDY ASSASSINATION

On November 22, 1963, the president and first lady flew to Dallas on a political peace-making trip. As the Kennedy motorcade traveled through the downtown, shots rang out from a building, hitting the president. JFK died in a nearby hospital, and the assassin, Lee Harvey Oswald, was soon captured. Oswald was a highly disturbed loner who had lived in Russia for a time and backed Castro. The nation was further horrified two days later when Oswald was murdered by Jack Ruby, a local nightclub operator. On the spur of the moment, as Oswald emerged from a building in the custody of police, Ruby used his revolver, thinking he would be considered a hero for avenging the death of the president.

The tragedy of Kennedy's death was compounded by the fact that it was captured on movie film by a spectator. The media showed the twelve-second film repeatedly and made much of the highly moving burial service at Arlington National Cemetery. The entire nation mourned the loss of its youthful and handsome chief executive, whose reputation for brilliance, character, and leadership soon soared. The intense grief at the assassination of JFK may be seen as the close of the "best years" and the beginning, under Lyndon Johnson, of a much different era.

SUGGESTED READING

Alan Ehrenhalt, *The Lost City: Discovering the Forgotten Virtues of Community in the Chicago of the 1950s* (1995); John Kenneth Galbraith, *The Affluent Society* (1958); Edwin O. Guthman and Jeffrey Shulman (eds.), *Robert Kennedy: In His Own Words* (1988); Will Herberg, *Protestant, Catholic, Jew* (1955); Kenneth A. Jackson, *Crabgrass Frontier* (1986); Douglas Miller and Marion Novak, *The Fifties: The Way We Really Were* (1977); Gerald Posner, *Case Closed: Lee Harvey Oswald and the Assassination of JFK* (1993); David Potter, *People of Plenty* (1954); Thomas C. Reeves, *A Question of Character: A Life of John F. Kennedy* (1991); Elmo Richardson, *The Presidency of Dwight D. Eisenhower* (1979).

Chapter Ten

ERA OF UPHEAVAL

F ew Americans knew Lyndon Johnson well before he was sworn in as chief executive on board Air Force One. Almost everyone wished him well, especially after he expressed the desire to carry on in the tradition of the fallen president. Johnson told a joint session of Congress five days after taking office, "Let us here highly resolve that John Fitzgerald Kennedy did not live or die in vain."

Some forecasters predicted a new era in peace, prosperity, and reform. The economy was healthy, relations with the Soviet Union were reasonably calm, and civil rights legislation was in the works. Few could have foreseen the tumult that would erupt under the well-meaning president, a turbulence that would shake the very foundations of the United States, producing social and cultural changes that remain powerful to this day.

LBJ

Johnson was born in 1908 on a modest farm in southwest Texas. He graduated from a local teachers college in 1930, having taught school and held a number of jobs to support himself. What Johnson lacked in formal education, money, and social graces, he made up for in high intelligence, towering ambition, and incredible energy.

Johnson went to Washington in 1934 to assist a local congressman, and he soon became the Texas director of the New Deal's National Youth Administration. He entered Congress in 1937, a staunch Democrat with a great admiration for FDR. He won election to the Senate in 1948 and became Democratic whip in 1951. Only two years later he became his party's leader, serving in that capacity until chosen by Kennedy as his running mate.

A principal Johnson asset was his determination and uncanny ability to manipulate people. He was the consummate "wheeler and dealer," willing to use threats, tears, promises, anything necessary to have his way. Ideologically, he was a New Dealer with a strong desire to help the common man. He could also be friendly to business. Although largely ignored by the Kennedys while serving as vice president, Johnson could boast of a distinguished legislative record and an unparalleled grasp of Washington politics.

The nation soon discovered that President Johnson lacked the polish, style, and media skills of his predecessor. In public appearances he often seemed crude, corny, and shifty. Some Kennedy administration officials who continued to mourn the loss of Camelot turned against the new president. Robert Kennedy, who had never liked or trusted him, would become an outspoken critic. Privately, LBJ cursed the haughty Easterners, whom he called "the Harvards."

Among his first actions, Johnson appointed a commission headed by Supreme Court Chief Justice Earl Warren to investigate the Kennedy assassination. This was thought especially necessary because of the spread of a multitude of conspiracy theories. After painstaking studies, the Warren Commission concluded that Lee Harvey Oswald was the sole assassin. Many Americans had their doubts, and conspiracy charges would rumble through the media and academia for decades.

Determined to build a substantial record as chief executive, Johnson used his full powers of persuasion on Congress to pass several Kennedy administration initiatives. The result was impressive. A tax cut produced economic growth. The Civil Rights Act of 1964 virtually ended Jim Crow, making the segregation of African Americans in public places (hotels, restaurants, theaters, and the like) illegal, creating an Equal Employment Opportunity Commission, and protecting the voting rights of blacks. Congress also passed the Economic Opportunity Act, a major step in the "war on poverty" Johnson declared in his first State of the Union address. Among other things, the legislation created work-training programs and rural conservation camps, and provided loans to farmers and small businesses. Conservation, housing, and school aid bills also passed.

The Election of 1964

Johnson seemed unbeatable in the presidential election of 1964. His legislative record was impressive, and millions linked him with the memory of JFK. Republicans handed their nomination to Senator Barry Goldwater of Arizona, an affable right-wing ideologue. Nominated in August by confident Democrats, LBJ spurned Robert Kennedy and selected liberal Minnesota Senator Hubert H. Humphrey to round out the ticket.

The campaign was dull and uninspired. Goldwater plunged in the polls by promising to dismantle government programs and curtail benefits. His running mate, Congressman William Miller of New York, made a largely negative impression on voters. Johnson portrayed himself as a moderate and humane leader, eager to unify the nation and make Kennedy's visions a reality.

He labeled his reform proposals the "Great Society."

Johnson also claimed to be a man of peace, contrasting himself with Goldwater, who was portrayed in memorable television commercials to be a dangerous warmonger who might use nuclear weapons in Vietnam. The president declared, "I'll never send American boys to do what Asian boys should be doing for themselves."

When the votes were counted, LBJ won 61.1 percent of the popular vote, a larger margin than Roosevelt had enjoyed in his first reelection bid. Goldwater carried only Arizona and five southern states. Democrats made huge gains in Congress, controlling the Senate 68 to 32 (Robert Kennedy represented New York) and the House 295 to 140. Johnson now had the most liberal Congress since 1936 to work with.

The Great Society

In a moving State of the Union address, Johnson called for dramatic and path-breaking legislation. Throughout 1965, prodded by the president, Congress delivered. The first item on the agenda was Medicare, which provided health care for most people age 65 and older. It was funded by an increase in Social Security taxes. Medicaid was a program that used federal, state, and local funds to provide medical and dental care for low-income Americans. Both programs were bitterly opposed by the American Medical Association and conservatives concerned about the growth of the welfare state.

Education was another top priority for the president, and the Elementary and Secondary Education Act of 1965 provided over a billion dollars in federal aid to help students in both public and parochial schools. President Johnson was personally responsible for forging a landmark solution to widespread objections against federal aid to education, especially Catholic education.

Despite three civil rights acts and the Twenty-fourth Amendment to the Constitution (outlawing poll taxes as a device to keep blacks from voting), only some two million of the South's five million African Americans were registered to vote in 1965. Racism remained at the heart of the problem. This was illustrated in 1964 when two young white men from New York City and a local black man were murdered in Mississippi for their involvement in encouraging black voter registration. A Boston minister was later murdered in Selma, Alabama (where 97 percent of the registered voters were white), for engaging in the same activity. The whole nation watched on television as Martin Luther King, Jr., and his followers were beaten up while on a march between Selma and Montgomery, Alabama, to protest discrimination at the ballot box.

On March 15, 1965, President Johnson gave a forceful speech before a joint session of Congress, calling for an equal right to vote for all Americans. Congress responded slowly in the face of strong southern resistance, but leaders of both parties, aided by the arm-twisting chief executive, produced another landmark bill. On August 6 Johnson signed the Voter Rights Act, giving the attorney general of the United States authority to appoint federal registrars to register voters in districts where there was a historic pattern of discrimination. The elections of 1966 were the first in which most African Americans could vote.

Congress produced a torrent of additional legislation. The Immigration Act of 1965, for example, dropped the ethnic restrictions in force since 1924 and based admission largely on job skills, education, and family ties with American citizens. Two new cabinet departments—Transportation, and Housing and Urban Development—were created. (Robert Weaver, named to head HUD, became the first black cabinet member.) Almost $3 billion was authorized for urban renewal. More than $1 billion went to fund projects in economically depressed Appalachia. The Head Start program to help disadvantaged preschoolers began with a budget of $96 million. There was legislation to combat air and water pollution, beautify highways, help the elderly, protect consumers, combat disease, supplement rent for low-income families, aid financially strapped college students, and promote the arts and humanities.

In 1965 and 1966, the "fabulous Eighty-ninth" Congress tackled more social problems than any of its predecessors. When LBJ left office, there were 435 federal domestic social programs, 390 more than when Eisenhower departed.

Conservatives railed against the "nanny state" and expressed fears about the financial costs of huge federal programs. (Medicaid costs would swell from $770 million in 1966 to $6.6 billion in 1975; the food stamp budget would grow from $30 million in 1964 to $1 billion in 1975; Head Start costs would more than quadruple between 1965 and 1975.) At the time, however, these cries were largely in vain. The reforms were popular and a booming economy seemed able to fund them indefinitely. The Great Society ranked Johnson with FDR and Wilson as one of the nation's greatest reform presidents.

The Vietnam War

Like almost all of his Washington contemporaries, Johnson was a Cold Warrior. He was firmly anticommunist and believed in the containment policy and the domino theory. Moreover, Johnson, like Kennedy, had a macho self-image and would not shrink from using force if challenged. When it seemed in early 1965 that communists were launching an effort to seize power in the Dominican Republic, LBJ sent in marines and army paratroops. The military intervention proved successful (although it violated the OAS charter and angered many Latin Americans) and democracy was restored. Action in the Dominican Republic encouraged the president to rely on the military to stop the Reds.

Johnson's assessment of the war in Vietnam was predictable. Shortly after taking office, LBJ told the American ambassador to Saigon, "I am not going to be the president who saw Southeast Asia go the way China went." This stance was supported by three top Kennedy aides who served in the Johnson administration: Secretary of State Dean Rusk, Secretary of Defense Robert McNamara, and national security adviser McGeorge Bundy.

South Vietnam was plunged into political and economic chaos after Diem's assassination. The Joint Chiefs of Staff recommended massive military intervention, but in early 1964 Johnson chose merely to increase economic and technical assistance and help South Vietnamese troops in minor covert military activities. He insisted publicly, as Kennedy had, that the war had to be won by the South Vietnamese themselves.

This approach changed dramatically on August 1 when North Vietnamese torpedo boats attacked the American destroyer *Maddox* in international waters, apparently believing that the ship had been involved in a nearby raid by South Vietnamese. In response, the navy sent in the destroyer *C. Turner Joy*, and on August 4 the Pentagon announced that both ships had come under fire in the Gulf of Tonkin.

President Johnson ordered air strikes against North Vietnam naval bases and asked Congress to give him the authority to do whatever was necessary to resist communist aggression in Southeast Asia. Congress was not told that the *Maddox* was engaged in electronic espionage or that the Gulf of Tonkin attack was shrouded in confusion and may well not have actually occurred. The "Gulf of Tonkin Resolution" passed the Senate 98 to 2 and the House 414 to 0. Johnson sought the blank check from Congress to demonstrate to the North Vietnamese, pouring men and supplies into the South, that America meant business. He also sought to deny Barry Goldwater, who had just been nominated by the GOP, the allegation that the president was "soft."

American bombing raids against North Vietnamese military bases and infiltration routes began in early February 1965. The raids were in response to a deadly attack on American military advisers by National Liberation Front forces, the Viet Cong, backed fully by Ho Chi Minh's communist regime.

In March, two marine battalions were dispatched to South Vietnam to defend an air base. In April and May Johnson made peace initiatives to Hanoi, but they were flatly rejected. In June, a month after Congress voted $400 million to back the effort in Vietnam, American troops were engaged in a ground offensive for the first time.

In July, under pressure from American military leaders, Johnson agreed to employ saturation bombing in South Vietnam and send 100,000 troops. General William Westmoreland, the U.S. commander in Vietnam, was given a free hand to direct the fighting in the South. The president and his top advisers were persuaded that without this commitment the Reds would snap up a vital part of the free world, endangering the rest of Southeast Asia. Almost all members of Congress and the vast majority of Americans agreed.

By early 1966 South Vietnam had a reasonably stable government, led by the swashbuckling pilot Nguyen Cao Ky. That October, after an election, General Nguyen Van Thieu became president and Ky moved to vice president. Still, the prospects for military victory continued to dim. In January

Americans began massive bombing raids on North Vietnam. This effort did nothing to deter the will of Ho Chi Minh to rule the whole of Vietnam (an area about the size of Missouri), and indeed led to worldwide expressions of sympathy toward him and his people. As public opinion began to shift against the American effort, the number of American troops in Vietnam increased: 385,000 by the end of 1966; 486,000 by the end of the following year. (From 1959 to 1975, North Vietnam sent 976,849 soldiers into South Vietnam and provided the great majority of weapons and supplies used in the South.)

American troops, aided by small contingents of allies from Australia, New Zealand, the Philippines, Thailand, and South Korea, employed "search and destroy" operations against the enemy. All of South Vietnam was a combat zone. This often, inadvertently and sometimes deliberately, led to the destruction of entire villages and the deaths of many innocent people.

Massive bombing and the use of indiscriminate firepower, napalm, and chemical herbicides (including the infamous Agent Orange) devastated the landscape. Thousands of peasants were uprooted from their land in the wake of attacks by both sides. Resistance to the government of Thieu and Ky as well as to the Americans increased dramatically within South Vietnam.

Americans troops were frustrated by savage battles in steamy jungles and swamps, long combat assignments, and the frequent inability to distinguish friend from foe in peasant villages. Many were turned off by the corruption and inefficiency of the South Vietnamese government. Some Americans became addicted to the drugs easily available in the region. Many grew increasingly uneasy about the growing resistance, at home and abroad, to the conflict. That resistance escalated as the number of American deaths mounted: almost five thousand in 1966 and some nine thousand in 1967.

Antiwar forces often claimed that the Americans being sent to Vietnam were mostly draftees and more often than not black. In fact, most of those who went to Vietnam volunteered. Volunteers accounted for 77 percent of combat deaths. Defense Department statistics later showed that 86 percent of those who died in Vietnam were white and 12.5 percent were black—from an age group in which blacks comprised 13.1 percent of the population.

Large-scale antiwar demonstrations began in the spring of 1965 and became an everyday part of American life for the next decade. College students, especially in elite institutions, seized campuses, burned their draft cards, and harassed military and industrial recruiters. Returning veterans staged protests. In May 1966, ten thousand protesters marched in front of the White House. In October 1967, 50,000 people demonstrated near the Lincoln Memorial in Washington, and some tried to force their way into the Pentagon. Protesters at such gatherings chanted, "Hey, hey, LBJ, how many kids have you killed today?" Many of these angry Americans were undoubtedly influenced by scenes on the nightly television news showing the worst features of the fighting overseas.

The American people had not been so divided since the Civil War. "Hawks" sought more support for the war and victory. "Doves" wanted out of the conflict. Most citizens were no doubt somewhere in the middle of these extremes, willing to back anticommunism but increasingly worried about the cost and the value of the property in question.

Ho Chi Minh had no illusions about defeating the American fighting machine. But he was confident that if his troops could hold on long enough public opinion would force Johnson to cave in. American military leaders were also confident that they could win in Vietnam—if given enough manpower, funding, and authority. They always wanted more. General Westmoreland and the Joint Chiefs of Staff gave the president consistently positive accounts of the fighting.

LBJ did not want to become involved in a full-scale war in Asia. He limited military activity on numerous occasions, and he made repeated peace overtures. Still, he was not going to "chicken out" or be one of the "nervous Nellies" who "will break ranks under the strain." He told a group of U.S. servicemen in 1966, "I pray the good Lord will look over you and keep you until you can come home with that coonskin on the wall."

In early 1966, Senator William Fulbright, chairman of the Foreign Relations Committee, broke with the president and held televised hearings on the war. Secretary of Defense McNamara, a major architect of the war, became disillusioned and resigned in late 1967. (In 1995 he declared that he and other U.S. policymakers had been "terribly wrong" in allowing the conflict to escalate.) Several others also left the administration because of the Vietnam policy. Liberals and intellectuals were now routinely opposed to the war, as were black leaders who feared that it was endangering the Great Society. Johnson's public popularity plunged, especially after he requested a tax increase to help fund the war. In November 1967, Senator Eugene McCarthy of Minnesota, a militant dove, announced his candidacy for the Democratic presidential nomination.

In early 1968, American ground troops reached the 500,000 mark. On January 30, about 80,000 Viet Cong and North Vietnamese troops began a massive series of surprise attacks on more than one hundred cities, towns, and military bases in South Vietnam. During the attack on Saigon, the U.S. embassy was raided. The old imperial city of Hue was destroyed. Television cameras sent horror-filled pictures into the living rooms of the world. One jolting sequence featured the street corner execution of a communist rebel by South Vietnam's chief of National Police.

In all, the "Tet offensive" left 1,113 Americans and at least 3,470 South Vietnamese dead. It was the turning point in the war. While Hanoi's forces were soon driven out of the areas they attacked (the attack cost them and the Viet Cong some 30,000 lives), their daring and well-planned effort had badly damaged the credibility of American military and political leaders. Johnson and Westmoreland had been reassuring the American people that victory in Vietnam was in sight. Now, it seemed, we were losing.

On March 12, dovish Eugene McCarthy won 42 percent of the vote in the New Hampshire Democratic primary. Four days later, Senator Robert

Kennedy, now also antiwar, jumped into the contest, exciting millions with memories of Camelot.

Reluctantly, sadly, and after much consultation, Johnson rejected the military's call for 205,000 more troops and decided to limit the bombing of North Vietnam in order to achieve peace talks. On March 31, in a dramatic television speech to the nation, he outlined his plan for ending the conflict and announced that he would not seek or accept his party's nomination for another term. Johnson, the supreme politician and reformer, had become another victim of the Vietnam War.

The Youth Rebellion

America had known "rebellious youth" in the 1920s and beatniks in the 1950s. But in the Johnson-Nixon years, a storm of dissent, coming largely from upper-middle-class young people, shook the country as never before. Critics blamed this left-wing rebellion on prosperity, mounting secularism, parental permissiveness, and a breakdown in the schools. Others saw it as a praiseworthy crusade, striking out against repressive and irrational laws and institutions and heralding the dawn of a glorious new era of peace and love. The movement preceded serious American involvement in the Vietnam War, but that conflict fueled the rebellion and propelled it into a force that significantly altered American culture.

The seeds of the rebellion could be seen in 1962 when fifty-nine delegates of the leftist Students for a Democratic Society issued the Port Huron Statement. This sixty-six page manifesto, written by activist Tom Hayden and others, seriously criticized American governmental and economic institutions, called for more freedom and democracy, and declared that "America should concentrate on its genuine social priorities: abolish squalor, terminate neglect, and establish an environment for people to live in with dignity and creativeness." This Kennedy-era statement would soon seem very tame, even innocent.

In 1964, at the University of California at Berkeley, the small Free Speech movement, led by civil rights activists Mario Savio and Jack Weinburg, shut down the campus and caused havoc for two months when university officials declared they could not use a campus area to solicit funds and volunteers for off-campus political activities. The FSM condemned the university as part of the corporate structure that oppressed blacks and the poor. (The turmoil did much to assist the rise of conservative Ronald Reagan in California.) Student teach-ins against the Vietnam War began at the University of Michigan in the following year and soon spread to campuses all over America.

In January 1967 thousands of young people, now being called "hippies," gathered in San Francisco for a "Human Be-In." *Newsweek* magazine called it "a love feast, a psychedelic picnic." The youthful rebels wore often outlandish clothes, sported beards and long hair, smoked marijuana (now a staple of hippie culture), frolicked with bells and balloons, and had sex on the lawn. Former Harvard psychologist Timothy Leary, dressed in white and wearing flowers in his hair, preached the glories of "acid" (LSD). Jefferson Airplane and the Grateful Dead played "acid rock." Jerry Rubin, a leader of the radical and sometimes violent Youth International party, the "Yippies," was on hand.

Historian Allen J. Matusow later observed, "the hippie impulse that was spreading through a generation of the young challenged the traditional values of bourgeois culture, values still underpinning the liberal movement of the 1960s—reason, progress, order, achievement, social responsibility." A counterculture had been created.

By this time, Haight-Ashbury had become the mecca of cultural radicalism. Young people from all over America poured into this San Francisco community of forty square blocks bordering Golden Gate Park to experience sex, drugs, and rock and roll. (They often drove the inexpensive and reliable Volkswagen Beetle, an icon of the youth culture. The Volkswagen station wagon, often hand-painted with peace signs and slogans, was also popular.) The glamor lasted only a short time, however, as the district appealed increasingly to the unstable and criminal. Reported crime at the end of 1967 included seventeen murders, one hundred rapes, and nearly three thousand burglaries.

In the spring of 1968, a year of shocking turbulence and violence, campus radicals and blacks shut down strife-torn Columbia University for more than a week. The initial complaints, involving race and the war, soon gave way to more basic issues. SDS leader Mark Rudd wrote to the University president, "We, the young people, who you so rightly fear, say that the society is sick and you and your capitalism are the sickness. You call for order and respect for authority; we call for justice, freedom and socialism." The often brutal tactics employed by New York police to regain control of the campus prompted sit-ins and demonstrations in more than one hundred colleges and universities across the nation. On some radicalized campuses like the University of Wisconsin-Madison, marches, rallies, demonstrations, and classroom disruptions were a part of daily life.

Civil Rights

The Civil Rights acts of 1964 and 1965, for all of their virtues, failed to satisfy the nation's 21 million African Americans. Blacks continued to face often severe economic problems (29 percent of black families lived on incomes below the official poverty level in 1970), and discrimination in employment, education, and housing remained part of their daily lives. Civil rights leaders contended that blacks fought and died in Vietnam in numbers far out of proportion to their percentage of the population. They also argued that the large percentage of black prisoners in the nation's jails and prisons stemmed in large part from racism.

In the summer of 1964, blacks rioted in Harlem and Rochester, New York. Five days after President Johnson signed the 1965 Voting Rights Act, a massive and shocking riot broke out in Watts, a predominantly black, lower-middle-class area of Los Angeles. What started as a protest against the arrest of a drunken motorist turned into a week-long binge of looting and violence that killed 34 people, injured 1,100 and left $40 million in property damage.

In the summer of 1966, urban riots occurred in seven major cities. In the following year, there were almost four dozen riots and over a hundred lesser incidents of civil unrest. In Newark, New Jersey, 26 people died and 1,200 were injured. A riot in Detroit lasted five days, cost 43 lives, injured 2,000, destroyed 1,300 buildings, and left 2,700 businesses looted. For the first time in the decade, federal troops had to be called in to restore order.

A later analysis revealed that the average rioter in Detroit was a young male African American who had graduated from high school and was both married and employed, often as an auto worker. Ironically, government and the unions in Detroit were largely integrated, and the Great Society had spent millions on the city.

In 1968, spurred on by the assassination of Martin Luther King, Jr., riots broke out in 125 cities. The violence in Washington, D.C., in April was such that routes to and from the city were sealed off and armed troops were braced to protect the capitol building. Within a few blocks of the White House, windows were smashed, stores were looted, and buildings were set on fire. In almost all of the urban riots of this period, the violence was largely contained within black ghettoes, and most of the victims were black.

The riots confirmed the worst prejudices of many whites about blacks. They were especially angered by black leaders who endorsed the violence. In June 1966, Congress of Racial Equality leaders Stokely Carmichael and Floyd McKissick preached "black power." Huey P. Newton and Bobby Seale organized the Black Panthers and declared the need for violent revolution. Martin Luther King, Jr., said in late 1967, "I am not sad that black Americans are rebelling; this was not only inevitable but eminently desirable. Without this magnificent ferment among Negroes, the old evasions and procrastinations would have continued indefinitely."

Some whites agreed with King, charging that the urban riots were legitimate and understandable protests against centuries of oppression. The National Advisory Commission on Civil Disorders, appointed by President Johnson, blamed white racism for the violence and called for numerous reforms and federal programs to heal race relations and promote equality. (In 1998, historians Abigail and Stephan Thernstrom strongly disagreed, noting the healthy economies of preriot Los Angeles and Detroit and the absence of serious rioting in the South, where life for blacks was undoubtedly more difficult. They concluded that "the causes of the violence remain obscure to this day.")

By the late 1960s "black pride" was the trend. Identifying with Africa, many blacks wore Afro hairstyles and dressed in African clothing. Some took African and Muslim names: black nationalist Malcom Little (who died in 1965) became Malcom X; famed heavyweight boxer Cassius Clay became Muhammad Ali; basketball star Lew Alcindor would later be known as Kareem Abdul Jabbar. "Afro-American" and "black" replaced "Negro," which reminded too many of historic discrimination. Black studies courses began to appear and multiply on college campuses. The popular soul singer James Brown declared, "Say it loud. I'm black and I'm proud."

Women's Liberation

By 1960, 40 percent of women over 16 were in the labor force, compared with 25 percent in 1940. Many chafed at the low salaries and lack of opportunities associated with "women's" occupations such as nursing, teaching, and clerical work. Many educated upper-middle-class women were especially eager to build careers outside the home.

The feminist movement was largely a thing of the past in the 1940s and 1950s. Fashionable femininity embraced maternity, humility, and self-sacrifice. But this would change dramatically in the turbulent 1960s, as feminism took on new life and became known as the "women's liberation" movement.

Betty Friedan, president of the National Organization of Women, in 1970. Source: UPI/Corbis-Bettmann

A catalyst for this powerful force was Betty Friedan's best-selling book *The Feminine Mystique*, published in 1963. Friedan, a well-to-do Vassar graduate, thought that housewives were slaves and victims and that the home was a "comfortable concentration camp." Self-fulfillment was vital, she argued, and required that women enter business and the professions.

Title VII of the Civil Rights Act of 1964 contained a provision banning job discrimination on the basis of sex. (It was placed there by civil rights opponents in an unsuccessful effort to defeat the legislation.) When the Equal Employment Opportunity Commission refused to enforce it, Friedan created the National Organization of Women. Although membership was small in 1966, NOW members were articulate and zealous. They were soon at work in state capitols, Congress, academia, and business circles demanding greater representation of women in employment, equal pay for equal work, the repeal of antiabortion statutes, easier divorce laws, more day care centers, tougher rape laws, and other reforms.

Backed by intellectuals, the major media, and the courts, feminists enjoyed rapid success. Seventeen state legislatures voted to abolish or liberalize abortion laws. "No-fault" divorce reform began in California in 1969, and within five years forty-four states had enacted such legislation. Feminists also sought the elimination of alimony on the explicit grounds that this would force women out of the home and into the work place where they belonged.

Women's Studies became a respected and popular academic discipline. Hiring goals and quotas were established in both public and private employment to ensure the presence of larger numbers of women. Occupations and professions previously dominated by men opened their doors. The prefix "Ms." became common as a substitute for the traditional "Miss" or "Mrs.", which identified marital status.

Feminists more radical than Friedan raged against the traditional images of women, calling for an end to beauty contests, refusing to wear bras or makeup or shave their underarms, spurning childbirth, objecting to the traditional family structure, and rejecting their husband's surname. They wanted to avoid, alter, or ban all masculine pronouns, including references to God. "Sexism" and "male chauvinism" were seen as the roots of almost every evil. Many radical feminists were proudly lesbian or bisexual.

In 1971, militant feminist Bella Abzug of New York became the second Jewish woman in Congress (Florence Prag Kahn served from 1925 to 1937), working earnestly through three terms to end the Vietnam War and promote feminist and gay issues.

Most women in the 1960s were not feminists, let alone radical feminists. A Gallup poll published in 1970 revealed that 70 percent of women thought they were treated fairly by men. (NOW leader Gloria Steinem, who called housewives "dependent creatures who are still children," said they were brainwashed.) Most married women continued to make home and family their top priority, even though by 1969 40.4 percent of them held a part-time or full-time job. Many right-wing Christians, men and women, opposed feminism because it rejected the subordinate view of women proclaimed in the Bible. Conservatives of all sorts saw in radical feminism an enemy from the far left.

Ethnic Power

Native Americans grew increasingly self-conscious in the 1960s. While many had moved to cities, over half remained on reservations and were plagued by poverty, high mortality rates, lack of education, and a high suicide rate. Militant leaders, inspired by the gains made by blacks, objected to the discrimination their people had suffered for centuries and demanded the restitution of lost lands, rights, and benefits from the federal government and the courts. In 1968, the American Indian Movement (AIM) was created to raise the banner of "red power." This mood was intensified by activist Vine Deloria, Jr.'s, *Custer Died For Your Sins* (1969), and Dee Brown's *Bury My Heart At Wounded Knee* (1971), which portrayed Indians as victims in American history.

Mexican Americans found a champion in migrant worker Cesar Chavez. In 1963 Chavez founded a trade union, the National Farm Workers Association, and worked hard to organize California lettuce workers and grape pickers. He led national boycotts of grapes in 1967–70 and 1973–78 that won broad support, and pressured most growers to sign labor contracts and give additional rights to farm workers. Stirred by the conflict, militant Mexican American leaders called themselves "Chicanos" and expressed pride in their heritage. In 1968, the first Mexican American studies program appeared on a college campus.

Everyday Life

Americans were increasingly on the move in the 1960s. More than 30,000 miles of the interstate highway system were in place by the end of the decade, enabling millions to move about the country as never before. As automobile and truck travel soared, railroads fell increasingly into disuse. More Americans than ever enjoyed air travel. The Boeing 727 and Douglas DC-9 set records for speed and comfort. The Boeing 747, the largest commercial plane in the world, with a range of 6,000 miles and seating 374 passengers, made its first flight on February 9, 1969. The supersonic Concorde was tested that same year. On September 26, 1973, it flew from Washington, D.C., to Paris in a remarkable three hours and thirty-three minutes.

Medical innovations and improvements enhanced the quality and length of life. The media were filled with stories of organ and corneal transplants, coronary bypass surgery, the pacemaker to regulate heartbeats, new uses for laser technology, and new drugs to treat a wide assortment of ailments. Still, modern medicine was hard pressed to understand and combat the Hong Kong flu, which killed 34,000 Americans in 1968–69.

Cigarette smoking, criticized by scientists since the 1950s, was declared by the U.S. surgeon general in 1964 to be a major cause of sickness and death.

In 1966 Congress required manufacturers to put a health warning on each pack.

In 1965 consumer activist Ralph Nader became famous for his book *Unsafe at any Speed*, a call for safety regulations for automobiles. In the next more than three decades, Nader would found dozens of consumer advocacy groups aimed at such industries as broadcasting and health care.

In the 1960s computer technology began to be widely used by newspapers, scholars, corporations, government agencies, and others interested in the rapid acquisition and analysis of data. The xerox machine for photocopying documents became an indispensable office tool.

Popular culture evolved during this period in ways that shocked millions of Americans. Many young women wore miniskirts (several inches above the knee), used birth control devices and pills, and rejected the sexual restraint long associated with femininity. Men and women increasingly abandoned formal dress, manners, and language. Rebellion was fashionable, and "doing your own thing" became a national standard, especially among the young.

Much of this conduct reflected trends in the media. Movie censorship was dropped in 1968, resulting in an explosion of violence, sex, and profanity in mainstream films. *Easy Rider* (1969) glorified two long-haired motorcycle riders who peddled heroin and engaged in casual sex. Theaters specializing in hard-core pornography multiplied rapidly all across the nation.

Rock music began to dominate the media, and performers routinely used four-letter words and promoted drug use, defiance, and alienation to attract audiences, particularly the young. The most popular rock group, however, was much less controversial. The Beatles, a quartet from the slums of Liverpool, England, made their national television debut in 1964 and quickly took the Western world by storm. Beatle John Lennon boasted in 1966, "We're more popular than Jesus now," and many agreed.

On Broadway, crowds delighted in the nudity and profanity featured in such plays as *Hair*, and *Oh! Calcutta!* Popular books and magazines were often of similar bent. Truman Capote's brutally frank *In Cold Blood* (1965) William Styron's *The Confessions of Nat Turner* (1967), and Philip Roth's steamy *Portnoy's Complaint* (1969) were best-sellers. Hugh Hefner's lecherous *Playboy* magazine (created in 1955 and selling a million copies a month within a year) had many imitators.

Still, the popular culture that most Americans enjoyed remained largely rooted in the 1950s and earlier. Millions watched the comedy programs of Carol Burnett and the Smothers brothers on television, and "Tonight" host Johnny Carson became famous for his topical humor. "Sweet music" bandleader Lawrence Welk and country singer Johnny Cash had enormous followings. Millions rooted for the Green Bay Packers, winners of five National Football League championships from 1961–67. Coach Vince Lombardi became a symbol of old-fashioned discipline, hard work, and success.

Moviegoers enjoyed such musicals as *My Fair* Lady (1964), *Mary Poppins* (1964), *The Sound of Music* (1965), *Oliver* (1968), and *Hello Dolly* (1969). Important films with serious themes included *In the Heat of the Night* (1967),

The Graduate (1967), and *Midnight Cowboy* (1969). Writer-actor-comedian Woody Allen brought out the first of his many movies in this period, and millions enjoyed films by playwright Neil Simon. James Bond thrillers, starring Sean Connery, were immensely popular. Veteran macho actor John Wayne won the Academy Award in 1969 for the western *True Grit.*

Classical music continued to appeal, largely to the educated and affluent. Symphonies existed in large and small cities all across the nation, and many larger cities could boast of having a local opera and ballet company as well. In 1966 the Metropolitan Opera House in New York opened its magnificent new building. College and university music, theater, and art programs continued to emphasize what had traditionally been considered the best of the fine arts.

Churches in Turmoil

While levels of public belief remained high, church membership, attendance, and the importance placed on religion dropped. The liberal Protestant churches—the American Baptists, the Disciples of Christ, the Episcopalians, the Evangelical Lutherans, the Presbyterians, the Methodists, and members of the United Church of Christ—were especially hard hit and began to shrink for the first time. Some critics thought this was a consequence of the secularization of these bodies. By abandoning many traditional biblical beliefs, adopting radical theology and "situation ethics," and endorsing and financing demands by feminists, civil rights activists, and antiwar demonstrators, these denominations had become mere echoes of the counterculture. Defenders of the "mainline" churches expressed great pride in their social and political activities, preferring to seek explanations for their falling numbers elsewhere. They noted correctly that many people stayed home on Sunday because they thought churches "behind the times" and irrelevant. Overall church attendance dropped from 49 percent in 1958 to 42 percent in 1969.

Still, conservative Protestant churches, which tended to stick to traditional biblical and cultural beliefs, continued to grow throughout the 1960s. Data on missionary personnel reflected the trend. Between 1958 and 1971, the United Methodist overseas task force dropped from 1,453 to 1,175. The number sent out by the conservative Southern Baptist Convention grew from 1,186 to 2,494.

American Roman Catholics were profoundly shaken by the modernization resulting from the Second Vatican Council (1962–65). The Mass was now said in English with the "pastor" facing the people. In most churches, traditional music, rituals, disciplines, and clerical vestments disappeared. Most nuns discarded or altered their habits. Many churches were stripped of altars, statues, and confessionals. Still, some on the left were disappointed that the changes did not go further to include married clergy, women priests, and approval of artificial birth control, abortion, and divorce. Mass attendance dropped sharply. Between 1966 and 1969, the num-

ber of nuns in America decreased by 14,000, and the number of seminarians by 30 percent. By 1976, some 35,000 nuns and 10,000 priests had departed.

By mid-1963, at least thirty states required or authorized Bible reading
in public schools. About half of the nation's schoolchildren began their
day with religious exercises that included Bible verses or the Lord's Prayer
or both. These practices, according to pollsters, had the overwhelming support of the American people. But the United States Supreme Court thought
otherwise. In 1963, continuing a trend that began in 1947, it struck down
state-sponsored Bible reading and recitation of the Lord's Prayer in public schools. Billy Graham said he was "shocked and disappointed." Liberal
church leaders, however, praised the decision of the Court.

Moreover, the media treated religion with increasing indifference. Many
Christian colleges and universities dropped religious requirements and practices. The mood of educated people (especially in the humanities and social
sciences) was moving sharply to the left in the 1960s, and this was reflected
in a growing hostility to traditional Christianity.

A Gallup poll of 1968 showed that 67 percent thought that religion was
losing its impact on society, five times the number who felt that way a decade
earlier. Two years later the figure rose to 75 percent.

The Backlash

By the late 1960s the majority of Americans were clearly upset by the direction in which the country was going. Most Americans were moderately
conservative. Michael Novak has reminded us that "the number of students
who ever demonstrated or marched or could by any public act have been
taken to be 'radical' or 'hippie' never exceeded 2 percent. Polling data show
that young people were more conservative than their elders."

Draft-dodgers, antiwar demonstrations, changing moral values, urban riots,
Muslim militants, campus uprisings, hippies, pot, acid rock, militant women,
assassinations, radical clergy, rising taxes and inflation—to many average,
white, hard-working, middle- and lower-middle class citizens, it seemed that
the nation was coming apart.

Tension and animosity were aimed especially at African Americans. They
were condemned for taking welfare and at the same time for bettering themselves and moving into traditionally white neighborhoods and schools. When
heavyweight boxing champion Muhammad Ali refused to be drafted into the
armed forces, many were glad he was stripped of his title. Millions were outraged when two victorious members of the U.S. track and field team at the
1968 summer Olympics raised clenched fists above their heads in black power
salutes during the playing of the national anthem.

In 1968 tensions all across the political spectrum were at their highest point
since the Civil War. The upcoming election seemed to many to be a referendum on the nation's future.

Demonstrators at the Democratic National Convention of 1968 in Chicago. Source: Roz Payne/Archive Photos

The Election of 1968

The Republicans met in Miami Beach in early August and turned to former vice president Richard Nixon to head the ticket. Nixon had retired from politics in 1962 after an unsuccessful race for governor in California. But he had continued to campaign and raise money for other candidates and was popular with party centrists and conservatives. Nixon chose Maryland governor Spiro Agnew as his running mate, a tall, tough-talking politico known for his advocacy of law and order.

The Democratic convention in Chicago, three weeks later, was a disaster. Some ten thousand hippies and radicals turned out to protest the war and President Johnson (who did not attend), and to disrupt the convention. Mayor Richard Daley, who detested the counterculture, vowed to keep the peace. When demonstrators blocked city traffic and pelted police with rocks and bottles, Daley sanctioned violent reprisals. Television cameras captured memorable scenes of police clubbing, gassing, and arresting young people. While the media routinely sided with the "victims" of the assault, millions of Americans cheered on the police and praised the mayor for his courage. The fissures in the culture were never more glaring.

Robert Kennedy's assassination in June left the antiwar forces without a viable candidate. The Democrats settled on Vice President Hubert

Humphrey on the first ballot. The nominee selected Senator Edmund Muskie of Maine to balance the ticket. Humphrey was a talkative, exuberant liberal known especially for his anticommunism, his personal integrity, and his support of civil rights. He entered the campaign leading a badly divided party.

Segregationist governor George Wallace of Alabama also chose to run. Heading the American Independence party, Wallace claimed to speak for the millions of average Americans who supported the Vietnam War, stood for traditional morality, and resented the intrusions of big government. His targets included hippies, "pointy-headed intellectuals," the Supreme Court, and civil rights activists. His angry call for law and order had strong racist overtones. By mid-September, Wallace had the support of 21 percent of the electorate, almost as many as Humphrey.

Sensing the frustrations of what he called "the great, quiet forgotten majority," Nixon presented himself as a man of the middle who stood for peace, unity, and patriotism. He spoke largely in generalities, giving the impression in his well- funded campaign that he was mature and capable. Spiro Agnew, on the other hand, attacked the left with harsh right-wing rhetoric that reminded many of the younger Nixon.

Nixon led in the early polls by a wide margin. Humphrey, short on funds and hounded by antiwar demonstrators, closed the gap substantially by announcing that if elected he would halt the bombing of North Vietnam. Antiwar Democrats now rallied behind Humphrey, as did organized labor. Five days before the election, President Johnson announced that he was suspending the bombing, and the Humphrey campaign gained more momentum. Nixon countered with talk of a secret plan he had to end the war.

On election day Nixon won 43.4 percent of the vote to Humphrey's 42.7 percent. Wallace, who won in five states of the deep South, received 13.4 percent. Nixon had an easier time of it in the electoral college, winning 321 to 191 over Humphrey, with Wallace collecting 46. Democrats retained control of Congress with substantial majorities in the House and Senate.

Race played a major role in the campaign. African Americans voted overwhelmingly for Humphrey. But 90 percent of southern whites voted either for Nixon or Wallace. The solid South the Democrats had enjoyed since Reconstruction was now permanently shattered. Election analysts also recognized the power of the cultural backlash. The militant left had driven millions of Americans to the right.

Rather than being a mandate for the right or left, the election of 1968 mostly revealed the sharp divisions within the American people. And it was clear that if the new chief executive could not somehow end the war and restore national unity, the frightening turmoil of the Johnson years would surely continue.

SUGGESTED READING

Michael Beschloss (ed.), *Taking Charge: The Johnson White House Tapes, 1963–1964* (1997); Sara M. Evans, *Personal Politics: The Roots of Women's Liberation in the Civil Rights Movement and the New Left* (1979); David R. Farber, *Chicago '68* (1988); David J. Garrow, *Martin Luther King, Jr., and the Southern Christian Leadership Conference* (1988); Kenneth J. Heineman, *Campus Wars: The Peace Movement at American State Universities in the Vietnam Era* (1994); George Herring, *America's Longest War: The United States and Vietnam, 1950–1975* (1986); Abbie Hoffman, *Revolution for the Hell of It* (1968); Doris Kearns, *Lyndon Johnson and the American Dream* (1976); Richard Krickus, *Pursuing the American Dream: White Ethnics and the New Populism* (1976); Theodore H. White, *The Making of the President, 1968* (1969).

Chapter Eleven

NIXON'S AMERICA

Richard Nixon, age 56, had long been a controversial politician. Admirers praised him for his high intelligence, determination, and energy. Born in southern California of middle-class Quaker parents, he excelled in his studies and graduated from Duke University Law School. He served in the navy during World War II and went into politics in 1946. In the House he became known nationally for his role in the Alger Hiss case. He won a Senate seat in 1950 and was vice president during the Eisenhower administrations. He lost the presidential election in 1960 and lost again two years later when running for the governorship of California. But his drive and ambition were such that he snared the GOP nomination in 1968.

Millions admired Nixon for his advocacy of traditional values and patriotism. He seemed willing and able to restore peace at home and abroad and halt what many saw as a calamitous decline in the nation's morals.

Nixon's detractors said he was ruthless and unprincipled, often calling him "Tricky Dick." There was a case for this. In his congressional and presidential campaigning, Nixon used irresponsible "soft on the Reds" smears against opponents. In 1952, Eisenhower came close to kicking him off the ticket for accepting irregular campaign funding. Nixon was a close friend and ally of Joe McCarthy until Eisenhower turned against the Wisconsin senator.

In private Nixon puzzled many, including those who knew him well. At times, like LBJ, he seemed personally insecure and filled with self-pity. He was given to angry denunciations of the liberal media, the Eastern political establishment, and assorted minorities. He could be secretive, devious, and ill tempered. Like that of JFK, his language was often peppered with four-letter words. At other times, however, Nixon appeared self-confident, charming, and high-minded. Evangelist Billy Graham, courted by the president, saw only the pious manifestation of Nixon and was later shocked to learn that there was another side to the man.

Without hobbies, Nixon devoted himself entirely to politics and the presidency. He was determined to be a moderately conservative, productive, and popular chief executive. But the obstacles facing Nixon were formidable. His electoral mandate was extremely thin. A Democratic Congress would check any meaningful changes in the welfare state. And he could count on intense opposition from the counterculture and its supporters. During the inaugural parade to the White House, Nixon's limousine was attacked by a mob of young people and antiwar demonstrators.

Domestic Programs

More interested in foreign affairs, Nixon turned over much of his domestic policy to loyal aides H. R. Haldeman and John Ehrlichman. His chief White House adviser on domestic affairs was Harvard professor Daniel Patrick Moynihan, whom Michael Barone has described as "a font of liberal ideas."

Among the achievements of Nixon's first term was the policy of revenue sharing, an effort to decrease the power of the federal government and give more authority to state, county, and city authorities. AMTRAK was created to relieve railroads of money-losing passenger trains. The Post Office Department, long an inefficient and often corrupt servant of the spoils system, became a government-owned corporation. In 1971, Congress created the Environmental Protection Agency (EPA), and Nixon named an effective administrator, William Ruckelshaus. Walter Hickel, the secretary of the interior, encouraged the many efforts by Congress to clean up the nation's air and water. With Nixon's backing, a constitutional amendment was ratified in 1971 lowering the nation's voting age to 18.

Despite an unsuccessful effort to reform the nation's welfare system, the president seemed willing to go along with liberal proposals to expand federal benefits. Congress passed, and Nixon signed, legislation increasing funding for Social Security, public housing, food stamps, Medicaid, Medicare, and other programs. Between 1968 and 1974 the number of people on food stamps grew from 2.4 million to 13.5 million.

The city of Washington boomed during the Nixon years as bureaucracies expanded to administer federal activities. Federal civil service employment reached almost three million in 1967, 1968, and 1969, peak peacetime records. In 1970 federal regulatory agencies employed 69,773 full-time employees. A decade later the number would rise to 121,791. EPA staffing grew during this same period from 4,093 to 14,045.

During his first term, Nixon seemed not only to be in favor of government expansion, but he proposed a deficit in the federal budget. He declared, "We are all Keynesians now," the first chief executive to endorse officially the federal deficit-spending policy of the English economist. Nixon was also favorable to the demands of organized labor. Inflation, which had remained low between 1953 and 1967, now became troubling, rising to 5.4 percent in 1969 and 5.9 percent in 1970.

The economy slipped into a recession in 1970, the first in almost a decade. By the summer of 1971 both inflation and recession seemed out of control, and the nation's balance of international trade was worrisome. In August 1971, Nixon announced the New Economic Policy, devised by Treasury Secretary John Connally. The program offered an assortment of tax breaks and imposed a ninety-day freeze on wages and prices, to be enforced by a new federal bureaucracy. Critics noted that such an assault on the free market, unprecedented in peacetime, ran counter to everything Nixon had traditionally stood for. The president tackled the balance of trade issue by imposing a 10-percent surcharge on imports. He took the dollar off the gold standard. The medicine seemed to work, and the economy blossomed in 1972. Inflation dropped to 3.5 percent, the stock market boomed, unemployment dropped, and the balance of international trade improved.

Civil Rights

Nixon seemed both for and against the civil rights movement. On the one hand, his administration was the first to impose "goals" to advance racial equality. In October 1969, Labor Secretary George Schultz approved the "Philadelphia Plan," which required contractors bidding on a federal construction project to make a "good faith" effort to hire minorities as a percentage of the work force. The administration also encouraged the Equal Employment Opportunity Commission to force private employers to accept hiring and promotion quotas for minorities and women. (Critics blasted affirmative action as a policy of "race-based preferences.") During Nixon's first term, the EEOC budget more than doubled and its staff more than quadrupled.

Still, the president had a "southern strategy" which catered to southern white voters by attempting to slow down school desegregation. Both the Justice Department and the HEW argued for delay. Senate liberals defeated two Nixon Supreme Court nominees, Clement F. Haynsworth of South Carolina and G. Harrold Carswell of Florida, because of their less than enthusiastic approach toward civil rights.

In April 1971, in a landmark decision written by Nixon appointee Chief Justice Warren E. Burger, the Supreme Court unanimously agreed to permit busing to achieve racial integration in the public schools. When federal judges began issuing such orders, public outrage erupted in numerous cities across the nation. Whites in Pontiac, Michigan, torched ten school buses. In response, both the president and Congress took steps to limit busing. But the practice continued.

Racing to the Moon and Beyond

In May 1961 President Kennedy had promised to put a man on the moon by 1970. The project remained a top priority throughout the decade, and at a cost of billions of dollars the historic event occurred on July 20, 1969. As some one billion people from around the world watched on television, astronauts Neil Armstrong and Edwin E. "Buzz" Aldrin, Jr., eased the lunar landing vehicle "Eagle" into the dust of the Sea of Tranquility, 240,000 miles from Earth. Michael Collins, a third astronaut, remained in orbit above them in the command module of the Apollo 11 spacecraft. The first person to step out on the surface of the moon, Armstrong declared, "That's one small step for man, one giant leap for mankind." On June 26, 1971, the first manned lunar roving vehicle made its debut.

The lunar landings were part of a spectacularly impressive American space program, inspired in part by Soviet successes. Weather and communications satellites were launched in 1970. The following year, NASA sent the spacecraft *Mariner 9* to photograph Mars and conduct an assortment of tests. *Pioneer 10* blasted off for Jupiter in 1972, and the next year *Mariner 10* headed for the planet Mercury by way of Venus.

In May 1973, the United States launched *Skylab*, a space station orbiting at about 270 miles from earth. An Apollo spacecraft soon took three astronauts to the space station where they spent twenty-eight days conducting experiments and taking photographs. That November, astronauts spent eighty-four days aboard *Skylab*.

On July 15, 1975, millions watched on television the first docking of two spacecraft, one American and one Soviet. In 1976, *Viking 1*, in orbit around Mars, sent a unit to test the soil of the red planet. Later that year plans for the space shuttle were announced. This would be the first reusable spacecraft ever developed, used in part to repair satellites while orbiting the earth. (The space shuttle *Columbia* took its first full test flight in April 1981.) In 1978 NASA selected Sally Kristen Ride to be the first woman astronaut, and she would serve as a mission specialist on a space shuttle.

In 1977 the United States launched two unmanned interplanetary space probes. *Voyager 1* reached Jupiter and Saturn. *Voyager 2* would eventually go by Jupiter, Saturn, Uranus, and Neptune, transmitting invaluable data and photographs.

These and similar developments gave millions of Americans confidence in the power of science and technology to solve virtually any problem. National pride soared as the United States regained the lead in space.

Détente

Nixon had a strong interest in foreign affairs. In 1969–70 he made three major trips across the world to strengthen NATO, to examine Asian policy firsthand, and to cement relations with a broad assortment of leaders.

With the invaluable assistance of National Security adviser Henry Kissinger, the president took numerous steps to create a policy of détente, a relaxation of tensions, with the Soviet Union. This shift away from the traditional Cold War stance was based in large part on the increasing danger of nuclear war between the two superpowers. The administration also sought to enlist the

India's Prime Minister, Mrs. Indira Ghandi, welcomes U.S. Secretary of State Henry A. Kissinger in 1974. Source: Reproduced from the Collections of the Library of Congress

Russians in the effort to win a satisfactory peace in Vietnam, and it was eager to open Soviet markets to American products. America's NATO allies were already making agreements and deals with the Soviets on their own.

In 1969 Nixon signed a Nuclear Nonproliferation Treaty with the Soviets. Strategic arms limitation talks (SALT) began the following year. In 1972, both sides signed three major arms agreements. When Congress approved, the United States declared its willingness to abandon the race to secure nuclear superiority over the Soviets and settle for a policy of sufficiency. At the same time, trade between the two superpowers increased significantly and several sticky diplomatic issues, including an agreement on the political status of Berlin, were settled.

China

It was ironic that Richard Nixon, a supreme Cold Warrior throughout his political life, was, as president, the apostle of détente with the Soviet Union. Equally ironic was his startling and highly significant approach to China, officially recognizing its diplomatic existence and cementing an alliance with

the communist nation. Critics noted correctly that had any previous chief executive made such a move, Nixon would have led the outcry, claiming that
the president was "soft on the Reds."

Since 1949, when Mao Zedong assumed power, the United States had refused to extend diplomatic relations to the world's most populous nation and
did its best to persuade other nations to join the boycott. The initiative for
improved relations came from China. Nixon and Kissinger responded affir-
matively. For one thing, the current policy was failing; a robust trade was
developing, and there was pressure to seat China in the United Nations in
place of pro-American Taiwan. Then too, the communist Chinese might be
helpful in achieving peace in Vietnam. A friendly China might force the Soviets to agree to further efforts to achieve detente. Moreover, a dramatic trip
to China would enhance the president's reelection campaign in 1972.

Nixon made a historic five-day visit to China in February 1972. Flocks of
reporters were on hand, and live television coverage drew the attention of
millions. The agreement that grew out of the visit included steps to normalize relations between the two countries; the United States lifted all restrictions on trade and travel; and the United States acknowledged that Taiwan

*Richard and Pat Nixon at the Great Wall of China, February 24, 1972. Source: Na-
tional Archives*

(expelled from the United Nations Security Council a year earlier) was part of China. The opening of China was the greatest achievement of Nixon's presidency.

Vietnam

In the first year of his presidency, Nixon proclaimed a new Far East policy. Under the Nixon Doctrine, America would provide Asian governments with economic and technical support but would no longer send troops. This was in harmony with the administration's general policy of backing away from the traditional containment policy and depending increasingly on negotiation. While there might not be any more Vietnams, the president was under terrific pressure to end the war going on.

An honorable peace in Vietnam was a top presidential priority. But Nixon was determined to maintain the existence of a noncommunist South Vietnam state, and this was unacceptable to Hanoi. In the spring of 1969, American forces began secretly bombing Viet Cong and North Vietnamese sanctuaries in neutral Cambodia. The bombing of a neutral nation was illegal, but the sanctuaries harbored troops, weapons, and supplies that were used to pursue a Communist victory in Vietnam.

At the same time, Nixon announced a phased withdrawal of American combat troops. He tried to negotiate further with Hanoi. He attempted to persuade the Soviets to intervene. Nothing worked: the North Vietnamese demanded an immediate and complete withdrawal and the formation of a coalition government that did not include General Thieu.

In April 1970, shortly after pro-American General Lon Nol led a successful takeover of the government of Cambodia, Nixon sent American troops into the country to protect it from North Vietnam. The United States now had two allies to defend; Nixon had expanded the war.

News of the Cambodian incursion caused a firestorm of dissent at home. At Kent State University four students were killed and nine wounded as National Guard troops opened fire on a crowd of demonstrators. A memorable photograph taken at the scene (a young woman weeping over the body of a fallen student) helped stir nationwide demonstrations against the nation's policy in Indochina. Hundreds of campuses were closed down. At the University of Wisconsin-Madison, protesters blew up an entire building, killing a young researcher who was working inside. There was trouble in Washington as well. The Senate repealed the Gulf of Tonkin resolution and voted to cut off all funds to Cambodia. (The House did not concur on the funding bill.)

With much of the country in an uproar, Nixon stepped up what he called "Vietnamization"—the gradual withdrawal of American troops and the building up of South Vietnamese forces. There were 234,000 American military personnel in Southeast Asia at the end of 1970, and 156,000 at the conclusion of 1971. While 14,589 Americans lost their lives in Vietnam in 1968, the number was down to 1,831 in 1971.

On March 29, 1971, a military court convicted Lieutenant William Calley
of multiple murders committed at My Lai-4. Calley and his men had been
ordered to destroy a hamlet suspected of harboring Viet Cong troops. Instead of first evacuating the inhabitants, the troops opened fire, killing over
a hundred civilians. The media made much of this and similar atrocity stories that shocked millions of Americans and accelerated the antiwar movement. Calley defenders saw the junior officer as a scapegoat. They noted the
unique horrors of this struggle: for one thing, it was extremely difficult to
identify the enemy; even friendly looking little children sometimes threw
hand grenades. They also recalled the fact that the Viet Cong and North Vietnamese troops had massacred hundreds of thousands of villagers over the
years. Nixon reduced Calley's sentence.

On June 13, 1971, the *New York Times* caused a sensation by publishing
the first installment of the "Pentagon Papers," an extensive and secret study
of American involvement in Vietnam from World War II through 1968. The
study was stolen from the RAND corporation by a former employee and one-
time Pentagon researcher, Daniel Ellsberg. Numerous classified documents
showed that American leaders had lied repeatedly, ignored peace offers, and
deliberately escalated the war.

By the summer of 1971 polls showed that two-thirds of the American people were ready to withdraw all American troops from Vietnam by the end
of the year, even if that meant a communist takeover. The Senate pushed
hard for troop withdrawal. Privately, President Nixon grew increasingly frustrated, convinced he was surrounded by forces eager to damage his presidency, defeat his Vietnam policies, and help the communists.

Included in a clandestine counterattack was the creation of "the plumbers,"
a small band of men led by White House staffer Egil "Bud" Krogh dedicated
to preventing leaks of secret government documents and discrediting Daniel
Ellsberg. In September, former CIA man E. Howard Hunt, ex-FBI agent G.
Gordon Liddy, and three Cubans broke into the office of Ellsberg's psychia-
trist, but failed to find relevant materials.

The North Vietnamese stepped up their assault in 1972. Nixon responded
with an increase in bombing, a naval blockade of North Vietnam, and appeals to both China and the Soviet Union to apply pressure on behalf of
peace. These steps prompted Hanoi to resume peace talks. An agreement
was tentatively hammered out in October between Kissinger and a North
Vietnam official, but the Thieu government balked and the fighting resumed.

Sixties Culture

The counterculture that began under Lyndon Johnson continued through the
Nixon years. Indeed, it flourished. All over the country and in almost all
walks of life one could witness the impact of a life style that stressed narcissism, free sex, illegal drugs, pornography, rock and roll, informal and outlandish dress, long hair and beards, leftist politics, feminism, gay and lesbian

rights, and an abiding concern for racial minorities. No institution was immune. The major media, for example, fell in line quickly, offering the baby-boomer rebels and their followers what they wanted to see, read, and hear. Education at all levels embraced radical changes, frequently lowering admission standards and academic requirements, and abandoning rules for student conduct. Liberal and even moderate churches jettisoned numerous doctrines, practices, and moral standards, in a sometimes frantic effort to seem relevant.

Polls, election returns, and the growth of conservative churches showed that most Americans failed to embrace at least much of the counterculture. But the traditional views of the majority seemed to matter little during the cultural whirlwind that swept through the nation between 1965 and 1975. Even the gray-haired could be seen sporting long sideburns and mustaches, wearing miniskirts and "granny" eyeglasses, experimenting with marijuana, "digging" rock, and enjoying the pornography now common in movie theaters. The film *Deep Throat*, which featured eleven separate acts of oral sex, was a huge money-maker in 1973.

On August 15, 1969, some 400,000 young people attended the Woodstock festival near Bethel, New York. It was the pinnacle of sixties culture: rock blared, drugs flowed, sexual inhibitions fled, and "flower child" conformity in apparel, manners, and speech prevailed. Andrew Kopkind observed, "No one in this country had ever seen a 'society' so free of repression. Everyone swam nude in the lake, balling was easier than getting breakfast, and the 'pigs' just smiled and passed out the oats." The frolic continued for three days and nights.

On June 29, 1969, homosexual patrons of Stonewall Inn, in Greenwich Village, violently resisted police who were attempting to arrest them. It was a turning point in the growing effort by "gays" (as homosexuals increasingly preferred to be called) and lesbians to gain public acceptance. In 1973 the American Psychiatric Association stopped listing homosexuality as a psychiatric disorder. "Gay pride" parades and demonstrations soon became routine in major cities, and colleges and universities began offering courses stressing the same theme.

The women's liberation movement was an especially powerful force during the Nixon years, and the administration contributed to its impact. In 1970 the secretary of labor announced that federal contracts would henceforth contain clauses requiring the employment of specific quotas of women. The attorney general began using Title VII of the Civil Rights Act of 1964 to prevent job discrimination against women. Federal agents investigated colleges and universities in search of discrimination in hiring and salaries.

In August 1970, the House of Representatives approved the Equal Rights Amendment, first proposed in 1923, and the Senate concurred two years later. The ERA, backed by the National Organization for Women, proposed that "Equality of rights under the law shall not be denied or abridged by the United States or by any State on account of sex." Women were supposed to have the same constitutional protections as racial minorities. Proponents noted that in 1970 women constituted only 7.6 percent of the physicians, 2.8 percent of the lawyers, and 9 percent of the full professors on campus. A male high-school graduate earned more on the average than a woman with four years of college. Critics (more often women than men) portrayed the ERA as a ploy by radical feminists to make societal changes, including the abolition of single-sex colleges and the placing of women in military combat roles.

Militant feminists were often in the news. In 1970 some 50,000 women participated in NOW's "Strike for Equality" parade down New York's Fifth Avenue. Some marchers burned their bras to protest sexual stereotyping, and others waved such signs as "Don't Cook Dinner—Starve a Rat Today."

Election of 1972

Four major Democrats, buoyed by congressional victories in 1970, actively sought their party's presidential nomination. Former vice president Hubert Humphrey and Edmund Muskie of Maine were moderately liberal, George Wallace was on the right, and Senator George McGovern of South Dakota represented the left. Senator Edward "Ted" Kennedy was not in the race. In 1969 he had been at the wheel of a car that went over a bridge, killing a young woman who was with him. His highly controversial behavior after the incident left him in disgrace.

Front-runner Muskie failed to excite voters. He had a difficult time winning the New Hampshire primary and lost to McGovern in Massachusetts and Pennsylvania. Wallace's bid was ended in May when a Milwaukee man shot and severely wounded him. Humphrey and antiwar activist McGovern wrestled through several primaries and waged a heated battle at the convention. McGovern won in large part because of racial and sexual quotas governing delegate selection. The 50-year-old ex-history professor selected liberal Senator Thomas Eagleton of Missouri as his running mate.

As expected, the GOP unanimously nominated Nixon and Agnew, who were heavy favorites to win reelection. But the president was taking no chances: his campaign leaders raised a war chest of $60 million, in part by promising wealthy corporate leaders government favors in return for company cash. An unprecedented number of "dirty tricks" against Democratic candidates were carried out with the encouragement of administration leaders. In June a squad created by the Committee to Reelect the President (CREEP) broke into the Democratic National Committee's offices in the Watergate complex in Washington in search of confidential party documents. The burglars were caught, and the president quietly ordered the CIA to keep the FBI off the investigation. While the discovery of this illegal move would later force Nixon from office, the Watergate incident had little impact on the campaign. The White House categorically denied allegations by *Washington Post* reporters Bob Woodward and Carl Bernstein, hot on the trail of clandestine and illegal administration activities.

The election provided voters with a rare and clear choice. McGovern was an outspoken advocate of the counterculture. He saw the Vietnam War as a crime committed by the United States and demanded immediate withdrawal. (In fact there were only 27,400 troops left in Vietnam, and the draft was virtually ended. On October 26 Kissinger announced, prematurely, that "peace is at hand.") He called for a host of sweeping social and cultural changes that included the liberalization of abortion and drug laws and the redistribution of wealth. The Democratic party platform, for the first time, endorsed much of sixties culture.

Nixon portrayed himself as a responsible and moderate candidate of the more traditional "silent majority," one who would end the war responsibly and reject "the far out goals of the far left." He appealed to many on the right by opposing busing, as well as the very racial quotas in hiring and promotion that his administration had encouraged. Vice President Agnew declared, "Will America be led by a president elected by a majority of the American people or will it be intimidated and blackmailed into following the path dictated by a disruptive radical and militant minority—the pampered prodigies of the radical liberals in the United States Senate?"

The campaign was dull and one-sided. If Nixon was crafty and dishonest, McGovern was inept and uninspiring. When Thomas Eagleton was revealed to have undergone shock treatment for depression years earlier, McGovern backed him for a week, panicked, and forced Eagleton from the ticket. He then fumbled a search for a replacement, winding up with Sargent Shriver, a little-known Kennedy clan member and former director of the War on Poverty. A Harris poll in early September had Nixon ahead 63 percent to 29 percent. Many long-time Democratic leaders refused to endorse the ticket. The AFL-CIO, normally a strong Democratic backer, remained neutral.

On election day, Nixon carried forty-nine of fifty states, won 61 percent of the vote, and rolled up an electoral margin of 521 to 17. Despite the fact that 18- to 21-year-olds could now vote, turnout at the polls was the lowest it had been since 1948. Democrats retained control of Congress, suggesting along with other evidence that voters were not as much turned on by Nixon as turned off by McGovern.

Winding Down the War

After the election, Nixon stepped up air attacks on North Vietnam, hoping to force Hanoi to the peace table. The fiercely destructive "Christmas bombing," aimed at military installations and electric power stations, lasted from December 17 to 30. It stirred often violent protest at home and abroad. Congress moved to terminate all funding for the war. Nixon then offered to halt the bombing if North Vietnam would resume negotiations. The offer was accepted and Henry Kissinger and Le Duc Tho of North Vietnam hammered out an agreement in January. The agreement, which Nixon imposed on the Thieu government, called for an immediate cease-fire, the withdrawal of all

American troops, and the exit of the North Vietnamese from Cambodia and Laos, which had been used to attack South Vietnam. It permitted the North Vietnamese to remain in the South, and left the future of the Thieu regime in the hands of the nation's assorted factions. Nixon announced "peace with honor."

Neither side in Vietnam, however, was sincerely committed to negotiation, and the fighting continued. Rampant inflation and corruption seriously weakened the South Vietnamese government. The North labored intensively to beef up its military capability.

The war concluded after Nixon left office. In the spring of 1975 a North Vietnamese offensive caused the collapse of South Vietnam. On April 23, President Gerald Ford announced that the United States' commitment to the Vietnam War was over, and six days later Saigon fell to the communists. Television cameras captured the frantic efforts of South Vietnamese to escape in the last departing American helicopters.

This most unpopular and divisive of America's wars, the first war America lost, cost some $150 billion over the span of twenty one years. It left 58,000 Americans dead and 300,000 wounded. In 1994, Vietnam put its own death toll at three million soldiers and civilians—a third from the North and two-thirds from the South—and claimed that U.S. chemical defoliants hurt two million more.

The conclusion of the war prompted a major reevaluation of the nation's containment policy. The "dominoes" did not fall, and Asia did not become communist. American alliances were not imperilled. American authority in the world did not diminish. Moreover, once Saigon was renamed Ho Chi Minh City, communist nations began turning against each other. Vietnam attacked the murderous (as many as 2 million died over four years) Pol Pot regime in Cambodia. China attacked Vietnam, and the Soviet Union backed Vietnam. At least in one part of the world, the realities of the struggle for power were more complex than the "free world versus communism" approach popular in 1947.

George Kennan, the so-called "father" of the containment policy, called the Vietnam War "the most disastrous of all America's undertakings over the whole two hundred years of its history." By 1975 most Americans agreed, including untold numbers of bitter, disillusioned, and unappreciated veterans of the struggle.

And yet a Harris poll taken in 1980, the most comprehensive ever taken of those who Vietnam veterans, found that 91 percent who served in combat were "glad they'd served their country," 74 percent "enjoyed their time in the military," and 80 percent disagreed with the statement that "the U.S. took unfair advantage of me." Nearly two out of three said they would go to Vietnam again, even if they knew how the war would end.

Determined to limit the ability of future presidents to involve the United States in a similar conflict, Congress passed the War Powers Act in the autumn of 1973—over President Nixon's veto. Henceforth when the president committed the nation to hostilities abroad or took action involving a significant increase in the number of combat troops committed to a foreign nation, he had forty-eight hours to submit the details to Congress. He was required to terminate the commitment or withdraw the troops after sixty days if he lacked congressional approval. The act also provided that by a concurrent (veto proof) resolution, Congress could terminate a presidential commitment to foreign hostilities or the deployment of troops abroad.

Chile and the Middle East

Elections in Chile deeply concerned President Nixon. In 1970, Marxist Salvador Allende Gossens secured 36.3 percent of the votes in a three-man race, and was selected as president by the Chilean Congress. Fearing that Chile would become another Cuba, Nixon asked the CIA to explore the possibility of a coup d'etat to prevent Allende's inauguration. This was in the tradition of every president since Truman. Nothing came of the secret request, however.

Marxist policy and rampant inflation soon led Chile to the brink of civil war. In September 1973 the military staged a successful coup, and Allende died in the struggle. Many in the world saw the hand of the United States behind the takeover, but Henry Kissinger later wrote that there was "no involvement with the plotters" and stated that the administration had only supplied opposition parties and local media with modest financial support.

In October, Arabs and Israelis began the fourth of their wars for control of the tiny (in 1997 more than a thousand square miles smaller than the state of New Hampshire) piece of land on the shores of the eastern Mediterranean that both peoples considered sacred. The last major struggle had occurred in 1967, when Israel won the Six Day War against Egypt, Jordan, and Syria and greatly expanded the territory under its control. This marked the third consecutive victory for the Israelis, who enjoyed strong support from the United States. The Soviets quickly helped the Arabs to rearm. The hatred between Arabs and Jews had international implications.

During the Olympic games in 1972, members of the terrorist Palestine Liberation Organization (PLO), headed by Yasir Arafat, murdered two and kidnapped nine members of the Israeli team. All nine athletes died in the attempt to free them.

On October 6, 1973, while vast numbers of Israelis were observing Yom Kippur, the Day of Atonement, Egyptian and Syrian troops attacked. During the first week of the war, the Soviet Union backed the invaders with equipment and supplies. The Nixon administration sent large-scale assistance to Israel. Within two weeks, Israeli forces had routed the attackers and were headed for the capital cities of Egypt and Syria.

Henry Kissinger (now secretary of state as well as national security adviser) and Soviet leader Leonid Brezhnev worked out a cease-fire agreement that both sides accepted on October 24. The Americans and Russians argued bitterly over the details of ensuring the peace, however, and Nixon placed

United States military forces around the world on alert. The crisis ended when United Nations troops were dispatched to the area to keep the peace.

The Energy Crisis

During the Yom Kippur War, six Arab nations unilaterally raised oil prices 70 percent. On October 20, eleven Arab states stopped shipping crude petroleum to the United States because of its support of Israel. Since America imported more than a third of the petroleum energy it needed, the nation was vulnerable to what amounted to blackmail. (With only 7 percent of the world's population, the United States consumed about 30 percent of its energy.) In December, the Organization of Petroleum Exporting Countries (OPEC) nearly quadrupled prices, causing economic havoc all over the world. Western Europe and Japan imported 80 to 90 percent of their oil from the Middle East. Congress approved Nixon's request for an oil pipeline from Alaska and set the highway speed limit at 55 miles per hour to conserve fuel.

Until the embargo was largely lifted in mid-March 1974, Americans endured a severe shortage of gasoline, often waiting in long lines at service stations. Even when supplies increased, heating oil and gas prices rose sharply. The era of cheap energy, which had long helped propel the economy, was over (for the time being). Automobile sales slumped and inflation soared, hitting double digits in 1973 and 1974. The gross national product plummeted during 1974–75. Some economists concluded that America had lost its long-enjoyed economic dominance in the world.

Feminism to the Fore

By the early 1970s, the women's liberation movement was busily at work attacking sexual discrimination and stereotypes. While there were significant tensions between feminists, they agreed on the general goals: equal employment opportunities and equal pay, equality before the law, and equality in sexual relations. Feminists started and supported abortion and birth control clinics, day care centers, and shelters for battered wives. They lobbied federal and state governments for financial and legal support. They badgered businesses to hire and promote women. They encouraged the media to feature women in a variety of roles once open only to men. The movement's overall success, despite failure of the states to ratify the Equal Rights Amendment, was among the most significant developments of the era.

By 1973, 61 percent of women in their 20s were in the labor force. Among college women that age, the figure was 86 percent. Seven years later, more than 50 percent of mothers with children under the age of 6 worked outside the home. Polls showed that a vast majority of women were committed to a lifetime of paid employment. Child-rearing and housework ranked low in female priorities, especially among younger and more educated women.

Between 1970 and 1974, the number of women in medical schools, law schools, and graduate business schools doubled. Earned doctorates by women in the 1970s increased from 11 percent of the total to more than 25 percent. Women entered the United States Military Academy at West Point in 1976. That same year they were welcomed to become Episcopal priests and bishops. The number of female mayors grew from 566 in 1975 to 1,680 in 1981. Women drove race cars and huge tractor-trailer rigs, piloted jet planes and helicopters, worked in construction, and became action heroes in the movies (where they often outfought as well as outsmarted men).

Large families were now seldom desired. Indeed, the birthrate fell to an all-time low in the 1970s. The divorce rate increased 66 percent in the 1970s; from 1975 on more than a million marriages ended in divorce every year. The connection between women at work outside the home and divorce was well established. Many women were not willing to sacrifice income, status, and self-fulfillment to preserve an unhappy marriage. The strain on women of bearing occupational as well as family responsibilities (men were notoriously reluctant to care for children and do housework) was widely noted. No-fault divorce laws, enabling either spouse to end a marriage unilaterally, were also a major factor in the escalation of divorce.

Polls showed that women worked outside the home far less from ideological commitment than from what was perceived to be economic necessity. But the two-income family was becoming the norm even in many upscale communities, leaving affluent neighborhoods largely empty of people during the day.

By the late 1970s, some 75 percent of American families did not share breakfast. The average family sat down to dinner fewer than three times a week, and the meal seldom lasted more than twenty minutes.

This dramatic change in the role of women generated much controversy. Conservative David Gelernter has written, "The average working mother sits at her desk in a big noisy room with a hundred other women at some insurance company in Peoria, and worries about her children. A generation ago she would have been at home taking care of them. Are we better off as a society now that she spends her day processing claims instead?" On the other hand, Lt. Col. Roxanne W. Cheney of the United States Marine Corps declared, "we are opposed to suggestions that we subordinate our authority or desires to someone else based solely on gender," adding, " 'Goodbye and good riddance' to Scarlet O'Hara-style subservience."

Premarital sex in the early 1970s became commonplace and was widely approved, especially on campus, where all restrictions on personal activity were being dropped. One study of college students showed that 76 percent of women (and 75 percent of men) had experienced sexual intercourse before their junior year. This striking change in sexual attitude and practice was in part due to the availability of oral contraceptives. The legalization of abortion also played a role.

In 1970, efforts to repeal antiabortion laws were defeated in thirteen states. Two years later, 61 percent of the voters in Michigan and 77 percent in North Dakota voted down repeal. But in January 1973, the United States Supreme

Court invalidated all state abortion laws. In *Roe* v. *Wade*, and the companion case *Doe* v. *Bolton*, the Court discovered (critics said invented) an absolute constitutional right to abortion during the first trimester of pregnancy. In practice, the Court virtually permitted abortion on demand through all three trimesters. Within the next quarter century, some 21 million American women would choose to have 35 million abortions.

Conservatives (often Roman Catholics) decried "the silent holocaust," and some picketed and harassed abortionists. The struggle between "pro-life" and "pro-choice" organizations became intense, one camp referring to the target of the medical procedure as an "unborn baby" and the other saying "fetus." Efforts to reverse *Roe v. Wade* proved futile. Most Americans did not want to make abortion illegal, although many approved of restrictions on the procedure.

Environmentalism

The 1970s have been called the Environmental Decade. Concerns about air and water pollution, pesticides, the destruction of the wilderness, dams, urban sprawl, and nuclear power plants, while not new, were accelerated. The "back to nature" movement by the counterculture played a role in making environmental protection fashionable. But many others were also concerned, for there were warnings that the very future of the planet was at risk.

Rachel Carson's *Silent Spring*, published in 1962, had caused a sensation by warning against the invisible consequences of pesticide. Both the Kennedy and Johnson administrations took steps to improve the environment. Lady Bird Johnson's "Keep America Beautiful" campaign and the Highway Beautification Act of 1965 were especially helpful in focusing the nation's attention on the need to reduce pollution. In 1968, biologist Paul Ehrlich's best-seller *The Population Bomb* contended that humanity was headed for self-destruction unless dramatic steps were taken to stop its natural increase. That same year, biologist Garrett Hardin warned that individual liberties would have to be curtailed to solve population and environmental problems.

The following year, a massive oil spill in Hardin's beautiful hometown of Santa Barbara, California, seemed to crystallize pollution problems for a great many Americans. Historian Hal K. Rothman has observed, "Only when the problems reached the lives of the privileged did the problems truly attract national attention. The bad air, the poor conditions in factories and plants, and the consequences of working with toxic materials were common and accepted." Almost overnight, the environment became a major political issue.

Most of those concerned were upper-middle-class whites. Many minorities and blue-collar workers feared that cleanup efforts by idealists might cost jobs and lead to higher taxes. One bumper sticker declared, "Out of work? Hungry? Eat an environmentalist." Nevertheless, there was a general consensus that pollution was bad and that government should lead the fight against it.

Led by Senator Gaylord A. Nelson of Wisconsin and others, environmentalists succeeded in persuading Congress to pass the National Environmental Policy Act of 1969. This landmark legislation committed the federal government to preserve and improve environmental quality. Among the NEPA provisions was the requirement that every federal or federally supported project had to be accompanied by an environmental impact statement, available to the public.

In February 1970, President Nixon gave the first "Message on the Environment" to Congress, an action mandated by the NEPA. A three-member Council on Environmental Quality, created by the NEPA, helped shape the Nixon agenda for the environment. In December 1970, the president signed into law legislation creating the Environmental Protection Agency. Within two years the agency had a $2.5-billion budget and employed more than seven thousand people. The EPA signaled an unprecedented commitment by the federal government to stop the wanton pollution and destruction of the continent that had been going on for centuries.

In April 1970, the first Earth Day was held, with as many as 20 million people across the nation participating in a variety of educational efforts and counterculture entertainments. Environmentalism had become a sort of secular religion of liberal, economically secure urbanites.

Conservatives scoffed when, under the Endangered Species Act of 1973, efforts to preserve a small fish called the snail darter temporarily blocked a $116-million dam project in Tennessee. (By 1998, there were 1,126 species on the endangered list, with about 80 added each year.) The timber industry was in a perpetual struggle with federal authorities over the nation's forests.

Watergate

In secretly ordering a cover-up of the Watergate burglary during the 1972 campaign, President Nixon was guilty of obstructing justice, a federal crime. Two young *Washington Post* reporters, Bob Woodward and Carl Bernstein, assigned to cover what was thought to be a minor incident, began to uncover the larger political overtones of the story almost immediately. In September and October, the reporters charged that the burglary could be traced to the upper levels of the White House, as high as Nixon's chief of staff H. R. Haldeman. Presidential spokesmen flatly denied the allegations, and the rest of the media largely ignored them during the campaign.

Following his overwhelming victory at the polls, Nixon demanded total personal loyalty of those around him, requiring all of his appointees, including members of the cabinet and White House staff, to submit their resignations, which he would accept or reject as he saw fit. He vowed to reverse the generally liberal tone of his administration, and declared war on

Congress by "impounding," refusing to spend, billions of dollars designed for purposes he disapproved of. He bristled at critics of his Vietnam War policies, and vetoed the War Powers Act. White House tape recordings later revealed that a source of this intense combativeness was concern about the Watergate investigation. Nixon was keenly aware that it had the potential of destroying his presidency.

The Watergate burglars went on trial in January 1973. Two were convicted and five others pleaded guilty. Sensing more to the story than a mere burglary, U.S. District Court Judge John Sirica imposed stiff sentences, hoping to compel the defendants to talk. The tactic worked. On March 19, James McCord confessed that he and his accomplices were under pressure to keep silent and that perjury had been committed during the trial.

Meanwhile, the Senate created a special Watergate Committee, headed by 76-year-old conservative Democrat Sam Ervin of North Carolina. Ervin was highly respected for his integrity, learning, and folksy sense of humor. The ranking Republican, Howard Baker of Tennessee, was honest, articulate, and ambitious. Knowing he was in deep trouble, Nixon said that he would invoke executive privilege and refuse to let any staff members testify before the committee.

At the same time, the Senate Judiciary Committee held hearings on the confirmation of L. Patrick Gray as FBI head. Gray had been acting director since May and had been in charge of the Watergate investigations. On March 22, Gray admitted that White House counselor James Dean had "probably" lied to the FBI during its probe.

The full Watergate story quickly began to unfold. Following rumors of their direct involvement, Nixon aides Haldeman and Ehrlichman resigned. Dean was fired. Attorney General Richard Kleindienst was replaced by Defense Secretary Elliot Richardson. The administration suffered another blow in early May when Nixon campaign leaders Maurice Stans and John Mitchell were indicted for perjury and obstruction of justice in connection with campaign contributions made by convicted financier Robert Vesco.

On May 17 the Watergate Committee began televised hearings that lasted twelve weeks. Nixon was forced to abandon his claim of executive privilege, and witness after witness, under incisive questioning, told senators of administration intrigue and corruption. In July, James Dean linked Mitchell, Haldeman, and Ehrlichman directly to Watergate, and charged that Nixon had been personally involved in the cover-up. Soon the existence of secret White House tape recordings became known, tapes that might prove whether Dean or Nixon was telling the truth. The Watergate Committee and special prosecutor Archibald Cox demanded certain of the tapes. Nixon refused, and the committee sued. Whether the tapes became public or not, Nixon's reputation was badly damaged, especially among Washington insiders and students of politics, and his administration was crippled.

Watergate thrust political humor into the mainstream for the first time. Comedian Mark Russell became famous for his withering ridicule of the president. Nixon impersonator David Frye drew howls with lines like, "There is a bright side to everything. My administration has taken crime out of the streets and put it in the White House where I can keep an eye on it."

Making matters worse, on October 10 Vice President Spiro Agnew pleaded guilty to tax evasion on bribes he had taken while governor of Maryland. He resigned the same day. Nixon quickly named 60-year-old Congressman Gerald R. Ford, Jr., of Michigan as Agnew's successor. While some critics questioned his intelligence, Ford was widely admired on Capitol Hill for his experience and integrity. At his confirmation hearings, Ford expressed confidence in Nixon's innocence in the Watergate matter but urged the president to cooperate in the investigations.

Over a million letters, telegrams, and telephone calls flooded congressional offices in late October after Nixon fired the attorney general, deputy attorney general, and special prosecutor Cox, and ordered the FBI to seal all executive office files.

The noose around Nixon's neck tightened swiftly. In November the president replaced special prosecutor Richardson with Leon Jaworski, a move that proved to be to Nixon's disadvantage. In March 1974, Mitchell, Haldeman, and Ehrlichman were indicted for obstructing justice in the Watergate affair. In April, the House Judiciary Committee subpoenaed earlier requested tapes and documents. When Nixon submitted edited transcripts of the tapes, the public was disgusted by the foul language and devious behavior they revealed. The committee rejected them as inaccurate and soon began impeachment hearings.

The American people were not eager to see the president driven from the White House. A Gallup poll found in May that 49 percent of respondents thought Nixon's actions insufficiently serious "to warrant his being impeached and removed from the presidency." In another poll taken that month, 40 percent called the president a man of integrity. As late as July 1974, 55 percent of those interviewed in a Harris poll agreed that Nixon "is trying to do his best in an almost impossible job."

Still, Nixon's popularity had dropped sharply from the 68-percent job approval rating he had enjoyed in January. Political scientist and pollster C. Everett Ladd thought later that the wobbly economy in 1974 (80 percent of respondents in August identified economic matters as the most important problem facing the country, and 70 percent referred specifically to the high cost of living) did as much as anything to undermine the public's confidence in Nixon.

In May, special prosecutor Jaworski went before the Supreme Court seeking vital tape recordings from the president. On July 24 the Supreme Court voted unanimously that the president had to turn over sixty-four tapes to Jaworski. The House Judiciary Committee soon voted to send three articles of impeachment to the floor of the House. On August 5 the special prosecutor learned from a tape recording that Nixon had known about the Watergate burglary long before he admitted it and was clearly guilty of obstructing justice. After hearing from Republican congressional leaders that his impeachment and conviction were certain, Nixon resigned on August 9. President

Ford quickly assured the American people that "our long national nightmare is over."

Few now mourned Nixon's forced retirement. People were exhausted and disillusioned by the corrupt administration. (In all, sixty-nine individuals were charged with Watergate-related crimes. Twenty-five served prison terms, including ten top Nixon aides. By contrast, only a single high official in the "scandal-ridden" Harding administration went to jail.) Many blamed the president for the return of double-digit inflation. Republicans, who had dropped four special elections earlier in the year, were generally pleased to see a change in leadership. The left condemned Nixon as a war criminal and social reactionary.

In fact, Nixon's record in office contained achievements that liberals should have applauded. The president wound down the Vietnam War, opened China to the West, stabilized relations with the Soviet Union, and made significant moves to expand the Great Society. For all of his rhetoric against the sixties counterculture, Nixon proved to be an ally in certain ways.

Still, there was no denying that Nixon had disgraced the presidency and temporarily shaken the nation's confidence in government. And there was more to the dark side of the president and his men than people realized in 1974. Nixon would spend the remaining twenty years of his life justifying his actions and raising funds to prevent the American people from hearing the rest of the tape recordings made in the Oval Office during his administration.

SUGGESTED READING

Carl Bernstein and Bob Woodward, *All The President's Men* (1974); David Garrow, *Liberty and Sexuality: The Right to Privacy and the Making of Roe v. Wade* (1994); Frank Graham, Jr., *Since Silent Spring* (1970); T. A. Heppenheimer, *Countdown: A History of Space Flight* (1997); David Horowitz, *Radical Son: A Journey Through Our Times* (1997); Stanley Kutler (ed.), *Abuse of Power: The New Nixon Tapes* (1997); Richard M. Nixon, *RN: The Memoirs of Richard Nixon* (1978); Richard Scammon and Benjamin Wattenberg, *The Real Majority* (1974); Robert Spitz, *Barefoot in Babylon: The Creation of the Woodstock Music Festival, 1969* (1979); Tad Szulc, *The Illusion of Peace: Foreign Policy in the Nixon Years* (1978).

Chapter Twelve

YEARS OF
DISILLUSIONMENT

Gerald Ford entered the White House with credentials to be both popular and effective. A native of Grand Rapids, Michigan, he had been an outstanding football player at the University of Michigan, had graduated from Yale Law School, served in the navy during World War II, and had entered Congress in 1949. His amiability, moderation, and hard work prompted House Republicans to name him their leader in 1965. He had become known nationally by teaming with Senate leader Everett Dirksen in televised press conferences. Republicans especially liked and trusted Ford. During his eight months as vice president, he had traveled more than 100,000 miles and made more than five hundred appearances to rally the GOP.

Most political experts and media leaders thought that Ford's good character and knowledge of Washington would do much to reestablish the dignity of his office and revive national confidence in political institutions. Initially, Ford enjoyed solid public support.

Ford named 66-year-old Nelson Rockefeller, a prominent liberal Republican and former governor of New York, his vice president. For the first time in American history, the presidency and vice presidency were occupied by unelected officials. Without a mandate from voters, Ford lacked influence over Congress.

Less than a month after taking office, Ford ruined his presidency by granting former President Nixon a "full, free, and absolute" pardon for any crimes he may have committed while in the White House. Sensing an earlier deal between Nixon and Ford, the American people expressed outrage. Even though Ford testified under oath that the pardon had not been prearranged, millions of Americans refused to believe him.

The president stirred more controversy by offering amnesty to the thousands of young men who had violated draft laws or deserted during the Vietnam War. Up to two years of public service would reduce or cancel their prison terms. Meant to bind the nation's wounds, this policy angered both

219

hawks and doves, the former considering it lenient and the latter seeing it as punitive. When the program ended in 1975, only about 20 percent of those eligible had applied.

Ford further undermined his popularity with millions by vetoing nearly sixty bills in his first two years, including federal aid to education, housing, and health care, and an effort to increase the power of organized labor. The president's conservatism, however, was consistent with the Republican party's long-declared desire to limit federal authority, balance budgets, and cut taxes.

In the 1974 elections, Democrats gained forty-three seats in the House and four seats in the Senate, giving them commanding majorities on Capitol Hill. Many Republicans, losing most of the state and gubernatorial elections as well, blamed Ford.

In 1975, already weakened by the energy crisis, the economy fell into its worst recession since the 1930s. By May, unemployment rose above 9 percent. Rampaging inflation compounded the misery. Ford agreed to tax cuts but opposed large public works programs to stimulate the economy. He relied on voluntary measures to hold down inflation, asking Americans to wear a lapel button reading WIN—"Whip Inflation Now." Conditions improved slightly by mid-1976, but the economy remained far from healthy. Crude oil that had sold from $2 to $3 a barrel in 1973 now averaged $12 a barrel.

Startling disclosures in Washington also fueled public discontent. In 1976, a commission headed by the vice president revealed that the Central Intelligence Agency had spied on political dissenters in the United States and disrupted their activities. The CIA had also attempted to assassinate Fidel Castro of Cuba and Patrice Lumumba of the Congo. A Senate investigation headed by Frank Church of Idaho confirmed the Rockefeller findings. When a CIA report revealed that Presidents Eisenhower, Kennedy, Johnson, and Nixon were involved in plots or coups against eight foreign leaders, President Ford issued an Executive Order declaring that "No person employed by or acting on behalf of the United States government shall engage in, or conspire to engage in, assassination."

The Church committee also revealed clandestine, illegal, and scandalous actions by the Federal Bureau of Investigation (to this point an almost sacred American institution) against thousands of Americans, including Martin Luther King, Jr. In addition, the committee detailed John F. Kennedy's "secret war" in Laos, and triggered the first of many probes into the popular president's extramarital affairs and relations with gangsters.

The last flickerings of the Vietnam War bred further disillusionment and cynicism. Many felt bitterness and sorrow at seeing the Viet Cong flag fly over Saigon. Others on the left, however, were jubilant. At the 1975 Academy Award ceremonies, the audience greeted the news that Hanoi had "liberated" South Vietnam with a standing ovation.

In May 1975, President Ford dispatched 350 marines to rescue the crew of the United States merchant ship the *Mayaguez*, seized by communist Cambodia off its coast. After some mishaps, the mission proved successful, and many Americans thought that national pride had been in some measure restored. Critics, however, blamed Ford for failing to rely more on diplomacy and noted that forty-one Americans lost their lives in the rescue effort. Ford's job approval rating was down to 45 percent by summer.

Ford and Foreign Affairs

Ford traveled around the world during his term of office, hoping to strengthen NATO, achieve nuclear disarmament, and promote better relations with the Soviet Union. Secretary of State Henry Kissinger was the major force in forging the administration's foreign policy.

In August 1975, Ford met with Soviet leader Leonid Brezhnev in Helsinki to conclude negotiations that had been under way since 1973. In the interest of détente, the United States agreed to recognize east-west boundaries established at the end of World War II, thus officially acknowledging the legitimacy of East Germany and the Soviet takeover of the Baltic states of Estonia, Latvia, and Lithuania. (Ronald Reagan and many other conservatives were scandalized by the concession.) Brezhnev promised to respect freedom of thought, conscience, and religion in the Soviet bloc and ease restrictions on Soviet Jews who sought to emigrate.

Secretary of State Kissinger labored intensively throughout the Nixon and Ford administrations to establish peace between Israel and its Arab neighbors. In September 1975, following pressure from President Ford on Israel, both sides came to terms. Israel made a modest withdrawal from the Sinai. Egypt permitted Israeli ships to pass through the Suez Canal and renounced war as an instrument of policy against Israel. The United Nations agreed to maintain a peacekeeping force in the area. And the United States provided massive economic and military assistance to both sides. Egyptian President Anwar el-Sadat soon traveled to the United States, where he was greeted warmly by Ford and addressed Congress.

Ford and Kissinger visited China in November 1975. But efforts to restore normal diplomatic relations failed due to the continued policy of the United States to recognize the pro-American Chinese Nationalists on Taiwan as the "true" Chinese government.

The Election of 1976

The Nixon pardon, the sagging economy, the vetoes, and the failure to make significant strides in foreign affairs made Ford's chances for reelection slim. Moreover, he was perceived by many to be a sort of brainless bumbler, always tripping and bumping his head and hitting people with golf balls. After surviving two assassination attempts in September 1975, he became the butt of cruel jokes. Even his participation in the lavish bicentennial celebrations of 1975 and 1976 failed to win him great public confidence and affection.

In November 1975, Vice President Rockefeller announced that he would not be on the ticket the following year. Two weeks later former California Governor Ronald Reagan officially declared his candidacy. By January 1976 Reagan trailed the incumbent president in the polls by only 53 percent to 42 percent. The former movie star and conservative activist ran as an outsider, condemning the Washington establishment. To Reagan, Ford was part of the problem.

Reagan won primary elections in California, Indiana, and several southern states, but Ford won more. (Most states now held presidential primaries, which reduced the importance of the political parties and their national conventions.) When the GOP met in convention in Kansas City in August, the president had a commanding lead. Ford named Senator Robert Dole of Kansas, a disabled veteran and skilled campaigner, to be his running mate.

By May it was clear that former Georgia governor James "Jimmy" Earl Carter would win the Democratic presidential nomination. Carter, like Reagan, had campaigned as an anti-Washington outsider, separating himself from the political establishment. Many admired his credentials and found his folksy charm and perpetual smile irresistible.

Born in 1925 in Plains, Georgia (the first president to be born in a hospital), Carter was the son of an ambitious farmer and a nurse. He excelled in his studies from an early age and graduated from the U.S. Naval Academy in 1946, ranking fifty-ninth in a class of 820. After graduation he married Rosalynn Smith, an attractive, industrious, and highly intelligent young woman who grew up near the Carter family.

Carter served in the navy for almost seven years, spending five of them on submarines. He was part of a team under Admiral Hyman G. Rickover that worked on the nation's nuclear submarine program. At his father's death in 1953, Jimmy resigned his commission and returned to Georgia. He and his wife made a success of the family's peanut seed business before Carter entered politics.

Intensely ambitious and politically shrewd, Carter was elected to the Georgia state Senate in 1962 and won the governor's race in 1970. As governor, Carter actively supported racial integration, worked to reduce and reorganize state government, and supported a number of reforms. He announced his candidacy for the White House in late 1974.

Carter promised to end waste in government, balance the budget, and restore integrity in Washington. His lifelong Baptist faith, he said, would guide his conduct in the Oval Office. He pledged repeatedly, "I'll never tell a lie." The Georgia Democrat won nineteen of thirty-one primaries. When nominated, Carter led Ford by 30 percentage points in the polls, one of the largest leads ever held by a presidential candidate. Liberal Senator Walter Mondale of Minnesota completed the ticket.

Both Ford and Carter accepted federal campaign funds for the first time, a practice designed to minimize the abuses, illustrated during the Watergate scandals, commonly associated with private fund-raising.

Carter's lead diminished as the campaign proceeded. Ford wrapped himself in the flag ("I'm feeling good about America" was his campaign song) and stressed his superior experience. But during a television debate with Carter, the president contended that Eastern Europe was not dominated by the Soviet Union. This incredible gaffe persuaded many that at least some of the Ford jokes were true. On the other hand, Carter, in a *Playboy* magazine interview, said, "I've committed adultery in my heart many times," an unsophisticated revelation that convinced many he was not of presidential caliber. Public opinion polls showed large majorities believing that neither candidate had leadership ability. The intellectual level of the campaign was not enhanced by Robert Dole's charge that "Democrat wars" during the century had killed 1.6 million Americans.

On election day, only 53 percent of the electorate went to the polls. Carter beat Ford 51 to 48 percent, and the Democrats retained control of Congress. Carter's coattails were minimal, however: only three congressmen owed him their seats. To emphasize the freshness of his approach to government, on inauguration day Carter wore a business suit rather than a cutaway, and

Jimmy and Rosalynn Carter surprised spectators by walking from the Capitol to the White House after the inauguration ceremony. Source: Courtesy of the Ronald Reagan Library

strolled bareheaded and hand in hand with his wife from Capitol Hill to the White House.

The Carter Style

Once in the Oval Office, Jimmy Carter continued efforts to portray himself as folksy and compassionate. He sold the presidential yacht, conducted a telephone call-in show, attended a New England town meeting, and held a televised "fireside chat" on energy while wearing a cardigan. But his style of leadership proved to be frustrating and unproductive.

While diligent and studious about details, Carter lacked vision and long-range goals. His principal adviser was the first lady, and he would often not listen to others. The president was self-righteous and often aloof. He refused to negotiate with Congress, and treated members of both houses with disdain. The result was governmental deadlock.

As the Carter administration increasingly revealed its inability to deal effectively with the nation's problems, jokes spread about the president. Even Democrats began saying such things as "Carter does the work of two men— Laurel and Hardy."

The Economy

More than two-thirds of the nation's voters listed the economy as their primary concern. When Jimmy Carter took office, the country was just recovering from the Ford recession. In early 1977 unemployment stood at 8 percent, and the inflation rate was 6 percent. After legislation creating federal service jobs and raising the minimum wage, unemployment fell 2 points. But inflation soared to 10 percent in 1978 and 13 percent in 1980. (Consumer prices rose an average of 9.2 percent per year between 1973 and 1982.) Monetary adjustments by the Federal Reserve designed to counter this trend drove interest rates upward without curbing inflation. The result was "stagflation," economic misery worse than the American people had suffered in decades.

In 1980, the country entered another severe recession. Tens of thousands of businesses went bankrupt. Productivity was sharply down, and hundreds of companies began moving their operations to Third World countries in order to benefit from cheap labor. Unemployment was at the highest level since the Great Depression. The federal budgetary deficit climbed to $59.6 billion (from $44.9 billion in 1977). People had less money to spend, as income dropped by 2 percent every year from 1973 through 1981. In 1980, the purchasing power of working-class families had dropped to 1960 levels.

The continuing energy crisis was part of the problem. A Department of Energy was created, and Carter made impressive speeches on the issue. But Congress and the president squabbled about details of reform until 1978 when the Energy Tax Act was passed. While requiring a number of reforms to cut use of petroleum products, the legislation failed to lower consumer prices or reduce the nation's dependence on foreign oil.

A revolution in Iran stopped the flow of oil from the world's second largest exporter, and prices soared again. In the year ending September 1979, heating oil prices had increased 73 percent, and gasoline prices were up 52 percent. By 1980, the country was spending in excess of $90 billion on imported oil, up from $40 billion in 1978 and $5 billion in 1970. Angry Americans waited in long lines to pay record prices for gasoline.

The American automobile industry was especially hard hit by the drop in purchasing power and the energy crisis. Sales fell from 9.3 million in 1978 to 5.8 million in 1982. Employment in the industry dropped by 250,000 during those years. In 1979, the government had to give Chrysler a guaranteed loan to keep the Big Three auto company from bankruptcy.

Foreign auto sales were also cutting into the market, imports amounting to 18 percent of total sales in 1978. Japanese auto makers in particular prospered because they understood, more clearly than their counterparts in Detroit, that the public wanted better made, less costly cars. In 1980, driving a Cadillac or Lincoln, long a status symbol, seemed to many Americans ostentatious and wasteful.

Military and Foreign Affairs

Carter's first official act as president was to grant pardons to all Vietnam War draft evaders. To many veterans this was a repudiation of their efforts in the prolonged and bloody war. Some conservatives later thought this one of many efforts by the president to win favor with establishment liberals who sneered at him because of his southern and agricultural roots.

Having virtually no experience in foreign affairs, Carter relied heavily on his secretary of state, Wall Street lawyer Cyrus Vance, and National Security Adviser Zbigniew Brzezinski, a Columbia University expert on international relations. Carter said he would emphasize human rights, and he signed several treaties and made numerous speeches supporting this agenda. But little specific was achieved beyond the deterioration of relations with the Soviet Union, often the target of administration rhetoric.

Bowing to charges of American imperialism by Panamanian leaders, Carter signed two treaties in September 1977 permitting Panama to take full control of the canal by the year 2000. The United States retained the right to intervene if the canal were closed, and to retain priority of passage in a foreign crisis. Many conservatives howled about the "giveaway" of American property, and polls showed voters solidly against the treaties. By a narrow margin the Senate ratified both agreements, but the action was unpopular and later cost several senators their jobs.

In early 1979, the United States and China extended each other full diplomatic relations. To reach this agreement, the administration was forced to sever relations with Taiwan. The vice premier of China visited the United

States, and the two major powers later signed a major trade agreement. American business leaders were particularly interested in opening up the vast Chinese market.

Carter worked hard to improve Arab-Israeli relations. In September 1978, he invited Israeli Prime Minister Menachem Begin and the president of war-weary Egypt, Anwar el-Sadat, to the chief executive's retreat in Maryland. The thirteen-day meeting, during which Carter took the lead, produced the much-heralded Camp David Accords, a "framework" for peace containing compromises on both sides. On March 26, 1979, prodded by Carter, Begin and Sadat signed an Israeli-Egyptian peace treaty on the White House lawn. Most Arab states, however, quickly rejected the agreement and broke relations with Egypt. Israel continued to expand its settlements in the West Bank, terrorism on both sides continued, and the outlook for a Middle East peace appeared as dim as ever.

Détente with the Soviet Union had been declining since 1975, when the United States pulled out of Vietnam. Perhaps thinking that their opportunity for military superiority in the world had arrived, the Soviets ordered a massive military buildup and made aggressive moves in Africa, the Middle East, and Cuba. Still, in September 1979, Carter and General Secretary Brezhnev signed the Salt II agreement, establishing limits on nuclear missiles and launchers. Senate critics argued that the treaty was inadequate and left the Soviet Union with military superiority in some areas.

In December, while the debate raged, Soviet troops invaded Afghanistan to defend a waning Marxist regime under attack by Muslims. Stunned by this aggression (which would prove to be the Soviet Union's Vietnam), President Carter withdrew Salt II from Senate consideration, imposed economic sanctions, and ordered a boycott of the Olympic games scheduled for Moscow. He also ordered an American defense buildup and issued the Carter Doctrine: "Any attempt by any outside force to gain control of the Persian Gulf region will be regarded as an assault on the vital interests of the United States of America and such an assault will be repelled by any means necessary including military force." The president now seemed much more a hawk than a dove.

The Hostage Crisis

In January 1979, a public loyal to Ayatollah Ruholla Khomeini overthrew the unpopular, corrupt, and repressive government of Iran and drove out the pro-American shah. Khomeini was a 79-year old Islamic cleric intent on transforming an increasingly Westernized and secular nation into an Islamic republic. America had a keen interest in the revolution because Iran was a major supplier of oil and the chief ally of the United States in the Persian Gulf. Overtures by Carter to Khomeini got nowhere; the Iranian leader called America the "Great Satan" and halted the flow of oil.

Under its new leadership, Iran's tottering economy collapsed, and a terror was waged against allies of the shah. When the Carter administration permitted the shah to seek medical assistance in the United States, riots erupted in Iran. On November 4, 1979, several hundred youths seized control of the American embassy in Tehran and took sixty-six Americans hostage. Khomeini gave his blessing to this action and warned that the hostages would be executed if the United States came to their rescue. (Thirteen hostages, blacks and women, were soon released, and a man who developed multiple sclerosis was later freed.)

The American people were shocked by numerous anti-American rallies staged by the Iranian government, and by similar activities conducted by many Iranian students living in the United States. The hostage situation, like the flag-burning seen on television, seemed to be a direct attack on the nation's honor. Jimmy Carter made the safe return of the hostages the top priority of his presidency.

The Carter administration chose not to engage in immediate military action in large part out of fear that it would alienate the entire Islamic world and build sympathy for the Soviets in Afghanistan. Instead, Carter froze Iranian assets in American banks, stopped shipment of goods to Iran, and persuaded the United Nations to condemn the embassy takeover. Extensive diplomatic efforts were launched. Five months later, nothing had worked, and the more than fifty Americans remained in captivity. Famed television newscaster Walter Cronkite ended his program nightly by reporting the number of days the hostages had been held.

On April 11, 1980, Carter approved a daring military plan to rescue the hostages. (Secretary of State Cyrus Vance, who opposed the decision, submitted his resignation.) The operation failed from the start due to the mechanical failure of key helicopters. Making matters worse, eight servicemen died in a helicopter crash during the retreat. Iranian militants proudly displayed and mutilated the corpses on television.

America's humiliation in the hostage crisis contributed to the widespread belief that Jimmy Carter's reelection bid was doomed from the start. Carter Democrats had talked a good case in the campaign of 1976, but they had not delivered. Double-digit inflation, soaring interest rates, huge federal deficits, congressional deadlock, the Panama Canal, and now Iran left millions, liberals and conservatives, eager for a change.

Some critics linked Carter with Ford, dismissing both as generally inept and counterproductive. Historian Paul Johnson would later write, "The years 1974–80 were among the more doleful in America's history."

Still, Jimmy Carter was a man of high intelligence and good character who worked extremely hard at his job. His record on civil rights was good. (He named former civil rights activist Andrew Young the U.S. ambassador to the United Nations.) At home and abroad, he had shown a genuine compassion for those suffering from poverty and injustice. He traveled all across the globe seeking peace. Supporters also noted that much of what had gone wrong in

America during Carter's four years was either unsolvable or, like the Iran fiasco, just plain bad luck.

Culture in the Post-Vietnam War Years

America began to calm down after the conclusion of the Vietnam War. College campuses were relatively quiet, urban rioting ceased, and many sixties militants got jobs, donned business suits, moved to the suburbs, and became "yuppies"—young, upwardly mobile professionals. The faltering economy, as well as the return of international peace, prompted much of this sobriety. With real income declining every year, people in all economic brackets were more inclined to think about paying their bills than demonstrating on street corners. Then too, there was a growing cynicism about politics and the possibility of meaningful reform.

Gains of the sixties culture were also a factor in the restoration of tranquility. Feminists and gays, for example, found their demands increasingly accepted. Few Americans publicly condoned racial discrimination any longer. Affirmative action was standard procedure in government and business. Rock took over much of the popular music world. Censorship all but vanished. Marijuana smoking was routine in many places. (Studies showed that nearly half of the nation's college students used it.) Lowered academic requirements and admission standards satisfied many campus radicals. The major media grew increasingly comfortable with the vast majority of intellectuals on the political left. In short, much that was controversial just a few years earlier was now conventional. Traditional moral standards and conservative politics were common targets of ridicule in influential circles—like short haircuts on men, and the polyester pantsuits popular among blue-collar women.

Despite the troubled economy of the 1970s, the American people, numbering 220.6 million at the end of the decade, enjoyed unparalleled comforts. In 1979, 44.1 percent of homes had air conditioning, up from 7.8 percent in 1960. More than 60 percent of the nation's homes had washers, and almost half had dryers. (In 1960, 28.6 percent had washers, and 10.1 percent had dryers.) Almost 80 percent of homes had vacuum cleaners. By 1975, 48.1 percent of occupied housing units owned one car, and two years later 7.8 percent had three or more. Sales of recreational vehicles soared from 192.8 thousand in 1965 to 526.3 in 1978, before declining in the wake of the new energy crunch.

Mass communications became an ever-growing influence in the lives of all Americans. By 1979 79.2 percent of homes had television, up from 50.8 percent in 1960. Radio was in 79.3 percent of homes. Television advertising almost doubled between 1975 and 1979, to more than $10 billion. (Children who had once memorized poetry versus now spouted only tv commercials and jingles.) Satellites in orbit enabled news to be transmitted live from all over the globe. More than four thousand cable systems served 14 million subscribers in 1979, providing a wide variety of programming. Citizens' band radios (CBs) were installed in many trucks and cars, enabling motorists to converse with each other while driving. Tens of thousands had computers by the end of the decade. The videocassette recorder (VCR) made its debut in 1975.

In part because of television coverage, sports became more popular than ever. Millions watched the Olympic games. At the summer events in Montreal, Bruce Jenner broke records in winning a gold medal in the track and field decathlon. Boxers "Sugar" Ray Leonard, Leon Spinks, and Michael Spinks won gold medals. In the Winter Olympics in Innsbruck, Dorothy Hamill took a gold medal for women's figure skating. She reminded many of Peggy Fleming, who won her gold medal in 1968, and in a sensational career also took five U.S. and three world titles.

More than 44 million attended major league baseball games in 1979, up from 29 million in 1970. Forty-year-old Hank Aaron thrilled the nation in 1974 by hitting his 715th career home run, breaking Babe Ruth's record. College football drew huge crowds (over 39 million in 1979), and professional football was coming into its own (nearly 14 million in 1979). In 1976, the popular Boston Celtics won the National Basketball Association championship, their thirteenth title in twenty years. Horse racing drew the largest audiences (almost 74 million in 1979), and greyhound racing was growing in popularity, from 12.5 million spectators in 1970 to more than 21 million by the end of the decade.

By mid-decade, with physical fitness the rage, nearly 88 million Americans went camping, about 56 million played tennis, more than 48 million were hiking and backpacking, and 68 percent of the population either jogged or walked for exercise. In 1979, more than 282 million Americans visited national parks, up from 172 million in 1970 and 79.2 million in 1960. Total recreational expenditures climbed from nearly $41 billion in 1970 to over $101 billion in 1979.

Americans spent nearly three times as much on movie-going in 1979 as they had at the beginning of the decade. Filmmaker Steven Spielberg was not yet 30 years old in 1975 when *Jaws* became one of the most profitable (budget $12 million, worldwide gross receipts $470 million) movies ever made. George Lucas, only two years older, also became a major force in Hollywood when *Star Wars*, the first in a series of science fiction thrillers, became an international favorite ($513 million gross on a budget of $11 million) in 1977. *Saturday Night Fever*, which focused on the disco craze of the 1970s, was a big hit in 1977 with both critics and moviegoers.

Americans spent record sums on operas, plays, Broadway musicals, and symphonies. Black prima donna Leontyne Price, who won the Presidential Medal of Freedom in 1965, continued to pack opera houses during the decade. Book and magazine sales climbed rapidly. In 1979, there were more than 18 million airline departures to foreign countries, up from just over 12 million in 1975.

Millions of Americans had the means to stay in school. More than 11 million were in college by the end of the decade, up from 8.5 million in 1970.

Federal expenditures supporting education at all levels climbed from $9.2 million in 1970 to $25.5 million in 1979. Median school years completed for people 25 years of age and older was 12.5 in 1979, up from 10.6 in 1960 and 8.6 in 1940. Illiteracy among those beyond their early teens dropped from 11.3 percent in 1900 to 1.2 percent in 1970.

Poverty and Crime

Of course, millions did not enjoy the affluence that distinguished Americans even in hard times. In 1979, the median annual wage for a full-time male worker was $17,533; for women it was $10,548. The median family income in 1978 was $17,640, up from $9,867 in 1970. But some 25 million people, 11.4 percent of the population, lived below the poverty line throughout the decade. (In 1960, nearly 40 million Americans, comprising 22.2 percent of the population, had lived in poverty.) Blacks were disproportionately poor. In 1978, 44 percent of black children living in the central cities existed below the poverty level. Families headed by women were especially in need and likely to be receiving government assistance.

Crime was a mounting public concern. The total number of reported crimes doubled between 1967 and 1979. Arrests increased more than 40 percent during the 1970s, sex crimes and assault leading the way. In 1979, a third of those arrested were black; about 41 percent of the jail inmates in 1978 were black. The racial data prompted many observers to link crime with poverty and charge police with bias.

The cost of the criminal justice system in America grew from $8.5 billion in 1970 to more than $24 billion eight years later. The prison population increased by nearly 98,000 between 1970 and 1978, to nearly 295,000. In 1972, the United States Supreme Court, in a 5 to 4 decision, invalidated virtually every death sentence in the country. Four years later, the Court resurrected capital punishment in certain cases. Critics noted the racial disparity in both sentencing and executions. A study by the American Civil Liberties Union in 1996 claimed that of the 232 executions carried out since 1977, only one white person was put to death for the murder of a black person.

The Family

The future of the family was another serious cause for concern. Families were getting smaller, especially among whites: the number of live births in 1978 was sharply lower than what it had been in 1960, and down from the 1970 level. Studies showed that a soaring divorce rate (1,181,000 in 1979) was causing millions of children to suffer often devastating psychological problems. Untold numbers of "latchkey" children used the hours after school until their working parents got home in destructive and wasteful activities.

Births to unmarried women more than doubled between 1960 and 1978, hitting a record 543,900 in the latter year. The number of children under age

18 living with only one parent increased from 11.9 percent of the nation's children to 19.7 percent in 1980. The number of unmarried couples living together tripled during the 1970s to 1.56 million.

The Election of 1980

Jimmy Carter fought off a challenge by liberal Senator Ted Kennedy and won the Democratic nomination on the first ballot. Numerous Republicans entered the presidential race, confident that the American people were ready, if not eager, for change. A Gallup poll taken in July showed Carter's job approval at 21 percent, still the all-time low. The president already trailed challenger Ronald Reagan in the polls.

Ronald Reagan, 69, was the favorite of the conservative wing of the GOP. A native of Tampico, Illinois, Reagan was the son of a shoe salesman. Bright, popular, athletic, and little interested in his studies, he worked his way through Eureka College, a Christian church school in Illinois. From 1932 to 1935 he was a successful sportscaster. Reagan took a screen test while in California and signed a contract with Warner Brothers. He was soon a star. During two decades in Hollywood, Reagan appeared in fifty-three films, including *King's Row* and *Knute Rockne—All American.* He married actress Nancy Davis in 1952, and from 1954 to 1965 appeared regularly on television.

As president of the Screen Actors Guild in 1947, Reagan supported the House Un-American Activities attack on Communists and their sympathizers in the film industry. A staunch New Dealer, he gradually moved to the right on most issues, and joined the GOP in 1962. Four years later he was elected governor of California by a million votes and was reelected in 1970. As governor, Reagan pushed for welfare and judicial reform, supported environmental issues, and significantly increased aid to schools and mental health facilities. He vetoed 994 bills, and all but one of the vetoes were upheld. Reagan's conservatism, good looks, and movie-actor charm attracted many. Critics dismissed him as dim-witted, reactionary, and dangerously hawkish. He ran for the presidency in 1968 and 1976.

By May 1980 Reagan had enough ballots to win the GOP nomination. Reaganites controlled the convention, producing a conservative platform that called for tax cuts, a balanced budget, increased defense spending, and constitutional amendments banning abortions and permitting prayer in public schools. Moderate George Bush of Texas, who had made a bid for the presidential nomination, was chosen to fill out the ticket.

Illinois Congressman John Anderson, a GOP liberal, ran as an independent with liberal Democrat Patrick J. Lucey, a former Wisconsin governor. The ticket received mild support from the left, and served only to draw support from Carter. In November, Anderson would win 7 percent of the votes cast.

On the campaign trail, Reagan called for smaller government, a more assertive foreign policy, and traditional morality. He pledged to restore "the great, confident roar of American progress and growth and optimism." Behind in the polls, Carter made personal attacks on the challenger and called for a televised debate. The October 28 confrontation enhanced Reagan's image as a firm, amiable, and knowledgeable leader. The Republican's most effective technique was to ask repeatedly if the American people were better off in 1980 than they had been four years earlier. The answer seemed obvious to millions.

The most fervent Reagan backers belonged to the "New Right," a loosely knit association of millions of Americans, often evangelical Christians, who were outraged by cultural developments of the past fifteen years. Led by "born again" clergymen Jerry Falwell and Pat Robertson, among others, the New Right opposed gay rights, the Equal Rights Amendment, busing, affirmative action, sexual permissiveness, pornography, abortion on demand, and efforts to drive religion from the public schools. They believed they spoke for the average American against a liberal elite that was systematically destroying the country. The voting strength of the New Right was difficult to measure, but pollsters noted that by the end of the 1970s evangelical Christianity claimed the support of more than 50 million Americans.

On election day, Reagan won 44 million votes to Carter's 35 million. Carter carried only six states and lost in the electoral college 489 to 49. It was the most stunning repudiation of an American president since Herbert Hoover's loss in 1932. Republicans won control of the Senate by gaining thirteen seats. They added thirty-three seats in the House, narrowing the Democratic margin to 243 to 192.

Of all of the components of the coalition that had brought him victory four years earlier, Carter was able to retain only the African American vote. Polls showed a drop in Democratic strength from 50 percent of the people in 1976 to 38 percent, the low mark, in modern times, for the party.

While some experts predicted the emergence of a popular Republican majority, others noted the comparatively low voter turnout. Nearly 47 percent of eligible voters chose to stay home. Reagan received only 28 percent of the total potential vote. Studies showed that working-class Americans especially had lost confidence in government and believed that their vote would not make a difference. Most of these nonvoters were former Democrats. Conservatives predicted that this unprecedented alienation and resignation would soon be reversed by the Reagan administration.

SUGGESTED READING

Barry Bluestone and Bennett Harrison, *The Deindustrialization of America: Plant Closings, Community Abandonment and the Dismantling of Basic Industry* (1982); Seth Cagin, *Hollywood Films of the Seventies: Sex, Drugs, Violence, Rock'n Roll, & Politics* (1984); Jimmy Carter, *Keeping Faith: Memoirs of a President* (1982); Gerald R. Ford, *A Time To Heal: The Autobiography of Gerald R. Ford* (1979); Edwin C. Hargrove, *Jimmy Carter as President: Leadership and the Politics of the Public Good* (1988);

Christopher Lasch, *The Culture of Narcissism; American Life in the Age of Diminishing Returns* (1979); Victor Marchetti and John D. Marks, *The CIA and the Cult of Intelligence* (1974); Winifred D. Wandersee, *On The Move: American Women in the 1970s* (1988); F. Clifton White, *Why Reagan Won: A Narrative History of the Conservative Movement, 1964–1981* (1981); Daniel Yankelovich, *New Rules: Searching for Self-fulfillment in a World Turned Upside Down* (1982).

Chapter Thirteen

DYNAMIC CONSERVATISM

Ronald Reagan enjoyed his years in the White House. He paid little attention to the work of government, took frequent vacations, and was known by insiders to be intellectually as well as physically lazy. One crisis, said a wag, "was causing president Reagan a lot of sleepless afternoons." A troika of aides—Michael Deaver, Edwin Meese, and James Baker—made many decisions in the president's name. Alexander M. Haig, Reagan's first secretary of state, said later, "You couldn't serve in his administration without knowing that Reagan was a cipher and that these men were running the government." The president's already low energy level was affected adversely by a near-fatal assassination attempt on March 30, 1981.

But Reagan was firm about his conservative principles, and he often employed his exceptional powers of persuasion on their behalf. His idol was Calvin Coolidge, whose portrait was placed in the cabinet room. Reagan labeled his formula for rescuing the country "dynamic conservatism."

Presidential appointees to the cabinet and federal regulatory agencies shared Reagan's desire to maximize personal freedom and private enterprise and minimize the role of government. Secretary of the Interior James Watt and Environmental Protection head Anne Gorsuch Burford, for example, largely opposed efforts by environmentalists. Secretary of Transportation Drew Lewis took steps to decrease recent pollution and safety regulations imposed on the automobile industry. David Stockman, the youthful director of the Office of Management and Budget, and Donald T. Regan, secretary of the treasury, strongly favored budget and tax cuts.

The president tried to eliminate the Energy Department, but settled for cuts in its budget. The Task Force on Regulatory Relief, chaired by Vice President Bush, was part of a major effort to scrap thousands of unnecessary federal regulations and save business, consumers, and state and local governments much time and billions of dollars. By 1985, federal regulatory agencies had lost 12 percent of their personnel and funding.

Reaganomics

Reagan could expect solid Republican support in Congress, but he often won the votes of "boll weevils," southern Democrats who agreed with the president's conservative principles. The first major target was the sagging economy. Following "supply side" economic theory, Reagan and his followers believed that prosperity would return when federal spending and taxes were cut and government regulations slashed. The private sector, it was thought, would expand dramatically, and that this growth would generate profits and jobs, cut inflation, generate tax revenue, and balance the budget. From this point of view, the liberal welfare state, in construction since the turn of the century, had brought the country to the brink of fiscal and moral disaster. Reaganites believed they had a mandate to reverse the course of recent American history.

Reagan and most of his fellow Republicans saw organized labor as part of the problem. When the air traffic controller's union, PATCO, conducted an illegal strike in the summer of 1981, the president fired 11,300 strikers and ordered Transportation Secretary Lewis to train and hire replacements. Reagan resisted all efforts to reverse this action and gave people all over the world the impression that he was tough and decisive. The destruction of PATCO was yet another blow against Big Labor, already reeling from the loss of manufacturing jobs and sharply declining numbers. (Total union membership dropped from 22.2 million in 1975 to 16.9 million in 1987). The only major growth in union membership came in the public sector, the target of many conservative legislators on the state and federal level.

David Stockman proposed some $64 billion in budget cuts and endorsed a 30-percent tax cut. In May, Congress endorsed most of the budget cuts. In July, despite several compromises and concessions to special interest groups, Congress passed the largest tax reductions in American history. Still, government spending would increase under Reagan, even for many social programs. The budget and the tax cuts simply ensured that federal outlays would not grow faster than the economy. The annual growth in federal spending dropped from 17 percent in 1979 to 5 percent during 1981–84. Tax levels dropped from 20.8 percent of gross national product to about 19 percent.

The Reagan economic policy did not bring relief in 1981, and the president's popularity dropped to below 50 percent by December. Moreover, major federal deficits began to loom: by early 1982 a whopping $200 billion was projected. That July, desperate for increased federal revenue, Congress passed a tax hike. The president signed it, but he continued to believe that his basic economic philosophy would eventually restore prosperity and balance the budget. There were promising signs: inflation dropped from 13 percent in 1980 to 5 percent in 1982. The Dow Jones industrial average climbed above 1000 for good.

The economy as a whole, however, continued to worsen throughout 1982. Toward the end of the year unemployment reached 10 percent. In the November mid-term elections, Democrats added twenty-six seats in the House, while the GOP held on to the Senate. House Speaker Thomas "Tip" O'Neill, a veteran pol and old-fashioned liberal from Massachusetts, promised to be a major obstacle in the furtherance of Reaganomics.

Deregulation was an integral part of the Reagan agenda. In 1982, to aid the savings and loan industry, Congress and the administration permitted firms to go beyond housing loans into more speculative ventures. White-collar thieves looted many financial institutions, leaving hundreds of them bankrupt. The problem was ignored until 1989, when President George Bush took action. By 1996, the savings and loan bailout cost had reached $480.9 billion, a sum exceeding the cost of the entire Vietnam War. The federal government borrowed money to cover the losses, and House banking chairman Jim Leach announced that taxpayer accountability due to bonds issued would continue through the year 2030. Reagan shared the blame for the most expensive scandal in history.

Social Issues

The president was more interested in economic than social issues. But he regularly defended his conservative principles and made unusual efforts to placate the New or Religious Right. Evangelist Billy Graham once told Reagan, "I would think that you have talked about God more than any other president since Abraham Lincoln." At times, conservatives expressed unhappiness, often blaming the "pragmatists" around the president for their disappointment. Historian William E. Pemberton has remarked, "Reagan's fire-breathing conservative rhetoric hid from many the fact that he was a very skillful politician who placed winning above ideological purity."

There was little enthusiasm in the administration for the demands of civil rights leaders. Reagan had long opposed many civil rights laws and favored a constitutional amendment to outlaw busing for the purpose of racially integrating the public schools. He had received the lowest percentage of African-American votes of any candidate in history.

Many of Reagan's supporters were known to be hostile to black aspirations and demands. Attorney General William French Smith and William Bradford Reynolds of the Justice Department opposed affirmative action and busing, cut funds for civil rights activities, filed fewer fair housing suits, and packed the Equal Employment Opportunity Commission with conservatives. Still, Reagan showed no personal animus toward African Americans and often boasted of his efforts throughout his career to end racism.

Throughout Reagan's terms in office, more men than women supported him, in large part because of his opposition to abortion and ERA. The president was said not to take women seriously. And yet Elizabeth H. Dole became secretary of transportation, Jeane Kirkpatrick was named ambassador to the United Nations, Peggy Noonan was an important speech writer, and Sandra Day O'Connor became the first woman to be appointed to the United States Supreme Court. Nancy Reagan was an inordinately powerful figure in the administration, intervening in personnel matters, helping with major policy decisions, and fashioning her husband's daily schedule in accordance with advice given by astrologers. She also headed a major national campaign against illegal drugs, telling young people especially to "just say no."

Foreign Affairs in the Early Eighties

Reagan reemphasized his well-known hostility toward communism early in his term of office, and went a step beyond, predicting the Soviet Union's downfall. On June 8, 1982, he declared publicly that the Soviet Union belonged to the "ash-heap of history." Nine months later, in a speech before the National Association of Evangelicals, he declared that the "evil empire" was doomed.

On March 23, 1983, Reagan proposed the Strategic Defense Initiative (SDI), a startlingly new and controversial defensive umbrella that would intercept and destroy nuclear weapons headed toward the United States. The technological feasibility of what critics called "Star Wars" was uncertain, and the financial costs were likely to be staggering. But Reagan was convinced that this system was the best way to prevent nuclear war. He did not believe that the United States could develop a clear and lasting nuclear superiority, and he did not trust the reasonableness of the Soviets, who had been told for years that a nuclear strike would mean devastation on both sides of the Cold War.

Reagan's ignorance about foreign affairs was a quiet scandal among insiders. His predictions about the Soviet Union, it was said, were based on intuition rather than a knowledge of Russian affairs. Lack of presidential direction prompted infighting and, at times, paralysis within the administration. Struggles between Secretary of State George Schultz and Secretary of Defense Caspar Weinberger were particularly intense. But Reagan's convictions about defending the free world from communism, his commitment to rebuilding American military might, and his dreams of a world rid of nuclear fear, won considerable support.

Reagan demanded and achieved the largest defense buildup in history. In his first five years in office, military spending increased by over 50 percent in real terms, totaling nearly $1.5 trillion. The military share of GNP grew from 5.7 percent to 7.4 percent. The public, still smarting over Vietnam and the apparent weakness of Carter, was generally supportive.

Not surprisingly, Reagan was eager to display American military strength throughout the world. Patriotism and courage were dominant themes espoused by the "Great Communicator" both in public and in private. Throughout his adult life he enjoyed having his photograph taken with an American flag in the background.

In August 1981 Reagan authorized the use of force against Libya, widely considered to be a source of world terrorism and now claiming the Gulf of Sidra as Libyan waters. U.S. Air Force jets shot down two Libyan jets after the Libyan planes fired on them. Reagan said that he wanted the world to know "there was new management in the White House."

Against the advice of key advisers, Reagan twice sent marines into Lebanon as part of a larger effort to secure peace between Muslims and Israelis. The confused effort failed, and Americans withdrew after a young Muslim blew up a marine barracks on October 23, 1983, killing 231 troops. Reagan later called the Lebanon venture "my greatest regret and my greatest sorrow."

The day after the bombing in Beirut, the president gave final approval for an invasion of the tiny Caribbean island of Granada, ostensibly to rescue about a thousand Americans but actually to overthrow hard-line Marxists who had staged a coup. Although eighteen U.S. servicemen were killed during the attack, Americans generally applauded the successful operation, which Reagan wrapped in patriotic rhetoric.

Reagan Prosperity

Prosperity returned by mid-1983, launching the longest period of economic growth in the nation's history. The gross national product grew at an average annual rate of about 4 percent from 1982 to 1988. Some 17 to 18 million new jobs were created during Reagan's presidency. Inflation and interest rates were down. Good times inspired faith in the wisdom of Reaganomics.

Critics, however, noted the growing federal deficit and pointed to the growing disparity of wealth between rich and poor. Changes in income taxes left families earning under $10,000 with a $95 loss, while families making more than $200,000 gained $17,403. Slashes in government social spending also widened the gap. In 1981, more than one in three households were receiving benefits from the federal government. Reagan vowed to limit aid to the "truly needy," and at his urging Congress made numerous cuts, including $2 billion from the $12 billion food stamp budget and $1 billion from the $3.5 billion school lunch program. Liberal Robert B. Reich complained in early 1984, "Even if Medicare and food stamps are included in the reckoning, over 21 million Americans are still impoverished, substantially more than four years ago."

Still the tide was rising significantly for most Americans, and the poverty rate was declining. Moreover, government cuts in aid were not nearly as drastic as critics contended. Total federal payments for individuals rose throughout the Reagan years, and so did spending on programs that benefited poor families. Housing and Urban Development outlays increased from $14.8 billion in 1981 to $28.7 billion in 1985, and the number of low-income households receiving household subsidies rose from 3.2 million to nearly 4 million. When Reagan announced his bid for reelection in January 1984, Richard Nixon commented, "You cannot beat an incumbent president in peacetime if the nation is prosperous."

Election of 1984

Some thought that Reagan, at age 73, was too old to serve a second term. Eisenhower had left office when he was 70, to a chorus of complaints about his mental and physical agility. Insiders knew that Reagan's mental stamina was minimal. But he could still deliver a written speech ably, flash his winning smile, and manage to persuade millions that he was personally responsible for the renewal of American prosperity and pride. Polls showed that Americans liked and trusted their president.

Democrats chose 56-year-old Walter F. Mondale of Minnesota to head their 1984 ticket. An articulate and well-informed liberal, Mondale had served in the Senate for two terms before becoming Carter's vice president. With the encouragement of the National Organization of Women, Mondale selected a woman to be his running mate, Congresswoman Geraldine Ferraro of New York. This was the first time a woman was nominated for vice president by a major party. Forty-nine-year-old Ferraro's feminism, her violations of campaign spending laws, and her husband's business and financial ties proved controversial. Still, she revealed competence and determination in her televised debates with George Bush.

Reagan led in the polls almost from the beginning of the year, and he used slick television commercials that stressed patriotism, optimism, and harmony and avoided specific issues. Speech writer Peggy Noonan provided the president with the campaign's best line: "America is back: it's morning again." Despite careful and extensive preparation, Reagan faltered badly during the

Ronald and Nancy Reagan at the White House, January 10, 1984. Source: Courtesy of the Ronald Reagan Library

first of two television debates with Mondale. But he recovered in the second confrontation and fended off charges that he was too old to serve another term.

Mondale's most effective line of attack was the growing gap between rich and poor. But Republicans dismissed him as a typical "tax and spend liberal" and linked him with the failures of the Carter years. GOP strategists also portrayed Mondale and Ferraro, and not without reason, as advocates of unpopular cultural changes that had swept the nation in the Vietnam War years.

On November 6, Reagan carried every state but Minnesota, which he lost by only a 3,761 vote margin. He won 59 percent of the popular vote to Mondale's 41 percent. His victory in the electoral college, 525 to 13, was second only to Roosevelt's landside in 1936. All age groups voted for the incumbent. He swept the once solid South by a huge margin. Even half of the union members voted for Reagan, despite the determined opposition of labor leaders. Mondale's highest vote levels were in black ghettos and university towns. Ferraro's largely blue-collar East River-Queens district went for Reagan. Republicans gained thirteen seats in the House and retained control of the Senate by a fifty-four to forty-six majority.

Growth and Change

The population in the 1980s grew from 226.5 million to 248.7 million. While the number of whites increased 6.0 percent, the Asian population jumped 107.8 percent, Hispanics increased 53 percent, and blacks grew 13.2 percent. The percentage of foreign-born residents increased from 6.2 percent to 7.9 percent during the decade. California, with a large Hispanic population, led the nation in foreign-born residents at 21.7 percent.

Educational levels continued their long climb. By the end of the 1980s, 75.2 percent of adults had completed high school and 20.3 percent had a bachelor's degree or more. Median family income, adjusted for inflation, climbed from $33,381 to $35,225.

Seeking jobs, people poured into urban areas (communities of 2,500 or more) during the decade. The cities themselves were expanding and absorbing some 30,000 square miles of land during the 1970s and 1980s. In 1990, for the first time, fewer than one American in four lived in the countryside. The percentage of the population living in suburbs climbed from 41.6 percent to 46.3 percent. Three-fourths of Americans lived on less than 3 percent of the nation's land. Slightly more than 115 million Americans were suburbanites, and 17.3 percent of households had three or more cars.

The growing disparity between rich and poor was a reality as well as a political contention. Between 1979 and 1989, the percent of families living in poverty increased from 9.6 percent to 10.0 percent. The number of children living in poverty climbed from 16.0 percent to 17.9 percent. Much of this latter statistic stemmed from the increase in births to unmarried women, a figure that nearly doubled between 1975 and 1990 to 28 percent of all births. This was a particular problem for blacks, for by 1990 65.2 percent of all births to African American women occurred out of wedlock, up from 37.6 percent twenty years earlier.

African American Progress

Political scientist Julia Vitullo-Martin has observed, "Racial integration is a uniquely American, twentieth-century ideal. None of the societies that represent our heritage so much as thought of it, much less practiced it. This is not a Greek, Judeo-Christian or Anglo-Saxon idea. It is ours alone." During the 1980s, integration was well advanced, and there were many success stories.

Job opportunities, especially in the defense industry, prompted many blacks to head north. The black populations in the Northeast and Midwest increased by more than 250 percent by the 1980s. By mid-decade, some 60 percent of all black families were middle class or working class, twice the proportion in 1947. Home ownership had doubled. The number of affluent black families doubled in the 1980s, increasing from 266,000 in 1967 to more than a million in 1989.

Still, on the whole, the nation's 30 million African Americans trailed whites in nearly every category of economic and physical well-being. Black family income was 61 percent that of whites in 1969, but only 56 percent as high in 1989. The poverty rate for blacks had remained at just above 30 percent for two decades. Infant mortality was twice as high for black babies as for white babies. Urban ghettos continued to be a national disgrace, trapping millions in a cycle of poverty, crime, and despair.

Hispanics and Native Americans, as well as blacks, lagged behind whites in education. In 1989, 86 percent of whites between the ages of 25 and 29 had high-school diplomas, compared with 82.2 percent of African Americans and 61 percent of Hispanics. Still, African Americans' high-school completion rate rose more than 7 percentage points during the decade.

Educational Woes

It seemed that many schoolchildren were learning less than they used to. Scholastic Aptitude Test scores, which had peaked in 1963, were plummeting by the early 1980s. This despite dramatic increases in expenditures. In 1960, the nation spent (in constant 1990 dollars) an average of $2,035 per student. In 1990, the figure had climbed to $5,247. Conservatives often blamed the permissive life style of the 1960s and low teacher training standards. Liberals usually contended that more money would solve educational problems. They also noted that falling SAT scores were due in part to the larger number of students taking the test, a reflection of the growing desire for higher education.

A 1983 report by the National Commission on Excellence in Education warned of "a rising tide of mediocrity" that threatened "our very future as a nation and a people." In the 1960s, most people would have turned to the federal government for solutions. (Mondale wanted immediately to spend $11 billion more in federal funds.) But now, with Reagan in the White House, there was widespread agreement with the commission that Washington would only make things worse, and that the best answers to the education woes would come at the state and local levels, from those people closest to the students and their needs. This clamor against federal authority, which was linked with bungling and excessive spending, was one of several examples that the country was no longer enamored of conventional liberal thought.

Toward the Information Superhighway

The computer chip was invented in the late 1950s, and before long an assortment of popular new products were on the market using it. The calculator appeared in 1967, the car-trip monitor in 1975, the speak-and-spell toy in 1978, the compact-disc player in 1982, the digital chassis in television in 1985, and digital wireless phones in 1988.

The number of transistors that could be placed on a silicon chip (commonly known as a microprocessor) advanced dramatically, from 3,500 in 1972 to 1.2 million by the end of the 1980s. This propelled the development and sale of the computer, chips being the computing engines in all personal computers. Engineers, needing more power, were the first customers and corporations were next, followed by the general public. The 80286 models (named after Intel chip speed) appeared in 1982, followed by the improved 80386 in 1985. About two years after the 80486 machines came out in 1989, the price of a personal computer dropped below the $2,500 level, and PCs began appearing in thousands of American homes.

The Internet, a communication network between computers, was started in 1969 when four major computers at universities were connected, for defense purposes, under a contract let by the federal government. E-mail was developed in 1972. (Queen Elizabeth II of the United Kingdom sent an e-mail message in 1976.) News groups, discussion groups focusing on a single topic, appeared in 1979. In 1989, computer scientists at McGill University in Montreal created Archie software to index sites on the Internet. That same year, Tim Berners-Lee and others at the European Laboratory for Particle Physics proposed a new protocol for information distribution that in 1991 became the World Wide Web. During the 1980s, the Internet was highly complex to operate and was limited by the federal government to research, education, and government users.

Rising Tide of Crime

The population of the United States increased 41 percent between 1960 and 1990. But total crimes increased over 300 percent, and violent crimes increased more than 500 percent. One study estimated that the aggregate cost of crime to victims in 1984 was $92.5 billion. The fastest growing segment of the criminal population was the nation's children. Juvenile violent crime arrest rates (per 100,000 population) soared from 137.0 in 1965 to 338.1 in 1980 and to 430.6 in 1990.

By 1989, prisons held 235,000 more convicts than six years earlier. One of every 364 Americans was in prison, with another 296,000 in local jails, 362,000 on parole, and 2.4 million on probation. In short, one of every sixty-nine Americans was currently in the purview of the corrections establishment. The nation was in the midst of the biggest prison construction boom in history.

A great many prisoners were in jail for drug-related crimes. Millions of Americans seemed to have an insatiable desire for illegal drugs. Untold numbers of people used marijuana. By the end of the decade, a million Americans were heroin addicts, and there were between 1.5 and 2.5 million cocaine addicts and crack cocaine users. Efforts by government, including the Reagan administration's much heralded "war on drugs," proved largely unsuccessful. Still, drug use reached a peak in the early 1980s and subsided slightly during the remainder of the decade. Drug-related emergency room visits in twenty-one cities dropped from 40,000 in 1988 to 33,000 in 1990. The percentage of high-school seniors who had tried marijuana fell from 59.5 percent in 1981 to 36.7 in 1991. Seniors who had tried cocaine fell from 16.5 in 1981 to 7.8 percent in 1991.

The AIDS Epidemic

In 1981, scientists recognized the spread of the HIV (human immunodeficiency virus), the virus believed to cause the deadly disease of AIDS (acquired immune deficiency syndrome). Public awareness mounted in 1985 when actor Rock Hudson acknowledged his illness shortly before his death. Since in the United States the disease was associated almost exclusively with anal sex by homosexuals and infected needles used by people on drugs, many thought that finding a cure was not a top priority. A 1987 Gallup poll showed that 43 percent thought AIDS a punishment for moral decline. Television networks refused to carry announcements advocating the use of condoms. The Reagan White House objected on moral grounds to procondom messages.

Under pressure from AIDS activists and concerned about the spread of the disease among heterosexuals in Africa, federal health officials launched a massive information program in the spring of 1988 portraying AIDS as a menace to everyone. A poll soon showed that 69 percent of Americans thought AIDS "was likely" to become an epidemic. In fact, as one study showed later, 85 percent of AIDS cases in the United States were concentrated among men who had sex with men. Another study showed that nationally, the HIV infection rate for women was 1.6 per 100,000 women.

Federal funds for AIDS-related medical research soared from $341 million in 1987 to $655 million in 1988. By the end of the decade, however, the hideous disease continued to baffle scientists.

The War on Tobacco

Cigarettes have been part of American life since the mid-nineteenth century. Between 1892 and 1930, thirty-seven states and territories considered legislation to ban them, and sixteen states enacted such laws. The prohibition of cigarettes, like the ban on alcohol, failed, the victim of public demand.

Cigarette smoking became truly fashionable during World War I, when they were freely supplied to the troops at the request of the military. By 1928, sales had reached the 100-billion-a-year mark. In 1947, three of every four adult males were regular or occasional smokers. Decades of health warnings by antitobacco crusaders about "coffin nails" and "cancer sticks" had obviously made little impression.

This began to change in 1952, when the public became aware of scientific studies pointing to a link between smoking and lung cancer, a disease first diagnosed in 1923. Other warnings from researchers appeared throughout the 1950s and early 1960s. In 1964, the surgeon general of the United States issued a report calling cigarettes a "health hazard" and strongly linked them to lung cancer and other diseases. The first health warnings appeared on cigarette packages in 1966. In 1971, Congress banned cigarette advertising on radio and television, and throughout the decade smoking was curtailed or isolated in a variety of public places. By the end of the decade, some 30 million Americans had kicked the habit, but many more millions persisted.

During the 1980s, states passed antismoking laws, government agencies issued restrictive regulations, and businesses routinely banned smoking on their premises. Smoking was no longer fashionable for much of the middle class. Historian Cassandra Tate observed, "Smokers retreated to the back of the plane, the back stairs at the office, the back porch at the dinner party."

In 1988, another surgeon general's report contended that smoking was as addictive as heroin and opium. That same year, a jury for the first time awarded damages to a former smoker (overturned on appeal). Angry voices in Congress talked about taxing cigarettes out of existence, and in a few years states would begin suing Big Tobacco to compensate for medical expenses.

Still, the tobacco industry was legal, its controversial advertising was still tax deductible, and tobacco farmers continued to receive federal subsidies. In 1998, some 50 million Americans smoked cigarettes.

The Soaring Economy

The troika responsible for much of Reagan's legislative achievements in the first term broke up after the election of 1984. Treasury Secretary Donald Regan became chief of staff. Intelligent and hard working, but often abrasive and at odds with the first lady, Regan was not as effective as his predecessor James Baker had been.

At Regan's suggestion, tax reform became the administration's top priority. Because tax reduction and smaller government were central to the president's philosophy, he labored hard to persuade Congress and the public that change would spur the economy and benefit all Americans. The result was the Tax Reform Act of 1986, the first major overhaul of the modern income tax system since its inception during World War II. The new code reduced personal income tax rates, bringing relief to a majority of Americans, and took nearly six million poor people off the tax rolls. It simplified the system, closed many loopholes, and destroyed thousands of tax shelters. The some sixty giant corporations that had largely escaped federal taxes were now required to pay more.

Noting that the maximum rate for individuals was cut from 50 percent to 28, critics called the new tax law a boon for the wealthy and predicted that it would hurt the economy. In fact, there were more wealthy Americans than ever before, and they did not escape the revenue collectors: in 1981 the top 1 percent paid 17.6 percent of total federal individual income taxes; in 1988, their share had increased to 27.5 percent. And the economy continued to soar.

Corporation profits broke records and the stock market shot upward. Inflation fell from over 12 percent under Carter to below 10 percent. Civilian unemployment dropped from over 7 percent to about 5 percent. From 1982 to 1989, real after-tax income per person rose by 15.5 percent, and real median income of families, before taxes, went up 12.5 percent. Mortgage rates fell from 15.2 percent in 1981 to 9.31 percent in 1988. Charitable giving in what critics called the "Decade of Greed" expanded in real dollars by 56 percent to $121 billion in 1989.

Budget deficits climbed, however, exceeding $200 billion in 1986. The deficits were largely the result of entitlement programs established before 1973. But federal spending was up, too, and while Reagan fumed about the Democrats who controlled the House and Senate after 1986, not once did he propose a balanced budget to Congress. Despite his commitment to smaller government, the president knew the obvious truth that cutting public benefits is bad politics. He was also determined to rebuild the American military, an extremely costly undertaking. A record stock market crash in October 1987 finally convinced the president and Congress to take serious steps to reduce the budget deficit.

The national debt, which first reached the trillion-dollar level in 1982, reached nearly $3 trillion in 1989. Paying interest on it trailed only Social Security and defense in the federal budget. The debt as a percentage of GDP rose from 19 percent in 1980 to 31 percent in 1989. Still, that was far lower than what it had been in 1946 (127 percent of GNP) when postwar expansion got under way. And the United States was not uniquely burdened with debt. In 1989, the figure for the United Kingdom was 31 percent of GDP, in

France it was 25 percent, in Canada it was 40 percent, and in Italy it was 96 percent.

Immigration Reform

Illegal immigrants, often from Latin America, poured into the United States in record numbers during the 1980s. It was estimated that in 1980 alone, some 1.5 million entered the country illegally, joining the 2 million illegal immigrants already in the country. The country seemed unable to police its borders. This occurred on the heels of the coming of hundreds of thousands of Indochinese, Cubans, and Haitians who fled politically repressive governments and were permitted by the Carter administration to enter the country legally. Many Americans worried that the nation would be overrun by bearers of strange languages and cultures, and argued that the United States could not accept all the poor and persecuted of the world.

After several failed attempts to grapple with the issue, Congress, with administration support, passed the Immigration Reform and Control Act of 1986. This landmark legislation offered amnesty for illegal aliens who could prove residence since before January 1, 1982, and created a temporary resident status for agricultural workers. The act also imposed fines and jail terms for employers who thereafter knowingly hired illegal aliens.

The law had economic dimensions, of course; immigrants traditionally worked hard for low wages. But there were higher motivations as well. Many proponents, often remembering their own ethnic roots, cherished the idea of America as a land of opportunity. More than half of all Americans, including President Reagan, could trace at least one ancestor back to the huge immigrations of 1840–1924. New York's Ellis Island, the entry port of 16 million immigrants from 1892 to 1954, was being refurbished as a museum, celebrating the immigrant in American life. (It would open in 1990, following an eight-year, $156-million renovation.) In the census of 1992, Americans claimed dozens of different ancestries, emphasizing the significant fact that the United States had always been a land of immigrants.

During the 1980s, Asians became the latest wave of peoples to reach American shores in great numbers. From 1981 to 1989, almost 2.5 million men and women were granted legal permanent residence. The intelligence and hard work of many Asian Americans often produced rapid socioeconomic advancement.

The Supreme Court

Predictably, the president was eager to put conservatives on the Supreme Court. Reagan infuriated many supporters on the right by naming Sandra Day O'Connor, who was suspected of being proabortion. O'Connor, however, turned out to be generally conservative and largely silenced her critics. In 1986, the president named Associate Justice William H. Rehnquist, a conservative, to be chief justice, replacing retiring Warren Burger. He selected a fiery conservative, Antonin Scalia, to take Rehnquist's seat.

In 1987, Reagan failed to get another hardliner, Robert H. Bork, approved by the Senate. Liberals, led by Ted Kennedy, waged an intensive campaign to keep Bork off the Court, in part because he opposed *Roe* v. *Wade* and might help overturn the controversial abortion decision. The Senate rejected the nomination 58 to 42. The successful tactics employed in the struggle prompted right-wing partisans to invent a new verb, "to Bork," which they likened to McCarthyism.

A second Reagan nominee, Douglas Ginsburg, had to withdraw his candidacy after he admitted using marijuana as a student (confirming the still basically conservative outlook of most Americans). A third nominee, judicial conservative Anthony M. Kennedy, was unanimously confirmed in February 1988.

Reagan moved the Court toward the right, but the shift was not dramatic. The leftist intensity of the 1960s was moderating by the late 1980s, and the mood of the country was in general accord with Court decisions. The president named nearly four hundred federal judges during his eight years in office, and only three of his nominees were rejected.

The Iran-Contra Scandal

The Reagan administration was plagued with scandals. According to one study, over 190 administration officials were indicted or convicted of illegal activity. After former troika member Edwin Meese became attorney general in the second term, the Department of Justice was wracked with charges of corruption. While Meese was not prosecuted, the federal prosecutor publicly labeled him a "sleaze," and the independent counsel in the case said that Meese had probably violated the law on four occasions. Meese resigned in July 1988. Michael Deaver, another former troika member, tried to use his White House connections as a lobbyist and was convicted in 1987 on perjury counts.

The most famous scandal, Iran-Contra, stemmed from two secret overseas operations that the president knew about and indeed helped direct. One was in Nicaragua and the other in Iran. When an underling merged the clandestine activities, and word leaked out, the result was a political explosion that shook public confidence in the chief executive for the first time.

The Sandinista government in Nicaragua, headed by Daniel Ortega Saavedra, grew militantly leftist and pro-Soviet soon after the downfall of dictator Anastasio Somoza in July 1979. Administration officials deadlocked after lengthy internal arguments about an appropriate response. Liberals, in the administration, in Congress, and throughout the country, tended to believe that the Sandinistas were mere idealists, committed to much-needed reform. Many throughout the political spectrum warned about Vietnam-style involvements in the affairs of other countries. Many conservatives, on the other hand, clung to long-established Cold War doctrine, warning that communism was at work in Latin America and would spread unless the United States took action against it.

The president, not surprisingly, held the latter view. In February 1981, he suspended aid to Nicaragua. In March and December Reagan quietly authorized a covert war to bring down the government. This involved the creation by the CIA of an anti-Sandinista force, the contras, among Nicaraguan exiles living in Honduras. Reagan saw the contras as the best hope for the return of freedom in Nicaragua. Many on the left in America portrayed them as killers and drug dealers. The struggle in Nicaragua would eventually cost hundreds of millions of dollars and kill thousands.

In the fall of 1982, following newspaper reports of the struggle, Congress passed the Boland Amendment, limiting aid to the contras and prohibiting the CIA and the Department of Defense from using any funds against the government of Nicaragua. Since the vote was 411 to 0, the president had no choice but to sign the bill. In 1984, the National Security Council largely took over the direction of the anti-Sandinista campaign, and marine Lt. Col. Oliver North began directing covert military actions.

North, a decorated veteran of Vietnam, was attractive (striking some as the model of a gung-ho marine), zealous, flamboyant, and cocky. He claimed privately to have a personal relationship with Reagan (who later denied it), and held Congress, and liberals in general, in contempt. His superiors, National Security advisers Robert McFarlane and John Poindexter, were military men of similar temperament and devotion to the president.

In early 1984, with funding for CIA activities in Nicaragua running out and Congress hostile, Reagan had to find other ways to keep aid flowing to the contras. He told McFarlane, "I want you to do whatever you have to do to help these people keep body and soul together." McFarlane took this as an order, and he and North began collecting funds from other countries and private donors. In June, Saudi Arabia pledged a million dollars a month. (After a visit with Reagan in February 1985, Saudi King Fahd agreed to pay $2 million per month.) The sultan of Brunei and the governments of Taiwan, Israel, South Africa, and South Korea made contributions. Reagan personally helped raise millions from such wealthy individuals as beer magnate Joseph Coors.

The anti-Sandinista effort was made more difficult in 1984 when Ortega Saavedra was elected president with more than 60 percent of the vote. In October, Congress passed Boland II, to close loopholes in the earlier legislation barring aid to the contras. But North and his NSC allies continued their efforts, believing that the legislation did not apply to them. Using the millions raised privately, North and a network of supporters throughout the government quietly set up "the Establishment," a miniature sort of CIA headed by retired air force Maj. Gen. Richard V. Secord and his partner, Iranian-American businessman Albert Hakim. A small military force was soon in the making.

On October 5, 1986, one of Secord's airplanes was shot down in Nicaragua, and the Sandinistas captured crewman Eugene Hasenfus, who talked about his efforts. Reagan publicly denied any government connection. At about the same time, headlines began screaming about America's covert action in Iran.

In early 1979, followers of the Islamic fundamentalist Ayatollah Khomeini overthrew the pro-American shah. Relations between the new government and the United States quickly deteriorated, and the staff of the American embassy was taken hostage. Even after its release, there was much bitterness between the two nations. When Iran went to war with Iraq in 1983, the administration launched Operation Staunch to stop international arms sales to Iran. Secretary of State Schultz branded Iran a backer of international terrorism, and the president called it "Murder Inc."

In November 1984, exiled Iranian businessman Manucher Ghorbanifar told the administration privately that he could rally moderates within Iran and save the country from Soviet control. He wanted to prove his worth to the moderate faction by arranging an arms sale to Iran and win favor with Americans by helping to gain release of four American hostages held in battle-torn Lebanon. Israeli intelligence forces believed that a moderate body existed in Iran. The CIA discounted the story. Ghorbanifar, in fact, was a con man, and the so-called moderates were agents of the Khomeini government.

McFarlane and Poindexter accepted the Israeli account, and so did the president. Reagan not only wanted to reach the antiCommunist moderates, he had a passion about freeing the hostages in Lebanon, and believed that the extremists in Lebanon could be swayed by fundamentalist Iranians. When Israel reported that Iran wanted to purchase TOW antitank missiles, it asked the administration for approval. The deal was to involve the release of four or more hostages. Against the wishes of several advisers, including Schultz, Reagan quietly agreed to sell the weapons, using Israel as the go-between.

In July 1985, Reagan gave a speech in which he called Iran part of a "confederation of terrorist states," and vowed that "America will never make concessions to terrorists." In August, Israel sold ninety-six TOW missiles to Iran. No hostages were released. In September, Israel sold 408 more, Iran making payment through Ghorbanifar. Finally, one hostage went free. This had become strictly an arms-for-hostages transaction with the Ayatollah, which Schultz had predicted. It was against the law and contrary to declared American policy.

In November, Reagan approved another proposed trade that sent more sophisticated missiles to Iran. At this point, Oliver North, on his own, mingled the Nicaraguan and Iranian activities, leaving the missile transfer details to Robert Secord and his private CIA. No hostages were released. Administration leaders argued intensely against the entire course of action. But Reagan, determined to free hostages in Lebanon, elected to continue.

In January 1986, the president agreed to let Israel sell four thousand antitank missiles to Iran. Iran increased its demands throughout the year. Meanwhile, North was quietly siphoning off funds from the millions passing through several hands and sending them to the contras. He stunned McFarlane by telling him what he was doing. While several hostages were released, the militants in Lebanon took others. When the operation finally ended, there were more American hostages in Lebanon than when Reagan and the others began trying to open dialogue with Iranian moderates.

The covert actions in both Nicaragua and Iran began leaking out late in the year. On November 19, despite being warned by advisers to let the world know what had been going on, Reagan held a press conference and denied everything. After being confronted by an angry Schultz, the president asked Ed Meese to investigate the full story. North was frantically shredding documents to conceal his activities. Meese found out anyway, and when Reagan learned shortly that North had diverted funds to the contras, he was shocked, and expressed his dismay to reporters. There were numerous resignations within the White House, and Schultz took command of the nation's foreign policy.

Several formal investigations got under way, an independent counsel was named, and reporters scurried to discover every detail of the scandal. Reagan's approval rating dropped in one poll from 67 percent to 36 percent. Former senator John Tower, who headed a presidentially appointed Special Review Board, learned to his dismay the extent to which the president was passive, out of touch, and honestly unable to recall much of what he had done. McFarlane, who acknowledged that he had not told the president about the transfer of funds, said that Reagan had "the attention span of a fruit fly." (In 1994, Nancy Reagan would reveal that her husband was diagnosed as having Alzheimer's disease.)

Tower's report concluded, as did three other probes, that Reagan was responsible for the scandal. The president acknowledged the blame publicly. Independent counsel Lawrence E. Walsh, following a seven-year, $48 million probe, secured eleven convictions but sent no one to jail—in part because President Bush later pardoned six people and two convictions were overturned on appeal. Televised congressional hearings, reminding many of the Watergate debacle, battered the administration's reputation and forced Vice President Bush, running for the presidency, to acknowledge his minor role in the machinations.

Many Americans, however, credited Reagan with good intentions; he was trying to release hostages and contain communism. Few wanted to see another president driven from office in disgrace.

Oliver North, who was outspoken and unrepentant during his testimony, became something of a hero on the right, the symbol of a patriot who would risk all to stop the Reds. (His conviction was one of those overturned.) Congress soon gave generous support to the contras. Daniel Ortega fell from liberal favor after losing his bid for reelection in 1990, but the Sandinistas remained a powerful force in Nicaragua. Fifteen hostages were released through 1991 (one was killed, one died, and one escaped). Iran remained fervently anti-American.

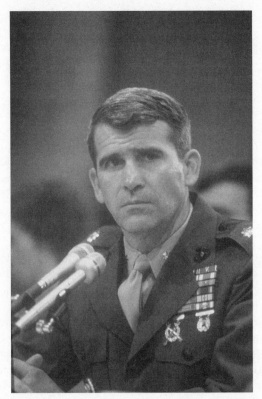

Col. Oliver North at the Iran-Contra trial. Source: Archive Photos/Consolidated News

Ending the Cold War

Mikhail Gorbachev became general secretary of the Communist party of the Soviet Union in 1985. At age 54 he was the youngest Soviet leader since Josef Stalin came to power in the 1920s. His youth and intelligence helped him recognize the serious economic and social problems facing his vast empire. Seventy years of communism had failed to match the wealth of the West and many Asian countries. (A secret CIA study concluded that the Soviet Union was in an advanced state of decay.) And millions chafed at the repressive government that denied them freedoms common in the more advanced nations.

Gorbachev was deeply concerned as well about the military buildup under way during the Reagan administration. He lacked the financial resources to match it. An aide noted later that Gorbachev was obsessed by the economic cost of the arms race and realized "we had to put an end to the Cold War." Moreover, the SDI, "Star Wars," threatened to give the United States the ability to mount a counterattack in a nuclear war. Even if the

SDI proved technologically impossible, the billions being spent to develop it might well produce innovations that would leave the Soviet Union militarily vulnerable.

Gorbachev also worried about the Reagan Doctrine, the public commitment by the administration to launch an active counteroffensive throughout the world against Soviet imperialism. In his 1985 State of the Union address, Reagan pledged to back "those who are risking their lives—on every continent, from Afghanistan to Nicaragua—to defy Soviet-supported aggression and secure rights which have been ours from birth."

This was more than rhetoric. In 1982 and 1983, the president signed secret National Security Decision directives pledging the United States to use diplomatic, economic, and psychological efforts to weaken Soviet power. The administration supported anti-Soviet efforts in Poland, and by 1985 was secretly spending $8 million a year to back the Solidarity party. It extended covert aid to the anti-Soviet forces in Afghanistan. The CIA led a successful effort to persuade Saudi Arabia to increase oil production, a move that reduced Soviet hard currency income by half. Political scientist Jay Winik wrote later, "Under Ronald Reagan, everywhere the Soviets had turned, their pressure was met by U.S. counterpressure."

The Reagan Doctrine also involved the defense of allies. In 1983, despite intense pressure from the Soviets and an assortment of peace organizations, the president ordered intermediate-range missiles to Western Europe to counter similar weapons aimed at the area by the Russians.

Gorbachev tried to restructure (*perestroika*) the Soviet economy with a program of moderate and controlled reforms. To make it more appealing, the Russian leader permitted more freedom and openness (*glasnost*). Turmoil rapidly ensued, and the Communist party began to lose its grip over the more than one hundred nationality groups under its authority. The taste of freedom quickly proved contagious.

Reagan thought the United States was winning the Cold War, but he feared the possibility of nuclear war and strongly desired to improve relations with the Soviets and achieve mutual arms reductions. In the fall of 1985, the Soviets made it clear that they had the same goals. In November, Reagan and Gorbachev held a cordial summit meeting in Geneva. While Reagan refused to budge on SDI, agreements included a 50-percent reduction in strategic arms, cultural and scientific exchanges, and additional summits. A formal statement declared that nuclear war could not be won and should not be fought. Both leaders sensed that they could deal with each other reasonably. Gorbachev aide Anatoly Chernyaev said later that the Geneva meeting was the beginning of the end of the Cold War.

Plagued with a faltering economy and a restless population, Gorbachev grew bolder. In January 1986, he proposed startling reductions in nuclear weaponry if the United States would give up SDI. At the Soviet Union's party congress in February and March, Gorbachev argued that the two superpowers had to learn to live in peace with each other, maintaining the lowest possible balance of weapons and without nuclear missiles. In declaring that capitalism and communism must coexist, the Soviet leader was conceding a basic premise of Marxist ideology, international class warfare.

At the Soviet leader's request, he and Reagan met at Reykjavik, Iceland, on October 11–12. Gorbachev made sweeping disarmament offers, and at one point the two leaders agreed in principle to eliminate all nuclear weapons within ten years. But when Gorbachev announced that his offers were contingent on the elimination of SDI, Reagan angrily refused and left the meeting.

The Reykjavik summit had major consequences. Details were worked out on missile reductions. The Soviets agreed to talk about human rights issues in future negotiations. Above all, Gorbachev realized that SDI was not a negotiable matter. The Soviet leader then chose to take another approach: he would wind down the Cold War in the hope that the decreasing threat would persuade the United States to scrap SDI.

Gorbachev came to Washington in December 1987, working crowds like a seasoned politician. The summit meeting led to the INF (Intermediate Nuclear Forces) Treaty, which eliminated an entire class of nuclear missiles with ranges of 600 to 3,400 miles. It was the first time that nations agreed to destroy nuclear weapons. Both sides agreed to permit on-site inspections of missile bases.

When Reagan visited Moscow in May 1988 and was well received and allowed to speak freely on television, it was clear that the Cold War was winding down. Reagan and Gorbachev embraced publicly at the site of Lenin's tomb.

In December 1988, Gorbachev told the United Nations that the Bolshevik Revolution was a thing of the past and that henceforth nations must free their foreign policy of ideology. Contending that force should not be the basis of foreign policy, he announced the unilateral reduction of 500,000 troops and the withdrawal of 50,000 troops and 5,000 tanks from Eastern Europe.

The following year, the Soviet Union collapsed. The Berlin Wall came down, and the two Germanies were united in 1990. In 1991, the Communist party was outlawed and most of the republics that had once been the Soviet state joined a loose economic federation called the Commonwealth of Independent States. The terrifying international struggle that had dominated much of the world's attention since 1946 was at last over.

Some observers gave Reagan credit for ending the Cold War. Conservative British Prime Minister Margaret Thatcher wrote in her memoirs, "President Reagan's Strategic Initiative, about which the Soviets and Mr. Gorbachev were . . . so alarmed, was to prove central to the West's victory in the Cold War." Others emphasized Reagan's belief in the fall of communism, his commitment to counter Soviet aggression throughout the world, and his diplomatic pursuits to rid the world of nuclear weapons. Columnist Bruce Chapman argued that Reagan deserved the Nobel Peace Prize. Howard Baker, Reagan's chief of staff after Donald Regan's departure in early 1987, said of the president, "He knew who he was, he knew what he believed, and he knew where he wanted to go."

Liberal critics have frequently disagreed, citing long-term Soviet economic and political ills, noting Gorbachev's boldness, and asking among other things how a man who knew so little in other matters could have been the guiding force in a highly complex military and diplomatic initiative. Washington insider Clark Clifford called Reagan an "amiable dunce."

In his impressive study of Reagan, historian William E. Pemberton argues that the president must share the plaudits for the end of the Cold War with Secretary of State George Schultz. But he does not discount the president's vital contribution. "The usually passive Reagan could exert great leadership on matters central to his vision of the future."

The distinguished historian John Lewis Gaddis is less certain, giving the Reagan administration credit for abandoning the fixation about obtaining nuclear superiority but adding, "whether it did so out of ignorance or craft is still not clear." What we do know, Gaddis concludes, "is that the United States began to challenge the Soviet Union during the first half of the 1980s in a manner unprecedented since the early Cold War. That state soon exhausted itself and expired—whether from unaccustomed over-exertion or Gorbachev's heroic efforts at resuscitation is also still not completely clear."

SUGGESTED READING

Archie Brown, *The Gorbachev Factor* (1996); R. McGreggor Cawley, *Federal Land, Western Anger: The Sagebrush Rebellion and Environmental Politics* (1993); Michael K. Deaver and Mickey Herskowitz, *Behind the Scenes* (1987); John Lewis Gaddis, *We Now Know: Rethinking Cold War History* (1997); Mikhail Gorbachev, *Memoirs* (1995); James Davison Hunter, *Before the Shooting Starts: Searching for Democracy in America's Culture War* (1994); Haynes Johnson, *Sleepwalking Through History: America in the Reagan Years* (1991); William G. Mayer, *The Changing American Mind: How and Why American Public Opinion Changed Between 1960 and 1988* (1992); William E. Pemberton, *Exit with Honor: The Life and Presidency of Ronald Reagan* (1997); Donald T. Regan, *For The Record: From Wall Street to Washington* (1988).

Chapter Fourteen

INTO THE NINETIES

Ronald Reagan, 78, left Washington with a 70-percent approval rating in the polls and with the personal impression that he had been a successful president. The Cold War was over and communism was on the run all over the world. The nation's military prowess had been restored. The economy was booming. Millions had lower expectations of government and higher respect for private enterprise and individual freedom. The disdain of the sixties for traditional values and patriotism was waning. People told pollsters that the president had made them proud of America again.

Despite mounting budget deficits, the huge national debt, scandals, and the continued growth of the federal government during the 1980s, conservatives were especially loyal to Reagan. William F. Buckley, Jr., said later that Reagan had accomplished 60 percent of the conservative agenda and that the administration was 60 percent successful.

Those on the left, of course, were generally horrified by the Reagan administration, condemning it for racial, sexual, and ecological insensitivity as well as greed, aggression, and ignorance. Reagan, said Robert Hughes, "left his country a little stupider in 1988 than it had been in 1980, and a lot more tolerant of lies, because his style of image-presentation cut the connective tissue of arguments between ideas and hence fostered the defeat of thought itself." A poll of historians put Reagan in the "below average" category. Democrats eagerly awaited their chance to see the executive branch once again in safe hands.

Election of 1988

Vice president George Bush was widely thought to be Reagan's natural heir. The backgrounds of the two men were vastly different. Bush, age 63, was the son of a wealthy investment banker and United States senator. Raised in Connecticut, he attended a prep school and went on to Yale University, where he was the captain of the varsity baseball team and graduated Phi Beta Kappa in economics. In World War II he earned his commission and wings at age 18, the youngest pilot in the navy. He went into combat at age 19 and won the Distinguished Flying Cross and three air medals. Bush had been a successful oil executive in Texas, a congressman, the nation's top United Nations delegate, head of the nation's first liaison office in the People's Republic of China, and chief of the CIA.

Bush was a moderate conservative, a skilled campaigner, and an effective fund raiser. When he announced his candidacy in October 1987, he had already accumulated a $12 million campaign chest. In primaries, Bush defeated such competitors as "televangelist" Pat Robertson and Senate Minority Leader Robert Dole, sweeping the South, where Reagan's policies were especially popular. At the GOP convention, Bush chose 41-year-old Indiana Senator Dan Quayle as his running mate. Party strategists thought that Quayle, handsome and conservative, would win the votes of women and the Reagan right. But his inexperience and persistent verbal blunders proved embarrassing.

A large number of Democrats sought their party's nomination, including civil rights activist Jesse Jackson, Missouri Congressman Richard Gephardt, Illinois Senator Paul Simon, Tennessee Senator Albert Gore, and Massachusetts Governor Michael Dukakis. Dukakis, whose campaign was highly organized and well-financed, emerged the winner.

Dukakis, 55, was the son of a Greek immigrant who had become a wealthy physician. He went to Swarthmore College and Harvard Law School. He had

George Bush, August 18, 1988, promising "Read my lips, no new taxes." Source: George Bush Presidential Library

been a state representative from 1963–70, and governor from 1975–79 and 1983–91. In sharp contrast to Bush, Dukakis lacked a military record and experience in the federal government and was a staunch liberal. At the party convention, 67-year-old Texas Senator Lloyd Bentsen was named to fill the ticket. Bentsen had once defeated Bush in a Senate race, and it was hoped he would appeal to the no-longer-solid South.

The campaign was less than inspiring. Bush rejoiced in the continuation of Reagan peace and prosperity, and rejected even the thought of increasing taxes: "Read my lips . . . no new taxes." He promised to be the "education president" and the "environmental president." He said he had the vision of a "kinder, gentler nation."

At the same time, Bush portrayed his opponent as soft on crime, noting the Democrat's support of a Massachusetts law granting furloughs even to prisoners serving life sentences without parole. The case of black murderer Willie Horton, who had escaped during such a parole and committed assault and rape, became a prominent theme in Bush television commercials. A Dukakis cover-up of the case became widely known in a devastating *Reader's Digest* article.

Dukakis and his backers dismissed Bush as a "wimp" and a "preppie" and made much of his Iran-Contra involvement. They stressed an assortment of alleged failures of the Reagan administration and dismissed the Horton campaign theme as racism. At one point, Dukakis had his picture taken in a military tank, attempting to look fierce and prove his toughness. The result was widespread ridicule. The television debates between the candidates amounted largely to a contrast in appearance—Bush was tall, good-looking, and self-confident; Dukakis was short, swarthy, and edgy. The debates increased Bush's lead in the polls.

In November, Bush carried forty of the fifty states and won by a 54-to 46-percent margin. The electoral margin was 426 to 112. Voter turnout was the lowest since 1924. Dukakis scored well only with African Americans. Still, Democrats controlled both houses of Congress and two-thirds of state governorships.

The Bush Approach

Despite their wealth and Ivy League backgrounds, George Bush and his wife Barbara (who attended Smith College for two years) sought to identify with average Americans. They stressed devotion to the family and talked about having good character. They enjoyed country-western music, pork rinds, horseshoe pitching, and their dog Millie. Mrs. Bush, the mother of five (a younger daughter had died in 1953 of leukemia), refused to dye her silver hair and was proud of being a homemaker. She told women at Wellesley, an elite women's college, "What happens in your house is more important than what happens in the White House." The White House during the Bush administration was more like Main Street than Camelot or Hollywood.

It was commonly said in the media that Bush was not a deep thinker and lacked a vision for America. There was no doubt some truth to the charge. But the new president had proposals about the environment and education that he thought vital, and he was determined to take advantage of the collapse of the Soviet Union and make the world a safer place. Bush's initial concerns were economic: paying for the huge savings and loan debacle and taking action to contain the ever-growing federal deficits.

Three members of the Bush cabinet were Reagan holdovers, including Secretary of Education Lauro F. Cavazos, the first Hispanic American cabinet member. In less than a year, Bush set a record for the number of women appointed to top federal positions. Elizabeth H. Dole was the new secretary of labor, and Dr. Antonia Novello was named surgeon general. Long-time Bush friend James A. Baker became secretary of state. The highly respected environmentalist William Reilly headed the Environmental Protection Agency.

Supreme Court Appointees

There were signs in the late 1980s that the Supreme Court was moving to the right. Cynics said the justices were again "following the election returns." Decisions restricting affirmative action programs and abortions, and approving capital punishment, worried the left. The 5–4 decision of July 3, 1989, upholding the right of states to impose sharp restrictions on abortions prompted feminists to ponder whether *Roe* v. *Wade* itself was in danger of being overturned.

Bush's initial appointment to the Supreme Court was David Souter, a centrist who did not arouse much opposition. Souter was a Rhodes Scholar and a graduate of Harvard Law School who had been on the New Hampshire Supreme Court from 1983 to 1990. He was on the U.S. Circuit Court of Appeals when named by Bush.

In 1991, civil rights champion Thurgood Marshall retired. To please the right wing of his party and retain the "black seat" on the Court, Bush nominated conservative African American Clarence Thomas. Thomas, age 43, was a Yale Law School graduate who had won favor with the Reagan administration because of his opposition to racial quotas and government paternalism in general. In 1981 Thomas was named head of the civil rights division of the Department of Education, and from 1982 to 1990 he headed the Equal Employment Opportunity Commission (EEOC). Thomas was a U.S. Court of Appeals judge when nominated to the Supreme Court.

Liberal opposition to the confirmation mounted when black University of Oklahoma law professor Anita Hill leveled sexual harassment charges against the nominee. Hill claimed that the actions, which did not involve physical contact, occurred when she worked with Thomas at the Department of Education and the EEOC.

Televised hearings magnified the charges and countercharges, and Americans divided sharply over the issue. Feminists and civil rights activists vehemently championed Ms. Hill, making the case a symbol of sexual harassment in the work place. Conservatives tended to believe Thomas, who angrily denied the charges and claimed he was the victim of racial discrimination. When the shouting died down, the Senate approved the nomination by the narrow margin of 52 to 48.

Thomas would prove to be as staunch a conservative on the Court as his partisans hoped and his opponents feared. Often shunned and constantly criticized, Thomas lashed out publicly at his detractors in 1998, calling them racists who refused to take his ideas seriously.

Tiananmen Square

During the years following Nixon's initiative, Chinese-American relations slowly improved. After 1979, when formal diplomatic relations were established, tens of thousands of Chinese students poured into American colleges and universities, and even more Americans traveled to China as tourists. Trade between the nations mounted steadily. Some thought that the dictatorship in Beijing might soon abandon communism and embrace free enterprise and democracy.

But China's rulers proved to be less willing to embrace independence and change than many hoped. In early 1989, troops put down Tibetans who were clamoring for more autonomy. On June 4, the army crushed prodemocracy demonstrators, mostly young people, in Tiananmen Square in Beijing, killing as many as two thousand. The world reacted in horror at the massacre, seen on film and covered extensively in the press.

President Bush extended visas of Chinese students, who might have feared to return home, and suspended the sale of military hardware to the communist government. Some critics thought this response half-hearted, but Bush was determined not to destroy a vital link with the world's most populous nation. The relationship with China would remain one of the most important topics of American foreign policy for the rest of the century.

The Invasion of Panama

With the end of the Cold War, Soviet financial contributions to Cuba were curtailed and stopped in Nicaragua. The United States appeared to be in a dominant position in Latin America. One sore spot remaining was Panama, ruled by military dictator Manuel Noriega. Once pro-American, Noriega had backed the Sandinistas and become personally wealthy as a drug trafficker. U.S. federal grand juries had indicted Noriega on several charges. In May 1989, the dictator nullified an election that a hand-picked candidate had lost and sent thugs to beat up his opposition.

When Noriega declared a state of war with the United States and threatened the lives of Americans living in his country, President Bush, on December 20, 1989, dispatched some 12,000 troops to Panama to join the 12,000 troops already there. The goal, of dubious legality, was to take over Panama and install a pro-American government. Most Panamanians welcomed the intervention. Noriega eluded capture but soon surrendered and was sent to Florida to face trial. In 1992 he was convicted on numerous counts of drug smuggling and racketeering and went to prison.

Only twenty-three Americans were killed in Panama, but thousands of Panamanians, many of them citizens, were casualties. The invasion was widely admired in the United States, and George Bush's popularity soared. Even his harshest critics admitted that he had shed the "wimp" image.

The War on Drugs

During his election campaign, George Bush declared that he would take bold steps to win the so-called war on drugs. The need for such a war was obvious. The link between crime and drugs, for example, was well documented. Among jail inmates arrested in 1989, 44 percent used drugs in the month before the offense, 30 percent used drugs daily in the month before the offense, and 27 percent used drugs at the time of the offense. Twenty percent of Hispanic state prison inmates said they committed their offense to get money for drugs, compared with 15 percent of white inmates and 17 percent of black inmates.

In 1989, 1.3 million Americans were arrested by state and local police for drug violations, up from 780,000 in 1984. Between 1975 and 1993, the federal government seized 6,605 clandestine drug laboratories. In fiscal year 1993, the U.S. Customs Service would seize 507,249 pounds of marijuana, 175,318 pounds of cocaine, and 17.9 million dosage units of drugs such as LSD and barbiturates.

To coordinate the federal effort, Bush named William Bennett, Reagan's iconoclastic education secretary from 1985 to 1989. The federal drug-control budget increased from $1.5 billion in 1981 to $9.7 billion in 1990, and would reach $12.2 billion in 1993. During fiscal 1991, state and local governments spent $15.9 billion on drug-control activities, a 13-percent increase over the $14.1 billion spent the year before.

In February 1990, Bush held a summit in Cartagena, Colombia, with the presidents of Peru, Bolivia, and Colombia, the three major illegal-drug-producing nations. The heads of state agreed that the need to reduce the demand for illegal drugs in the United States was as important as the reduction of supplies from abroad.

The Persian Gulf War

In the late 1980s, the United States backed Iraq in its war with Iran, fearing that an Iranian victory would threaten Saudi Arabia and American oil supplies. The Reagan and Bush administrations approved nearly $1 billion in economic and technical aid to the government of Saddam Hussein. Some of this aid was capable of providing Iraq with powerful weaponry.

When the war ended, Kuwait unilaterally increased its oil production, causing a drop in world prices and damaging the already precarious economy of Iraq. This and Hussein's anger at the refusal of Kuwait and Saudi Arabia to forgive Iraqi debts, prompted Hussein to prepare for war. Asserting historical claims to Kuwaiti territory, Hussein marched into Kuwait on August 2, 1990. This unexpected move caused grave concern in Washington because the Iraqi leader was now in a position to disturb the flow of oil from the Saudis, who controlled more than a fifth of the world's proven oil supplies.

President Bush declared, "This aggression will not stand," and rapidly forged a thirty-nation coalition, including Arab nations, to oppose Iraq's aggression. The United Nations authorized a trade embargo on Iraq and sent a quarter of a million troops, mostly Americans, to defend Saudi Arabia. Operation Desert Shield was commanded by American army General Norman Schwarzkopf. By late 1990, plans were being laid for a military offensive against Hussein, and the U.N. military force grew to 550,000 troops.

The House and Senate debated the issue at length, with liberals generally opposing military action and hoping that the economic boycott of Iraq would prove effective, and conservatives portraying the struggle as a stand against aggression and a fight for Kuwait's freedom. On January 12, 1991, Congress narrowly approved the use of American troops in the Persian Gulf. Four days later, Operation Desert Storm began.

On February 23, following weeks of air strikes, Schwarzkopf sent 200,000 troops into Iraq. Although coverage was censured by the Pentagon (excluding the gore of actual combat and focusing on high-technology weapon systems), television carried much of the war live. Millions watched round-the-clock programming on the Cable News Network (CNN). Within one-hundred hours after the invasion, fire-breathing Hussein humbly accepted a cease-fire. Iraq left Kuwait after setting its oil fields on fire and dumping huge quantities of crude oil into the Gulf. The United States lost only 148 Americans in the six-week conflict, while some 100,000 Iraqi soldiers and citizens died.

Americans rejoiced, Schwarzkopf and his troops were celebrated as heroes, and Bush's approval rating reached 91 percent, the all-time high. It now seemed clear that America was the dominant force in the world and would set the agenda for the post-Cold War era. The Persian Gulf War made many Americans dismiss the defeat in Vietnam and talk again about national pride and global duty.

Bush was later criticized for failing to pursue the war until Hussein was killed or at least driven from power. Hussein brutally suppressed two internal rebellions following the conflict, chafed at the military inspections of Iraq that were required after the cease-fire, and was often thought to be harboring vast poison gas reserves. But the president and the allies feared the dissolution of Iraq and a resurgence of Iranian authority should Hussein be ousted. The Middle East would remain a volatile region throughout the decade.

The Sagging Economy

While domestic oil prices dropped after the Persian Gulf War, the economy slid into a recession. In the spring of 1991, Bush reluctantly agreed to demands by congressional leaders to raise some new taxes. Breaking his iron-clad campaign pledge put the president at odds with GOP conservatives and persuaded millions that the man in the Oval Office could not be trusted. The impact of the tax increase on the future of the Bush administration was compared by some with the disastrous political outcome of Ford's pardon of Nixon.

By 1992, all of the key elements in the economy were retracting, and consumer confidence set a record low. Unemployment rose to 7.8 percent. While the Federal Reserve Board slashed interest rates, the economy failed to pick up.

Cutbacks in military and aerospace spending played a role in the slump, and so did the replacing of workers by computers and computer-driven machines. Many companies laid off workers while shifting their manufacturing to low-wage developing nations. "Staying competitive in the world market" was a slogan often repeated by business leaders in the 1990s, and many workers bore the brunt. Those who kept their jobs often found themselves working longer hours and depending on income from a spouse to maintain or improve their standard of living. In 1967 the number of dual-income families amounted to 33 percent of American households. By 1998 the figure had jumped to 66 percent.

The economic slump proved to be temporary. But the eventual recovery was too late to help George Bush, whose popularity plummeted from the heights of the Persian Gulf War to below 30 percent.

Racial Explosion

Despite the enormous and unprecedented progress in civil rights that the country had experienced over the past several decades, racial tensions remained a major part of American life. Millions of whites feared blacks, convinced that they were given somehow naturally to crime, drugs, and illegitimate births. Nearly all-black Washington, D.C., seemed to illustrate the point: it was the murder capital of America, inheriting the title from heavily black Detroit. A rampage of assault—a "wilding"—by black teenage boys in New York's Central Park in April 1989 shocked the nation.

Millions of African Americans resented what they saw as a persistent racism that trapped them in urban ghettoes, packed them into prisons, denied them educational and occupational opportunities, and prevented them from the wealth and respect that other Americans enjoyed. The often rapid social mobility of Asian and Near Eastern immigrants served to intensify the frustration and anger.

On April 19, 1992, an all-white jury in suburban Los Angeles acquitted four white policemen charged with beating a black motorist. Twenty-five-year-old parolee Rodney King had been drunk when police finally stopped him after a high-speed, eight-mile chase. A bystander recorded on videotape what followed: four police officers repeatedly kicking and savagely hitting King with steel batons. The incident occurred on March 3, and the media showed the videotape repeatedly for weeks. Many blacks and civil rights activists were convinced that this was a typical example of white oppression. Defenders of the police officers pointed to King's wild and dangerous driving and his "menacing" resistance when arrested. (King was 6 foot 4, 240 pounds, and of arguably fearsome appearance. His initial actions when police confronted him did not appear on the tape shown by the media.)

The jury verdict was followed by the most violent race riot in American history. The three-day rampage of destruction and violence focused on South Central Los Angeles and disbursed across a huge swath stretching from Long Beach to Hollywood. Fifty-five people were killed, at least 4,000 were injured, more than 12,000 were arrested, and 5,270 buildings were destroyed or badly damaged, including some 200 liquor stores. The often confused Los Angeles police were aided by 4,000 National Guard troops sent in by Governor Pete Wilson and 1,200 federal law officers and armed service personnel supplied by President Bush. The immediate cost of the riot exceeded a billion dollars.

When analyzed, the incident defied simple explanation. While the King verdict triggered the outburst, the appalling violence seemed to have deeper roots, including a complex of ethnic tensions. Stores owned by Koreans, for example, suffered greater damage than those owned by African Americans. Television reporters interviewed blacks who admitted harboring a grudge against the Koreans for treating them with suspicion and condescension. During the riot, Hispanics attacked both blacks and whites and engaged in looting and burning of their own.

Federal authorities soon indicted the four police officers on federal charges of violating Rodney King's civil rights. Critics claimed this was a classic case of double jeopardy, prompted by fear of further riots. On April 17, 1993, a jury found two of the officers guilty. Each was sentenced to thirty months in prison. After serving their sentences, they faced a new crisis: the Clinton administration, which had close ties to civil rights leaders, tried to get the pair resentenced to longer terms. This move proved unsuccessful.

Rodney King sued the City of Los Angeles and in 1994 came away with $3.8 million. Before and after his sudden wealth, he had further run-ins with the law, being convicted of drunk driving and hit-and-run driving.

Five years after the great riot, a third of the buildings destroyed had not been replaced, and some two hundred vacant lots scarred the landscape of South Central Los Angeles. Forty-four businesses had spent $400 million for recovery, and government funneled in $1.3 billion in loans and grants. But this was far short of the $6 billion needed to revitalize impoverished areas of Los Angeles.

Race relations again grew tense in 1995 when a jury of nine African Americans, two whites, and one Hispanic declared the famous black football player and actor O. J. Simpson innocent of two charges of murder. The victims were Simpson's ex-wife Nicole and her friend Ronald Goldman, both whites. The case had been in the headlines for more than a year, and millions watched the televised trial. Polls showed that African Americans and whites had very different opinions about the case: six out of ten blacks thought Simpson innocent, while three out of four whites were convinced of his guilt. Defense attorneys had portrayed Simpson as another black victim of the white justice system. After the swift verdict was announced, journalist Lou Cannon observed, some black Americans said it was "payback for Rodney King." Families of the victims soon sued Simpson, and a jury ordered him to pay $33.5 million in damages.

International Disarmament

Bush was keenly interested in foreign affairs, and was especially concerned about the disintegration of the Soviet Union, which took place during his administration. In 1990, the Berlin Wall came down and Germany was reunified. Lithuania, Latvia, and Estonia declared their independence a year later. In December 1991, The Commonwealth of Independent States was created, dominated by Boris Yeltsin, president of Russia. Gorbachev, without a Soviet Union to preside over, resigned.

Bush worked well with Gorbachev and his successors. He negotiated START (Strategic Arms Reduction Talks) I (1991) and START II (1993), the first agreements of the nuclear era designed to dismantle and destroy strategic weapons.

Domestic Policy

Bush was far more pragmatic than Reagan and often took steps designed to appeal to the broad political spectrum. The result was that to many, especially on the right, he seemed indecisive and expedient. Still, the president could boast of considerable achievement in domestic policy. He signed the Americans With Disabilities Act, a renewal of the Voting Rights Act, and the Clean Air Act, often described as the most significant environmental legislation ever passed. Bush proposed sweeping educational reforms, including national achievement examinations in core subjects. He signed the Civil Rights Act of 1991, which made it easier for workers to sue for job discrimination. (Employment discrimination lawsuits climbed from 12,962 in 1993 to 23,796 in 1997.) And he signed a bill greatly increasing Head Start funding.

On the other hand, Bush alienated many by vetoing an earlier civil rights bill, which he feared mandated racial quotas, reducing several hundred social programs, and vetoing a minimum-wage bill. The war on drugs seemed to be making little headway by the end of the term. (Things would soon get worse. According to the Substance Abuse and Mental Health Services Administration, between 1992 and 1995 teen drug use skyrocketed 105 percent, including a jump of 183 percent in monthly use of LSD and other hallucinogens and a jump of 141 percent in use of marijuana.) Environmentalists were disturbed that Bush opposed efforts to draft stricter rules to decrease the threat of global warming. He also refused to prevent corporations from exploring for oil in the Alaskan wildlife preserve.

Huge deficits, which would have been even larger had Congress not placed Social Security surpluses into the general fund, concerned many. The national debt hit $4 trillion in 1992, up from $2.8 trillion in 1989. The economic recession and the president's reversal on his pledge not to raise taxes left him especially vulnerable as elections neared.

The Election of 1992

Most of the top Democrats declined to run for the presidency in 1992, thinking that Bush, like Reagan before him, was certain to be reelected. This paved the way for the candidacy of the little-known governor of Arkansas, Bill Clinton.

William Jefferson Blythe IV was born in Hope, Arkansas, on August 19, 1946 (he later took the name of his stepfather). His mother was a nurse and his stepfather was an automobile salesman. Exceptionally bright and charming, Bill starred in school as a student, musician, and athlete. In 1968 he graduated from Georgetown University with a degree in international affairs and was named a Rhodes Scholar. He graduated from Yale Law School in 1973, taught law at the University of Arkansas, and went into politics.

After losing a congressional race in 1974, Clinton was elected attorney general two years later, and in 1978, at the age of 32, became governor. He failed to win reelection in 1980, but was reelected in 1982 and altogether served twelve years as governor.

Clinton married Hillary Rodham in 1975. A native of Chicago, she was a graduate of Wellesley and Yale Law School. She too possessed good looks, charm, high intelligence, and burning ambition. Her political bent was decidedly to the left. Insiders knew that Ms. Clinton's influence on her husband was considerable.

Clinton ran as a centrist, opposed to both Reagan economics and "tax and spend" liberalism. On the primary trail, he tended to avoid direct answers to questions, stick with generalities, and tell audiences what they wanted to hear. Clinton's campaign was handicapped by his avoidance of military service during the Vietnam War, by his admission that he once smoked marijuana but "didn't inhale," and by woman trouble. Gennifer Flowers of Arkansas said that she had been Clinton's mistress for twelve years. (Clinton denied it, but years later, under oath, admitted having sex with Flowers once.) This and rumors of similar activities prompted a senior Clinton aide, Betsey Wright, to oversee a campaign operation to handle what she called "bimbo eruptions."

There was also evidence of dubious Clinton financial transactions in Arkansas, dismissed by some on the grounds that politics in that state had long been corrupt. The candidate portrayed himself as a serious Southern Baptist of the highest integrity.

Clinton won the Democratic nomination at the party convention in New York and named liberal 42-year-old Senator Al Gore of Tennessee as his running mate. It was the first baby-boomer presidential ticket. The Democratic party found itself with young, attractive, and articulate candidates; unity; plenty of money; and an early lead in the polls.

The Republicans enjoyed less harmony, for the Religious Right, disturbed especially about abortion and the growing secularization of American life, was less than pleased with Bush moderation. Conservative Pat Buchanan, who had served in the Nixon administration and was a familiar figure in the media, was especially critical of the GOP for failing to tackle directly an assortment of moral issues and refusing to limit immigration.

The campaign was enlivened by the independent candidacy of eccentric Texas billionaire H. Ross Perot. Appearing often on television with a feisty, witty, homespun approach that employed simple arguments and folksy analogies, Perot drew much applause from those who thought that politicians avoided the real issues facing citizens in favor of slick imagery and empty promises. In mid-July, however, Perot suddenly withdrew from the race and backed Clinton.

Influenced by Perot and eager to contrast his youthful vigor with the administration's alleged torpor on domestic issues, Clinton called himself an "agent of change" and promised to work for health care reform, lower taxes, job creation, and college scholarships. Like his idol, JFK, Clinton made hundreds of promises on the campaign trail.

Bush and Quayle blamed the Democrat-controlled Congress for the nation's economic ills, stressed the president's foreign policy achievements, and challenged Clinton's patriotism and integrity. Democrats answered in kind. Perot jumped back into the race during the final month of the campaign, and the three candidates participated in three inconsequential televised debates.

Clinton led in the polls throughout the campaign, and on election night he collected 43.7 million votes to Bush's 38.1 million and Perot's 19.2 million (the largest total ever achieved by a third-party candidate). In the electoral college the margin was even larger, Clinton leading Bush 370 to 168. Clinton scored especially well among minorities, women, and young people. Still, he was elected by only 43 percent of the voters.

Almost 55 percent of eligible voters went to the polls in 1992, up 5 percent from 1988. Democrats did well in congressional races and now had commanding majorities in the House and Senate. Five women, all Democrats, won Senate seats, and Carol Moseley Braun of Illinois became the first African American woman to sit in the Senate. Colorado sent Native American Ben Nighthorse Campbell to the Senate.

Clinton had promised during the campaign to appoint many women and minorities to the executive branch, and he followed through once elected. Janet Reno, for example, became the first woman attorney general, Donna

Shalala became secretary of health and human services, and women headed the Council of Economic Advisers and the Environmental Protection Agency. Surgeon General Jocelyn Elders was a black, as was Commerce Secretary Ron Brown. Housing and Urban Development Secretary Henry Cisneros was a Hispanic. Feminist Ruth Bader Ginsberg was named to the Supreme Court in 1993.

Ideologically, the White House staff tended to be from the left, which since the McGovern campaign had gained supremacy in the Democratic party. This general consensus meant that many of the attitudes and practices of the sixties were to be expected. A Secret Service agent told the House Government Reform and Oversight Committee in 1996 that he had seen references to cocaine and crack usage in the FBI files of more than forty White House aides.

Clinton Controversies

Controversy marked the new administration from its inception. In January, the president, who was prochoice on abortion, lifted the ban on fetal tissue research. This deeply upset the Religious Right. Late in the month he announced plans to integrate gays and lesbians into all branches of the armed forces. This action produced a firestorm of protest. In July, a compromise was reached between the White House and the Pentagon in which the military would no longer ask about sexual behavior when recruiting and would not drum people out of the military who were merely suspected of being gays and lesbians. But gays and lesbians could not engage in homosexual behavior on or off the military base or openly acknowledge their sexual preferences. This "don't ask, don't tell" policy failed to satisfy many and eventually led to even larger numbers of gays and lesbians being expelled from the military.

At the same time, the Clinton administration was adamant about integrating the sexes in the armed forces. This proved easier to swallow for the military, and women were soon serving aboard ships at sea and undergoing basic training with men while living in sexually integrated barracks. Many conservatives condemned the change, noting lower physical requirements and contending that morale would be jeopardized in combat. Military leaders, soon faced with a string of sex scandals (U.S. troops in their gender-mixed tents in Bosnia produced roughly one pregnancy every three days), were forced to impose a broad ban on personal relationships between superiors and subordinates and issue guidelines designed to curb adultery. By 1998, about 14 percent of the active-duty force of 1.4 million were women.

In September 1993, the Justice Department filed a brief with the United States Supreme Court advocating the liberalization of child pornography laws to make it harder to convict pedophiles. The Senate, in November, voted 100 to 0 for an amendment criticizing the administration for this proposal.

The Whitewater investigation was a probe of a real estate deal along the White River in north central Arkansas that the Clintons had been part of from

1978 to 1992. Allegations of criminal activity swirled around the project, and investigations eventually led to the conviction of three Clinton friends and business associates on charges of fraud and conspiracy. White House Deputy Counsel Vince Foster, Jr., a close friend of the Clintons involved in the White-water project, committed suicide in July 1993. Vital documents were reportedly taken from his office before investigators arrived.

Webster Hubbell, a personal friend and law partner of Hillary Clinton's, resigned as associate attorney general in March 1994, and soon pleaded guilty to felonious mail fraud and tax evasion while in private practice. Clinton associates provided him with more than $700,000 in job payments, and there were charges that the funds were provided to keep Hubbell from talking about Whitewater. A deputy treasury counsel and treasury counsel resigned in mid-August over their activities in the Whitewater case.

In August 1994, Kenneth Starr, a Texas appeals court judge who had once been seriously considered for a seat on the Supreme Court, was appointed by a three-judge panel to be the special prosecutor in the Whitewater matter. Attorney General Reno and the three-judge panel later assigned Starr's office at least five separate probes, including Whitewater, and Starr found himself locked in fierce legal and media battles with the Clinton administration.

In March 1994, the press discovered that Hillary Clinton had a few years earlier made a swift and almost miraculous $100,000 coup in cattle futures. The first lady said little about the transaction. Critics called it a well-disguised bribe from Arkansas business interests.

And then there was the case of Paula Jones. This young Arkansas woman sued the president for sex harassment in May 1994, charging that three years earlier the then governor had invited her to a hotel room, dropped his pants, and requested oral sex. Jokes about Clinton's sexual appetite and duplicity became routine in the media. Critics often referred to him by his Arkansas nickname, Slick Willie. But the president denied that he had ever done anything wrong, and the American people, polls showed, tended to believe him. Jones had financial backing in the case from the conservative Rutherford Institute, persuading many, including leading feminists, that the lawsuit was a right-wing effort to smear the president.

Scandal haunted the administration. From August 1994 through May 1995, independent counsels were named to probe the activities of Secretary of Agriculture Mike Espy, Commerce Secretary Ron Brown, and HUD Secretary Henry Cisneros.

In June 1996, it was revealed that the White House had requested and obtained hundreds of raw FBI records on people without their permission. Many of the individuals were former employees of the Reagan and Bush administrations. Personnel Security Office Director Craig Livingstone of Arkansas (whom no one could remember hiring) was allowed to resign, but that did not resolve the issue. In June 1996, the president referred to the "Filegate" scandal as a "completely honest bureaucratic snafu." FBI Director Louis Freeh told a different story, saying that he and his agency were "victimized" by the White House.

Domestic Initiatives

Among the president's first actions was the appointment of the first lady to head a task force charged with designing a major reform of the nation's health care. Some 37 million Americans were without health insurance. The highly complex plan, as it evolved, seemed to create a bureaucratic giant that would curtail personal freedoms and be enormously expensive. In early 1994, the Congressional Budget Office predicted that the health plan would increase the deficit by $74 billion. In August, the CBO estimated that the plan would cost more than $1 trillion in its first eight years. The medical establishment fought hard to kill the proposal. Many small businessmen said they would go bankrupt were they required to purchase health insurance for all their employees. Many liberals were unenthusiastic about the mechanics of the plan.

After six months of hearings, the administration conceded defeat. According to the Government Accounting Office, it cost taxpayers $13.4 million dollars to design the plan, and another $433,000 to defend the government against a lawsuit that challenged the secrecy in which the initiative was assembled.

In August 1993, Congress passed a five-year economic renewal program that raised top marginal income tax rates from 31 to 36 percent, cut taxes on 15 million low-income families, cut spending by $255 billion over five years, and laid out the largest deficit-cutting plan in history, saving more than $1 trillion over seven years. Republicans, who fought the program at nearly every step, called the $280 billion hike on the top 1.2 percent of the wealthiest taxpayers the largest tax increase in history.

With Republican support, Clinton successfully backed the North American Free Trade Agreement (NAFTA), which added Mexico to the free trade zone already created for Canada and the United States during the Reagan administration. Liberal Democrats, trade union leaders, and isolationists argued that jobs would be moved to low-wage Mexico. But NAFTA supporters, who convinced Congress, said that the proposal would create new jobs by opening the vast Mexican marketplace to more American products. Exports to Mexico rose 23 percent in the first eleven months of 1994.

Clinton and the Congress supported the latest round of GATT agreements. (The General Agreement on Tariffs and Trade was created in 1947 to alleviate trade problems that had contributed to the economic collapse of the 1930s; it was updated periodically.) In 1994, Congress approved the latest changes, which reduced tariffs by a third, eliminated trade quotas, and protected intellectual property rights. Tariffs were to be lowered worldwide by $744 billion over ten years.

The Contract with America

All of the controversies of Clinton's first two years contributed to the election shock wave that hit in November 1994. The Republicans gained fifty-two seats in the House and eight in the Senate, winning control of Congress for the first time since 1954. In addition, the GOP gained eleven governorships and nineteen new majorities in state legislatures. Not a single incumbent Republican governor, senator, or representative lost.

The new Speaker of the House was Congressman Newt Gingrich of Georgia. Articulate, well educated, highly aggressive, and at times irascible and shifty, Gingrich was convinced that the GOP victories were the result of a ten-point "Contract With America" platform for "national renewal" that conservatives had proposed and publicized. Calling himself a "genuine revolutionary," Gingrich promised to carry out what Reagan had begun. A group of seventy-three mostly young conservatives, many representing the Religious Right, agreed that the voters were demanding change and that Congress had the obligation to deliver.

The 104th Congress proceeded to alter the way the House of Representatives operated, overhaul the nation's welfare system, deregulate telecommunications, stop several new federal regulations, pour funds into the fight against crime at all governmental levels, restore funds to the defense budget, cut foreign aid, and give the president the line-item veto. Gingrich was named *Time* magazine's "Man of the Year" for 1995.

At first, Clinton reacted stoically to these dramatic moves by Congress. He even appeared to have moved to the right himself, remembering that he had been elected as a centrist Democrat. By late 1995, eager to achieve some re-election ammunition, Clinton decided to resist Congress on balancing the federal budget and cutting Medicare benefits. The government was partially shut down twice in the course of a bitter budget struggle that went on for months. The president was able to persuade millions of Americans that Gingrich and his "extremists" were to blame for the turmoil.

Republicans caved in on the budget, but they could boast of a major achievement in welfare reform. In August 1996, the president resisted the pleas of leading Democrats and signed into law the first major reversal of liberal welfare state policy in sixty years. Food stamp spending was cut and time limits and work requirements imposed, and some federal aid was transferred to the states.

Clinton's struggles with Congress in the election year presented the agenda of both parties fairly clearly. In April, the president, expressing his concern for women's rights, vetoed a ban on partial-birth abortions, a particularly gruesome form of late-term abortion that many Republicans and their pro-life supporters had hoped to stop. In May, he vetoed limits on product liability suits, a nod to the trial lawyers who were strong Clinton backers. Clinton won a hike in the minimum wage, to $5.15 an hour, and agreed with Congress on minor health insurance reforms.

International Peacekeeping

Clinton was far more interested in domestic than foreign affairs. When he thought at all about international relations, it was usually in connection with economic issues. Secretary of State Warren Christopher was known to be competent and hard working, but he was of little assistance in providing the president with a vision of America's role in the post-Cold War era. There was a distinctly ad hoc approach to international relations throughout the Clinton administrations.

Clinton inherited a humanitarian effort in Somalia by the Bush administration. In December 1992, American troops were sent in to end months of anarchy and famine in the northeast African nation. Clinton turned over command of U.S. forces in Somalia to the United Nations and toyed with the idea of attempting a nation-building effort. On October 3, 1993, army Rangers were involved in a disastrous raid on a warlord's headquarters. Eighteen soldiers were killed, seventy-eight wounded, and captives were paraded before television cameras. At that point, Clinton called for withdrawal of all American forces within six months. Secretary of Defense Les Aspin was removed as a sop to military leaders who said they had been denied necessary armored support in Somalia. Chaos in the impoverished country continued.

Early in Clinton's term, a major breakthrough was announced in the lengthy and bitter struggle between Israel and the Palestine Liberation Organization (PLO). In September 1993, at a ceremony hosted by Clinton, Israeli Prime Minister Yitzhak Rabin and PLO leader Yassir Arafat signed an accord and shook hands. The PLO was to have self-government in the Gaza strip and portions of the West Bank; Arafat renounced terrorism and extended diplomatic recognition to Israel. Incidents of violence soon continued, but some progress had been made.

By the time Clinton arrived at the White House, civil war was raging in Bosnia and Herzegovina, former members of the defunct Yugoslav federation. Ethnic fighting in this region was a very old story, contributing to the outbreak of World War I. Warfare broke out again in 1991, and by 1993 the struggle between Serbs, Croats, and Bosnian Muslims had killed over 100,000 people and left 3.5 million refugees. NATO bombardments and stiff resistance by Croats and Muslims persuaded Serbia to enter into peace negotiations.

In 1995, Clinton brought leaders of the warring factions together in Dayton, Ohio, and in December a settlement was announced. The Dayton Accord stated that Bosnia would remain a single nation but be governed as two republics. The North Atlantic Treaty Organization was to send an international peacekeeping mission into the area. The administration prevailed over much opposition in Congress and elsewhere, and stationed about 15,000 troops in Bosnia and roughly 5,000 support personnel in Croatia, Hungary, and Italy. Congress approved initial funding of $2.26 billion. All NATO nations contributed personnel, along with eighteen non-NATO nations, for a total of 54,000 troops. The fighting largely ceased, and municipal elections were held in 1997.

In 1999, between 25,000 and 30,000 American troops were still in Bosnia, and America (without the support of NATO allies) had provided more than $100 million in military assistance to the region. President Clinton wanted the troops to stay indefinitely.

American troops were also part of a multinational force sent into Haiti in 1994 to "restore democracy" and the rule of an elected president, leftist Jean-Bertrand Aristide, who had been ousted by a military junta in 1991. The military had conducted a reign of terror on the chronically impoverished nation, killing some five thousand and driving tens of thousands into exile. America was the most popular destination of those fleeing their country. The Coast Guard rescued more than 68,000 of them off the coast of Florida between 1991 and 1994.

Clinton was a driving force behind the invasion. The United States sent 21,000 troops to Haiti at a cost of about $3 billion. Order was restored and illegal immigration slowed to a trickle. Aristide served out his term of office and transferred power in January 1996 to President Rene Preval.

Terrorism at Home

In February 1993, Muslim terrorists used a car bomb to rock the 110-story World Trade Center, killing six people and injuring more than a thousand. The four men convicted said the attack was to avenge U.S. support for Israel and to protest American Middle East policy. The tragedy prompted many Americans to wonder about the safety of their own environment. A study by the Rand Corporation spanning the years 1981–92 later reported 670 terrorist acts in the United States by right- or left-wing ethnic or issue-oriented groups.

In April 1995, medal-winning veteran and right-wing extremist Timothy McVeigh used a car bomb to blow up the federal building in Oklahoma City. The explosion killed 168 people, including many children in a preschool nursery housed on the second floor, and injured hundreds. McVeigh and an accomplice were convicted. The media carried the story for months, showing photos of victims and again pondering the vulnerability of American society to the assaults of extremists. President Clinton had a portion of Pennsylvania Avenue sealed off to traffic in the hope of preventing a bomb-ridden vehicle from reaching the White House.

Some on the right were just as deeply concerned about the role of the federal government in suppressing dissent. In 1992, the FBI had attacked a white separatist and his family living in the hills of Idaho, and a sharpshooter killed an unarmed woman holding her baby. The Ruby Ridge case resulted in a shakeup of the FBI and a conviction of a top Bureau official for obstruction of justice and destroying internal FBI reports. In April 1993, the FBI launched an assault on the premises of a religious community, the Branch Davidians, near Waco, Texas, and seventy-six of the occupants died, including many women and children. Attorney General Janet Reno was widely criticized for her role in the controversial incident.

Election of 1996

Following the brief slump under Bush, the economy grew at a healthy pace. This contributed in no small way to Clinton's reelection campaign. The Dow

Jones industrial average that had been at 3168 in 1991 hit 6448 in 1996. Corporate profits after taxes were $437.1 billion in 1996, up from $256.6 billion in 1990. In 1994, real GDP growth was the highest in a decade.

Median family income was up, high enough to enable Americans in 1995 to spend $37 billion in commercial participant amusements, a Census Bureau category that included bowling alleys, amusement parks, and the like. Unemployment had fallen to 5.6 percent. The Federal Reserve had kept inflation in check. Clinton could boast of $600 billion in deficit reduction. Welfare roles had shrunk 37 percent since 1992. Persons living below the poverty line had dropped from 15.1 percent of the population in 1993 to 13.8 percent in 1995.

Republicans were unable to come up with a highly attractive alternative to Clinton. Senator Robert Dole of Kansas, age 72, was not to be denied after three attempts at the presidential nomination. Dole had entered Congress in 1961, was elected to the Senate in 1968, had served as chairman of the Republican National Committee, had been Ford's vice presidential candidate in 1976, and was Senate Republican leader from 1985 to 1996. Considered a moderate or pragmatic conservative, Dole did not appeal to the Religious Right. A distinguished military record in World War II appealed to many, but to others it merely emphasized his age. The candidate's major strengths were his decades of experience in Washington and his sound personal character.

At the GOP convention, Dole named conservative Congressman Jack Kemp as his running mate. A listless campaign followed, and Clinton never lost his lead in the polls. In November, Clinton won 49 percent of the vote to Dole's 41 percent. Ross Perot, again running as an independent, took 9 percent. In the electoral college, Clinton beat Dole by a margin of 70 percent to 30 percent. Republicans retained control of Congress but lost ten seats in the House.

In his inaugural address in January 1997, the president spoke of the progress evident throughout the twentieth century and vowed to continue the pursuit of the highest ideals of humanity. At one point he expressed his specific hope for those engaged in his own craft: ". . . in this land of new promise, we will have reformed our politics so that the voice of the people will always speak louder than the din of narrow interest, regaining the participation and deserving the trust of all Americans."

But even as he spoke, stories of illegal Clinton campaign fund-raising activities were stirring interest in the media. There was soon evidence of a conspiracy to violate campaign finance laws involving the president's close friend and legal adviser Bruce Lindsey. Several Asian donors were said to have tried to purchase influence in the White House. The Lincoln bedroom was reported to have been virtually rented out to wealthy donors. Large AFL-CIO donations were of questionable legality. Still, Republicans enjoyed a traditional advantage in fund raising and outspent Democrats in the election.

The presidential election of 1996 cost about $800 million, well over double the estimated $311 million spent just four years earlier. Another $800 million was raised for House and Senate races. Only 54.2 percent of the voting-age population cast ballots. The Congressional Research Service said it had not recorded such a low turnout since it began keeping records in 1948.

SUGGESTED READING

Phyllis Bennis and Michel Moushabeck (eds.), *Beyond the Storm: A Gulf Crisis Reader* (1998); Lou Cannon, *Official Negligence: How Rodney King and the Riots Changed Los Angeles and the LAPD* (1998); James Carville et al., *All's Fair: Love, War, and Running for President* (1994); Newt Gingrich et al. (eds), *Contract with America: The Bold Plan by Rep. Newt Gingrich, Rep. Dick Armey and the House Republicans to Change the Nation* (1994); Peter Irons, *Brennan v. Rehnquist: The Battle for the Constitution* (1994); David Maramiss, *First in His Class: A Biography of Bill Clinton* (1996); Herbert Parmet, *George Bush: The Life of a Lone Star Yankee* (1997); Sam Roberts, *Who Are We? A Portrait of America Based on the Latest U.S. Census* (1994); James B. Stewart, *Blood Sport: The President and His Administration* (1997); James Trabor and Eugene Gallagher, *Why Waco? Cults in the Battle for Religious Freedom* (1995).

Chapter Fifteen

THE CLOSE OF
THE CENTURY

By the late 1990s, ruminations about the meaning of the past century began flooding newspapers, magazines, and scholarly journals. The more popular accounts stressed "progress," long a common word in the national lexicon. America's 270 million people, it was said, were more prosperous, healthy, educated, equal, tolerant, and law abiding than their forbears of the nineteenth century. With the conclusion of the Cold War, the opportunities for world peace were never better. The facts substantiating this thesis were abundant.

But a stream of pessimism was also present in this literature, especially among scholars and the deeply religious. William Bennett, who headed the National Commission on Civic Renewal, noted in 1998 that while the United States led the industrialized world in wealth, power, and influence, it also led in the rates of murder, violent crime, imprisonment, divorce, abortion, sexually transmitted diseases, teen suicide, cocaine consumption, and pornography production and consumption. Robert Bork, in *Slouching Towards Gomorrah*, was convinced that "the traditional virtues of this culture are being lost, its vices multiplied, its values degraded—in short, the culture itself is unraveling." Roman Catholic philosopher Peter Kreeft wrote that "night is falling" in "the worst century," adding that "If the God of life does not respond to this culture of death with judgment, God is not God."

Prosperity

The economy in the late 1990s remained extraordinarily strong. The gross national product in mid-1998 stood at a whopping $7.28 trillion. During the first three months of 1999, the economy grew at a robust 5.6 percent. The Dow Jones industrial average closed at the 11,000 mark for the first time on May 13, with experts believing that half or substantially more of all households held stock. Interest rates were low, new contruction spending had soared, real estate was selling at a record pace, unemployment was at 4.3 percent in January, and inflation was at 1.7 percent.

Companies involved with the development and production of computers were booming. The market for PCs and related products and services grew from $85 billion in 1992 to a projected $240 billion in 1998. Microsoft was one of the world's most wealthy and powerful corporations, and billionaire Bill Gates, the company's youthful and aggressive founder and leader, was widely admired and hated. By mid-1998, Yahoo, an internet search engine company, was worth more ($8.2 billion market capitalization) than the New York Times Co. ($7.6 billion). American Online, the nation's largest commercial on-line service provider, was worth about as much ($26 billion) as network giants ABC, CBS, and NBC combined.

As a result of the robust economy, federal and state governments enjoyed fat budget surpluses. In January 1999, the Congressional Budget Office projected that federal surplusers would total $2.6 trillion over the next decade.

Workers were enjoying high wages and benefits. Total compensation increased 3.5 percent over the twelve months ending in June 1998, the biggest gain in more than four years and roughly double the 1.7-percent increase in consumer prices over the period. The median household income in 1997 was $37,005, the third consecutive annual rise.

A study by the Federal Reserve Bank of Dallas, published in 1998, showed that factory workers' average hourly wages bought more than ever. A refrigerator in 1915 cost a worker 3,162 hours of labor to purchase. In 1970, the figure was 112 hours. In 1997, the cost was 68 hours. A color television set in 1954 cost workers 562 hours. In 1970 it was 174 hours. In 1997 the cost was 23 hours. Noting that a cellular phone cost just 2 percent of what it did a decade and a half earlier, and computing power was less than 1 percent of its 1984 real price, bank president W. Michael Cox declared, "Within the space of just one generation—not two or three as in yesterday's economy—capitalism's delivery system now spreads the wealth."

In the summer of 1998, consumer spending remained strong. Shopping malls were packed. Home buying was heavy. People enjoyed travel and vacations at a record pace. In South Dakota, attendance at the Badlands and Mount Rushmore national parks was up 53 percent and 16 percent respectively from a year earlier. Yellowstone, Yosemite, and Grand Canyon national parks had major traffic problems. Walt Disney World in Orlando, Florida, flourished despite nearby forest fire devastation earlier in the year. Las Vegas continued to be the site of new and ever more lavish casinos.

Americans devoted vast sums of money to gambling. In 1994 alone, they spent $482 billion on it, more than they spent on movies, sports, music, cruise ships, and theme parks combined. By 1996, ten states had casinos, thirty-six and the District of Columbia operated lotteries; six ran video poker, and twenty-four allowed Indian-run gambling. In 1998, gambling Web sites on the Internet were a $2 billion industry. A Powerball lottery jackpot that year reached $250 million; people lined up all over the country to buy tickets and face odds that were 80 million to 1.

There were warnings about the fragility of America's prosperity. By the fall of 1998, the stock market was fluctuating wildly. Financial woes in Asia and Latin America prompted fears by many investors; Russia seemed on the verge of economic and political collapse. Personal indebtedness was high, and personal savings fell to an all-time low by mid-1998. Between June 1996 and June 1997, a record 1.4 million people filed for bankruptcy. Agriculture was in a slump. The *Wall Street Journal* pointed out in early 1998 that GDP growth from 1950 to 1973 averaged 3.9 percent a year, and that since then it had slowed to an annual average growth of 2.6 percent. Federal entitlement programs, such as Social Security, threatened to raise tax burdens in the next century. In early 1999 the country was more than $5 trillion in debt. The trade deficit with China alone had reached a billion dollars a week.

Most people chose to ignore the warnings and get on with the business of enjoying prosperity. Emperors and kings of the past had not enjoyed the comforts now available to millions of Americans. By mid-1998, the median home price nationally was $131,000, up 6 percent from a year earlier. Over 65 percent of Americans owned their own homes (70.5 percent in the Midwest). Three quarters of the homes in 1997 had air conditioning, 77.5 percent had washing machines, 53.7 percent had automatic dishwashers, 58 million homes enjoyed warm-air furnaces. As recently as 1940, two out of five homes had lacked a shower or bathtub, air conditioning was almost nonexistent, and heat often came by feeding wood or coal into a furnace; many homes were still lighted with kerosene lamps.

In 1998, about 98 percent of American homes had television sets, and two out of three had cable television. Personal computers found a place in about 45 percent of all homes. In 1999, PCs for under $600 were becoming popular. America Online had a membership that topped the combined readership of *The New York Times, The Wall Street Journal, USA Today,* and a handful of other newspapers thrown in for good measure.

About 74 million Americans used the Internet by early 1999, about 41 percent of the nation's adults. (Some 100 million people worldwide were using it.) By mid-1998, the World Wide Web contained at least 320 million pages, making it one of the largest libraries in the world. Nearly 90 percent of Americans who had access to the Web sent or received e-mail. On-line retail sales rose from $2.6 billion in 1997, to $5.8 billion in 1998, and was expected to be $15.6 billion in 2000.

Of course, not all Americans wallowed in the unprecedented economic growth and wealth. In 1998 the federal government's poverty line for a family of four was $16,400 in annual household income. More than 30 million Americans were living in poverty, the Census Bureau reported. Still, the poverty rate dropped to 13.3 percent, marking the fourth consecutive decline.

Even America's poor were wealthy by the standards of most people in the world. In 1995, 41 percent of all poor households owned their own homes,

70 percent owned a car, 97 percent had a color television set, two-thirds had air conditioning, 64 percent owned a microwave oven, and half had a stereo system. Policy analyst Robert Rector observed in 1998 that "total spending per person among the lowest-income one-fifth of households actually equals those of the average American household in the early 1970s—after adjusting for inflation."

Health

Never had a people enjoyed such good physical health. The fruits of medical research, technology, and training were abundant. In 1996, the infant morality rate in the United States dropped to an all-time low: 7.2 infant deaths per 1,000 live births. That was 5 percent lower than in 1995. The life expectancy for children born in 1996 was 76.1 years, with males expected to live 73.1 years and women 79.1 years. The long-standing gap between whites and blacks had narrowed: 76.8 years for whites and 70.2 years for blacks.

Smallpox, once a scourge of the human race, was nearly eradicated from the planet in 1980. By mid-1998, the syphilis rate in the United States had plummeted 84 percent since 1990 to the lowest level on record, and scientists thought themselves within striking distance of stamping out the disease. Pneumonia, influenza, and tuberculosis, the major killers in 1900, could usually be controlled by drug therapy. From 1990 to 1996, heart disease decreased 1.7 percent, and deaths from cancer declined 5 percent.

Since the first discovery of a specific marker for a genetic disease in 1983, scientists had made remarkable progress in the field. The gene responsible for cystic fibrosis was isolated in 1989. In 1994, a team of American researchers discovered the BRCA1 gene, believed to cause about 5 to 10 percent of breast cancers.

People lived longer with artificial heart valves and heart, lung, and kidney transplants. Drugs eased pain, stopped disease, and mitigated high blood pressure. At the close of 1998, Pharmacists racked up an estimated $102.5 billion in sales, up eighty-five percent in just half a decade. (In 1998, Viagra, designed to help the some 30 million men who suffered from impotence, became the best-selling drug in history.) Hormonal therapy radically improved the lives of millions of menopausal and postmenopausal women. Artificial joints enhanced physical mobility. Lasers, invented in 1960 by Theodore Maiman, were used in surgery, dentistry, and ophthalmology. Dentists could stop tooth decay, and oral surgeons repaired facial deformities and used implants to make false teeth unnecessary.

Millions of middle- and upper-middle-class Americans were greatly concerned about their health. In 1996, a poll showed that 52 percent of Americans got vigorous exercise at least three days a week. Fat-free and calorie-free foods were popular, although nutritionists claimed that Americans were eating more calories than at any time in the century. Billions of dollars were spent annually on vitamins, herbs, diet books, health clubs, and sports equipment. Close to 90 percent of Americans were covered by health insurance, half of those belonging to a health maintenance organization (HMO).

Birthrates in the United States continued to fall in the late 1990s, reflecting in large part a greater use of birth control devices and pills. Teenage birthrates, which dropped an estimated 3 percent in 1997, continuing a six-year trend, accounted for much of the decline. Still, nearly a million teenage girls became pregnant each year, and more than 200,000 had abortions.

There was a quiet epidemic of sexually transmitted diseases among teenagers. In a study published in 1998 of 3,200 Baltimore teens ages 12 to 19, mostly girls, nearly a third tested positive for chlamydia, the most commonly reported infectious disease in the United States. Still, the Centers for Disease Control and Prevention reported that in a 1997 survey of the nation's high-school students, 52 percent said they had never had sexual intercourse, a sharp reversal of practices reported in the 1970s and 1980s. (The percentage of black high schoolers who said they had sex dropped 8 percentage points to 73 percent between 1991 and 1997. The change for Hispanics was less than 1 percentage point, to 52 percent. For whites, the decline was 6 points to 44 percent.)

The top five causes of death in the United States, according to the National Center for Health Statistics, were heart disease, cancer, stroke, chronic lung diseases, and accidents. AIDS, which received most of the attention in the media, dropped to number 14 in 1997. But the disease was not to be taken lightly. By 1996, AIDS had killed 320,000 Americans. Between 650,000 and 900,000 others were infected with HIV, although the rate of new infections, in the United States, Europe, and other wealthy parts of the world, declined sharply from its peak in the mid-1980s. African Americans accounted for about 57 percent of all new infections in this country. Powerful drug-combination therapies provided some relief for victims by the late 1990s, but new strains of the virus proved resistant.

Women and the Family

The Census Bureau reported in mid-1998 that the decline of the traditional family—a married couple with children under 18—was slowing. A quarter of American households fit that description in 1997. (In 1957, the figure had been 50.8 percent, and in 1967, 50.1 percent.) The percentage of single-parent families, which had doubled between 1970 and 1990, was also leveling off, amounting to 13 percent in 1997. The divorce rate was dropping, from 5.0 per 1,000 people in 1985 to 4.3 percent in 1997. Ralph Monaco, a University of Maryland researcher, said, "The wild, carefree years are over. The average boomer is now older and wiser" and settling down with spouses and children.

But a return to the 1950s was unlikely. In 1997, 85 percent of black females with children under 6 years of age had never been married. The same was true of about three-quarters of Hispanic women and 56 percent of white women. In 1998, 33 percent of women aged 25 to 29 had never married; it was 48 percent for men in the same age group. Living together out of wedlock, which became popular in the sixties, was an accepted way of life for millions.

A national survey sponsored by the *Washington Post* and published in 1998 revealed that large majorities of both men and women said it would be better if women could stay home and take care of the house and children. But at the same time, equally large majorities wanted equality for women in the work place, and men approved of women working outside the home.

Sociologists Suzanne Bianchi and Daphne Spain reported that between 1970 and 1995, the percentage of women ages 25 to 54 who worked outside the home climbed from 50 percent to 76 percent. Seventy-five percent of college-educated women were in the paid labor force. In 1996, women were 29 percent of lawyers and judges, and 26 percent of all physicians. In 1998, a third of all professional athletes were women, almost double the proportion in 1983. The U.S. Census Bureau reported in 1998 that the woman working outside the home was responsible for the 154-percent increase in married-family real median income over the past half century, from $20,620 in 1947 to $51,591 in 1997.

In 1998, Washington state could boast that 41 percent of its state legislators were women. (The national average was 22 percent.) Arizona became the first state to have an all-female elected line of succession: governor, secretary of state, attorney general, treasurer, and superintendent of public instruction.

Education

The quality of education being offered by the nation's public schools was one of the hottest topics of the late 1990s. National test scores were often woeful. SAT combined scores plunged nearly 80 points between 1960 and 1990. In 1994, only 7 percent of 17-year-olds could solve multistep math problems and had mastered beginning algebra; only 2 percent of eleventh graders were judged as writing effectively. The education of teachers was often severely criticized. Lack of discipline and incidents of violence in the schools were all too common. Perceptive observers were generally agreed that anti-intellectualism was pervasive. Conservative Charles Sykes, in *Dumbing Down Our Kids*, contended that "America's schools are in deep trouble, not because they lack men and women who care about children, but because they are dominated by an ideology that does not care much about learning."

Polls showed that television watching consumed much of the lives of America's young people. A 1991 survey showed that 56 percent believed that television had the greatest influence on children's values—more than parents, teachers, and religious leaders combined.

Many wanted a voucher system that would permit parents to send their children to a school of their choice at public expense, even if that school was religious. Milwaukee and the State of Wisconsin led the nation in this direction. In the late 1990s, cases challenging this approach were working their way toward the United States Supreme Court. Others looked to charter schools, for-profit schools, and home-schooling as alternatives. (By 1998, about 1.5 million American children were participating in some form of home schooling. One study showed home-schooled students outperforming their public-school counterparts by up to 37 percent when measured by standardized tests.) Teachers' unions and the Clinton administration, among others, defended the public schools, emphasizing their historic value in a democracy and seeking increased funding.

While an unprecedented 60 percent of high-school graduates went on to some form of higher education, controversy also swirled around what they might be learning in America's colleges and universities. Academia seemed to many critics to lack any sense of design or purpose beyond the graduation of more than a million people a year. Open admission was common, courses were offered in almost anything (a study of fifty top schools showed 70,901 undergraduate courses offered in 1993, up from 36,968 in 1964), graduation requirements were often minimal, instruction was frequently impersonal, and athletics were routinely overemphasized.

Conservatives contended that "political correctness," a term that became popular in 1990 to express a knee-jerk sympathy with all things to the left, reigned supreme in academia. Marxism, moral relativism, and deconstructionism, the idea that all literature is without meaning, seemed everywhere on campus. Liberals, on the other hand, often complained about the persistence of racism and sexism, the teaching of "outdated" ethics, and required reading that focused on the works of "dead white males." They sought "diversity" through a wide variety of often required "multicultural" courses they said would sensitize students to the values and customs of other races and cultures.

Many liberals and conservatives decried the lack of attention paid to the liberal arts. Only 2 percent of colleges and universities required a single course in history. The most popular major in college was business.

Worship and Morality

America's churches remained in a pattern that was set in the 1960s. Leaders of the mainline denominations such as the Presbyterians, Episcopalians, and Methodists still clung to the standards and tastes of contemporary liberalism, and their churches continued to shrink in size. In 1995, a researcher observed that the Methodist church, which had flourished in America during the nineteenth and early twentieth centuries, had lost one thousand members every week for the last thirty years. The Episcopal church had as many active members (1.6 million) as it enjoyed during World War II. Mainline seminaries were often proud bastions of leftist thought and practice, echoing the prestigious nondenominational institutions such as Harvard Divinity School and Union Theological Seminary.

Conservative and fundamentalist denominations grew at a steady pace. In 1994, the 15.6 million Southern Baptists comprised the largest Protestant denomination in the country. Between 1965 and 1989 the Assemblies of God grew 121 percent. The major metropolitan areas boasted large and affluent Bible-based nondenominational churches. The Christian Coalition, the major expression of the Religious Right, claimed in 1994 to have 1.5 million dues-paying members and the support of up to 20 percent of Americans.

The Roman Catholics, buoyed by Hispanic immigration, passed the 60-million member mark. Mormons, highly active in missionary efforts, grew to more than 4 million in 1994. The Jewish faith continued to become smaller, largely due to intermarriage.

Gallup pollsters continued to show that about 40 percent of Americans went to church on a given Sunday. A 1994 poll found that 70 percent belonged to a church or synagogue, that nine adults in ten believed in a heaven, and that 79 percent believed in miracles. A Harris poll taken in July 1994 revealed that 95 percent of those surveyed believed in God. Of the four in five Americans who described themselves as Christians, 85 percent believed in the virgin birth of Jesus Christ. Even 52 percent of the non-Christians surveyed expressed belief in the Resurrection! A 1994 survey of 4,809 Americans found that almost nine of ten said they had "old fashioned values about family and marriage."

The demand for religious literature remained strong. About half of the some 55,000 new trade books published each year were religious. Sales in 1993 were at about $2.7 billion, up from about $1 billion in 1980. Bible sales amounted to more than $400 million a year. The Catholic sociologist Andrew Greeley declared in 1993, "In some countries, most notably Ireland and the United States, religious devotion may be higher than it has ever been in human history."

And yet America had a particular kind of religiosity by the 1990s. There was a fierce independence; polls showed that for most Americans religious authority resided in the believer, rather than the church or the Bible. And there was vast ignorance of the faith. Gallup referred to "a nation of biblical illiterates" and presented solid evidence: fewer than half of all adults could name the four Gospels of the New Testament; only four in ten Americans knew that Jesus delivered the Sermon on the Mount.

This resulted in what has been called "Consumer Christianity," a religion based on selective teachings of the historic faith that was highly permissive, self-centered, and indistinct. This modern, convenient religion posed few if any challenges to the public's way of life.

It is difficult to say how much of this came from individual Americans themselves and how much was absorbed from the very secular leadership of the media, education, and the legal profession. American newspapers and movies virtually ignored religion and churches, while on television and on stage they were sometimes mocked. (A flurry of interest in angels in the late 1990s had more to do with entertainment than anything else.) Nonreligious and state schools at all levels usually shunned even religious history. Religion and morality were often treated in the classroom and on the screen as two separate topics.

The courts, in the name of the separation of church and state, were a major force in restricting the impact of the Christian faith. Among other things, they outlawed prayer in the public schools and drove Christian symbols out of public places. The highly influential *New York Times* and the American Civil Liberties Union, among others, applauded these rulings. Conservative Catholic and evangelical intellectuals were scandalized, often appealing to American history to show the novelty of this approach. Right and left found little or no common ground on the issue by the end of the 1990s.

Moral Ascendancy?

In 1997, the nation's crime rate fell for the sixth straight year. Murder and robbery showed the sharpest decline. Violent crimes dropped 5 percent between 1996 and 1998, helping to push down the overall U.S. crime rate by 4 percent to its lowest level in more than a decade. The nation's big cities showed the steepest decline, with a 5-percent decrease. In 1998 the crime rate declined 7 percent, continuing the remarkable streak.

In July 1998, the Justice Department noted that the incidence of work place violence was declining. Police officers, security guards, and taxicab drivers, the workers most likely to be attacked or threatened on the job, were safer.

Explanations included the aging of baby boomers, the relatively small population of teenagers and young adults, the addition of police officers, better policing practices, and a boost in prison terms. By mid-1998, America had the largest system of incarceration in the world, with 1.8 million people behind bars. One in every 150 Americans was locked up, a rate of incarceration double that of a dozen years earlier.

Tough city officials, like Mayor Rudolph W. Giuliani of New York, were also given credit for the drop in crime. Elected in 1993, Giuliani brought about a renaissance in the Big Apple, lowering crime an unprecedented 44 percent in five years and reducing murder 48 percent. In 1998, New York was the safest large city in America.

In July 1998, syndicated columnist Donald Lambro contended that the United States was in "a moral ascendancy." Beyond the crime figures, he noted, "Teen-age births have fallen. So have all out-of-wedlock births. Abortions are way down, too. The divorce rate has been declining. Overall drug use has been falling. Per capital alcohol consumption is the lowest it has been in a quarter century. Community volunteerism is up." Lambro quoted economist Richard McKenzie of Washington University who reported that 93 million Americans devote 20 billion hours a year to charitable causes. *The Chronicle of Philanthropy* soon reported that contributions to the nation's most popular charities rose 13 percent in the last year. The Salvation Army received nearly $1.2 billion in cash and donated goods.

Conservative economist Lawrence A. Kudlow, in *American Abundance: The New Economic and Moral Prosperity*, argued that the recent decline in the welfare state had produced a new sense of individual responsibility and enhanced general moral conduct. Work and prosperity, he argued, produce positive "cultural and material change."

Minorities and Progress

In *America in Black and White: One Nation Indivisible*, historians Abigail and Stephan Thernstrom showed in 1997 that African Americans were doing increasingly well in the quest for prosperity and dignity. Between 1970 and 1995, seven million blacks moved to the suburbs. During those two and a half decades, as the white suburban population grew 63 percent, the black suburban population increased by 193 percent. In the late 1990s, one-third of all blacks lived in suburbia, twice the proportion of twenty-five years earlier.

Moreover, the typical central city neighborhood had become more integrated. By 1990, the typical black resident of a metropolitan area lived in a census "block group" that was only 60-percent black. A few years later, five out of six blacks said they had white neighbors. Contrary to the woeful depictions of many civil rights leaders, the Thernstroms contended, African Americans were more integrated and affluent in the 1990s than ever before.

Critics of the Thernstroms pointed, among other things, to the persistence of hideous inner-city slums, the fact that in 1997 26.5 percent of blacks lived below the poverty line, and the alleged presence of racial bigotry in all walks of American life. The chance of going to state or federal prison during one's life for black men was 28.5 percent; for white men, 4.4 percent.

In 1998, black newspaper columnist William Raspberry cited data showing that the percentage of black high-school graduates aged 25 to 29 nearly equaled the percentage for whites—86 percent compared with 87 percent for whites. In 1985, 8 percent of college-age African Americans were in college; by 1995 the figure had jumped to over 10 percent. "That's a rate of increase that exceeds the rate for whites," Raspberry wrote, "and that's significant."

Also significant was the continued rise of blacks in professional sports and the warm public reception these athletes received. By 1998, 80 percent of the players in the National Basketball Association and two-thirds of National Football League players were black. Baseball players as a group were 58 percent white, 24 percent Hispanic, 17 percent black, and 1 percent Asian. All three leaders in product endorsements by athletes—Michael Jordan, Tiger Woods, and Grant Hill—were African Americans. Basketball great Jordan brought in between $40 and $60 million a year.

In 1998, the Census Bureau reported that there were 29.7 million Hispanics in America, about 11 percent of the population. Los Angeles and its environs contained nearly six million Hispanic residents, a number greater than the population of most individual states. The Hispanic rate of growth prompted bureau officials to predict that the number of Hispanics might sur-

The athlete know on seven continents simply as "Michael." Source: Reuters/Jeff Christensen/Archive Photos

pass that of African Americans (12.8 percent of the population) as early as the year 2000.

Roberto Suro's *Strangers Among Us: How Latino Immigration Is Transforming America* noted the general success these immigrants had found in the United States. Families were strong, the crime rate was low, wages were rising, and the number of Hispanic-owned businesses was escalating to more than a million in the late 1990s. Still, the Census Bureau reported that 27.1 percent of Hispanics lived below the poverty line in 1997.

"Bilingual education," a product of the 1970s, was an emotional issue in the late 1990s. The debate was about the proper pathway to academic achievement. Proponents contended that teaching should be carried out in a native language while students also learned English. Opponents argued that nonnative English speaking children should be required to learn English and learn it quickly. Under bilingual instruction, tests showed, nonnative English speakers were emerging with poor reading skills in both English and their native language. But the reasons for this were hotly debated.

On June 5, 1998, California voters overwhelmingly (61 percent) approved Proposition 227, an initiative that largely eliminated bilingual education from the state's public schools. About a third of California's population was Hispanic. A day after the vote, civil rights leaders went to court to challenge the measure. Compounding the issue was the "English Only" movement, a desire by many to make English the nation's official language. (Eighty-one languages were spoken in Los Angeles.)

Affirmative Reaction

Polls showed that Americans opposed racial quotas but favored affirmative action. One 1998 poll showed 51 percent of adults favoring the programs, including 82 percent of blacks and 55 percent of women. That affirmative action very often involved quotas (often called "hiring goals") made the policy all the more controversial.

To proponents, affirmative action ensured equality of opportunity in hiring, college admissions, and government contracting, and was reparation for centuries of racism. To critics, racial preferences amounted to reverse discrimination and were thus immoral and unconstitutional. They were also expensive: hiring and contracting "goals" were calculated to be adding $10 million to the cost of building Milwaukee's new baseball stadium. In the 1990s, the case made by critics grew increasingly popular.

In 1995, the Supreme Court in the so-called Adarand decision ruled that federal affirmative action programs had to meet a "strict scrutiny" requirement, allowing narrowly tailored preferences. In March 1996, the U.S. Fifth Circuit Court of Appeals ruled that the University of Texas could not use race as a factor when admitting students. That November, California voters approved Proposition 209, ending affirmative action in state programs and state schools. Minority enrollment at the prestigious University of California at Berkeley plummeted without preferences. Still, in May 1998, the House of Representatives defeated an amendment that would have barred race- or sex-based preferences in admissions to public colleges and universities that received federal funds. By mid-year, African American leaders were organizing to preserve affirmative action and expand civil rights legislation.

The Role of Government

Both major political parties declared their support for smaller government. But few politicians were willing to cut programs that voters wanted. In 1998 the Congressional Budget Office and the Office of Tax Analysis in the Treasury Department reported that taxes took between 26 percent and 30 percent of a typical family's paycheck. The federal tax bite had remained steady at about 20 percent for the last two decades.

Using slightly different data, Republicans claimed that the typical family paid more than 38 percent of its income in taxes. In mid-1997, financial journalist Tam Saler said that "tax freedom day," that point in the year when all of a person's taxes and attendant costs were paid, was May 23rd, the 143rd day of the year. In 1960, it had been the 106th day. In 1913, one worked only thirty-one days to pay the entire year's tax obligations. Saler predicted that a continuation of the rate of increase since 1900 would mean that by the year 2226, Americans would need to work 365 days a year just to pay their federal, state, and local taxes.

The power of the federal government was recognized by virtually everyone, from food stamp recipients to the titans of industry. In 1998, a study showed that businesses, interest groups, and labor unions were spending $100 million *a month* to lobby the federal government. The Washington influence game was at least a $1.2 billion-a-year business. Topping the list of interest groups was the American Medical Association, which dispensed $8.5 million for lobbying in the first six months of 1997.

The Political Spectrum

A *Wall Street Journal*/NBC News poll published in December 1997 reported that 41 percent of all adults identified themselves with the Democratic party and 32 percent with the Republicans. Nearly a quarter of those polled, 23 percent, declared themselves independents. Both the elderly and the younger voters tilted toward the Democrats. Experts thought that the GOP effort to trim Medicare benefits accounted for the disenchantment among seniors.

But these data disguised the fact that more Americans saw themselves as conservative rather than liberal. In mid-1998, pollster Richard Wirthlin reported that when respondents did not have the option of answering "moderate," they said 58 to 33 percent that they were conservative. This figure had held steady for years, and other studies substantiated it.

Los Angeles attorney and broadcaster Hugh Hewitt published a provocative argument in May 1998, contending that the United States in fact had a six-party system and that "Each of our major political parties is really three smaller parties stacked in a pyramid." The Party of Faith consisted of conservative Christians who normally backed the Republican party. The Party of Race contained minorities who overwhelmingly voted for the Democrats. The Party of Wealth historically linked itself to the GOP, but unhappiness with the Party of Faith had driven many to the left and to the Democrats. The Party of Government comprised the labor unions (especially the public employee and teachers' unions), environmentalists, consumer advocates, and all others who needed direct government support and sought expanded tax revenue. The Party of Patriotism appealed to the Reagan right, including conservative intellectuals and members of the armed forces, who backed Republicans. And the Party of License—the academic left, feminists, and the gay community—supported Democrats.

To Hewitt, civil rights activist Jesse Jackson personified the Party of Race, Vice President Al Gore the Party of Government, feminist Betty Friedan the Party of License, Dr. James Dobson of "Focus on the Family" the Party of Faith, billionaire Warren Buffet the Party of Wealth, and Senator John Mc-

Cain the Party of Patriotism. Hewitt thought that in the long run the GOP was at a disadvantage, in part because of the internal friction surrounding the moral demands of the Party of Faith. The rapid growth of the Party of Race worked in the same direction.

In 1998, Congressional Democrats and Republics got into a heated row over "statistical sampling" of the 2000 census. Census data, taken every decade, were used to redraw House district lines and to distribute hundreds of billions of dollars in federal spending. Republicans sought to rely upon actual people counted, the traditional method. Democrats, arguing that too many poor people and minorities, who usually voted Democratic, were missed by census takers. The Census Bureau admitted that in 1990 it had failed to count some 4 million people, or just below 2 percent. A Democratic motion to use both census forms and a statistical input that would help tally hard-to-reach Americans failed in the House 227-201, on a largely party-line vote. Republicans filed suit to block sampling, and the initial response from a lower court was supportive.

During the battle in the House, Minority Leader Dick Gephardt of Missouri said, "The census is today's great civil rights issue, and once again Republicans are standing against what is right." The number three Republican, Rep. Tom DeLay of Texas, said an administration that had been accused of illegally using FBI files could not be trusted with census statistics. He asked, "Can we trust this president to do what's right?"

The Second Clinton Administration

After his reelection, Clinton moved again to the left, engaging in numerous skirmishes with the Republican majority in Congress. He employed the line-item veto to eliminate "pork" from legislation until the Supreme Court declared the new authority unconstitutional. Although barred by the Constitution from running again, Clinton spent much time traveling about the country, fund raising and campaigning for others. The first lady, who after the health care battle deliberately softened her public image from ideologue to homemaker and child advocate, also traveled extensively, sometimes accompanied by daughter Chelsea.

From June 25 to July 3, 1998, the Clintons visited China. By this time China's relationship to American prosperity was obvious; people saw "made in China" labels on much of what they purchased. But many were concerned about reports of slave labor and political and religious persecution by the communist government.

Clinton, along with many business leaders, preferred to divorce the human rights and trade issues. But at one point in his trip the president engaged in a spirited debate on human rights with Chinese President Jiang Zemin. Clinton also gave a talk in which he seemed to say that the United States was abandoning Taiwan for the "one-China" policy that the communist government had long desired. The Senate soon voted 96 to 0 to clear the air of that false impression. Critics again raised the issue of alleged Chinese campaign contributions in 1996, implying that Clinton was paying the piper during his visit.

Monicagate

Monica Lewinsky was an attractive, aggressive, uninhibited 22-year-old college graduate from southern California. In June 1995 she began work as an intern in the office of Chief of Staff Leon Panetta. In December she was moved to a paid position, and in April 1996 she was transferred to the Pentagon. White House logs showed that Lewinsky was cleared to visit the White House thirty-seven times between April 1996 and December 1997, while she worked at the Pentagon.

In late 1997, attorneys for Paula Jones heard rumors of an affair between Lewinsky and the president, and demanded the young woman's testimony. They also subpoenaed gifts allegedly given by the president to the intern. Lewinsky signed an affidavit saying there had been no such affair.

In January 1998, Linda Tripp, a former White House employee, presented prosecutor Starr with twenty hours of tape recordings she had secretly made of telephone conversations with Lewinsky. The young woman told Tripp of a romance with Clinton and said she had engaged in oral sex with him. Tripp also took detailed stenographic notes of Lewinsky's revelations, which she turned over to Starr.

Tripp, a personal friend, had tape recorded the emotional story, she said later, because she was angry at what she knew had been going on in and around the Oval Office and did not want the president to get away with it. Tripp also knew about crude sexual advances allegedly made by the president toward White House aide Kathleen Willey, who went on national television in March to describe the incident.

Starr had the FBI provide Tripp with a concealed recording device, and Lewinsky repeated the story to her friend in person, noting that the president had asked her to hide their relationship. Lewinsky showed Tripp a "talking points" document that detailed ways in which she could deny her involvement with the president during the Paula Jones case.

On January 17, testifying under oath in the Jones suit, Clinton denied having had an affair with Lewinsky. (The Jones suit was later settled with a payment of $850,000 by the president.) He said he did not recall ever being alone with the young intern at the White House. Word of Tripp and Lewinsky soon reached the press, and the most devastating of the Clinton scandals burst into the headlines.

The central issue was whether the president had lied under oath about his relationship with Lewinsky and whether he was guilty of obstructing justice by counseling her to commit perjury. On a deeper level, the case involved Clinton's personal integrity and the dignity of the office of chief executive. With Attorney General Reno's approval, Starr added this investigation to his

already lengthy series of Clinton probes. Starr was probing a pattern of behavior by the president.

In his sworn testimony and on two television appearances, Clinton em-
phatically denied ever having had "sexual relations" with Lewinsky. Several
of the president's senior aides assured the public that Clinton was not employing a linguistic loophole to exclude oral sex and that the president had
denied any sort of intimate relationship with the young woman.

Clinton refused further public comment on the matter. White House lawyers
and "spin doctors" then began a lengthy series of attacks on Tripp, Lewinsky, Willey, and Starr. Numerous delaying tactics and legal challenges by the
Clinton forces were invariably followed by their complaints that Starr was
taking too long to end his investigation. The story was told that Lewinsky
was merely visiting Clinton secretary Betty Currie during her thirty-seven
White House visits. The first lady attributed the entire body of Clinton investigations to a "vast, right-wing conspiracy" and later blamed her husband's
difficulties on anti-Arkansas bias as well.

Despite much resistance from White House lawyers, Starr succeeded
through the courts in acquiring the sworn testimony of Clinton's Secret Service agents and White House lawyers and top officials. In July, after months
of stalls, leaks, confusion, and media frenzy, Starr granted Lewinsky and her
mother, Marcia Lewis, full immunity for their testimony. By this time, Starr's
four-year investigation had cost some $40 million, and Starr was under in-
vestigation for leaking information to the media.

*On January 26, 1998, President Bill Clinton insists, "I did not have sexual relations
with that woman, Miss Lewinsky." Source: Reuters/Win McNamee/Archive Photos*

Lewinsky testified before a federal grand jury in August, providing graphic detail about an eighteen-month affair she had with the president. She turned over a dress she said was stained with the president's semen. Clinton was also reported asking Lewinsky to deliver to his secretary gifts he had given her, to keep them from Paula Jones's attorneys.

Following unsuccessful legal ploys, Clinton agreed to respond to a Starr subpoena by giving videotaped testimony to the grand jury, accompanied by three attorneys. Clinton was the first incumbent president to give testimony in a criminal investigation into his own conduct.

Polls showed that nearly 75 percent of Americans believed the president was lying about a sexual relationship with Lewinsky. But Clinton's popularity was extremely high, 65 percent at the point Lewinsky won full immunity. Starr, Lewinsky, and Tripp had consistently low approval ratings.

Journalists and historians struggled with the meaning of the polls. Much could be said for the president's powers of persuasion. Some thought the polls provided further evidence of the public's moral indifference. Others noted that Starr had made mistakes and that Lewinsky had a tarnished reputation. A common explanation was that the country was enjoying peace and record prosperity, and that Clinton was receiving the credit. To most people, it was said, Dow Jones was more important than Paula Jones.

The stain on Lewinsky's dress forced Clinton to change his story. He knew that the DNA test would link him with the young intern. (It did.) On August 17, following more than four hours of questioning by Starr and the grand jury, Clinton made a four-minute, nationally televised address. It was as defiant as it was apologetic. The president admitted that he had been lying about the Monica Lewinsky affair for seven months, and conceded that what he had done was wrong. But he refused to acknowledge the nature of the "relationship" with the young intern, he denied asking anyone to lie, he denied lying under oath (which meant he was taking refuge in the linguistic ploy that distinguished oral sex from "sexual relations"), and he attacked independent counsel Starr for prying into personal matters and taking too long to complete his investigation. The speech was quickly and almost unanimously acknowledged to be a failure.

The Starr Report

On September 9, Kenneth Starr issued a 445-page report to Congress, which the House made public two days later. The report focused on the Lewinsky-Clinton relationship and included detailed descriptions of sexual conduct, including incidents of oral sex, in and just outside the Oval Office. Starr listed eleven possible grounds for impeachment, including five instances of the president lying under oath. In addition, thousands of pages of documentation were made available to the public, and more were promised as investigations of the Whitewater affair and similar matters proceeded. A videotape of Clinton's grand jury testimony, which Starr had turned over to Congress, was also made public and shown on television.

While not condoning Clinton's affair with Lewinsky, leading Democrats argued that it only involved sex by mutually consenting adults and was thus insufficiently serious to warrant resignation or impeachment. Union leaders, blacks, feminists, and gays, the heart of the Democratic coalition and the beneficiaries of many administration appointments and favors, were highly supportive. (Cabinet secretaries Rodney Slater of transportation and Alexis Herman at labor were blacks. Madeleine Albright was the nation's first woman secretary of state. Elizabeth Birch, of the Human Rights Campaign for gay and lesbian rights, said that Clinton had named more than 100 openly gay and lesbian Americans to his administration.)

Leading Republicans declared that the overriding issue was perjury, not sex, and contended that no one, let alone the president of the United States, was above the law.

Given the evidence at hand and the president's unwillingness to step aside, GOP leaders had little choice but to proceed. On October 8, by a largely partisan vote of 258 to 176 (31 Democrats supported the Republican-backed resolution), the House voted to launch an impeachment inquiry against Clinton for his conduct in the Lewinsky scandal. The vote marked just the third time in American history that Congress had begun impeachment proceedings against a president.

Democrats fared unexpectedly well in the November elections, picking up five House seats and holding their own elsewhere. In the fallout, House Speaker Newt Gingrich, the most visible Republican in the country, announced his decision to leave Congress. Many thought the elections a mandate for Clinton. If so, the public had spoken, and the impeachment hearings seemed likely to get nowhere.

Beyond Politics

Most Americans placed politics low on their scale of personal priorities, and "Zippergate," as the Clinton-Lewinsky affair was often called, failed to interest many. Some Americans interviewed by pollsters even dismissed the idea of voting. "It's hard to get really excited," said waitress Beth Ann Corrigan. "What does the Clintons' sex life have to do with me? What does the investigation have to do with me?" This sense of disengagement, said pollster Robert Teeter, reflected the view that the "political system since Watergate has become seedy, not very ethical and has not performed very well."

In 1998, there were other things capturing the public's imagination. Major league baseball, for example. Mark McGwire of the St. Louis Cardinals hit seventy homeruns, and Sammy Sosa of the Chicago Cubs hit sixty-six, both breaking the hallowed single-season record of Roger Maris. Cal Ripken, Jr., of the Baltimore Orioles ended his record-setting pace of playing in 2,632 consecutive games. The New York Yankees won a record 114 regular-season games and swept the world series, prompting some to rank them the greatest baseball team of all time.

The movie *Titanic* won the hearts of millions and the academy award in 1998 for best picture. By that fall, the film had grossed more than three times its cost of $200 million, breaking all box-office records, and Paramount pictures had shipped more than 20 million copies of the film on videotape.

Videotape sales in 1997 stood at $9.3 billion and videotape rentals amounted to $11.2 billion. Between watching movies and videos and working and playing at computers, Americans spent much of their time staring into screens. What they saw, of course, had a huge impact on their lives.

High Priests

Most Americans got their news primarily from television. Complaints of bias were common and often well documented. Accounts of the bizarre, the tragic, the deadly, and the corrupt dominated the programs. At times, stories seemed to have lives of their own. Millions became emotionally involved in the death of England's jet-set Princess Diana, for example, due to accounts that lingered for more than a year. (Television journalists quickly forgot saintly, Nobel Prize-winning Mother Theresa, who died five days earlier.)

Television dominated the lives of a great many Americans. Millions mourned the end of the popular "Seinfeld" television series. Millions watched daily "soap operas" and talk shows that often vied with each other to present the most controversial programming. Among the most popular was talk show host Oprah Winfrey, and many accepted her recommendations about the rights and wrongs of life even to the point of what books to read. (Worth $550 million, Winfrey was the only black on the *Forbes* list of the 400 wealthiest Americans.)

Sex and violence on television and in the movies concerned a majority of Americans, and with good reason. Before entering junior high school, a child would witness eight thousand on-screen murders on television and in such movies as *Die Hard 2,* which featured 264 killings.

Radio continued to attract millions daily. Right-wingers enjoyed Rush Limbaugh and Paul Harvey, and the left listened avidly to National Public Radio. All-news stations, such as WBBM in Chicago, had huge audiences. Enormously popular rock and country music stations drove out virtually all jazz and classical programming.

Despite the virtual disappearance of serious books from best-seller lists, and a steady decline in newspaper readers, the print media continued to make an impact, especially upon the educated. Giant publishers such as Random House and Penguin Putnam, and powerful newspapers such as the *New York Times, Wall Street Journal, Washington Post, Chicago Tribune,* and *Los Angeles Times* were often highly influential.

Increasingly the media were coming under the authority of fewer and fewer people, such as billionaires Ted Turner and Rupert Murdoch, and the heads of huge conglomerates (Disney owned and operated both ABC and ESPN). The impact of this development was uncertain, but some critics were pessimistic about the long-term consequences to entertainment, to culture, to public morality, and even to democracy.

The media, more than any other institution at the close of the century, had the power to define truth, beauty, and virtue; to determine the very confines of reality. The authority of churches, schools, government, and often even the family paled in comparison. Media moguls and their employees were the high priests of the secular, consumer society.

IMPEACHMENT

On December 19, 1998, the House of Representatives impeached President Clinton on two articles, emphasizing perjury and obstruction of justice. (Two other counts were defeated.) This was only the second time a president was impeached and marked the first time that an elected chief executive was so accused. The voting was highly partisan, with Democrats overwhelmingly in support of Clinton and Republicans, with a few defectors, backing impeachment. The public strongly sided with Clinton; although a CBS News poll found that 84 percent believed him guilty of the charges raised by the House, the great majority admired his administration of his duties and did not want him removed from office. Republicans contended stubbornly that principle was more important than popularity. After the vote, Democratic pollster Mark Mellman said of Republicans, "They were digging their own political graves."

The president responded to the impeachment with angry defiance, blasting the GOP and promising never to resign. Conservative William Bennett called the president "a sociopathic liar" and "a malignant presence in American politics and culture." It was an ugly period in the nation's political history, reflecting a culture war between the right and left that was increasingly tense.

The Senate impeachment trial, held behind closed doors, began on January 27. It was predictably partisan and passionate. After more than a month of rancorous debate and media frenzy, the House leadership, presenting the case against Clinton, failed to come close to the necessary two-thirds majority to convict. The charge of perjury was defeated 45 in favor to 55 against. The vote was 50 to 50 on the obstruction of justice article. Not a single Democrat voted for either article of impeachment, while ten Republicans cast their ballots against the charge of perjury and five voted against the obstruction of justice article. A harshly worded motion to censure the president, written by liberal California Democrat Dianne Feinstein, died as well. While twenty-nine Democrats signed it, sixteen did not.

The impeachment vote failed to quell the issue of Clinton's character. In February, a wealthy Arkansas woman, Juanita Broaddrick, asserted that Clinton had raped her in 1978. No other president had been the target of such an allegation. After weighing the available facts, which were persuasive, feminist leaders and others declared the charge credible. Most Clinton partisans said little. The president's only response was a brief denial issued by his attorney.

KOSOVO

On March 24, 1999, the United States and its NATO allies began a series of air and cruise-missile attacks on military targets around Yugoslavia. The effort was designed to end brutal Serbian violence against tiny (half the size of New Hampshire) Kosovo. Ethnic Albanians in the area, Muslims who made up ninety percent of the 1.5 million population, were seeking independence from Yugoslavia. Their rebel army, the Kosovo Liberation Army (KLA), had also engaged in terrorism.

Clinton, who had not prepared Americans in advanced for the sudden strikes, blamed Yugoslav leader Slobodan Milosevic for the turmoil, comparing him to Hitler. In fact, Milosevic had been persecuting neighboring peoples since the collapse of communism in 1989. Kosovo was especially important to the Yugoslav autocrat as it was the historic home of Serbian nationalism, the Serbian people's "holy land."

The attacks marked the fourth time in a ten-month period that Clinton had rained bombs on a country. Afghanistan and Sudan were hit in August 1998 to punish terrorist Osama bin Laden. Widespread attacks on Iraq occurred in December and afterward, attempting to punish Saddam Hussein. Both bin Laden and Hussein survived, and positive results of the attacks were difficult to find. (The Center for Strategy and Budgetary Assessments put the price tag on U.S. military operations from 1991 to 1999, before Kosovo, at $21.4 billion.) Getting involved militarily in the Balkans, an area with an 800-year history of ethnic fighting, was particularly controversial and dangerous.

Supporters of the attacks contended that Clinton was defending the integrity of NATO as well as attempting to end brutal aggression and "ethnic cleansing." Liberal newspaper columnist Sandy Grady wrote, "For a superpower and NATO to avert their eyes from massacres in a European cockpit would have been dishonorable." The president claimed that America had a "moral imperative" to act.

Some critics claimed that Clinton was attempting to bolster his image as a national leader. As bombs and missiles slammed into Yugoslavia, Serbian television showed "Wag the Dog," an American movie about a president who fabricates a war in Albania to distract attention from a sex scandal. Others noted that Molosevic was hardly a Hitler, and that he was not even attempting to take over a foreign country; Kosovo had been part of Yugoslavia since the country's creation in 1918. Critics also doubted that air power alone could stop the violence in Kosovo. Clinton said he did not "intend" to send ground troops into the area.

Many people, including members of Congress, were simply confused by the issue. Most Americans could not find Kosovo on a map. They wondered about the importance of peace in Yugoslavia to the United States, and they were deeply concerned about possible American casualties. Then there was the question of cost: John Pike, a defense expert at the Federation of American Scientists, estimated that the first 24 hours of the Kosovo operation cost taxpayers more than $100 million.

The NATO strikes were equally controversial throughout the world. Russia denounced them as "naked aggression," and China followed suit. Greece, a NATO member, supported the Serbs, and its air force took no direct role in the air strikes. The German army participated, marking the first time it had fired a shot since the end of World War II, and prompting unrest in Germany and elsewhere. Anti-American riots broke out all over Europe. Eastern Orthodox Christians, who shared the faith of most Serbs, were outraged by the NATO attacks. The Islamic world showed little enthusiasm for the warfare.

After 78 days and more than 35,000 NATO sorties, Milosevic agreed to peace terms. Albanians, including the some 900,000 who had recently fled Serb violence, could return to Kosovo under the protection of an international military force. But Kosovo was to remain under Serbian authority, and the KLA was to be disarmed. The overall agreement was more advantageous for Serbia than prewar demands made by the U.S. Secretary of State Albright.

The victory of the 19 western nations over an economically poor country the size of the state of Ohio was not entirely surprising. But it was the first such victory won exclusively through the air (some 90 percent of Allied weaponry was precision-guided), and it was achieved without a single Allied casualty.

In June, 50,000 NATO troops (including 7,000 Americans) entered Kosovo, encountering evidence of numerous Serb atrocities. Some 10,000 Kosovars were said to have been murdered, matching the estimated number of Serbs killed by NATO weapons. Americans and Europeans faced billions of dollars in foreign aid to the region.

The move against Yugoslavia marked the first time NATO forces had attacked a sovereign nation. The action was taken without a clear United Nations mandate. NATO had been created a half century earlier to protect Western nations from a Soviet-led invasion. Its new role, containing ethnic rivalries and other challenges to European stability, might prove equally demanding. It was widely acknowledged that the world's only superpower would be the dominant force in future NATO actions.

CONCLUSION

The twentieth century posed unprecedented challenges to the American people. Among other things, they grappled with the Industrial Revolution, massive immigration, urbanization, reform, economic depression, two world wars, two Red scares, the restoration of war-torn Europe, the Cold War, nuclear power, civil rights, women's rights, educational change, conservation efforts, energy crises, a revolution in medical technology, massive cultural change, mounting crime, unprecedented prosperity, and the superpower status of post-Cold War America.

Change is the most persistent theme of the century. A businessman in downtown Boston in 1900, looking at often dilapidated wooden buildings and streets frequently filled with debris, mud, dead horses, and ragged children would think himself almost on another planet were he transported to that same spot in our time. The Iowa farmer of 1900, having slaved behind a mule in the hot sun all day with only a chance of making a profit, could only dream of the security and comfort that rural Americans frequently experienced a hundred years later. The black southern sharecropper at the turn of this century, toiling in poverty and persecution, could surely not believe predictions of the equality and economic opportunity that awaited his great-great-grandchildren. Barely literate women who toiled with hot irons and steaming washtubs to keep huge families clean and presentable would look with astonishment at the trim, independent, educated, often childless stereotype of the 1990s woman. People who wobbled on bicycles with huge wheels might shriek as building-size airplanes roared overhead. Those who frequented vaudeville in William McKinley's time might go into cardiac arrest during a modern film festival in the Bill Clinton years.

Much of what has happened in the twentieth century is clearly progress. The great strides in medicine, the wealth generated by industrialism and technology, the increased availability of education, and the equality brought about by the civil rights revolution, for example, have few serious detractors today. Not many would like to see the role of government diminished to the point that the disadvantaged were again left to die in the county poorhouse. Few would want the nation's military presence again so small that we could be threatened by virtually anyone. Hardly any Americans would like to repeal the religious tolerance that holds sway in our largely secular era.

Critics can also make a strong case against much of the change that transformed twentieth-century America. The bloody wars (more people died in 1945 than in any other single year in history), the descent of popular culture, the breakdown of the traditional family, the waning of traditional religious faith and morality, the pervasiveness of consumerism, the sharp decline in good manners, the disintegration of educational standards, the continued destruction of the environment—many books have lamented these and other features of modern life.

A major lesson most Americans learned in this century is the truth that they are a major part of the world. In an age of supersonic aircraft, intercontinental ballistic missiles, and stock markets reacting to developments all over the planet, isolationism is impossible.

And the world of which we are a part remains extremely dangerous. In 1998, the Pentagon launched a new agency to deal with threats of weapons of mass destruction. Defense Secretary William Cohen said, "Today's harsh reality is too powerful to ignore—at least 25 countries have, or are in the process of developing, nuclear, biological or chemical weapons, and the means to deliver them." There was considerable concern as well about the fate of the massive arsenal of missiles in unstable Russia.

Given the unprecedented dominance of the United States at century's end, the American military bears much of the responsibility for keeping world peace. The United Nations and NATO will play a role, of course, but much of the financing and fighting in crucial situations will be carried out by Americans. In the Balkans, the Middle East, Africa and elsewhere, the planet's most powerful nation will be summoned in a time of crisis.

A sign of genuine progress and hope at century's end is the fact that democracy was the most widespread system in the world. Zbigniew Brzezinski, Jimmy Carter's chief national security advisor, observed in 1998 that "The majority of states today are elected democracies (117 out of 191), and 1.3 billion people (22 percent of the world population) live in free societies." Thirty nine percent lived in countries with partially democratic systems, and the remaining 39 percent lived in basically antidemocratic systems.

At the close of the twentieth century, the freedom and the prosperity enjoyed by Americans were the envy of much of the world. But millions around the globe also feared the secularism, the crime, the popular culture, the cynicism, and the growing disparity of wealth that were part of American life.

The overwhelming challenge facing the United States as the year 2000 dawned was to respond to rapid change with enough intelligence, integrity, compassion, and courage to warrant the world's full-scale admiration as well as respect. The globe's leading nation had the responsibility not only to lead militarily but to create a society that could live up to its highest ideals, which were, in fact, the aspirations of a great many people everywhere at the dawn of the new century.

SUGGESTED READING

Elliott Abrams (ed.), *Close Calls: Intervention, Terrorism, Missile Defense, and "Just War" Today* (1998); Richard Bernstein, *Dictatorship of Virtue: Multiculturalism and the Battle of America's Future* (1994); Michael Cromartie (ed.), *No Longer Exiles: The Religious New Right in American Politics* (1993); William Damon, *Greater Expectations: Overcoming the Culture of Indulgence in America's Homes and Schools* (1995); Lawrence Kudlow, *American Abundance: The New Economic and Moral Prosperity* (1997); Thomas C. Reeves, *The Empty Church: The Suicide of Liberal Christianity* (1996); Michael J. Sandel, *Democracy's Discontent: America in Search of a Public Philosophy* (1996); Charles J. Sykes, *Dumbing Down Our Kids: Why America's Children's Feel Good About Themselves but Can't Read, Write, or Add* (1995); Roberto Suro, *Strangers Among Us: How Latino Immigration Is Transforming America*; Stephen Thernstrom and Abigail M. Thernstrom, *America in Black and White: One Nation Indivisible* (1997).

INDEX